Infinite Hope and
Finite Disappointment

Legal Thought
Across Disciplines
Published in Cooperation with
The University of Akron School of Law

Elizabeth Reilly, editor, *Infinite Hope and Finite Disappointment: The Story of the First Interpreters of the Fourteenth Amendment*

Infinite Hope and
Finite Disappointment

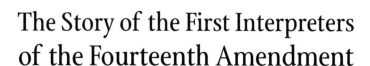

The Story of the First Interpreters
of the Fourteenth Amendment

Edited by Elizabeth Reilly

The University of Akron Press
Akron, Ohio

15   14   13   12   11   5   4   3   2   1

LIBRARY OF CONGRESS CATALOGING-IN-PUBLICATION DATA

Infinite hope and finite disappointment : the story of the first interpreters of the Fourteenth Amendment / edited by Elizabeth Reilly.—1st ed.
    p. cm.
    Summary: "Infinite Hope and Finite Disappointment details the hopes and promises of the 14th Amendment in the historical, legal, and sociological context within which it was framed. Part of the Reconstruction Amendments collectively known as "The Second Founding," the 14th Amendment fundamentally altered the 1787 Constitution to protect individual rights and altered the balance of power between the national government and the states. The book also shows how initial Supreme Court interpretations of the amendment's reach hindered its applicability. Finally, the contributors investigate the current impact of the 14th Amendment. The book is divided into three parts: "Infinite Hope: The Framers as First Interpreters," "Finite Disappointment: The Supreme Court as First Interpreter," and "Never Losing Infinite Hope: The People as First Interpreters.""—Provided by publisher.
Includes bibliographical references and index.
    ISBN 978-1-935603-00-9 (pbk.)
    1. United States. Constitution. 14th Amendment. 2. Constitutional history—United States.
3. United States—Politics and government—1865–1877. I. Reilly, Elizabeth (Elizabeth A.)
    KF45584TH .I54 2011
    342.7302'9—DC22
                        2011008195

The paper used in this publication meets the minimum requirements of American National Standard for Information Sciences—Permanence of Paper for Printed Library Materials, ANSI Z39.48–1984. ∞

Infinite Hope and Finite Disappointment was designed and typeset by Amy Freels, with assistance from Zac Bettendorf. The typeface, Stone Print, was designed by Sumner Stone in 1991. *Infinite Hope and Finite Disappointment* was printed on sixty-pound natural and bound by BookMasters of Ashland, Ohio.

Contents

Constitution of the United States

PREAMBLE

We the People of the United States, in Order to form a more perfect Union, establish Justice, insure domestic Tranquility, provide for the common defence, promote the general Welfare, and secure the Blessings of Liberty to ourselves and our Posterity, do ordain and establish this Constitution for the United States of America.

FOURTEENTH AMENDMENT

Section 1. All persons born or naturalized in the United States and subject to the jurisdiction thereof, are citizens of the United States and of the State wherein they reside. No State shall make or enforce any law which shall abridge the privileges or immunities of citizens of the United States; nor shall any State deprive any person of life, liberty, or property, without due process of law; nor deny to any person within its jurisdiction the equal protection of the laws.

Section 2. Representatives shall be apportioned among the several States according to their respective numbers, counting the whole number of persons in each State, excluding Indians not taxed. But when the right to vote at any election for the choice of electors for President and Vice President of the United States, Representatives in Congress, the Executive and Judicial officers of a State, or the members of the Legislature thereof, is denied to any of the male inhabitants of such State, being twenty-one years of age, and citizens of the United States, or in any way abridged, except for participation in rebellion, or other crime, the basis of representation therein shall be reduced in the proportion which the number of such male citizens shall bear to the whole number of male citizens twenty-one years of age in such State.

Section 3. No person shall be a Senator or Representative in Congress, or elector of President and Vice President, or hold any office, civil or military, under the

United States, or under any State, who, having previously taken an oath, as a member of Congress, or as an officer of the United States, or as a member of any State legislature, or as an executive or judicial officer of any State, to support the Constitution of the United States, shall have engaged in insurrection or rebellion against the same, or given aid or comfort to the enemies thereof. But Congress may by a vote of two-thirds of each House, remove such disability.

Section 4. The validity of the public debt of the United States, authorized by law, including debts incurred for payment of pensions and bounties for services in suppressing insurrection or rebellion, shall not be questioned. But neither the United States nor any State shall assume or pay any debt or obligation incurred in aid of insurrection or rebellion against the United States, or any claim for the loss or emancipation of any slave; but all such debts, obligations and claims shall be held illegal and void.

Section 5. The Congress shall have power to enforce, by appropriate legislation, the provisions of this article.

ARTICLE IV

Section 2, Clause 1. The Citizens of each State shall be entitled to all Privileges and Immunities of Citizens in the several States.

Section 2, Clause 2. A Person charged in any State with Treason, Felony, or other Crime, who shall flee from Justice, and be found in another State, shall on Demand of the executive Authority of the State from which he fled, be delivered up, to be removed to the State having Jurisdiction of the Crime.

Section 2, Clause 3. No Person held to Service or Labour in one State, under the Laws thereof, escaping into another, shall, in Consequence of any Law or Regulation therein, be discharged from such Service or Labour, but shall be delivered up on Claim of the Party to whom such Service or Labour may be due.

Section 3, Clause 2. The Congress shall have Power to dispose of and make all needful Rules and Regulations respecting the Territory or other Property belonging to the United States; and nothing in this Constitution shall be so construed as to Prejudice any Claims of the United States, or of any particular State.

Section 4. The United States shall guarantee to every State in this Union a Republican Form of Government, and shall protect each of them against Invasion; and on Application of the Legislature, or of the Executive (when the Legislature cannot be convened) against domestic Violence.

Contributors and Acknowledgments

Richard L. Aynes, Professor and John F. Seiberling Chair of Constitutional Law, Director of the Constitutional Law Center, The University of Akron School of Law. B.S. Miami University, Ohio; J.D. Cleveland State University. The Constitutional Law Center was one of four established by the U.S. Congress in order to commemorate the Bicentennial of the U.S. Constitution in 1987.

David S. Bogen, Professor Emeritus of Law, University of Maryland School of Law. B.A. Harvard University; LL.B. Harvard University; LL.M. New York University.

C. Ellen Connally, Retired Judge of the Cleveland Municipal Court, former President, Board of Trustees of Bowling Green State University. B.S. Bowling Green State University; J.D. Cleveland State University; M.A. Cleveland State University; Ph.D. candidate (history) The University of Akron.

Garrett Epps, Professor, University of Baltimore School of Law, and author, *Democracy Reborn: The Fourteenth Amendment and the Fight For Equal Rights In Post-Civil War America* (Henry Holt, 2006). B.A. Harvard University; M.A. Hollins College; J.D. Duke University; LL.M. Duke University.

Paul Finkelman, President William McKinley Distinguished Professor of Law and Public Policy and Senior Fellow, Government Law Center, Albany Law School. B.A. Syracuse University; M.A. University of Chicago; Ph.D. (History) University of Chicago.

James W. Fox, Jr., Professor of Law and Associate Dean of Faculty Development, Stetson University College of Law. B.A. University of North Carolina; J.D. University of Michigan.

Wilson R. Huhn, C. Blake McDowell, Jr. Professor of Law, The University of Akron School of Law. B.A. Yale University; J.D. Cornell University.

Gwen Hoerr Jordan, Assistant Professor University of Illinois-Springfield. J.D. University of Denver; Ph.D. (History) University of Illinois-Chicago.

Elizabeth Reilly, C. Blake McDowell, Jr. Professor of Law, The University of Akron School of Law. A.B. Princeton University; J.D. University of Akron.

William J. Rich, Professor of Law, Washburn University School of Law. B.A. Oberlin College; J.D. University of California, Berkeley.

Michael A. Ross, Associate Professor of History, University of Maryland at College Park. Dr. Ross won the 2005 Alpha Sigma Nu Jesuit Book Award in the discipline of history for his book, *Justice of Shattered Dreams: Samuel Freeman Miller and the Supreme Court during the Civil War Era*. Ph.D. (history) University of North Carolina at Chapel Hill; J.D. Duke University.

Introduction

Elizabeth Reilly, The University of Akron School of Law

We must accept finite disappointment, but we must never lose infinite hope.
—Martin Luther King, Jr.

The 14th Amendment embodies hope. An outgrowth of the Civil War and its aftermath, the Amendment profoundly reconstituted "the People of the United States" and redefined what it meant "to form a more perfect Union, establish Justice, insure domestic Tranquility ... promote the general Welfare, and secure the Blessings of Liberty."[1]

The importance of the 14th Amendment is hard to overestimate; some have called its adoption the "second founding." The Amendment has a wide scope and is one of the most frequently invoked sources of protection for individual liberties.[2]

Among the many reasons to enshrine the 14th Amendment in a position of Constitutional primacy is the fact that the Amendment was designed to have, and has had, profound effects upon all three of the structural principles undergirding the Constitution: federalism, individual rights, and separation of powers. As the 39th Congress struggled with correcting the wrongs that had divided the Union before, during and after the Civil War, altering the constitutional understanding of each of these principles was essential. The vast reach of this enterprise was not lost on the Amendment's framers or on the American people.

From its stunning opening phrases through to its final section on congressional power, the Amendment recast national and state power and the individual's place within the governing structure. After decreeing that "All persons born or naturalized...are citizens of the United States," Section 1 limited state power to infringe individual rights—"No State shall make or enforce any law" to "abridge the privileges or immunities of citizens," or to "deprive any person of life, liberty or property without due process of law" or to "deny to any person" the "equal protection of the laws." To emphasize the national power to protect those rights, Section 5 explicitly granted Congress the power to enforce all of the provisions of the Amendment. The 14th Amendment left no doubt that the powers reserved to the states were altered and that the powers granted to the national government were expanded.

The Amendment also tackled significant questions of the terms of reunification. Section 2 directly reduced apportioned representation in any state that denied a male citizen of age the right to vote in a federal or state election. This section negated the excess allocation of representatives to slave states that had been accomplished through the infamous Three-Fifths Clause, and counted freedpeople only if they were also granted the right to vote. Section 3 disqualified from federal or state office all of those who betrayed their previous oaths of office by engaging in insurrection against the United States and granted the pardoning power over this disability to the Congress, not the President. Together, Sections 2 and 3 prevented the antebellum Slave Power structure from reasserting itself in the readmitted states and in the branches of the federal government. Section 4 prohibited the nation or any state from assuming or paying any debt incurred in aid of insurrection, prevented claims for compensation based upon emancipation of the slaves and validated national debt incurred in preserving the Union. Thus, Section 5 both placed Congress in charge of the reconstruction, and expanded its role in the constitutional system of government.

Despite its high purpose and its structural changes to the constitutional framework, the 14th Amendment was not universally embraced. The United States Supreme Court promptly eviscerated much of the meaning of Section 1's guarantees of citizenship, privileges and immunities, due process, and equal protection. In short order, the Court also limited Congress's power to enforce rights and narrowed the federal power to protecting the rights in the Amendment only from state action, not the actions of private parties like the Ku Klux Klan. By 1883, the Supreme Court's interpretations appeared to render the Amendment all but impotent.[3] The precedental impact of that legacy continues to haunt constitutional law.

The Amendment regained some of its power when the twentieth-century Court began using the Due Process Clause to incorporate guarantees of the Bill of Rights and make them applicable to the states. Congress resurrected the Amendment as a source of the equal protection principle during the Civil Rights era of the 1960s, using the Commerce Power to support its legislation. The Supreme Court upheld those statutes, and began to articulate an interpretation of Section 5 (and its companion Section 2 of the 15th Amendment) that accorded Congress the power to guarantee rights through far-reaching legislation.[4] But citizen activism kept the spirit and promise of the Amendment alive during the intervening century.

This book grew out of a symposium held in October 2009 at the University of Akron School of Law celebrating the 140th anniversary of the ratification of the 14th Amendment. Anniversaries provide fruitful occasions to reflect. The book seizes upon that opportunity to ask a central interpretive question: How did the First Interpreters of the 14th Amendment interpret and use the Amendment and thereby affect its meaning?

In addressing this question, several subsidiary questions become important. First, how did the framers and adopters of the Amendment, the 39th Congress, interpret their work? Second, how did the Supreme Court initially interpret the Amendment, and how did their interpretation affect future cases and readings? Third, how did the American people interpret and use the Amendment? The chapters in this book examine different aspects of these questions, explicating the initial interpretations by the Congress, the United States Supreme Court and the public, and examining their lasting impacts.

The 39th Congress labored on the Amendment from December 1865 until June 1866. Ratification occurred during and after the critical 1866 elections, which functioned as a referendum on the Amendment and clarified the strength of public support for it. On July 28, 1868, Secretary of State William Seward issued the proclamation recognizing that the 14th Amendment had been ratified.[5]

The work of interpreting the Amendment began as soon as the 39th Congress began framing it. The senators and representatives were well aware of the importance of their work. The framers crafted the Amendment to achieve the critical goals of securing immediate and long-term peace and Union. The succeeding Congresses took seriously their role to effectuate the Amendment. In response to the abuses of rights being practiced in the former slave states, those Congresses passed a significant number of measures to make rights real and provide protection for their exercise.[6] Federal prosecutors and judges between 1866 and 1876 interpreted and applied the Congressional statutes consistently with their understanding of the Amendment. Their enforcement had a positive impact on conditions in the South, an impact that collapsed after the Supreme Court intervened.[7]

The Supreme Court's first occasion to interpret the Amendment came in 1873. Although cognizant of the consequences its interpretation would have on the future of the nation,[8] the Court, unfortunately, seemed to be overwhelmed by the potential breadth of the Amendment. Into the early twentieth century, the Court acted repeatedly to limit the Amendment's scope, opining that "we do not see in those amendments any purpose to destroy the main features of the general system."[9] The early Court decisions derailed the propulsive force of the Amendment for legal change, and the Amendment remained nearly impotent for seventy years.

Even as the Court limited the scope of the Amendment and of Congress's power pursuant to it during the 1870s and 1880s, the people engaged in interpreting the Amendment's guarantees through their own civic and political actions. The rebirth of the Amendment's legal force is a testament to the power of the ideals embodied in the Amendment and embraced as a key part of the national consciousness.

Interpretation matters. This collection of work elucidates the interpretations of those who created the 14th Amendment, as well as those charged with applying it initially. Those first interpretations are significant because they influenced later interpretations. As both Garrett Epps and Richard Aynes point out, despite the many competing theories of how to interpret the Constitution, none reject the relevance of the history of the framing of that constitutional provision or the likely meaning it held to the framers or others at the time of framing. As Wilson Huhn notes, no theory rejects the use of Supreme Court precedent in interpretation.

Interpretation differs from intent. Interpretation is a public process of giving and explaining meaning, of representing meaning by actions taken pursuant to events and words. Interpretation is directed toward others. Interpretation translates and applies principle; it fleshes out the principle in action. Interpretation is capable of being collective, more forward-looking and external. To determine interpretation, we examine text, contemporaneous action pursuant to text, and the political and historical background of text and action.

Intent, conversely, is an internal process of "directing the mind," the "state of one's mind at the time one carries out an action." Discerning "intent" is an attempt to parse the motives and understandings of individual participants. Intent, therefore, is limited to the understanding of the drafters (assuming one can divine it), which is inevitably located in a single context, including the inability to foresee the various futures the text is designed to address. The synonym for *interpret* is *explain* and for *intend* is *mean*. Explicating interpretation is an objective inquiry, whereas revealing intention is a subjective inquiry.[10]

Interpretation is a public act of witness and requires full context. This book is dedicated to enriching the historical context within which we examine the 14th Amendment, an historical context that is intrinsically fascinating.

The context within which the Amendment was drafted reveals how the framers interpreted their own history and times and incorporated their understanding into the language and structure of the Amendment. Garrett Epps details the fear and suspicion that surrounded the Republican framers as they sought to behead the hydra of the Slave Power "conspiracy" by reshaping the Constitution at its most fundamental levels. Paul Finkelman investigates the nascent progressive movements toward racial equality in the North that formed the political milieu that influenced the key framers of the Amendment. He also recounts the horrendous practices in the South that the Joint Committee on Reconstruction responded to in framing the Amendment and legislation pursuant to it. Richard Aynes leads us into the halls and chambers of the 39th Congress, revealing the framers themselves; their aspirations both to secure a peace to end the ongoing unrest and also to fashion a Union where specific rights would guarantee future peace; and their resolve in the face of serious obstacles during the drafting process.

Equally compelling are the stories of the Amendment's first interpreters after ratification. Michael Ross transports us to the streets of New Orleans, where the public health legislation to restrict butchers to using a slaughterhouse located away from the city and below its water supplies spawned the first interpretive challenge to reach the United States Supreme Court. He reveals the underlying tensions among the butchers, the city and the lawyers in the case, as well as the influences on Justice Miller, whose interest in protecting the public health led to his majority opinion which supported local reconstruction legislative initiatives by limiting the impact of the Amendment. Ellen Connally recounts the prosecution of Jefferson Davis, the president of the Confederate States. She explains the inherent dangers in trying Davis for treason, and the creativity of the lawyers and judges who sought to preserve the fragile peace without either vindicating secession or claiming victory by making Davis a martyr. The interpretations of these judges and lawyers were heavily influenced by the political realities they confronted, both as individuals and on behalf of a nation struggling to understand the permanency of "union" and the meaning of the cataclysmic bloodshed of the Civil War. Gwen Jordan documents how Myra Bradwell and the women's movement claimed that the equal protection guarantee of the Amendment applied to women. She shows how Bradwell carried that struggle to the courts, creating not only arguments about the reach of equal protection but also an entire interpretive method that continues to influence the application of the 14th Amendment. James Fox points out the importance of the African American conventions, which infused vitality into the concept of national citizenship. He explains how the newly created and recognized Black citizens emphasized the primacy of suffrage for defining citizenship and helped shape the meaning of civil and political rights.

Supreme Court interpretation profoundly affects constitutional meaning. Supreme Court precedents often control the impact that constitutional guarantees have on the people, leading some to argue that the high court's interpretation carries too much weight. My contribution details the importance of pre-Civil War Supreme Court precedents and the impact of those precedents and their ideological basis on the framers of the Amendment. It also illuminates the framers' purpose to increase congressional power. David Bogen reanalyzes the Court's initial interpretation in *Slaughter-House Cases*, arguing that later Court decisions misread that precedent. He contends that a more accurate reading of the decision opens up possibilities for expanding the Amendment's reach. William Rich argues that the 39th Congress interpreted "privileges or immunities" as encompassing rights created by congressional legislation, and demonstrates that his interpretation is not inconsistent with early Court interpretations. Wilson Huhn carefully parses the first three Supreme Court interpretations of the Amendment and the effect of those rulings at the time they were made. He shows how those decisions became the starting point for further interpretation, eclipsing the starkly contrasting interpretations of the framers and their direct congressional descendants.

Interpretation of the meaning of the Amendment, especially in the Supreme Court, has often started with these early 14th Amendment decisions. Sometimes, the Court has relied on precedents and constitutional provisions that predate the 14th Amendment to constrict its meaning. The modern tendency to treat the Court as both the "first" and the final interpreter ignores the primacy of the framers as interpreters and reads the framers' interpretations only through the narrow lens of subsequent Court interpretations. This Supreme Court-centric focus overlooks the value and impact of those who first breathed life into the guarantees of the Amendment—succeeding Congresses, federal prosecutors and judges, and participants in powerful social movements inspired by the promises of the Amendment.

This book contributes to the explosion of work that illuminates the early history of the adoption and use of the 14th Amendment by telling the stories of its very earliest interpreters. The contributors make no sweeping claims as to the precise role that the first interpretations should play in the modern interpretive enterprise. However, each chapter explores one or more of the first interpreters within their historical and ideological context to produce a more accurate and accessible understanding of their interpretations of the Amendment. The importance of historically accurate understandings as a guide to applying the Amendment was foreshadowed by counsel for the butchers in *Slaughter-House Cases*:

> The comprehensiveness of this amendment, the natural and necessary breadth of the language, the history of some of the clauses; their connection with discussions, contests, and domestic commotions that form landmarks in the annals of constitutional government; the circumstances under which it became part of the Constitution, demonstrate that the weighty import of what it ordains is not to be misunderstood.[11]

Part I of the book examines how the 39th Congress interpreted its own work. First, that Congress had to interpret the past and present events that led to the necessity for the Amendment. What problems in the original constitutional framework needed to be addressed? What solution would uproot those problems and prevent them from recurring? Second, the framers had to interpret the structure and language of the proposed Amendment. Were both adequate, comprehensive and clear enough to accomplish their goals?

The framers were both interpreters of what they wanted and needed to say and interpreters of what they had said in the Amendment. They shared a well-developed political ideology of the constitutional inadequacies that had led to the Civil War and needed to be eradicated. As the framers drafted and adopted the Amendment, they interpreted their present circumstances in order to address them effectively. After ratification, the framers enacted legislation to implement the Amendment, giving early and nearly contemporaneous interpretations of the Amendment's ability to address new and continuing inequities.

Parts II and III examine how the early interpretations of others, including the Supreme Court and the polity, affected the reach and power of the Amendment.

Part II closely examines the infamous *Slaughter-House Cases*, the Court's initial interpretation of the Amendment. The Court interpreted Section 1 of the

Amendment narrowly with the avowed purpose of preserving the existing framework of government. This work's contributors disagree about the extent to which the Court intended to eviscerate the Amendment's meaning; later Court decisions and legislation used alternative paths including the Due Process and Commerce Clauses, respectively, to reinstate virtually all of the rights or powers withheld by the earliest Court interpretations. The authors note that the early Supreme Court decisions blocked some interpretive paths but either opened another interpretive trail or, at the very least, left openings later used to reinvigorate the promises of the Amendment and achieve its framers' goals.

Part III looks directly at how the public response to the Amendment shaped its meaning. The contributors investigate how public movements kept alive the Amendment's potential to revise the fabric of American life and law. For instance, lawyers and judges interpreted Section 3 of the Amendment to achieve overriding goals like maintaining peace, stability and reconciliation while protecting the constitutional theory of Union that prevailed with the North's victory in the Civil War. Even though the Supreme Court ignored the Equal Protection Clause when upholding Illinois' refusal to admit Myra Bradwell to the practice of law, Bradwell and the women's movement continued to invoke the Amendment and equal protection to further civil rights. Bradwell's interpretive strategies still affect the concept of equal protection as used today. The black conventions illustrate the importance of political participation in defining constitutional meaning. This movement enabled the freedpeople to participate in the political life of the country and use their personal experiences to define citizenship and infuse meaning into the broad guarantees of Section 1 of the Amendment. These social movements wove the Amendment's promises into the public consciousness, keeping its ideals alive despite the initial Supreme Court rulings and the end of Reconstruction.

The story of the 14th Amendment is one in which the infinite hopes of its framers became finite and bitter, disappointments in the hands of the Court. Yet, the spirit of hope in the Amendment survived. Ultimately the fate of hopes for liberty and equality rests, and always has rested, with people who make the Constitution a force in their lives.

I would like to thank Richard Aynes, Wilson Huhn, and Sarah Cravens for their comments and assistance on earlier drafts, and Ellen Lander and Christy Wesig for their editorial assistance. If any historical or other errors appear, they are solely my responsibility.

I: Infinite Hope

THE FRAMERS AS FIRST INTERPRETERS

1 The Antebellum Political Background of the 14th Amendment

Garrett Epps, University of Baltimore School of Law

For the viability of a progressive American constitutionalism, no question of meaning is more important than that of the 14th Amendment. Much of American constitutional law, at least that part of it that concerns individual rights, consists of a series of footnotes to the 14th Amendment.[1]

The Amendment was the work of a particular group of practical politicians, the Republican congressional majority in the 39th Congress, a group concerned with their own political futures, the future of their party, and the rights and desires of their constituents, as well as the future course of American society.

The 39th Congress that framed the 14th Amendment was not a "Reconstruction Congress," but one overwhelmingly shaped by the practical concerns of the Civil War. The 39th Congress, which opened its deliberations in December 1865 and the draft Amendment in June 1866, had been elected in late 1864 as part of the same wartime election cycle that reelected President Abraham Lincoln. Though the framers of the 14th Amendment had reacted to specific events in the South after the surrender at Appomattox, their sense of the issues facing the nation was that of the Northern Republican leadership that fought the war.

Specifically, the framers were operating on the assumption that the cause of the Civil War was neither the institution of slavery itself, nor Northern moral disapproval of it, but a complex political institution called the "Slave Power"— a political term that referred not only to Southern whites who owned slaves but

to constitutional provisions and political practices that gave them disproportionate power in the federal government. As antebellum free-soil and antislavery
politicians saw it, the complexity of the Slave Power meant that the war's aims
could not be realized by merely freeing the slaves and guaranteeing their freedom
in the 13th Amendment. Because the chief threats of the Slave Power lay in its
negative effect on national politics and the rights of white citizens outside the
South, eliminating it would require far-reaching changes in the state–federal
balance, the federal separation of powers, and the internal political systems of
the individual Southern states.

My contention is that if, in 1856, an antislavery politician had been asked to
propose a constitutional amendment to eliminate the dangerous influence of
the Slave Power, an amendment very much like the 14th Amendment would have
been produced. In this regard, I argue that we should pay close attention to the
antebellum political arguments forged by the men who later framed the 14th
Amendment. Their ideas are essential to understanding the interpretation given
by them to the words and structure of the Amendment they adopted.

In relating the final Amendment to antebellum politics, I do not wish to
slight the influence on Northern public opinion of the Civil War itself or of the
events of 1865, but I do suggest that it is extremely useful to note that the Republican response to the events of 1861–1865 flowed out of prewar political thought.
In that configuration of antislavery ideas, the idea of the Slave Power deserves
a more prominent place than most legal and constitutional thinkers (though not
necessarily most professional historians of the period) have heretofore given it.[2]
In fact, I suggest that we grant the theory of the Slave Power the same kind of
attention paid to the intellectual background of the framing of the Constitution.
The framers of the 14th Amendment were shaped by a background of political
history and theory quite different from the eighteenth-century history and philosophy that informed the work of framing in 1787.

The five-section Amendment is by far the longest ever adopted through the
amendment process. Much scholarship and caselaw refers to the far-reaching
effects on individual rights that resulted from the Citizenship Clause, the Privileges and Immunities Clause, the Due Process Clause, and the Equal Protection
Clause. In addition, there is power bestowed upon Congress by Section 5 to interfere with state laws that violate the previous four sections. The middle three sections imposed unprecedented (if now obsolete) federal limitations on state voting
laws, qualifications for state offices, and debt-repayment schemes. Section 3 also
changed the separation of powers created by the original Constitution, transfer-

ring from the President to Congress the power to grant "reprieves and pardons for offenses against the United States" to officials who have engaged in "insurrection or rebellion" or have given "aid and comfort" to the nation's enemies.[3]

The changes the 14th Amendment wrought in our system were profound, with implications not only for the substance and procedure of state government, but also for the relationship between states and the federal government and among the branches of the national government. In many ways, the totality of the 14th Amendment has shaped American democracy to this day.

Much of the interpretive work on the 14th Amendment has occurred in the courts and, while the reach of the Amendment is quite expansive, its judicial interpretation has often relied on a decidedly crabbed vision of its meaning. American judges maintain an odd dual consciousness about the 14th Amendment. On the one hand, they admit, over and over, that the 14th Amendment changed many details of our legal system. On the other hand, they seem unaware that the number of details, and the direction of the changes they represent, amount to something more than a series of isolated, almost idiosyncratic, results of the amendment process. Even in important decisions construing the 14th Amendment, judges often seem to regard it as a minor editing change to the Founders' Constitution—interpreting it first and foremost through an assumption that it was not designed to change the structure and workings of the 1787 document.[4]

For instance, in the first major decision interpreting the 14th Amendment, the *Slaughter-House Cases*, Justice Miller explained that it was necessary to interpret the Amendment extremely narrowly, because otherwise it might be held to have changed the Constitution:

> The argument we admit is not always the most conclusive which is drawn from the consequences urged against the adoption of a particular construction of an instrument. But when, as in the case before us, these consequences are so serious, so far-reaching and pervading, so great a departure from the structure and spirit of our institutions; when the effect is to fetter and degrade the State governments by subjecting them to the control of Congress, in the exercise of powers heretofore universally conceded to them of the most ordinary and fundamental character; when in fact it radically changes the whole theory of the relations of the State and Federal governments to each other and of both these governments to the people; the argument has a force that is irresistible, in the absence of language which expresses such a purpose too clearly to admit of doubt.[5]

The dismissive tone of the *Slaughter-House* majority reappears over and over in the United States Reports, the official record of the U.S. Supreme Court, and the current Supreme Court is committed to it. In *City of Boerne v. Flores*, the Court insisted that Congress lacks the power to set a broad prophylactic rule enforcing the congressional vision of the Free Exercise Clause of the 1st Amendment because the language of Section 5, which appears to empower Congress, is limited by an unwritten requirement that congressional enforcement legislation be "congruen[t] and proportional" to the constitutional violations Congress seeks to remedy. Perhaps, the Court does not realize that the framers of the 14th Amendment may not have reposed the same implicit trust in the wisdom of federal judges that the current justices do.[6]

The tone of denial is succinctly captured by Chief Justice Rehnquist in an opinion explaining that the 14th Amendment's Section 5, Enforcement Clause could never be construed to allow Congress to supplement state tort law with a federal tort cause of action against perpetrators of gender-based violence:

> [T]he language and purpose of the 14th Amendment place certain limitations on the manner in which Congress may attack discriminatory conduct. These limitations are necessary to prevent the 14th Amendment from obliterating the Framers' carefully crafted balance of power between the States and the National Government.[7]

I maintain that the odd tone and almost certainly wrong interpretation of these opinions arises from an impoverished historical understanding of the 14th Amendment. Some misunderstandings arise from the reticent tone of the legislative debates leading up to the Amendment.[8] However, some confusion also arises because contemporary interpreters read those legislative debates without a rich sense of the historical background against which the framers of the 14th Amendment based the change they were making to the Constitution.

The Slave Power background of the Amendment gives grounds to argue for a broad interpretation of its terms, one embracing the radicalism of some of its authors, reflected in the dissent in *Slaughter-House* by Justice Swayne:

> These amendments are a new departure, and mark an important epoch in the constitutional history of the country. They trench directly upon the power of the States, and deeply affect those bodies. They are, in this respect, at the opposite pole from the first eleven. Fairly construed these amendments may be said to rise to the dignity of a new Magna Charta.[9]

In order to put the Amendment into proper context, I will summarize the meaning of the term "Slave Power" as used by the practical politicians who built the Republican Party, brought it to power, and won the war against the South. I go on to demonstrate the ways in which antislavery politicians saw the strength of the Slave Power as flowing directly from flaws in the original Constitution of 1787, and the ways in which the antebellum political system strengthened the slaveowning interests of the South both within Southern politics and in the counsels of the nation. I then discuss the original Republican program for ending Slave Power influence before Southern secession and show its relevance to the political situation faced by the Republican members of the 39th Congress, who would eventually pass the Amendment. In the conclusion, I argue that reading the 14th Amendment against the political background of the Slave Power concept suggests that the somnambulists on the federal bench have misread the Amendment, both in its aim and in its scope.

I. ANALYSIS
A. The "Slave Power"—Conspiracy and Historiography

The Slave Power was a term coined by abolitionists in the 1830s, but it was not taken up and widely used by mainstream politicians until the 1850s. It had two related but not identical meanings. The first referred to a conspiracy of slaveholders and "dough-faced" Northern politicians (Northerners who sought office and influence by cultivating Southern support) to preserve and extend the prerogatives of slaveholders.[10] The second (discussed below) referred to the political advantages conferred on slave states by the Constitution and the antebellum political system.

In the conspiratorial sense, the Slave Power fits with other conspiracy theories of the antebellum era—the fears of Freemasonry and Catholicism that spawned the Anti-Masonic and American (or "Know-Nothing") Parties, respectively, for example. Throughout the period, and throughout history, Americans have shown credulity toward allegations that a secretive, alien, and undemocratic group or elite was conspiring to subvert the promise of American liberty.[11] That it seems implausible today does not mean that it was not sincerely believed at the time. For example, no less a figure than Abraham Lincoln accused Stephen A. Douglas of taking part in a conscious conspiracy to nationalize slavery, a conspiracy in which the other participants were Presidents Pierce and Buchanan and Chief Justice Taney. As Lincoln summarized his thoughts in a draft speech for the 1858 senatorial election against Douglas:

I clearly see, as I think, a powerful plot to make slavery universal and perpetual in this nation.... The evidence was circumstantial only; but nevertheless it seemed inconsistent with every hypothesis, save that of the existence of such conspiracy. I believe the facts can be explained to-day on no other hypothesis.

He repeated the charge, in somewhat more measured language, during his famous debates with Douglas, saying, "[T]here was a tendency, if not a conspiracy among those who have engineered this slavery question for the last four or five years, to make slavery perpetual and universal in this nation."[12]

Lincoln, a consummate politician, would of course not have made the accusation if he did not think voters would respond to it. But, that does not necessarily mean he did not believe it himself; indeed scholars believe he did. Nor was Lincoln alone; Salmon P. Chase and Joshua Giddings, The New York Times, The New York Tribune, David Wilmot and Benjamin Wade all made similar arguments.[13]

The idea of the Slave Power is relatively unfamiliar even to most educated Americans, and certainly has been little discussed by legal commentators. But an educated American during the half-century after the Civil War would have understood the antebellum era differently—as a struggle between "free soil, free speech, free men" on the one hand and the aggressive Slave Power on the other.

The Slave Power's role in bringing on the war was explored in two popular and well regarded histories published after Appomattox—Horace Greeley's *The American Conflict* and Hermann van Holst's magisterial *The Constitutional and Political History of the United States*. Both authors recognized the effect the idea of the Slave Power had upon Northern leaders and public opinion; beyond that, they both concluded that the term "Slave Power" had a discernible and objective meaning in the structure of American politics.

Horace Greeley's history of the Civil War era, written during Reconstruction, depicts the story as an assault on civil liberty, black and white, by the forces of the Slave Power. Von Holst, a German academic observer of American civilization, argued that as a result of the hybrid nature of the Union, two civilizations arose. The Southern, or "slavocratic," civilization was from the beginning inclined toward obtaining its way in national affairs by bullying and threatening Northern politicians into bartering sectional rights for Southern votes. This pattern of bullying South and appeasing North meant "that [the North] was governed, not by the black slaves of the south, but by its own white slaves." This mastery in national politics ensured that "a majority of the justices of the supreme court of the United States would profess the doctrines relative to slavery which were agreeable to the slave interest, whenever a legal question bearing on slavery arose." Secession and war was caused by "the doctrine of non-coercion [of states by the federal government], the slavocratic interpretation of state sovereignty, and slavery." Northern victory ensured the restoration "[o]f the Union, but not of the Union reduced to ruins under the constitution of 1789"—but instead, of a new nation purged of the constitutional influence of slavocracy.[14]

If writers and readers who had actual memory of the Civil War understood the Slave Power concept, how is it that we today have all but lost sight of it? The explanation lies in the highly politicized nature of Civil War historiography. Having lost the trial of arms, the unrepentant South won the postbellum battle of ideas. From the early twentieth century until at least the mid-1960s, the general understanding of the causes of the war and the nature of Reconstruction was one provided almost entirely by pro-Southern historians. In the Southern revisionist account, the Civil War was a needless conflict, brought on by a tiny minority of fanatical and deluded abolitionists and by a "blundering generation" of politicians who failed to see that compromise was always within easy reach.[15]

Revisionist historian Chauncey S. Boucher argued that antebellum Southern politicians saw themselves as divided by party and subregion. But as historian Leonard L. Richards points out, the principal argument of the Slave Power proponents was that when slavery was an issue, Southern politicians tended to unite and command considerable support from Northern allies. Most importantly, the political preconceptions of the Republican leaders who drafted the 14th Amendment and steered it to ratification reflected the latter vision of the Slave Power as a haughty, aggressive oligarchy.[16]

In the search for intent and meaning, the way in which legislators perceived the world is highly relevant, even if we ourselves do not fully share their perceptions. My contention is not that the Slave Power existed, but that these practical, antislavery politicians believed it did, and that their fear of the Slave Power, as a conspiracy or as a constitutional flaw, shaped the view of the world they wrote into the 14th Amendment.[17]

Sober constitutional and political analysts like Lincoln, William Henry Seward, and Salmon P. Chase—the practical politicians of the Free-Soil and Republican Parties—"made the Slave Power thesis popular."[18] These men cannot be easily dismissed as lunatics; they took over the country, won the Civil War, and founded the last new national party to emerge in American history. And they took the Slave Power thesis seriously.

The Slave Power concept had a second thread that functioned as a political and constitutional critique, which was at least as important as the conspiracy theory. This aspect was particularly important politically to Free-Soil and, later, Republican politicians because it offered a critique of the South and its power that did not entail a direct attack on slavery. Most Republicans, Lincoln included, believed that only a state's own government could abolish slavery in that state. Their political program forswore federal abolition of slavery where it existed as unconstitutional and undesirable. The term "antislavery," as affixed to these leaders, was most assuredly not a synonym for "pro-black" or even "abolitionist." Further, the Republican Party was not simply a moderate wing of the abolitionist movement.[19]

Republican leaders differed from abolitionists in their aims, assumptions, and tactics. Abolitionists were an important force in bringing the slavery issue to the forefront, and they helped shape Lincoln's response to the early setbacks of the Civil War. They reached their zenith of influence in the immediate post-bellum period, but at no time did abolitionists control the political movement against slavery and the Slave Power. That role fell to practical politicians—men like William Seward, John Sherman, Thaddeus Stevens, and Abraham Lincoln—who were far more concerned with electoral victory than moral purity, and who often did not feel even a token commitment to racial equality.[20]

The political meaning of the "Slave Power" is now enjoying a renascence in American historiography. Every major analysis of antebellum politics now notes that many of its central players used the term to denote a political and constitutional reality.[21] This reality recently received a thorough examination by Leonard Richards. As Richards notes, "[T]he notion that a slaveholding oligarchy ran the country—and ran it for their own advantage—had wide support in the years before and after the Civil War." Rather than the "lunatic fringe," the real authors of the Slave Power thesis were "the Free-Soil Party of the late 1840s and early 1850s and the Republican Party thereafter." These antislavery politicians contended that the Constitution and the political party system gave slaveholders and slave states control of the federal government:

> [S]lavemasters had far more power than their numbers warranted. In the sixty-two years between Washington's election and the Compromise of 1850, for example, slaveholders controlled the presidency for fifty years, the Speaker's chair for forty-one years, and the chairmanship of House Ways and Means for forty-two years. The only men to be reelected president—Washington, Jefferson, Madison, Monroe, and Jackson—were all slaveholders. The men who sat in the Speaker's chair the longest—Henry Clay, Andrew Stevenson, and Nathaniel Macon—were slaveholders. Eighteen out of thirty-one Supreme Court justices were slaveholders....

... [W]hile Yankees had disproportionate power in the national legislature
and in northern state houses, they seldom controlled the higher offices of the
national government. Slaveholders generally were in control.

The idea of disproportionate power, and the corollary idea that slaveholders were conspiring to make slavery a national institution, were "the heart and
soul of the Slave Power thesis." This thesis united the antislavery political movement, and under its aegis gathered a disparate set of political thinkers, agitators,
and office-seekers. Some were genuinely moved by the plight of the slave; others
were indifferent or hostile. But all could agree that the slave states and the slaveowners within those states had too much power. Because of its role in uniting
divergent antislavery views, this thesis was the primary force behind the antislavery struggle over the status of slavery in the territories and thus served as a
central feature of antebellum political thought.[22]

It is hard to give a precise definition of the disproportionate power concept
because each major political actor tended to give it his own definition. But most
agreed that key features of the Constitution as framed in 1787 gave Southern slaveholders and Southern states disproportionate political power within the Union.

The most important of these features was the Three–Fifths Clause, which
gave slaveholding states representation in the House of Representatives for their
slaves at the rate of three-fifths of the representation given to free citizens. The
additional House seats given to the South by the Clause were known to antebellum politicians as "slave seats." These excess House seats also gave the South
extra electoral votes, which tipped the balance of power toward the South in
presidential elections. Even in the early years of the Republic, this electoral
advantage proved decisive. In 1800, if electors had been assigned solely on the
basis of free population, John Adams would have been elected to a second term,
and the history of the next quarter century (marked by unbroken rule by Jeffersonian Presidents—Virginians and slaveowners all) might have been very different.[23]

But the Three-Fifths Clause was not the only feature of the Constitution that
free-state politicians criticized. Their critique also encompassed a series of guarantees given to the slave states that had proved a bad bargain between the two
sections of the country. The federal government was obligated to provide positive protection for slavery under the Fugitive Slave Clause,[24] which overrode the
laws of the free states and required them to assist in the return of escaped slaves.
Further, though it was never invoked for this purpose, antislavery writers were

aware that the Domestic Violence Clause[25] imposed on the federal government a duty to come to the aid of Southern states in case of slave revolts.

The critics of slavery differed among themselves about why the framers had structured the federal government that way. The abolitionists, particularly those of Garrisonian persuasion, argued that the framers had made slavery a central feature of the new nation, and that the Constitution, therefore, was a "Pro-Slavery Compact," a "covenant with death," and an "agreement with Hell." Antislavery politicians such as Lincoln, Seward, and Chase began during the 1850s to argue that the advantages given slavery by the Constitution were neither foreseen nor desired by the framers, who had expected and wanted slavery to die out in the years after the adoption of the Constitution. In this critique, the expansion and growth of slavery during the first half of the nineteenth century, and the exploitation by the slave states of their constitutional advantages, were signs that the Republic had strayed from its original aims, and that the Constitution was being perverted and misapplied.[26]

The constitutional critique was not expressed, as it might be today, by a demand for amendments. Before the Civil War, the country had little experience with the amendment process. The Constitution had been changed only twice after the first congress framed the Bill of Rights. Politicians tended to regard the original Constitution as a kind of holy writ not to be altered by lesser, post-founding mortals. There was a "widespread belief among all Americans that the constitutional text should remain static."[27]

And yet, there was a pervasive unease with the political order that had grown up under the shadow of the framers' Constitution; many thinkers in the North believed something had gone badly wrong under the Constitution of 1787.

B. Slavery and the Antebellum Political System

The North's sense that something was profoundly wrong was strengthened by the slave states' domination of the three branches of the federal government. The South's advantage, only marginal when the Constitution went into effect, grew during the antebellum era as the invention of the cotton gin sparked an explosion in the number of slaves in the lower South. The resulting imbalance was felt in the House of Representatives, in which the three-fifths rule between 1800 and 1850 consistently endowed the slave states with between fifteen and thirty "slave seats."[28] As scholar William Lee Miller notes, "[B]y 1860, the seven largest slave states, with a free population of 3,298,000, had forty-five representatives in the House, while the state of New York, with a free population of

3,831,590, had only thirty-one."[29] The overrepresentation of the free Southern population in the House also translated into overrepresentation of Southern voters in the Electoral College.

Augmenting the South's national influence was the brute fact that proslavery politicians—with federal collaboration—had suppressed free debate and democratic politics in the slave states in a way that seemed to mock the Constitution's promise of free speech and "a republican form of government."[30] After the Nat Turner revolt, a determined and successful effort was made to suppress any criticism of slavery or talk of abolition in the Southern states. Those who questioned the proslavery orthodoxy were often silenced or even killed by mob violence. Even more disturbing to those in the free states, Southern postmasters, with the active support of the federal government, began to exclude antislavery publications from the mail on the grounds that these publications might incite a slave revolt. The result was that the average Southerner was increasingly isolated from even moderate Northern antislavery opinion by what historian Clement Eaton has called an "intellectual blockade." Beyond the symbolic insult to the values of the Constitution, the political conformity imposed in the South had direct political effects on the national government and Northern society—effects most antislavery politicians and voters found threatening to their political interests and perhaps to their very liberties.[31]

Northerners had begun to feel uneasy about their own free speech rights during the famous controversy over the congressional Gag Rule. Under this standing congressional rule, adopted in 1836 and finally repealed in 1844 after prolonged, bitter controversy, the House of Representatives would not permit citizens to lodge petitions asking for the abolition or limitation of slavery. This prohibition seemed to many—even those not abolitionists—to undermine the liberties of free citizens of the North. The leader of the opposition to the ban, former President and current representative John Quincy Adams for the first time formulated and brought to wide attention the charge that the Constitution of 1787 was operating to grant illicit privileges to slaveowners and slave states.[32]

Beyond the Gag Rule, free-state citizens discerned threats to their own liberty in the mob violence increasingly used to silence abolitionists not only in the South but in the North, as with the 1837 murder of abolitionist editor, Elijah Lovejoy in Illinois. Southern states also demanded that Northern governors extradite slavery opponents to the South, where they could be tried and hanged for undermining slavery. The very demand dramatized both the arrogance of the Slave Power and the threat it posed to Northern liberty.[33]

Most serious of all, of course, would be a federal government ban of anti-slavery agitation—a gross violation of even a conservative reading of the 1st Amendment. By 1860, presidential hopeful Abraham Lincoln was warning audiences that his likely Democratic opponent, Douglas, had introduced a "sedition act" that would make antislavery agitation a federal crime.[34]

Once firmly in place, the South's enforced internal unity profoundly affected the two-party system. While both the North and South were split along party lines, after the rise of the intellectual blockade, party divisions tended to disappear when votes in Congress were important to the interests of slavery. Opponents of slavery experienced the South's congressional delegation as a monolith with the will and the power to block any legislation adverse to the broadest formulation of slavery's interests.[35]

A second feature of the party system augmented Southern power: the convention system of nominating presidential candidates. Beginning in 1832, candidates were nominated by national conventions, meaning any presidential candidate had to face the reality that nearly half of the delegates at his convention would be committed to a proslavery position. The new convention system in the Democratic Party—the nation's most powerful party—required a two-thirds vote to produce a nominee. As a result, Southern politicians could block the national hopes not only of any Democratic candidate who was antislavery, but even of those who were merely insufficiently proslavery.[36]

At about the same time, in the 1842 case of *Prigg v. Pennsylvania*, the Supreme Court gave what free-state politicians regarded as unmistakable evidence of its loyalty to slave states and their political interests. Interpreting the Fugitive Slave Clause for the first time in an opinion by Justice Joseph Story, the Court unanimously held that slaveowners entering free states carried with them the law of their home states, giving them the right of "recaption" of their slaves without any need to observe local state law or resort to local courts. Story wrote that the Clause, in effect, nationalized a policy favoring slaveowners and created "a positive, unqualified right on the part of the owner of the slave, which no state law or regulation can in any way qualify, regulate, control, or restrain." This was true even if the state laws were to ensure that free persons were not kidnapped, and dictum suggested even if the alleged slave had been born on free soil to a fugitive slave mother. In effect, this nationalized an all-but-absolute presumption that a black resident of the North was a slave to any Southern claimant.[37]

The *Prigg* decision sparked the radical, or Garrisonian, wing of the antislavery movement to break with the Constitution and declare itself in favor of dissolution of the Union. More moderate antislavery politicians were simply inspired to reflect on the fact that slaveowners dominated the Court. Jackson and Van Buren had appointed eight justices, and only one was even mildly antislavery. Six owned slaves as they sat on the bench.[38]

Antislavery politicians, then, could have been forgiven for concluding that structural flaws in the original Constitution had allowed the South to dominate all three branches of the government, and most particularly the judiciary. Using this dominance, the South had become increasingly aggressive in pursuing measures designed to upset the regional balance of power and harness the federal government in the service of slavery interests.

The first such measure was the annexation of Texas in 1845, which many historians view as the real beginning to the antebellum political struggle. The entry of Texas had the potential to upset the numerical balance between free states and slave states. But even worse, from the point of view of free-state politicians, was the provision of the admitting bill that granted Texas, at its sole option, the right to subdivide at any time into as many as five states, thereby granting Texas and the South as many as eight new senators at any time they might feel outnumbered in the federal legislature.[39]

The Compromise of 1850 produced the Fugitive Slave Law of 1850. This act, far more stringent than the Fugitive Slave Law passed by the first Congress, explicitly subordinated state officers and authority to federal mandates. To begin with, it overrode state personal liberty laws, denied the authority of state courts to adjudicate the cases of black residents claiming to be free, and barred habeas corpus relief for alleged fugitive slaves resisting return. Second, it required local law enforcement officials to cooperate with federal fugitive slave commissioners seeking assistance in returning alleged fugitive slaves to whites claiming to be their masters. Finally, and most galling to free-state whites, it empowered federal marshals to press ordinary citizens of free states into service as slave-catchers, on pain of imprisonment and fine for refusal to participate.[40]

Proslavery forces had begun to escalate the debate in other ways by the 1850s. Although Congress had banned the import of slaves in 1808, slave-state spokesmen began to demand that slaveowners be given access to the international market again, on the grounds that slave property was guaranteed to them by the Constitution and thus that restrictions on the slave trade, though clearly contemplated by the framers, were incompatible with the spirit of the Union. Alternatively, slave-state interests pressed for the annexation of Cuba or other parts of Latin America as sources of new slaves for Southern plantations. President Franklin Pierce, with the diplomatic help of future President James Buchanan, attempted to purchase Cuba, outraging antislavery politicians.[41]

Soon after the Compromise of 1850 (and despite the solemn assurances given by slave-state lawmakers that the compromise marked a definitive and binding solution to the quarrel over slavery in the territories), the Kansas-Nebraska Act violated the Missouri Compromise of 1820 by adopting "popular sovereignty" with respect to slave state or free state status for Kansas, which was north of the geographical boundary set by the Missouri Compromise. Evidence suggested the Buchanan Administration would respect "popular sovereignty" only if it favored making Kansas a slave state. Federal officials seemed unconcerned when the new territory was invaded by mobs of "border ruffians" who killed free-state settlers and openly cast fraudulent votes against antislavery measures and candidates in territorial elections. In 1856, proslavery vigilantes sacked the free-soil capital, Lawrence, which was followed by an unrepresentative constitutional convention that wrote a proslavery state constitution for Kansas. The Administration then reneged on a clear commitment to require a vote of the people to approve a state constitution and instead collaborated with the slave-state party in Kansas to impose the "Lecompton Constitution" on Kansas without a vote.[42]

Two final events in the late 1850s convinced many politicians and voters in the North that the slave states would not be satisfied until they had imposed the slave system on the North. The first was the decision in *Dred Scott v. Sandford*, in which the Supreme Court held Congress had no power to exclude slavery from the federal territories. Northern and Southern observers alike saw the decision, and the majority opinion written by Chief Justice (and former slaveowner) Roger B. Taney, as a complete triumph for Southern interests. "Southern opinion upon the subject of southern slavery . . . is now the supreme law of the land," exulted the Augusta, Georgia Constitutionalist, "and opposition to southern opinion upon this subject is now opposition to the Constitution, and morally treason against the Government." " 'There is such a thing as The Slave Power,' shrieked the Cincinnati Commercial when the decision was announced. 'It has marched over and annihilated the boundaries of the states. We are now one great homogeneous slaveholding community.' "[43]

Republicans, with an eye on the 1860 presidential election, walked a fine line between criticizing the decision and advocating equal citizenship for blacks. Many focused their critique on the idea that the decision was "incompatible with State rights and destructive of personal security."[44] Many also noted that a pending case in New York, *Lemmon v. The People*, might give the Taney Court an opportunity to hold that free states were required to maintain slaves as property whenever slave-state owners should bring them onto free soil for purposes of transit, sojourn, or visitation. From this holding it would have been a short jump to a rule that the Constitution required "free" states to permit slaves to be held permanently by residents who acquired them under the laws of slave states. Such a decision would have marked the culmination of the Slave Power conspiracy.[45]

The *Dred Scott* decision was seen as a watershed at the time it was announced, but another event loomed at least as large in the minds of free-state voters— giving lasting form and credibility to Northern fears that the South had the will and the power to transform the American system of government into something unrecognizable as a republic.

On May 22, 1856, Charles Sumner, the senior senator from Massachusetts, was nearly killed on the Senate floor by South Carolina Representative Preston S. Brooks, who objected to Sumner's intemperate criticisms of the South and of Brooks's cousin, South Carolina Senator Andrew P. Butler, in a widely publicized speech on the Kansas–Nebraska issue. The attack by "Bully Brooks," which occurred on the same day as the sack of Lawrence, seemed to Northerners to symbolize the intention of the South to behave toward the North as a master does to slaves. As poet and editor William Cullen Bryant wrote, "Are we, too, slaves, slaves for life, a target for their brutal blows, when we do not comport ourselves to please them?"[46]

The rhetoric was telling. In the wake of these events of the late 1850s, many Northerners had come to believe that the South intended to make slavery national, and would curb or eradicate the civil liberties enjoyed in the North, replace republican institutions of government with an aristocracy, and reduce the free white population of the North to "slavery," a state of subjection to political tyranny and the antithesis of self-government, at the hands of their own countrymen.

C. Republican Ideology, "States' Rights," and Federal Power

In January 1861, Ohio Representative, John Bingham, later one of the most important framers of the 14th Amendment, summarized the offenses of the Slave Power against the Union and the people of the North:

> the repeal of laws for the protection of freedom and free labor in the Territories; the conquest of foreign territory for slavery; the admission into the Union of a foreign slave State; the rejection by this sectional party of the homestead bill; the restriction of the right of petition; the restoration of fugitive slaves at

the national expense; the attempt to reward slave pirates for kidnapping Africans; the attempt to acquire Cuba, with her six hundred thousand slaves; the attempt to fasten upon an unwilling people a slave constitution [in Kansas]; the attempt to enact a sedition law, thereby restricting the freedom of the press and the freedom of speech, in direct violation of the Constitution . . . and the attempt, by extra-judicial interference[,] to take away from the people and their Representatives the power to legislate for freedom and free labor in the Territories.[47]

Running through Bingham's litany was a fear of the federal government as an instrument of the Slave Power, a political juggernaut that, having illegitimately seized control of the Republic, was attempting to use it to reduce free states to subjection and slavery.

The growing concern in the North between 1850 and 1860 about Southern control of the federal government illuminates the complex issue of "states' rights" as a feature of the sectional quarrel. During the early federal period, Southern statesmen had championed "states' rights," beginning with Jefferson and Madison, and progressing through John C. Calhoun. But by 1850, the South had become more confident in its hold over the federal government. Southerners began to address the nation in sternly nationalistic tones about their duties to the federal government, and the concern for states' rights became a Northern, and Republican, concern. The Republican message was that the Slave Power, or the "slavocracy," was bent on using the federal machinery to take over the free states and impose a slave system on them.[48]

In 1858, Senate candidate Abraham Lincoln warned that Stephen Douglas was part of a Slave Power conspiracy to nationalize slavery through federal power, forcing slavery, and thus black people, into a state that wanted no part of either:

> [W]hat is necessary to make the institution [of slavery] national? Not war. . . . It is simply the next Dred Scott decision. It is merely for the Supreme Court to decide that no State under the Constitution can exclude it, just as they have already decided that under the Constitution neither Congress nor the Territorial Legislature can do it. When that is decided and acquiesced in, the whole thing is done.[49]

Lincoln was not unusual among Republicans in expressing fear for free-state sovereignty against the federalized Slave Power behemoth. The Republican Party's national platform in 1860 demanded that "the Federal Constitution, the Rights of the States, and the Union of the States, must and shall be preserved."

The platform went on to guarantee "the maintenance, inviolate, of the Rights of the States, and especially of the right of each State to order and control its own domestic institutions according to its own judgment exclusively."[50]

Obviously some of this was election rhetoric. But it was by no means empty rhetoric. The federal government, as they saw it, had become the instrument of the Slave Power and was engaged in war against the free states.[51] Republicans, as late as 1860, had no program for federal abolition of slavery in the states where it existed, but opposed slavery's extension into the territories and the admission of new slave states. They were concerned that extension of slavery would subvert the republican institutions of the free states, change the nation from a republic to an aristocracy, and end by enslaving the whites of the North. This concern was the core of antislavery politics in the antebellum period, and the concept of the Slave Power was the embodiment of those fears.[52]

Lincoln is the best example of the narrow contours of political antislavery in the decade before Fort Sumter. He repeatedly forswore any belief in or desire for Negro equality with whites; his solution to the problem of slavery was that slaves should be freed gradually. His 1862 amendments prescribed that all persons of African descent be removed from the United States. To the extent that practical antislavery politicians like Lincoln "opposed" slavery, it was because of its negative impact on the freedom of Northern whites and the political power of free states.[53]

It is in order, therefore, to ask how Lincoln and those around him expected to deal with the Slave Power when he won election as President in 1860. Lincoln and the other Republican leaders in 1860 had not expected the South to secede. The Republican strategy had been to purify the federal government from the Slave Power, and then, without moving directly against slavery in the states, to use the power of the purified federal government to build a Republican Party and a democratic society like that of the North in the slave states. As free government and free speech were restored below the Mason-Dixon Line, states would freely choose to abolish the "peculiar institution." As they did so, their own newly opened political systems would abate the danger of undemocratic capture of the federal government.[54]

Lincoln never had the opportunity to try his plan; but the leadership of the 39th Congress saw not only the opportunity but the necessity to do something very similar. In fact, the Republican leadership found itself facing the political situation Lincoln had expected to face in 1861—attempting to govern a nation that included a significant minority of states whose political systems deliberately excluded Republican ideas and officials from public office and debate.

Despite the Union victory over the South, the Party of Union was still desperately weak in the restored nation. Republicans had never commanded a majority of the voters. The Party had won the 1860 election with a minority of the vote, had not captured Congress, and had lost ground legislatively in 1862. The Party had won congressional majorities in 1864, but only because the Southern states did not take part in the election. In 1864, Lincoln won reelection only by forming a coalition with War Democrats under the "National Union Party," and by dropping the reliably antislavery Hannibal Hamlin from the ticket in favor of Southern Democrat and former slaveowner, Andrew Johnson. Johnson was a lifelong Democrat, and he had little in common with the Republican leadership. They had sought to woo him as an ally after the assassination of Lincoln, but by the time Congress convened, they realized their efforts had failed, and many correctly suspected Johnson was actively working to restore the South in ways that might permit him to run for a full term as President in 1868 on something like the Democratic ticket.[55]

Johnson was building his own potential power base by claiming the executive power to restore the Confederate States to the Union after ratification of the 13th Amendment, and by using his pardon power to allow the antebellum leadership to assume control of the restored states. Under Johnson's proclamations, seceded states were allowed to elect legislatures and members of Congress under their prewar constitutions using all-white, restrictive prewar voting systems. The results, predictably, were state governments that seemed reluctant to give any but grudging support to the outcome of the war. And in fact, the states restored by presidential order had elected members of the 39th who, if seated, would have permanently altered the balance of power in the federal government.[56]

The 39th Congress featured solid Republican majorities in both houses. In the House, Republicans numbered 145 to a mere 46 Democrats, while the Senate had 39 Republicans to only 11 Democrats. But in December 1865, to Republican leaders like House Speaker Schuyler Colfax, Representative Thaddeus Stevens, and Senators Henry Wilson and John Sherman, the nose count must have seemed somewhat less favorable. The official historical totals do not include the delegations sent by the states readmitted by Johnson's order; when those numbers were added, the partisan picture must have looked a good deal chancier. In early 1865, the Southern states sent 55 claimants to the House of Representatives, and 20 putative senators.[57]

Elected by all-white voters, these presumptive delegations were made up either of conservative Southern Unionists who had opposed secession, but otherwise resisted any change in Southern society, or of outright secessionists and former Confederate officials. They included at least 9 former officers in the Confederate Army, 7 former members of the Confederate Congress, and 3 former members of Southern secession conventions. Their natural leader was Alexander H. Stephens, senator-elect from Georgia, who had until a few months before been vice president of the Confederate States of America.[58]

Had these officials, or even a significant minority of them, been added to the legislative mix, the partisan alignment would have looked far different. Consider the eventual votes on adoption of the 14th Amendment, which passed in the Senate by 33 to 11 and in the House by 138 to 36. Had every Southern representative been seated, proponents of the 14th Amendment would have needed 46 Senate votes and 163 House votes. The 14th Amendment itself was a compromise measure, much weaker than many of its proponents had hoped. Even so, it failed to attract the votes of every Northern Democrat and would have been unlikely to attract any additional votes from the South. In effect, congressional efforts to influence Reconstruction would have been stymied by the addition of these Southern members of Congress.

The prospect of the Slave Power's return to its former influence in Congress was a subject of general discussion during the months before 39th Congress assembled. Former Confederates no less than Republicans were keenly aware of the potential increase in their power. As the Richmond Examiner, the most irredentist of secessionist voices, put it:

> Universal assent appears to be given to the proposition that if the states lately rebellious be restored to rights of representation according to the Federal basis, or to the basis enlarged by the enumeration of all the blacks in the next census, the political power of the country will pass into the hands of the South, aided, as it will be, by Northern alliances. The South claims that this will be the fact, and the North does not dispute it.[59]

Nor did there seem to be much prospect of mounting effective electoral challenges to the conservative Southern governments Johnson was recognizing. None allowed freed slaves to vote. The "reconstructed" state legislatures quickly focused on enacting laws to keep former slaves in a state of subordination. The legislatures were made up of former Confederates or conservative Southern Unionists. The two groups were united in their conviction that subordination of blacks was essential to the proper functioning of the Southern economy and society. Freed slaves were required to maintain employment, often evidenced by a written contract, to avoid arrest for vagrancy. Black "vagrants" were to be auctioned off as contract laborers to white employers who paid their fines. Public whipping was the penalty for a wide variety of offenses by blacks, including "intrud[ing]" into public assemblies of whites or entering vehicles designated for whites only. Freed slaves were forbidden to own or carry firearms or knives. Authorities could seize children of freed slaves and force them into apprenticeship if a court concluded that their parents were unable to support them.[60]

Many Southerners believed their "Black Codes" were forward-looking reforms because they yielded to freed slaves the same legal rights free blacks had possessed before secession. But many Northerners, even those of moderate opinion, viewed the Black Codes as a defiant means designed to produce "a condition which will be slavery in all but its name."[61] The congressional Republicans acted quickly to block the Black Codes by enacting the Civil Rights Act of 1866. But concern remained that a future pro-Johnson Congress might repeal it or that the federal courts might invalidate it as unconstitutional.

The new system of labor in the former Confederacy seemed a continuation of slavery, this time as a social and political institution rather than as a system of property. Thus, the war seemed to have done nothing to bring a free labor system to the South; slowly but surely, the Slave Power seemed to be reassembling itself.

If the reassembly had been successful, the Slave Power would have been made more, not less, powerful by the war. The ratification of the 13th Amendment, days after the 39th Congress met, had rendered the Three-Fifths Clause a dead letter. Beginning with the reapportionment of 1870, the Southern states would receive full representation for each freed slave rather than a mere 60%, a change that would give the region 13 more House seats and electoral votes without the extension of minimal political rights, much less the franchise, to the freed slaves who formed the basis of the representation. It would be the "slave seats" problem all over again.[62]

This meant that the Republicans, despite having won the war, might be unable to prevent a coalition of Northern and Southern Democrats from giving away the peace. If the Southern members were seated, their numbers in the 39th Congress would make it all but impossible to block Johnson's presidential reconstruction. Moreover, their power in Congress would give them decisive influence over the Democratic presidential nomination in 1868. Finally, the electoral vote windfall given by nullifying the Three-Fifths Clause might even enable the South to swing the White House to their chosen nominee. As early as December 1865,

rumors began to circulate, North and South, that the next Democratic presidential nominee would be not Johnson but a popular war hero, Robert E. Lee.[63]

Once safely back in control of the federal government, the former slaveowners could recreate some new institution resembling slavery. They could also use
the federal treasury to pay off the debts owed by the Confederacy to Southern
and European bondholders, or conversely to repudiate bonds issued by the
Union to finance the war effort.

In short, the Republicans in late 1865 needed both a short-term and a long-
term strategy to prevent the complete reascendancy of the Slave Power—political domination of the federal government by skewed representation, one-party
rule in the South, and subordination in economic policy of the needs of the
industrial North. In the short term, the Republicans solved their political
dilemma with a desperate expedient: using their control of the House Clerk's
Office not to recognize any representatives from the presidentially reconstructed
states. This tactical move ensured Republican political dominance was maintained until the next election. But obviously a longer term solution was needed—
a mechanism that would check the recrudescence of the Slave Power so that
Lincoln's original plan could go into effect.[64]

Advanced thinkers in the party and the abolition movement favored giving
the vote to the freed slaves. But black suffrage was an unpopular idea in the
North.[65] Republicans were deeply concerned about physical violence and legal-
ized subordination of the freed slaves, but their commitment to black Southerners as full members of the political order was more equivocal. For conservative
Republicans, the vision was still of a white man's country, but one that lived by
open debate and republican values.

The long-term fix would need to permit not only free debate but genuine
political competition between the parties. At the same time, it would need to
prevent Southern leaders from using black populations for disproportionate
representation; states with large black populations would have to choose
between black suffrage and loss of representation. In addition, the solution
would need to proscribe the reascendance of disloyal conservative leaders of the
Slave South, permitting a new leadership to emerge. And it would need to
empower Congress, the only branch of the federal government under firm
Republican control, to override both the executive and the judiciary, and the
Southern state governments, in setting the terms of political life.

In short, the long-term fix for the danger of a new Slave Power looks remark-
ably like the 14th Amendment.

II. CONCLUSION

Of course, the Slave Power was not the only political current that powered Republicanism during the antebellum and immediate postwar periods. The ideology of "free labor," with its economic vision of independence and integrity as an individual value, also powerfully affected the Republican view of the world. In addition, many of those who took part in framing the 14th Amendment (even some known to history as radicals) were men of profoundly conservative instincts who, while they wished to preserve the result of the Civil War, wished also to preserve key features of the Republic they had known before the war. Finally, the political vagaries of 1866 shaped the specifics of the 14th Amendment's text. As Eric Foner notes:

> [T]he aims of the 14th Amendment can only be understood within the political and ideological context of 1866: the break with the President, the need to find a measure upon which all Republicans could unite, and the growing consensus within the party around the need for strong federal action to protect the freedmen's rights, short of the suffrage.[66]

However, the Slave Power thesis also played an important role in shaping an ideological response to the immediate needs of 1866, a result of multiple forces flowing together. Political actors must often react to events without adequate time to think; they always operate against a set of assumptions and beliefs, which are shaped both by the practical concerns of the moment and by the ideological lessons they have absorbed during their careers. We confront new problems with the tools we have learned to use, and this is true whether those tools are weapons or political ideas. In the case of the 14th Amendment, the events of 1865–1866 posed a complex question. The answer the 39th Congress constructed resembles, not coincidentally, the antebellum solution to the problems of the Republic: Cripple the Slave Power.

Read against a Slave Power background, an overriding aim of the 14th Amendment seems to have been predominantly defensive: to protect the federal government against former slave states, to ensure that the new government forged during the Civil War would be supreme in any future confrontation, and to require that reconstructed state governments of the South run their internal politics by the North's republican rules.

The Slave Power thesis and its history provide a fertile ground for scholars reading the congressional debates. A reading of the 14th Amendment as a measure against the Slave Power confounds certain assumptions of current jurisprudence. To begin with, since the *Slaughter-House Cases*, courts and commentators have tended to take for granted that the Equal Protection Clause of Section 1, and perhaps all of Section 1, were aimed specifically at the situation of the freed slaves. There is ample warrant in the history of antislavery thought to cast doubt on that interpretation. The 14th Amendment may be better seen as a source of political values than of specifically legal, formal guarantees. In light of the Slave Power thesis, the Privileges and Immunities, Due Process, and Equal Protection Clauses can be seen as guaranteeing a free and open society for all Southerners, white and black, with free speech and free elections (perhaps all white at first, but very soon open to voters of both races), and as reaffirming the interpretation of the Guarantee Clause that antislavery politicians had sought to advance before the Civil War.

The political background of the 14th Amendment suggests that it was designed to operate powerfully on the internal life of the states—to impose the nationalist vision implied by Madison's argument for an "extended republic," impervious to the claims of "faction," as the best guarantee of self-rule and liberty.[67] State governments were dangerous, not only to their own people but to the purified democratic republic forged on the anvil of Civil War. The normative preference for states as the political shapers of society that some claim to discern in the Constitution of 1787 would thus be negated or perhaps even reversed, with a new preference for national values of equality, participation, and open debate. The 14th Amendment read in this light would be a fertile source of arguments over the essential components of such an open society, in which political decisions are made by an informed process of critical discourse among free, equal citizens.[68]

The Slave Power reading also casts doubt on any argument that the purpose of the 14th Amendment was primarily to empower the federal judiciary and strengthen its role as arbiter of constitutional rights.[69] The framers vividly remembered the capture of the judiciary by the Slave Power, and they feared it had not yet fully freed itself.

In fact, it seems much more probable Congress intended to grant itself a coequal role with the courts in the clearly political work of defining what constitutes "privileges and immunities," "due process of law," and "equal protection of the laws." Congressional statutes might set the goals; the courts would enforce them. Both branches might be involved, but the Court's current vision of itself at the center, with Congress relegated to an occasional role as an auxiliary enforcer of court decisions, seems far from what Slave Power-minded framers intended.

Finally, the Slave Power reading calls into question any vision of American federalism inspired by the structure of the 1787 Constitution. The framers of the 14th Amendment surely believed they were making a far-reaching and significant change to that original design. "[W]e must never forget," wrote Chief Justice John Marshall in 1819, "that it is a constitution we are expounding."[70] Similarly, we must not forget that in construing the 14th Amendment, we are expounding an amendment, a change, one that is "to all intents and purposes" as much a part of the Constitution as any of the original Clauses.

The 14th Amendment was drafted at the end of a terrible war that transformed almost every feature of American life. It seems entirely logical to believe that the Amendment was intended to render permanent those changes. The record suggests that those who drafted it saw not just the glory of what was written at Philadelphia but its flaws as well.

An earlier version of this chapter was published in *Law and Contemporary Problems*, Vol. 67, No. 3, pp. 175–211. Copyright © 2004 Garrett Epps.

This paper was presented at the Fourth Annual Conference of the Duke Law School Program in Public Law on December 14, 2002. Of the many participants who offered suggestions there, I thank in particular Adrienne Davis, Pamela Karlan, Judith Resnik, and Clark Cunningham, as well as fellow panelists Richard Pildes, Michael Rappaport, and Robert Tsai. In addition, I thank these historians and legal scholars of the 14th Amendment and Reconstruction, who read and commented on earlier drafts of this article: Richard Aynes, Michael Kent Curtis, Michael F. Holt, Ward McAfee, James M. McPherson, Jack P. Maddex, Andrew Taslitz, and Michael Vorenberg. They share no responsibility for historical howlers that remain. I also thank my colleagues during my visit to Duke University School of Law in 2001–2002 for their encouragement and comments, particularly Paul Haagen, H. Jefferson Powell, Christopher Schroeder, and William Van Alstyne of the Duke faculty, and William Marshall, Louis D. Bilionis, Ann Hubbard, Eric Muller, and Melissa Saunders of the University of North Carolina School of Law. I am grateful, moreover, for the guidance of Peter Wood of the Duke History Department, as well as John Hope Franklin, an ideal teacher and my hero. Thanks, too, to Lawrence Goodwyn and Spencie Love of Duke; Senior Associate Dean Richard Danner and the staff of the Duke Law library; my former colleagues at the University of Oregon, particularly Rennard Strickland, Dave Frohnmayer, Jim O'Fallon, Keith Aoki, and Robert Tsai; and Judge David Schuman of the Oregon Court of Appeals. And I thank my research assistants, Kimberly Shore, Jacqueline Marks, and Emmett Soper; my editor at Henry Holt, John McCrae; and my agent, Wendy Weil. I also thank Sanford Levinson, Aviam Soifer, Peter Shane, Gerald Torres, William Forbath, Carl Tobias, John Paul Jones, Gary Leedes, Michael Gerhardt, David Garrow, Michael Dorf, Christopher Eisgruber, and Jane Harris Aiken.

2

The Historical Context of the 14th Amendment

Paul Finkelman, Albany Law School

In the mid-twentieth century, the 14th Amendment emerged as a central, indeed the central, provision in our constitutional jurisprudence. In the last half-century or so, Section 1 of the Amendment has been the driving engine of the judicial expansion of civil rights and civil liberties. During this period, scholars and jurists have combed the records of the 39th Congress, seeking a sure answer to the question of what the 14th Amendment meant.

In *Brown v. Board of Education*, the Supreme Court sought to understand the historical meaning of the guarantees of the Amendment. The Court explicitly asked in terms not just of "intention" or original contemplation, but of the "interpretation" the framers and ratifiers understood should be given to their work. In scheduling reargument for the fall of 1953, the Court asked lawyers to provide briefs on a number of questions including two historical issues:

1. What evidence is there that the Congress which submitted and the state legislatures and conventions which ratified the 14th Amendment contemplated or did not contemplate, understood or did not understand, that it would abolish segregation in the public schools?
2. If neither the Congress in submitting nor the states in ratifying the 14th Amendment understood that compliance with it would require the immediate abolition of segregation in the public schools, was it nevertheless the understanding of the framers of the [A]mendment (a) that future Congresses might in the exercise of their power under Section 5 of the [A]mendment abolish segregation, or (b) that it would be within the judicial power, in light of future

conditions, to construct the [A]mendment as abolishing such segregation of its own force?[1]

Paraphrasing those questions, we might ask: How did the Congress in 1866 interpret the Amendment, especially with respect to racial equality? Ever since *Brown,* scholars have been trying to answer the questions raised by the Court. To do this, the view of the framers and ratifiers as "intenders" should be seen in the context of the world they came from and the world they inhabited. Their experiences help us understand not only what members of Congress "intended," but how they interpreted what they accomplished. Context is critical to interpretation, but is often overlooked in the analysis of intent.

In *Brown* the Court and the litigants focused on the debates in Congress. During oral arguments Justices Felix Frankfurter and Stanley Reed asked Spottswood Robinson, counsel for the NAACP, about the intent of Congress.[2] The Court seemed to believe that the key to understanding the Amendment could be found in the records of the Congressional debate. Even today, many scholars seem certain that the records of Congress contain some Rosetta stone that will allow them to interpret the meaning of the terms in the 14th Amendment such as "privileges and immunities of the citizens of the United States," "due to process of law," or "equal protection of the law."

However, there is, in fact, no easy and clear way to determine the specific intentions of the framers.[3] Exploring the records of Congress can be useful, but certainly the debates in Congress do not tell the whole story of the origin and meaning of the 14th Amendment. These debates may not even tell the most important story. Moreover, it is possible that the debaters themselves were uncertain what they intended, in the most narrow and specific ways. For example, the man responsible for the language of Section 1, John A. Bingham of Ohio, liked the term "privileges and immunities" because its "euphony and indefiniteness of meaning were a charm to him."[4] This suggests that he intended that the Amendment be open ended and flexible.

To understand the meaning of the 14th Amendment we must get beyond the debates in Congress, and attempt to understand the context in which the Amendment was framed and ratified. What were the political and social realities of the age? What events were fresh in the minds of the framers as they sought to secure the victory of the Union cause? These other stories may be a better guide to what the drafters and supporters of the Amendment in Congress had in mind when they wrote the Amendment.

An understanding of the 14th Amendment begins, then, in the history leading up to the Amendment. One crucial aspect of the story is the striking changes (and attempted changes) in the law of race relations that took place across the North in the two decades before the Civil War. Section 2 of this chapter focuses on political and societal changes in Pennsylvania and Ohio, and how those changes affected two of the most important framers of the 14th Amendment, Thaddeus Stevens and John Bingham. The second story, told in Section 3, describes the legal repression and brutal racial violence in the South immediately after the Civil War. The Report of the Joint Committee on Reconstruction detailed this repression and violence. While preparing the Report, the Joint Committee also wrote the Civil Rights Act of 1866 and the 14th Amendment.

These two stories complement each other. The first gives us insight into the legal and political history that shaped Republican thought about race and the aspirations of Republican leaders for a racially just society. There are a number of key Republican leaders who are part of this history. Congressman John A. Bingham, the primary author of Section 1 of the 14th Amendment, is one of these leaders. So too is Thaddeus Stevens of Pennsylvania, the most powerful member of the House of Representatives. Stevens was a key player in the adoption of the 14th Amendment and in the shaping of Republican policy towards race. The second story helps us understand what the Congress was struggling against when drafting Section 1 of the Amendment, and thus illustrates what the Republican leadership of the Congress hoped the Amendment would accomplish and what it would prevent. Put together, this history affects our understanding of how the 14th Amendment was designed to protect both civil rights and civil liberties for all Americans.

I. RACE AND LAW IN THE ANTEBELLUM NORTH: A PRELUDE TO THE 14TH AMENDMENT

The general view of antebellum Northern race relations has been shaped by an odd mixture of progressive and conservative scholarship. In the 1960s, a number of scholars began to look carefully at the nature of race relations in the pre-Civil War North and concluded that the situation was abysmal. Influenced by the civil rights movement in the South, scholars like Leon Litwack and Eugene Berwanger discovered that the antebellum North was not a paragon of equality. On the contrary, these historians discovered racism, segregation, and other forms of discrimination. Thus, Leon Litwack asserted that on the eve of the Civil War "the Northern Negro remained largely disenfranchised, segregated and

economically oppressed" and, just as important, "change did not seem immi-
nent." Similarly, in *The Frontier Against Slavery*, Eugene Berwanger claimed that
"discrimination against Negroes in the Middle West reached its height between
1846 and 1860, the same years in which the slavery extension controversy became
most acute." Berwanger argued that "prejudice against Negroes was a factor in
the development of antislavery feeling in the ante-bellum United States." Even
abolitionists came under attack. Jane and William Pease argued that some lifelong opponents of slavery were uncomfortable in the presence of blacks and
that many abolitionists could never decide

> whether the Negro was equal or inferior to the white; whether social equality
> for the Negro should be stressed or whether it should be damped; whether civil
> and social rights should be granted him at once or only in the indefinite and
> provisional future; or whether, in fact, social and civil rights or only civil rights
> should be granted or whether only civil rights should be given him.[5]

Writing in the early years of the civil rights movement, the message of these
scholars was in part that Northerners should realize their racist past. Recognizing this past was a key to changing the nature of mid-twentieth century race
relations.

In an ironic twist, conservative scholars seized on this scholarship to reach
a different conclusion. If the antebellum North was inherently racist, these
scholars argued, then the Congress in the 1860s and 1870s could not possibly
have meant to create an integrated society. Thus, the conservative legal scholar
Raoul Berger claimed that the framers of the 14th Amendment could not have
intended to require integration or substantive equality for blacks. He asserted
that the "key to an understanding of the 14th Amendment is that the North was
shot through with Negrophobia."[6]

It is certainly true that in most of the antebellum North racial equality was
rare. But, it is also true that in this period a number of politicians, especially
Republicans or those who later became Republicans, worked hard to alter race
relations in order to move toward a more equal society. Many of the leaders of
the party had long been working for greater equality. The Republican congressional leaders in 1866 saw the 14th Amendment as an opportunity to achieve at
the national level what they had long hoped to achieve at the state level.

A. Thaddeus Stevens and Race in Pennsylvania

In 1866, Thaddeus Stevens was the most powerful member of the House of
Representatives, and perhaps the most powerful political leader in the nation. He

was also a key member of the Joint Committee on Reconstruction, which drafted the 14th Amendment. For more than four decades, Stevens had been an uncompromising supporter of black rights and racial equality. In 1866, as a member of the Joint Committee, he was in a position to implement his ideology.[7]

From the 1820s on, Stevens regularly argued fugitive slave cases pro bono. His most famous effort came in the dramatic prosecutions in the wake of the Christiana incident. In 1851, a Maryland slaveowner, his relatives, and a United States deputy marshal had attempted to seize a fugitive slave living with a number of other fugitive slaves in Christiana, Pennsylvania. The blacks refused to peacefully surrender, and instead opened fire on the approaching whites. A short battle ensued, which left the slaveowner dead and his relatives wounded. The fugitive slave, who had killed his owner, calmly traveled by train to Rochester, New York, where he visited Frederick Douglass before taking a boat to Canada. The federal prosecutor, following direct orders from President Millard Fillmore,[8] secured treason indictments against more than 40 blacks and 5 white men who had refused to help the marshal arrest the fugitive slaves. Part of the defense strategy included defying racial conventions; thus the black defendants entered the courtroom accompanied by white women to the horror of the proslavery prosecutors. Here Stevens, as a key strategist in the case, demonstrated his belief in fundamental racial equality and his willingness to challenge the racial status quo.[9]

As a politician Stevens was equally supportive of black rights. As a delegate to the 1837 Pennsylvania Constitutional Convention, Stevens worked hard to maintain black suffrage in the face of Jacksonian Democrats, who were intent on taking the vote away from blacks. Although Stevens was unsuccessful in his efforts, his commitment to the ideals of racial equality only intensified.[10]

Stevens' relationships with blacks were more than political. He saw them as social equals, and he acted on this belief in his personal life. Stevens had a long-time black housekeeper who was probably his mistress. However, whatever their private relations were, in public Stevens treated her with respect and dignity. "He always addressed her as 'Madam,' gave her his seat in public conveyances, and included her in social intercourse with his friends." Here, again, Stevens challenged prejudice. Indeed, throughout the last half century of his life Stevens challenged racism. Even in death the Congressman from Pennsylvania struck a blow for equality. Before he died, Stevens had left instructions to be buried in a cemetery that accepted the bodies of all people, without regard to race.[11]

Race relations in Pennsylvania during Stevens' lifetime were complicated and often in flux. The highpoint of antebellum Northern racism did not occur in the 1850s and on the eve the Civil War, as Litwack, Berwanger, and Berger claim, but in the 1830s. During the age of Jackson, "Jacksonian democracy" came to mean an expansion of rights for white men and a contraction of rights for blacks. This was a trend Stevens vigorously opposed.

Until 1837, black men could vote in Pennsylvania, but in that year a new constitution deprived them of that right. As I have already noted, Stevens was unsuccessful in fighting this change. By the 1840s, however, the racial climate in Pennsylvania had begun to move in a more progressive direction. The South's incessant demands for more slave territories and greater federal support for slavery led to greater Northern opposition to slavery. This opposition to slavery, and Southern demands for protecting and expanding slavery, also led to greater rights and legal protection for blacks.

Even while the Jacksonians were working hard to take rights away from blacks, Pennsylvania enforced its laws to protect black freedom. Pennsylvania's 1826 Personal Liberty Law,[12] for example, was designed to protect free blacks from kidnapping and also provide some measure of protection for fugitive slaves. In 1837, a justice of the peace invoked it to prevent Edward Prigg and three other Marylanders from removing Margaret Morgan and her children from the state. Prigg and his cohorts ignored the law, removed the blacks without legal authority, and were subsequently indicted for kidnapping. Pennsylvania's governor pushed hard to have the Marylanders extradited, and ultimately Maryland returned Prigg to Pennsylvania, where he was convicted of kidnapping. However, in *Prigg v. Pennsylvania*, the U.S. Supreme Court overturned Prigg's conviction and struck down the state's 1826 Personal Liberty Law.[13]

In response to this case, the state withdrew all support for enforcement of the federal Fugitive Slave Law of 1793 and the Fugitive Slave Clause of the Constitution, and prohibited its officials from aiding in the return of fugitive slaves. In 1847 Pennsylvania repealed a law of 1780 that had allowed visitors to bring their slaves in the state for up to six months. Thus, after 1847, any slave brought into Pennsylvania, even for a moment, became instantly free.[14]

Pennsylvania's position on fugitive slaves and on slaves in transit illustrates the complexity of race relations in that state during the time of Stevens' rise to political power. Increasingly, the state protected black liberty and offered African Americans safe haven from bondage. Even though Pennsylvania took the vote away from blacks in the 1830s, the state never attempted to limit their immigration. Indeed, the 1847 repeal of the "six months law" meant that any slaves brought into the state would remain there as free people. Blacks living in Pennsylvania could own property, enter the professions, attend schools, testify against whites in court, and fully exercise their rights to freedom of speech, press, assembly, and religion. The emergence of the African Methodist Episcopal Church (AME) illustrates the complexities of race relations and law in Pennsylvania. When a white Philadelphia church segregated blacks in the late eighteenth century, Richard Allen and Absalom Jones built Bethel Church and then organized and created the AME Church. Private racism set the stage for this new church, while Pennsylvania laws allowed free black to organize the church. This would have been impossible in the South, where laws prohibited blacks from gathering for such purposes without white supervision. For black church leaders like Jones and Allen, freedom of religion, antislavery, freedom of speech, and politics were all interconnected. In 1830 Allen would preside over the first National Negro Convention in Philadelphia. The fact that blacks could create their own churches, agitate for full political rights, and also protest private discrimination allowed them to participate in all sorts of protests against slavery. The state turned a blind eye to the active involvement of blacks and whites in the Underground Railroad, which of course led to a larger population of blacks. State officials also continued to prosecute whites accused of kidnapping free blacks,[15] and increasing numbers of the people of Pennsylvania voted for antislavery politicians, like Stevens, who were ready to fight against human bondage and for human equality.

These experiences and this history shaped the background that Stevens brought to Congress and to the Joint Committee on Reconstruction, which drafted the 14th Amendment.

B. John A. Bingham and Race Relations in Ohio

The experience of Congressman John A. Bingham of Ohio mirrors that of Stevens. Like Stevens, Bingham served on the Joint Committee on Reconstruction. Bingham, the author of Section 1 of the 14th Amendment, was equally a long time opponent of racial discrimination, and like Stevens, he had fought against slavery and segregation. In his home state of Ohio, Bingham had witnessed a dramatic change in the nature of race relations. In the first decades of the nineteenth century, Ohio was one of the most racially retrograde Northern states. However, by the 1840s, and continuing through the 1850s, Ohio's racial environment changed. These changes coincided with the rise to power of Bingham's new political organization, the Republican Party.[16]

In 1804 and 1807, Ohio adopted elaborate registration requirements for blacks entering the state. These laws were rarely enforced and were utterly ineffective in limiting the growth of the state's free black community. Indeed, while these laws were on the books Ohio's black population grew rapidly. Nevertheless, these laws always posed a threat to blacks, who might be forced out of the state if they could not prove their freedom or find sureties to promise to support them if they were unable to support themselves. Ohio also prevented blacks from voting, serving on juries, or testifying against whites. Ohio prohibited blacks from attending public schools with whites while also denying them meaningful access to segregated public schools.[17] Such laws led Raoul Berger to argue that the antebellum North was "shot through with Negrophobia."[18]

However, in parts of the North, a profound transformation of the law with regard to race took place in the last two decades of the antebellum period. This change was especially apparent in Ohio, at precisely the time that Bingham, Salmon P. Chase, Jacob Brinkerhoff, and other future leaders of the Ohio Republican Party were entering politics, or taking a leading role in the state's new Republican Party.[19]

In 1839, the Ohio legislature created an elaborate system to regulate the return of fugitive slaves. The law required that ownership of a fugitive slave "be proved" to the "satisfaction" of a state judge, while at the same time authorizing state officials to aid in the return of bona fide fugitive slaves. This law was consistent with Ohio's long-standing policy of protecting free blacks from kidnapping while supporting its constitutional obligation to return fugitive slaves. However, unlike earlier laws, which only punished kidnapping, this act had the potential to frustrate attempts by masters to recover fugitive slaves and would have made fugitives feel more secure in the Buckeye State.[20]

The adoption of this law cuts against the idea of a "negrophobic" Ohio; the law increased the state's black population and made the state a haven for runaway slaves rather than discouraging blacks from living in the state. A truly "negrophobic" Ohio would have passed laws similar to those in the South, which required law enforcement officers to incarcerate black strangers and travelers and advertise them as runaway slaves, unless they could document their status as free people.

In 1842, *Prigg* effectively struck down personal liberty laws of the free states, like Ohio's 1839 Act. A year later the Ohio legislature reacted by reinstating an earlier law which provided imprisonment "at hard labor" for up to seven years for anyone convicted of removing a free black from the state as a fugitive slave or even attempting to seize a free black with the intent to remove that person from the state. Again, a more negrophobic state would not have passed a new law to punish the kidnapping of free blacks.[21]

Starting in 1848, at a time when Bingham was beginning his political career,[22] Ohio began to rapidly change its racial laws while taking an increasingly strong stand against Southern slavery. These new laws were both antislavery and supportive of expanded rights for blacks. In 1848, the Ohio legislature sent Congress a resolution urging a prohibition on slavery in any territories acquired in the Mexican War.[23] More significantly for the background to the 14th Amendment, in that year Ohio passed a new law which provided two separate methods for educating blacks. Previously, blacks had no right to a public education and had been denied access to the public schools, although in fact some districts ignored the law and allowed African American children to attend local schools. The new law for the first time specifically allowed school districts to permit blacks to attend public schools. Furthermore, the law allowed blacks to attend public schools with whites, if local communities did not object. The law also authorized the creation of segregated schools for blacks funded by taxes collected from blacks if the local white community would not allow for integrated schools.[24] While segregated education was considered a mark of discrimination at the time (just as it is today), this law was nevertheless an important and positive step forward in the expansion of rights for blacks in Ohio because, for the first time in its history, Ohio acknowledged its obligation to provide for the education of black children.[25] In 1849 Ohio repealed the registration and surety bond requirements of the earlier laws, allowed blacks to testify against whites, and gave them even greater access to the public schools.[26] Laws passed in the 1850s, when Bingham was in Congress, provided blacks with new protections against kidnapping, and demonstrated Ohio's hostility to the Fugitive Slave Law of 1850.

By the eve of the Civil War, blacks did not have full equality in Ohio. They still could not vote, serve on juries, or serve in the state militia, but blacks had far more legal rights than they ever had before. Moreover, the thrust of the newly created Republican Party was towards greater racial equality. Far from being "shot through with Negrophobia," Ohio in this period was making steady and significant progress towards a more egalitarian polity that provided increasing rights for free blacks. Ohio did not entirely eliminate discriminatory laws at this time because a substantial number of voters were Democrats who opposed racial equality and were later hostile to emancipation. After antislavery, Free Soil Democrats like Chase and Brinkerhoff joined the new Republican Party, the Democratic Party in the state became the bastion of those who were most hostile to blacks. These Democratic voters, who were particularly powerful in southern Ohio, were able to block some changes, especially those like black suffrage, which required a constitutional amendment. They were also able to block Republican hegemony in the 1850s and 1860s by sometimes controlling the state legislature. Ohio in the late antebellum period was a divided polity, with the Republicans usually, but not always, able to control state government.

The key to understanding Bingham's Ohio background is that parts of his state were clearly negrophobic, but that in his northern Ohio district, and in much of the state, Free Soilers and Republicans gained enormous power in the 1840s and throughout the 1850s. These Republicans won elections while expanding the rights and liberties of blacks in Ohio. By the mid-1860s, Republicans were at the zenith of their political power nationally, and they brought with them a long history of civil rights advocacy as well as a track record of successfully moving Ohio forward in the march to civil rights.

It was in this context of statutes, court decisions, and executive actions against slavery[27] and in favor of expanded equality that John Bingham became a key member of the Ohio Republican Party and a rising star in national politics. His pedigree was deeply connected to antislavery and black civil rights. He brought these ideas to Congress and to his role in drafting the 14th Amendment.

When we consider what the Amendment meant to its drafters, we must begin with the backgrounds and experiences of key Republican leaders like Stevens and Bingham. We must further consider the racial trajectory of the North—and more significantly the Republican Party in the North. The evidence suggests that for Stevens, Bingham, and other Republicans, black civil rights mattered.[28]

II. THE SOUTHERN CONTEXT OF RECONSTRUCTION AND THE SHAPING OF THE 14TH AMENDMENT

Stevens, Bingham and other Republicans in the 39th Congress were not only influenced by their own long struggle against racism in the North and slavery in the South. The retrograde actions of Southern politicians and the racist brutality of Southern whites in the wake of the Civil War also affected their Constitutional views and interpretation of the work they were doing. A brief description of race relations in the South in 1865–1866 reminds us of why the 14th Amendment was passed and helps us understand what Stevens, Bingham and their Republican colleagues hoped it would accomplish.

A. *The Aftermath of Slavery*

In April 1865, the United States successfully suppressed what leaders at the time referred to as "the late wicked Rebellion."[29] The suppression of the rebel-

lion had involved more than 2,000,000 soldiers and sailors, 10% of whom were African Americans. The vast majority of these black soldiers—the "sable arm" of the United States Army—had been slaves when the rebellion began.[30] Most Northerners understood that these black soldiers had earned their freedom and a claim to political and legal equality.

Republican politicians like Stevens and Bingham assumed the end of slavery would lead to a new political reality in the South that would include the votes of the freedmen, as the former slaves were called. In much of the South, blacks constituted one-third to one-half of the population. These postwar Republican leaders venerated and celebrated the idea of a "republican form of government," in which the people of a society elected a legislature and in which all citizens had equal rights under the law. Thus, Northern politicians expected that emancipation, which was completed with the ratification of the 13th Amendment in December 1865, would lead to more than simply an end to slavery; they assumed it would lead to an entire revolution in the way blacks were treated, and in the rights they had.

Southern whites, however, had other ideas. Southerners still believed slavery was the best status for blacks. Georgia leader, Howell Cobb, claimed, even after the war ended, that "[t]he institution of slavery ... provided the best system of labor that could be devised for the negro race." He predicted that emancipation would "tax the abilities of the best and wisest statesmen to provide a substitute for it."[31]

In the fall of 1865, with the war barely over, Southern voters, most of whom had supported the rebellion, elected new state legislatures. Many of these state lawmakers had served in the Confederate government or in the rebellious state governments. Others had been soldiers, often officers, in the Confederate Army. The vast majority had either been slaveowners or members of slaveowning families. Although defeated in battle and deprived of their slaves by a combination of Congressional acts,[32] the Emancipation Proclamation, the brilliant military success of the United States Army, and the 13th Amendment, these former Confederates were unwilling to accept that the War had fundamentally altered the racial status quo in the South.[33] The newly-elected Southern legislators knew that African Americans could no longer be held as chattel slaves, to be bought and sold at the whim of a master; but Southern white leaders were unprepared to accept that the freedmen were entitled to liberty, equality, or even fundamental legal rights. In late 1865, the Southern states began to pass laws, generally known as Black Codes, which were designed to "substitute" a new form of repression to mirror prewar slavery.

Many Northerners were shocked by the statutes that unreconstructed Southern legislatures passed immediately after the war. The statutes indicated how the South planned to treat the former slaves. General Carl Schurz, after visiting the South in 1865, concluded that many, perhaps most, Southern whites conceded that blacks were no longer the slaves of individual masters, but intended to make them "the slaves of society."[34] The 14th Amendment was in large part a reaction to these black codes and the legal repression and the extra-legal violence and terrorism that accompanied them.

B. The Joint Committee on Reconstruction

In December 1865, Congress authorized the Joint Committee on Reconstruction to investigate conditions in the South. The Joint Committee consisted of six Senators and nine Congressmen. Thaddeus Stevens and John Bingham were key house members on the committee. Also on the committee were George S. Boutwell of Massachusetts and Justin Morrill of Vermont. Both had been life-long opponents of slavery and both came from states that gave free blacks full legal and political rights, including suffrage. The investigation of this committee led to the Civil Rights Act of 1866, reported out of the Committee on April 30, 1866 and to the proposed 14th Amendment, which Congress passed on June 13, 1866. Eleven members signed the final report. Three Southerners and a New Jersey Democrat did not sign the report.

The Report was massive, covering about 800 pages. The Committee members interviewed scores of people, including ex-slaves, defeated confederate leaders, former slaveowners, United States Army officers, journalists, and others in the South. In its Report, the Committee reminded the nation that the former slaves had "remained true and loyal" throughout the Civil War and "in large numbers, fought on the side of the Union." The Committee concluded that it would be impossible to "abandon" the former slaves "without securing them their rights as free men and citizens." Indeed, the "whole civilized world would have cried out against such base ingratitude" if the United States government failed to secure and protect the rights of the freedpeople.[35]

The Committee also found that Southern leaders still "defend[ed] the legal right of secession, and [upheld] the doctrine that the first allegiance of the people is due to the States." Noting the "leniency" of the policies of Congress and the President after the war, the Committee discovered that "[i]n return for our leniency we receive only an insulting denial of our authority." Rather than accept the outcome of the war, Southern whites were using local courts to prosecute loyalists and "Union officers for acts done in the line of official duty" and "similar prosecutions" were "threatened elsewhere as soon as the United States troops [we]re removed."[36]

The Committee understood that the task before the Congress and the nation involved three things: (1) preventing former Confederates from reinstating the same type of regime that existed before the War; (2) protecting the liberty of former slaves and guaranteeing them the power to protect their own rights within the new political regime that had to be created; and (3) protecting the rights and safety of white Unionists who were threatened by laws that discriminated against them and by the violence of unreconstructed Southern whites who had not accepted the political or social outcome of the war. Indeed, the laws and violence directed against whites in the South was an important aspect of the decision to nationalize fundamental protections of liberty. After investigating the situation in the South, the Committee concluded that nothing short of a constitutional amendment—what became the 14th Amendment—would protect the rights of the former slaves, Southern white Unionists, and Northerners who had moved to the South with the Army, with the Freedmen's Bureau, or with charitable organizations that were opening schools for blacks and in other ways helping former slaves in their transition to freedom.

Two categories of evidence were particularly important in setting out the need for civil rights legislation and a constitutional amendment to protect liberty in the states. First, Congress and the Joint Committee learned a good deal about conditions in the South by examining the statutes and constitutions adopted by the former Confederate states immediately after the war. Second, the Joint Committee interviewed hundreds of people familiar with conditions in the postwar South. The information from these interviews, along with some published materials, such as excerpts from Southern state constitutions, filled the nearly 800 pages of the Joint Committee's report. Both the legal documentation and the evidence from interviews led to the inescapable conclusion that the majority of Southern whites were not prepared to accept blacks as equal citizens and that many Southern whites were willing to use intimidation, violence, and even murder to prevent racial equality in the post war South.[37]

C. The Black Codes and State Constitutions, 1865–1866

The Southern black codes and constitutions passed in 1865 and 1866 acknowledged some significant changes in the legal status of blacks. Although facially extending some legal rights to former slaves, these laws actually placed blacks and their white supporters in continuing jeopardy. The laws also replicated, as closely as possible, the prewar suppression and exploitation of blacks and involuntary servitude. Many of the statutes were designed to control black labor in order to ensure that former masters had a sufficient, reliable, and pliable work force to maintain and operate their plantations.

For instance, the Alabama Black Code of 1865–1866 allowed blacks to testify in court, "but only in cases in which freedmen, free negroes, and mulattoes are parties, either as plaintiff or defendant." In addition, blacks were allowed to testify in prosecutions "for injuries in the persons and property" of blacks.[38] Mississippi enacted similar legislation, which more directly and unambiguously provided that blacks could testify against white criminal defendants, "in all criminal prosecutions where the crime charged is alleged to have been committed by a white person upon or against the person or property of a freedman, free negro, or mulatto."[39]

These laws certainly expanded the rights and legal protections of blacks. For the first time in the history of these states, blacks could testify against whites. However, such laws did not give blacks the same legal rights as whites. Under these laws, blacks could not testify in a suit between two whites or at the prosecution of a white for harming other whites. Thus, the laws in effect declared that blacks were not "equal" to whites and that their testimony was not as "good" as that of whites. These restrictions undermined fundamental justice and created dangerous possibilities for free blacks and their white allies. For example, a white suing another white could not use the testimony of a black to support his case. More importantly, under these laws, Southern white terrorists, such as those in the Ku Klux Klan, could kill a white in front of black witnesses, and those witnesses could not testify at the trial. This limitation on black testimony would undermine the safety of white teachers, army officers, Freedmen's Bureau officers, and Unionists who supported black rights and the national government. Thus, while these new laws gave some protection to blacks, the laws did not give them legal equality and did not even fully protect their civil rights.

The Black Codes also undermined the position of the freedmen by giving them the right to enter into contracts and to be sued. Alabama's code began by acknowledging the new status of blacks, declaring that "[a]ll freedmen, free negroes, and mulattoes" had "the right to sue and be sued, plead and be impleaded."[40] These were rights that slaves had not had. Certainly such rights were vital to freedom. But, blacks in the deep South were mostly illiterate, had virtually no experience with either the law or a free labor economy, and were only a few months out of slavery. Many had never even handled money and most had no meaningful experience with buying anything or earning money. They were vulnerable to signing contracts that committed them to long-term labor agreements, and being sued for breach of these contracts. Similar laws were found in other Southern states. Thus, Major General Christopher C. Andrews told the Joint Committee on Reconstruction that conditions in Texas were such that "[u]nless the freedmen are protected by the government they will be much worse off than when they were slaves" because the whites were prepared "to coerce" blacks into working for unfair wages under unfair contracts.[41]

Other provisions of the new laws more blatantly undermined black freedom. Alabama's law "Concerning Vagrants and Vagrancy" allowed for the incarceration in the public work house of any "laborer or servant who loiters away his time, or refuses to comply with any contract for a term of service without just cause."[42] Mississippi's Civil Rights Act of 1865 provided that if any laborer quit a job before the end of the contract period he would lose all wages earned up to that time.[43] If a black laborer signed a contract to work for a planter for a year, and left after eleven months, he would get no wages. This allowed employers to mistreat and overwork laborers, knowing they dare not quit. Indeed, a shrewd employer could purposefully make life excessively miserable for workers near the end of a contract term, in hopes that they would quit and forfeit all wages. Mississippi law also provided that any blacks "with no lawful employment or business" would be considered vagrants, and could be fined up to fifty dollars.[44] Any black who could not pay the fine—almost all blacks in the state at the time—would be forcibly hired out to whoever would pay the fine, thus creating another form of unfree labor. The same act created a one dollar poll tax for all free blacks. Anyone not paying the tax could also be declared a vagrant and assigned to work for a white planter.[45] These laws also prohibited blacks from renting land or houses in towns or cities effectively forcing blacks into the countryside where they would be doomed to agricultural labor.[46]

Laws such as these set the stage for a new system of forced labor. Southern states passed these laws just before, or immediately after, the ratification of the 13th Amendment. These laws attempted to reduce blacks to a status somewhere between that of slaves (which they no longer were) and fully free people (which the vast majority of white Southerners simply would not allow). The labor contract laws, coupled with vagrancy laws, were designed to create a kind of serfdom, tying the former slaves to the land, just as they were once tied to their masters.

The new state constitutions were equally oppressive. The Joint Committee on Reconstruction reprinted some state constitutions and excerpts from others in its report. The Florida Constitution, for example, limited suffrage to white men and prohibited any person employed by the United States from voting in the state unless he was a resident of Florida before entering federal service. The same constitution prohibited blacks from serving as jurors and limited black testimony to cases involving blacks. The Arkansas Constitution likewise limited voting to whites, banned federal officers from voting, and in other ways discriminated against blacks. The Georgia constitution was similar, limiting the vote to whites. The state used a statute to limit the testimony of blacks. The Committee included summaries of these laws in its report to Congress.[47]

These laws and constitutional provisions astounded Northerners. Having been defeated in battle, and forced to give up slavery, the South seemed as defiant as ever, unwilling to accept the outcome of the war, and refusing to accept the necessity of treating blacks as citizens. The reaction to these laws led to the Civil Rights Act of 1866 and later to the 14th Amendment.

D. Southern White Attacks on Blacks and the Report of the Joint Committee on Reconstruction

The Southern black codes were not the only cause of Northern astonishment at Southern behavior. Even more important, perhaps, was the violence directed at blacks and their white allies after the war. While Congress was debating what was to become the Civil Rights Act of 1866, Senator Charles Sumner of Massachusetts received a box containing the finger of a black man. The accompanying note read: "You old son of a bitch, I send you a piece of one of your friends, and if that bill of yours passes I will have a piece of you."[48] While not typical of the mail Northerners in Congress received, this box and note illustrated all too well the savage and murderous violence that Southern whites were prepared to use to suppress black freedom.

The evidence presented in the massive Committee Report documented the dangers to blacks and white Unionists—and the nation itself—posed by the refusal of most former Confederates to accept black freedom. Congressman Bingham chaired the subcommittee that investigated the situation in Tennessee. Everyone agreed that Tennessee had more Unionists than any other former Confederate state, and in the end, the Committee endorsed its immediate readmission to the Union.[49] Nevertheless, a sampling of the testimony gathered from Tennessee supports the understanding that the Committee which wrote the 14th Amendment was fully aware of the need for a powerful weapon to force change and protect freedom in the South. Testimony from the other former Confederate states showed that throughout the South whites were prone to use violence against blacks and Unionists. This testimony demonstrated, over and over again, how liberty and justice were imperiled virtually everywhere in the former Confederacy.

Major General Edward Hatch testified that many whites in Tennessee were unwilling to accept black liberty. General Hatch noted that "the negro is perfectly willing to work, but he wants a guarantee that he will be secured in his rights under his contract" and that "his life and property" be "secured." Blacks understood they were "not safe from the poor whites." Hatch noted that whites wanted "some kind of legislation" to "establish a kind of peonage; not absolute slavery but that they can enact such laws as will enable them to manage the negro as they please to fix the price to be paid for his labor." If blacks resisted this reestablishment of bondage, "[t]hey are liable to be shot."

Major General Clinton Fisk, for whom one of the nation's first black colleges, Fisk University in Nashville, Tennessee, would be named, testified about the murderous nature of former "slaveholders and returned rebel soldiers." Such men "persecute bitterly" the former slaves, "and pursue them with vengeance, and treat them with brutality, and burn down their dwellings and school-houses." Fisk pointed out this was "not the rule" everywhere in Tennessee, but nevertheless such conduct existed. And, as everyone admitted, Tennessee was the most progressive state on these issues in the former Confederacy.

Lieutenant Colonel R. W. Barnard was far less optimistic than General Fisk. Perhaps because he was a field officer, Bernard was more likely to see the day-to-day dangers blacks faced. Asked if it was safe to remove troops from Tennessee, he replied, "I hardly know how to express myself on the subject. I have not been in a favor of removing the military. I can tell you what an old citizen, a Union man, said to me. Said he, 'I tell you what, if you take away the military from Tennessee, the buzzards can't eat up the niggers as fast as we'll kill 'em.'" Barnard thought this might be an exaggeration, but told the Committee, "I know there are plenty of bad men there who would maltreat the negro." He did not need to emphasize that this threat to black life came not from a "bad" man, but from a Unionist.[50]

Thus, in Tennessee, where loyal Union men were more common than elsewhere in the South, the dangers to blacks were great. In other states the dangers were extraordinarily greater. Major General John W. Turner reported that in Virginia "all of the [white] people" were "extremely reluctant to grant to the negro his civil rights—those privileges that pertain to freedom, the protection

of life, liberty, and property before the laws, the right to testify in courts, etc."
Turner noted that whites were "reluctant even to consider and treat the negro
as a free man, to let him have his half of the sidewalk or the street crossing."
They would only "concede" such rights to blacks "if it is ever done, because they
are forced to do it." He noted that poor whites were "disposed to ban the negro,
to kick him and cuff him, and threaten him." George B. Smith, a Virginia farmer,
admitted that whites in the state, "maltreat [blacks] every day" and that blacks
had "[n]ot a particle" of a chance "to obtain justice in the civil courts of Virginia." He declared that a black or "a Union man" had as much chance of obtaining justice in Virginia as "a rabbit would in a den of lions." Others in Virginia
explained, over and over again, how the whites were trying to reduce blacks to
servitude with laws and violence. The white sheriff of Fairfax County noted that
the state was "passing laws" to "disfranchise" black voters and "passing vagrant
laws on purpose to oppress the colored people and to keep them in vassalage,
and doing everything they can to bring back things of their old condition, as
near as possible."

Perhaps the most powerful testimony on Virginia came from United States
District Judge John C. Underwood, who had lived in the state since the 1840s. He
described the cold blooded murder of a white Unionist by a returning Confederate medical officer. The state did not prosecute anyone for the crime. Underwood
also noted that the murderer of an army officer had "not yet been punished" but
was "still at large." He believed that white Unionists in Virginia were even more
vulnerable than blacks, because the army would intercede to protect the freedmen, while "a Union man could" not "expect to obtain justice in the courts of the
State." But if the army abandoned the state and left the fate of the freedmen to
the native whites of Virginia, the situation would be radically altered. Judge
Underwood quoted a "most intelligent" man from Alexandria, who declared that
rather "than see the colored people raised to a legal and political equality, the
Southern people would prefer their total annihilation."[51]

Testimony about North Carolina revealed the lethal danger to blacks in the
South. A black was shot down in cold blood near Camden. A United States Army
captain reported "numerous cases" of the "maltreatment of blacks," including
flogging and shooting, and that "instances of cruelty were numerous." He predicted that without United States troops schoolhouses for blacks would be
burned and teachers harassed. A minister in Goldsborough reported the cold
blooded shooting of a black in order to take his horse. When another former
slave led soldiers to the culprit, this black was also murdered. Lieutenant Colonel

Dexter H. Clapp told the committee about a gang of North Carolina whites who "first castrated" and then "murdered" a black, and when the culprits escaped from jail, the local police refused to even attempt to capture them.[52] This gang then shot "several negroes." One of these men, a wealthy planter, later killed a twelve year old Negro boy and wounded another.

A local police sergeant "brutally wounded a freedman...in his custody." While the man's arms were tied behind his back, the policeman struck him on the back of his head with a gun. It was later shown that this man had "committed no offence whatever." This policeman later "whipped another freedman" so that "from his neck to his hips his back was one mass of gashes." The policeman left the bleeding man outside all night. A black who defended himself when assaulted by a white was given twenty-two lashes with a whip over a two hour period, then "tied up by his thumbs for two hours, his toes touching the ground only," and then "given nine more lashes and then tied up by his thumbs for another two hours." A planter in the same area whipped two black women until their backs were "a mass of gashes." Clapp asserted that away from military posts "scenes like these" were "frequent occurrences" in "portions" of North Carolina.[53]

In South Carolina, General Rufus Saxton reported numerous atrocities. In Edgefield, local whites treated free people as if they were slaves. One "freedman [and] three children, two male and one female, were stripped naked, tied up, and whipped severely," while a woman was given a hundred lashes while tied to a tree. Another man was whipped with a stick, while two children were also whipped. Saxton reported shootings, whippings, various forms of torture, whipping of naked women, floggings, and beatings of all kinds. In addition to attacks on blacks by individual planters, ruffians, and gangs, Saxton reported a more ominous trend: "organized bands of 'regulators'—armed men—who make it their business to traverse these counties, and maltreat negroes without any avowedly definite purpose in view. They treat the negroes, in many instances, in the most horrible and atrocious manner, even to maiming them and cutting their ears off, etc."[54]

General George Armstrong Custer, who was stationed in Texas, reported that whites in that state blamed the black man for "their present condition," and thus they did not "hesitate" to use "every opportunity to inflict injuries upon him in order, seemingly, to punish him for this." Custer noted that in Texas more than 500 former Confederates had been charged with murdering blacks or white Unionists, but no one had been convicted. Blacks, however, were routinely convicted and jailed for minor offenses. Custer reported "it is of a weekly, if not of daily, occurrence that freedmen are murdered. Their bodies are found in different parts of the country," but no whites were ever charged in these cases, even when they were known. Custer reported that "[c]ases have occurred of white men meeting freedmen they never saw before, and murdering them merely from this feeling of hostility to them as a class."[55]

Testimony about the rest of the South mirrored the violence and denial of rights sketched out here. Blacks disappeared, were beaten, maimed, and killed. Legislatures passed laws to prevent them from owning land, moving to towns, voting, testifying in all court cases, or in any other way asserting and protecting their rights as free people. The Committee heard numbing reports of violence and hatred.

Perhaps even more horrible than the fear of violence, was the threat of reenslavement. Brigadier General Charles H. Howard, who was serving as an inspector for the Freedmen's Bureau, reported instances in Georgia of blacks being held on plantations against their will and of others being kidnapped and taken to Cuba, where slavery was still legal. At South Newport, Georgia, a woman escaped from the plantation of her former master "after much maltreatment." She reported that her former master had "insisted that she and her children were not free, [and] that he cared nothing for 'Lincoln's proclamation.'" When she insisted on leaving "she was confined on bread and water" until she escaped. However, she was forced to leave her children behind.

Howard also reported that at New Altahama, Georgia, army officers had investigated "a case where certain parties were charged with kidnapping colored children and shipping them to Cuba." Two children "mysteriously disappeared" but were then found in Florida after their former owner was placed "under bonds to produce the children." The former owner could not explain how the children got to Florida, or how he knew where they were. The implication was clear: the former master had kidnapped the children, sent them (or took them) to Florida, and was preparing to send them to Cuba where they could be sold as slaves.[56]

III. UNDERSTANDING THE 14TH AMENDMENT

It was in the context of this history that the Joint Committee on Reconstruction and Congressman Bingham wrote Section 1 of the 14th Amendment. What did Bingham and his colleagues desire to accomplish with this provision? We can never fully know, of course, but the context in which they framed the Amendment suggests that their goals were sweeping and broad. Bingham and others in the majority on the Joint Committee understood that they had to protect the life, liberty, safety, freedom, political viability, and property of the former slaves. They had to protect their rights to have meaningful contracts.[57] Bingham and his colleagues had to be able to protect former slaves' families in the courtroom and the voting booth, as well as in the market place. Former slaves had to be protected from whipping and other forms of cruel and unusual punishment. The newly freed blacks desperately needed the protections of the Bill of Rights— fair trials by fair juries, with legal counsel to represent these largely illiterate former slaves. They needed to be able to express themselves in public and to organize politically, to speak freely, and to be able to freely (and without intimidation) assemble and petition the government. They needed equal schooling to participate in the political process. They also needed to have the right to worship as they wished in their own churches, something that the slave states had denied to all blacks, slave and free.

It would have been impossible to detail all these needs with explicit constitutional protections. In fact, Bingham did not try. He used large phrases, encompassing grand ideas. He took John Marshall's admonitions in *McCulloch v. Maryland* to heart.[58] He did not try to turn the Constitution into a legal code. Rather, he produced language that would "endure for the ages," and could grow and develop over time. His goal was to reverse the racism and violence of slavery and its immediate aftermath.

At a more basic level, though, Bingham and the Joint Committee's efforts reflected the simple lesson of Major General John W. Turner's testimony. Turner noted that whites in Virginia were "reluctant even to consider and treat the negro as a free man, to let him have his half of the sidewalk or the street crossing."[59] Bingham's goal was to make sure that African Americans, and all other minorities, had full access to their "half of the sidewalk" in the social world, the political world, and the workplace. The concept was a radical change to the Constitution and to American notions of federalism. Indeed, the goal was nothing short of a Revolution in liberty and justice—trying to bring those concepts and rights to "all" Americans.

An earlier version of this chapter appeared in *Temple Political & Civil Rights Law Review,* Volume 13, 389–409, 2004. Reprinted with permission.

3 The 39th Congress (1865–1867) and the 14th Amendment

Some Preliminary Perspectives

Richard L. Aynes, The University of Akron School of Law

T he 14th Amendment is a very critical part of our distribution of government powers and the framework for protecting the rights of citizens. It has been considered by some to be a second founding and has been called by others a second U.S. Constitution.[1] In the work of interpretation, the courts frequently look to the legislative history of the Amendment, and use that history to help inform and develop a decision. Historians and lawyers do not always agree with the way the Court uses history, but nevertheless the court uses history in this way. Therefore, it is not only important to insist upon good history, but also, when considering that history, to place it within the context of the people living through it, to help inform the interpretive enterprise. For, if the Court now uses history as an interpretive guide, it stands to reason that the 39th Congress was interpreting both its own time and its own work when framing and passing the 14th Amendment.[2]

The 39th Congress met from March 4, 1865 to March 3, 1867. We do not often think about the Congress as a whole yet specific body. Normally we think about Congress through individuals—great individuals such as Henry Clay, Daniel Webster, or even John C. Calhoun. We might think of more controversial Congressmen like Reconstruction's Thaddeus Stevens and Charles Sumner or turn of the century Congressmen like Joseph Cannon or Henry Cabot Lodge. Though understanding the 39th Congress through this collective lens is still a work in progress, this chapter will attempt to give a collective overview of the 39th Congress while acknowledging its important leaders.[3]

If we look at the Congress in this collective sense, most people would say there have been great Congresses that were critically important. One such Congress would undoubtedly be the First Congress. The First Congress assembled many of those individuals who drafted the Constitution and many who had been in the ratifying conventions, which has given the First Congress an aura of authority with respect to how these legislators interpreted the Constitution. The U.S. Supreme Court often assumes that because members of that Congress were so familiar with the Constitution, those members must both have known what the Constitution meant, and also would not have passed a statute that was inconsistent with that meaning. This assumption may not always be a safe one, but it is an interpretative method that the Court uses.[4] Other Congresses people might look to as great are the Depression-era New Deal Congresses that enacted so much legislation, implemented so much change, and then became war Congresses during World War II.

I want to suggest that when someone creates the Hall of Fame of the Congresses we need to include the 39th Congress. The reason for this becomes more apparent when we look at its history. We can begin by drawing some comparisons between the 38th and the 39th Congresses. The 38th Congress was a "war" Congress and one that supported the efforts of the Lincoln Administration to bring the Civil War to a successful conclusion. Because there were so many different political affiliations—Republicans, Unionists, Unconditional Unionists, War Democrats, Peace Democrats, etc.—a contemporary publication divided the 38th Congress into two groups, "Administration" supporters and the "Opposition" party.[5]

Using those categories of *Harper's Weekly*, there was strong majority support for the Union in the 38th Congress. In the Senate, the split was 32–18, with the Administration having a 14-member majority. In the House, the split was 104–81, with the Administration having a majority of 23. In the context of the history of the nation, both of these margins are significant. At the same time, neither house had the two-thirds vote necessary to override a Presidential veto or to propose an amendment to the U.S. Constitution.

The national Republican Platform of 1864 called for a Constitutional Amendment to "forever prohibit the existence of Slavery within the limits of the jurisdiction of the United States." Similarly, the Platform of the Union Convention in Ohio, May 25, 1864, "pledge[d] the cordial sup[port]" and "especially" approved "the pending amendment of the Constitution to make States of the Union all free and republican, and therefore forever one and undivided."[6] In the nineteenth century, Congress came back after the elections for a "lame duck" session before the new Congress took office the following March. But with the Republicans needing 124 votes in the House to propose the Amendment and having only 104 votes potentially available from their own party, it did not seem likely that the 38th Congress would abolish slavery. While President Lincoln could have simply waited until the 39th Congress convened to propose the 13th Amendment, hindsight allows us to know that, had he done so, he would not have lived to see the proposal approved by Congress. Instead Lincoln worked, especially with Congressman James M. Ashley (R-OH), to push the Amendment through the 38th Congress. It was ultimately passed by the House of Representatives on January 31, 1865, though by the time of Lincoln's death it had only been ratified by 21 states. Ratification was not complete until December 6, 1865.[7]

The Union Party did well in the 1864 elections in which Abraham Lincoln was reelected President. When the 39th Congress convened in 1865, the Republican majorities had increased in both the House and the Senate. According to a contemporary source, there were 155 Republican members in the House of Representatives and only 46 Democrats. There were 44 Republicans in the Senate and only 12 Democrats. Thus, between the 38th and 39th Congresses, the Republican percentage in the Senate had increased from 64% to 79% and in the House from 56% to 77%. From a Constitutional point of view, the Republicans not only gained a veto-proof Congress—something that would become important when Andrew Johnson became President—but they also gained the supermajority necessary to propose constitutional amendments.[8]

The overwhelming number of Republicans, compared to Democrats, should produce caution in citing the members of the minority party's statements on the meaning of the 14th Amendment. Democrats knew the Amendment was going to pass the House and Senate without their approval and had motives to misstate its meaning for purposes of affecting the state ratifications, elections, or future litigation. Senator Reverdy Johnson (D-MD) is an example of a legislator who used such misleading comments as a method to defeat the Amendment.[9]

Though only a portion of the statistical analysis of the membership in the 39th Congress has been completed, one surprising aspect is that, in an era where less than one percent of the population had a college education, a striking number of members of the 39th Congress had attended college.[10] It appears that a clear majority of the members of the 39th Congress were lawyers or judges.[11] Two matters are of particular interest: First, many of the Congressmen took what could be called courses in law when they were in college. Some, including John Bingham, took world history courses which included studying the Magna Carta, Due Process Clause, and the meaning of the Constitution.[12] They were actually receiving a partial, formal, legal education as part of their college education. Second, though a small group, it is striking nevertheless that some members of the 39th Congress both attended law school and worked as legal apprentices.[13]

Over 40% of the members of the 39th Congress were freshmen and many others were second-term Congressmen. This put a premium on leadership, which provided opportunities for the more experienced Congressmen.[14]

The formal leadership in the Senate was provided by the president pro tempore of the Senate. Lafayette S. Foster (R-CT) was elected president pro tempore at the March 7, 1865 special session of the Senate and continued to serve until March 2, 1867. Benjamin F. Wade (R-OH) was elected to that position on March 2, 1867, serving on March 3rd and then into the 40th Congress. In the House of Representatives, prior Speaker Schuyler Colfax (R-IN) was again elected Speaker of the House.[15]

Of course, there are other formal positions of leadership as well as informal ones. Within the House of Representatives, Thaddeus Stevens was one of the key leaders. Next to Stevens, historian Benjamin Kendrick listed John A. Bingham (R-OH), Roscoe Conkling (R-NY) and George S. Boutwell (R-MA). Other members of the House had influence, depending on the issue, and we would number among them James F. Wilson (R-IA), Chairman of the Judiciary Committee, and James M. Ashley (R-OH), who played a critical role in the adoption of the 13th Amendment.[16]

In the Senate, Kendrick identified William P. Fessenden (R-ME), Chair of the Joint Committee on Reconstruction, James W. Grimes (R-IA), and George H. Williams (R-OR) as influential leaders. To that important group, we could add Charles Sumner (R-MA), Lyman Trumbull (R-IL), Chair of the Senate Judiciary Committee, and Henry Wilson (R-MA), later Vice President of the United States.[17]

Last of all, but a very important dynamic, is that the overwhelming membership of this Congress was Republican. The Republican dominance not only allowed the Congress to ignore the veto threats of the President, but also provided little incentive to negotiate with or care about the very small Democratic minority, especially since several members of the Democratic Party had been "Peace Democrats," who did not support the war and incorrectly predicted its failure. These Democrats would have had little credibility or influence with the Republican majority.

I. CHALLENGES FACING THE 39TH CONGRESS

The greatest challenge facing the 39th Congress may be surprising to many—how to bring the war to a close and, in the terminology of the day, "secure the peace" so that there would be no future war. Many people think the connection between the 14th Amendment and the Civil War is that winning the war allowed the Congress to pass the Amendment. However, the connection is much stronger: The war actually prompted the Amendment as a means of preventing a future war. Many Republicans viewed the Amendment both as embodying the terms upon which peace could be made and as providing guarantees that would prevent another outbreak of rebellion.[18]

Three of the challenges before the Congress will be considered: (1) the losses of life and property in the war; (2) the uncertainty about whether the war was really over at the time the Congress met; and (3) the enormity of the task of economic and political reconstruction to try to put the country back together again, especially with the President working against the Congress. All of these problems—and the people experiencing these problems—confronted the 39th Congress. It is useful for us to explore their understanding of those problems and what was required to address them, if we are to understand the Amendment they framed.

A. Loss of Life and Property

There were an estimated 620,000 soldiers who died in the Civil War. If one translates the percentage killed in terms of today's population, about six million soldiers would have been killed. There were also civilian casualties. There was an immense amount of property destroyed by the various armies, and an immense amount of wealth poured into nonproductive war support. After the war, it was estimated that the Confederate debt was over $2 billion, and the rebel states and local governments had another $1 billion in debt. Further, the value of the newly-emancipated people formerly held in slavery was estimated between $1.6 and $2 billion. These losses do not include the loss of property and livestock where battles were fought, the loss of food and property requisitioned for use by various armies, and the investment in the nonproductive goods of war. Nor do they include the Union expenditures in the war or the Union debt. Senator Henry Wilson (R-MA) indicated that in charity alone the North had contributed $75 million to the care of wounded and sick soldiers, and that the nation faced a "vast national debt."[19]

B. Was the War Really Over?

When the 39th Congress convened on March 4, 1865, the war was still ongoing. To be sure, within only slightly more than a month, the major Confederate Army had surrendered. But even then, the 39th Congress could not be sure the war was over. Robert E. Lee surrendered to Ulysses S. Grant on April 9, 1865, and we know that this marked the end of the war for all practical purposes. However, this view is overly simplistic and comes only from the benefit of hindsight.[20]

Lincoln's assassination on April 14, 1865, the wounding and attempted assassination of Secretary of State, Seward, and the planned-but-unexecuted attempt to assassinate Vice President Johnson were clearly designed by John Wilkes Booth to disrupt the war effort and give hope for continued Confederate resistance. Whether his purported plan to kidnap Lincoln was supported by formal Confederate action or not is a matter of dispute. Despite earlier scholarly repudiations of this theory, modern authors have provided evidence that, if accurate, could link the Confederate government and its secret service to Booth's kidnapping plan. What is clear is that at the time, many people in the government and country believed that the assassination efforts were supported by the Confederate government of Jefferson Davis. Indeed, this was the very theory that the Judge Advocate General proceeded under in the trial of the Lincoln coconspirators.[21]

Thus, the feeling of the country at the time was that this unsettling conspiracy could portend new military action by the Confederates in the form of guerilla warfare and assassination, and this was further evidence that the war had not ended.

After President Lincoln's assassination, Secretary of War, Edwin Stanton estimated that there were over 90,000 Confederate soldiers still in the field. Many Confederate cabinet officers, military officers, and members of the Confederate Congress had fled the United States. They went to Mexico, England, and Brazil.[22] No one knew whether these Confederate leaders had really gone for good or if, as with the history of English kings, they were just trying to raise new support in foreign countries to return to fight at a later time.

Troops were still in the field, with fighting in different areas taking place almost to the end of 1865; Confederate military field commanders were prepared to continue fighting. Confederate President, Jefferson Davis, even after the surrender of the armies of Lee and Johnston, proposed joining Cavalry General and former slave-trader Nathan Bedford Forrest in Mississippi or General Kirby Smith in Texas to "carry on the war forever."[23]

Jefferson Davis was captured on May 10, 1865. That day, President Johnson issued a proclamation indicating that "armed resistance ... in the ... insurrectionary States may be regarded as virtually at an end." On that very day, May 10, guerilla forces under William Clarke Quantrill fought against irregular Union troops in Kentucky. Understandably, in spite of Johnson's proclamation, there were substantial uncertainties that military operations were actually over.[24]

What is considered the last major engagement of the war took place on May 12th, with the Confederate forces in Texas winning the battle. Yet, clashes between Union soldiers and guerillas continued in Missouri on May 14th, 20th, 22nd and 23rd, 27th, and 29th. Commander Kirby Smith did not surrender the Trans-Mississippi Department until June 2nd.[25]

Even with Smith's surrender of the last major Confederate army, fighting on a small scale continued. The Federal army spent most of May 1865 through December 1865 skirmishing against guerillas and former Confederates escaping into Mexico. Some Confederate battle units simply disbanded rather than surrender.[26]

President Johnson himself did not revoke the suspension of the *writ of habeas corpus* in the majority of states until December 1, 1865, almost 8 months after Appomattox, 7 months after the capture of Davis and 6 months after the 39th Congress began its first session.[27]

It took President Johnson until April 2, 1866 to declare that the insurrection in all of the Confederate states except Texas was over and until August 20, 1866— after three states had already ratified the 14th Amendment—to determine that the insurrection in Texas was at an end.[28]

When Lee contemplated surrender, one of his staff urged him to disband the army so that they could continue to fight a guerilla war. Though Lee rejected this suggestion, there was no way for Union commanders to determine if some of Lee's soldiers might follow such a policy. Concerns about guerilla tactics were also especially true of the Confederate battle units that disbanded but refused to surrender. Was this an abandonment of the war, or simply a shift in tactics? Would these soldiers reappear to fight the Union again? At what has been called the end of the war, thoughtful Union leaders had to consider the possibility that these were temporary exiles who would return to renew the conflict.[29]

Immediately after the war, violence in Memphis and New Orleans against white and black Unionists was orchestrated by local government employees trying to resist or overthrow the results of the war. In Memphis, the "riots" lasted three days and were led largely by white police and firemen attacking African

American areas of town, including areas where the families of African American U.S. soldiers lived. As summarized by one of the nation's leading historians of Reconstruction, "at least forty-eight persons (all but two of them black) lay dead, five black women had been raped, and hundreds of black dwellings, churches, and schools were pillaged or destroyed by fire."[30]

Twelve weeks later, it "appear[ed] certain that some members of the [New Orleans] city police, made up largely of Confederate veterans, conspired to disperse [a] gathering [of Radical Republicans] by force." Twenty-five delegates and about 200 African American veterans were attacked in what General Philip H. Sheridan termed "an absolute massacre." The son of former Vice President Hannibal Hamlin, a Union war veteran, termed it a "wholesale slaughter" that was worse than anything he had seen on the battlefield. Thirty-four black and three white Republicans were killed and it was estimated that over 100 people were injured.[31]

The enactment of the Black Codes indicated that the white governments of Andrew Johnson could not be trusted to protect the legal rights of African Americans or their freedom, notwithstanding the 13th Amendment. The actions of white police and former Confederate veterans in Memphis and New Orleans demonstrated that not only could the white Johnson-appointed governments not be trusted to enforce the law, but that they would actually take the lead in violating it. Further, the Ku Klux Klan was the terrorist wing of the Southern White Democratic Party, and its membership largely consisted of former Confederate soldiers resisting the results of the war and Reconstruction. The Klan was ultimately successful in resisting both constitutional requirements and the results of the war by using assassination, violence, and voter fraud.[32]

Thus, in many ways, former Confederate soldiers continued their resistance to the national government and Union supporters all the way into the 1870s and perhaps the 1880s. These events show that the situation was more ambiguous and nuanced than the simplistic use of the formal surrender of Confederate Armies or the Proclamation of President Johnson that resistance had "virtually" ceased might suggest.

Orchestrated hostilities continued throughout the time the 39th Congress was deliberating over the 14th Amendment. President Johnson himself did not proclaim a total end in the United States of hostilities related to the war until August 20 of 1866, approximately three months after the 14th Amendment was proposed by Congress. Thus, the debate, proposal, recommendation, and beginning of the ratification of the Amendment all took place during a time of great military uncertainty.[33]

C. Andrew Johnson and the Loss of Life

The third challenge before the 39th Congress was President Johnson, and involves the reasons for the attempt to remove him from office. During the pendency of the 14th Amendment, Johnson went far beyond simply disagreeing with and vetoing the Congress on certain policy issues.

Johnson was actively removing commanders who enforced congressional law and replacing them with commanders who would not enforce the law. Johnson even removed war hero Philip Sheridan from his position as a military governor because he was enforcing the law and supporting the Congress. Both houses of Congress adopted a resolution condemning Johnson's dismissal of Sheridan and censuring Johnson. The harshness of the times may be seen in a speech by Congressman Elihu B. Washburne (R-IL).

> His whole official career as President has been marked by a wicked disregard of all the obligations of public duty and by a degree of perfidy and treachery and turpitude unheard of in the history of the rulers of a free people; his personal and official character has made him the opprobrium of both hemispheres, and brought ineffable disgrace on the American name.[34]

Even while people were dying, Johnson encouraged the white Southern former slaveholders to resist Reconstruction. "A firm believer in the superiority of the white race, a prejudice he would never be able to overcome," Johnson considered himself successful because "[h]e had preserved the South as a 'white man's country.'"[35]

The standoff between the Congress and the President was not simply a philosophical disagreement. It was a disagreement that was resulting in thousands of people losing their lives because the President of the United States was trying to undermine the Congress and the results of the war, and was refusing to enforce the law as required by the Constitution.

II. ACTIONS BY THE 39TH CONGRESS

What did the Congress do when faced with all these problems? They did what any legislative body does; they legislated. The legacy of the 39th Congress is in the 807 pages of Volume 14 of the U.S. Statutes. If one reviews that volume, what one finds is that over the course of its term, the 39th Congress passed 714 pieces of legislation.[36] This was more legislation than any Congress had ever passed up to that time. The 39th Congress faced problems, and its members tried to come up with solutions to those problems. At least three of their statutory solutions merit mention.

First, the 39th Congress passed the Civil Rights Act in 1866, the first Civil Rights Act in U.S. history. The 1866 Act provided for the first time a statutory definition of citizenship and defined some of the rights of citizens. President Johnson vetoed the statute, but it was passed over his veto.[37]

Next, the Congress extended the existence of the Bureau of Freedmen and Refugees for another two years. People often view the Bureau as designed to only help people formerly held in slavery. While that was its predominant role, the Bureau also helped people of all races who were suffering because of the war. The Bureau provided substantial legal protections for those who were under the jurisdiction of the white, racist governments Johnson had established. Johnson also vetoed this bill, and the Congress passed it over his veto.[38]

These actions signaled Johnson's break from the Republican Party. In part because of Johnson's silence and in part because his allies in Congress had voted for the Freedman's Bureau Bill, Johnson's veto was an "utter surprise" to Congress. Similarly, because the Civil Rights Bill of 1866 was considered such a moderate proposal and had such widespread support, Johnson's veto of that bill was thought by many Republicans to be "a declaration of war against the party and the freedmen."[39]

Third, the Congress proposed the 14th Amendment, which will be discussed below. Though President Johnson was unable to veto the proposed Amendment, he opposed it and even supported a counter-14th Amendment designed to preserve the status quo.[40]

In these actions, as well as their other legislation, the 39th Congress made its mark upon the face of U.S. Constitutional Law.

III. THE OVERRIDING GOAL OF THE 39TH CONGRESS: ENDING THE WAR AND SECURING THE PEACE FOR THE FUTURE

If one looks at other wars in history, one will find that the 39th Congress was no different than those of other eras. In the aftermath of World War II, the Allies decided that they had to occupy Japan and Germany. Further, they determined that, in order to preserve peace in the future, they had to make sure that the militarists of Japan and the Nazis of Germany were no longer in positions of authority and power.

The 39th Congress acted exactly the same way. Time and time again, in countless speeches and newspaper articles, Unionists declared their desire to "secure the peace." The ultimate goal of the 39th Congress was to keep a civil war from happening again.

For example, in the Ohio Republican Convention of June 21, 1865, the Republicans stated that they desired a quick "reconstruction" of the "insurgent States[,]" but they also insisted "that such reconstruction shall be at such time and upon such terms as will give unquestioned assurance of the peace and security, not only of the loyal people of the rebel States, but also for the peace and prosperity of the Federal Union."[41]

Immediately after the recommendation of the 14th Amendment by Congress, the Ohio Union Republican Convention of June 20, 1866 endorsed the Amendment, demanding that "peace shall be established upon such stable foundations that rebellion and secession will never again endanger our national existence."[42]

Congressman Bingham himself, speaking on the campaign trail in the all-important congressional elections of 1866, touted the Amendment as the way in which to "[s]ecure a permanent peace by establishing freedom and justice throughout the whole land." Senator John Sherman (R-OH), the brother of General William T. Sherman, advocated for the Amendment by indicating that the government had the "right to take a bond of [the rebels] for the future safety of this country."[43]

These goals were confirmed after ratification by Major General Wager Swayne, winner of the Medal of Honor and son of Justice Noah Swayne, in a speech before the New York Commandery of the Military Order of the Loyal Legion: "The fruits of our war are gathered and preserved . . . in three short paragraphs which are amendatory of the Federal Constitution. They were adopted soon after the war, and with the express intention to make its results secure."[44]

During the Civil War, the Congress had created a Joint Committee on the Conduct of the War made up of members of both the Senate and the House to address the issues raised by the war.[45] The 39th Congress took the same approach as it addressed the issues involved in securing the peace. The Congress formed the Joint Committee of Fifteen on Reconstruction, made up of leading members of the House and Senate, to consider how to address these monumental issues. The Joint Committee was well balanced among the different factions of the Republican Party and at least some of the more reasonable leaders of the Democratic Party. The Joint Committee was chaired by Senator William P. Fessenden (R-ME), who has been described by a leading expert on Reconstruction as a "conservative," but the Joint Committee was clearly controlled by moderates.[46]

As a prelude to their proposals, the committee held hearings and produced a lengthy report. Approximately 150,000 copies of this document were published, and it was not only summarized in newspapers, but distributed across the country. There were over eighty amendments proposed to deal with Reconstruction. All were referred to the Joint Committee, and became the subject of public discussions outside of Congress. As the Joint Committee worked to craft this constitutional amendment, it is clear they built on all the background, thoughts, and ideas that have been discussed earlier in this chapter and in the chapters by Garrett Epps and Paul Finkelman.[47]

It is important to emphasize that, as the 39th Congress developed the terms of the 14th Amendment, these Congressmen were not writing on a clean slate. As Garrett Epps details, they were writing based on thirty years of antislavery debates, litigation, struggles for free speech and freedom of the pulpit, countless platforms of a variety of political parties, and the collective, shared experiences of their generation.

Even while fighting the war, Unionists were planning what needed to happen afterward: "'the North,' after conquering this rebellion, means to have guarantees for its rights." Those guarantees of rights included "going freely every where in the country, and of freely expressing every where his opinion." In other words, no longer could the Slave Power oligarchy keep someone out of South Carolina because he was a Republican judge who came down to file a suit arguing the unconstitutionality of a state law that required the jailing of Massachusetts-citizen sailors while their ships were docked in a South Carolina port. The leaders of a state could no longer punish people for expressing opinions that the state did not like.[48]

The 14th Amendment reads more like the Constitution than an amendment because there are multiple provisions. In Section 1, citizenship is defined, the privileges or immunities of U.S. citizens are guaranteed, and every person is guaranteed equal protection and due process of law. Section 2 treats the question of how members of Congress will be apportioned. Section 3 disqualifies people who had previously held office and taken an oath to uphold the U.S. Constitution from holding office if they had violated their oaths by engaging in insurrection or rebellion. Section 4 protects the public debt, bars payment of the debt of those involved in insurrection, and prohibits any claims for compensation for the emancipation of people previously held in slavery. Section 5 gives Congress the power to enforce the provisions of the Amendment through "appropriate legislation." In addition, the adoption of the 14th Amendment was analogous to the adoption of the Constitution: all of these Clauses were presented as a package, on a take it or leave it basis.

There may be some minor inconsistencies between the public understanding of the Amendment and what happened after the Amendment passed. But if so, some of these inconsistencies may result from the fact that some states may not have wanted to make all the changes contemplated by the Amendment, yet those states thought that adopting the Amendment was the lesser of two evils.[49]

The Amendment was reported out of the House of Representatives. Because of the overwhelming Republican majority in the House, and the fact that the Amendment was a moderate proposal that appealed to so many people, the vote was not even close. The Amendment passed the House 128–37. It was next considered by the Senate. After some preliminary debate, the Senate went into a private caucus. The results of the caucus led to two actions, the addition of the Citizenship Clause and a change to the Disqualification Clause. With that, after some debate and additional changes, the Senate approved the Amendment overwhelmingly by a vote of 33–11.[50]

The Senate was more conservative than the House, and the fact that no Republican Senator voted against the Amendment was seen as evidence that the Senate changes had eliminated all "vestiges of radicalism" from the proposal. When the Senate version of the Amendment went back to the House, the vote was again overwhelming: 120–32. The support for the Amendment in the Congress is beyond question. The legislative branch expressed its view with great clarity.[51]

The fact that the Amendment rejected what were considered to be "radical" proposals and became a moderate provision which would appeal to the mass of voters is confirmed by its reception by the *New York Times*. The *Times* was considered a "conservative" paper and had backed President Johnson in his dispute with the Congress. But the proposed Amendment convinced the *Times* to support the Congress against the President because the Amendment was a "good faith...measure of protection on the one hand and of reconciliation on the other."[52]

The question then became what would the states do in response?

IV. INTERPLAY AMONG THE CONGRESS, PRESIDENT JOHNSON, AND THE RATIFYING STATES

After passage by Congress, the Amendment went to the states for consideration of the people through their state legislatures. The first state to ratify was Connecticut, followed by New Hampshire. The third state to ratify the Amendment was Tennessee.[53]

The story of Tennessee is interesting for two reasons. First, most people think of the Southern states as monolithic Confederate states. But in reality, each of those states had individuals who were loyal to the Union. Estimates of the number of white Union soldiers from the eleven so-called Confederate states are between over 80,000 to almost 300,000, with slightly more than 100,000 probably being the most reliable estimate. Tennessee was one of the states with the strongest Unionist sentiment. It had the tradition of Unionist President Andrew Jackson. When the war came, it is estimated that 42,000 white soldiers from Tennessee volunteered and served in the Union Army.

Second, Tennessee was also the home of President Andrew Johnson. Johnson had been the only Southern Senator not to leave the U.S. Senate after secession and eventually was the Military Governor of Tennessee. Yet, Johnson sought to exercise influence in the state to defeat the Amendment. Johnson's connection with Tennessee, and the fact that its majority had fought against the Union, no doubt hurt it in the Congress. Nevertheless, at least the moderate Republicans wanted to recognize the Unionists in Tennessee and be able to readmit their representatives to the Congress.[54]

Contrary to revisionist claims, the desire to readmit Tennessee was not because the Republicans thought they "needed" the support of Tennessee to enable ratification of the 14th Amendment. Republicans consistently believed that only the votes of the loyal states that had active governments in the Union would count to achieve ratification. Rather, Tennessee's ratification was seen as a symbolic signing of the "peace treaty" of the war, and Tennessee's readmission would be an incentive for other rebellious states to come back to the fold in a like manner.[55]

Once again, the readmission of Tennessee demonstrates the power of the moderates in the story of the adoption and ratification of the Amendment. We think of Thaddeus Stevens (R-PA) as being the leader of House. However, Stevens was unwilling to guarantee admission to the rebellious states even if they ratified the 14th Amendment. Bingham, the "moderate," supported admission for Tennessee if it ratified the Amendment. The moderates won over Stevens.[56]

The 14th Amendment was clearly a moderate proposal that commanded the support of the overwhelming majority of the nation, as would eventually be demonstrated by the 1866 elections. Some may object here that the white Southern elite and their allies were not allowed to vote in this election, but neither were the white Unionists living in the South allowed to vote and, more importantly, neither were the new citizens under the 1866 Civil Rights Act allowed to vote. In order to contest the results of this election, one has to assume the propriety of disqualifying the African American vote in determining majority sentiment, and ally one's self with the white racist elite.

Despite its moderate nature, and contrary to the advice of many of his advisors, Johnson opposed the 14th Amendment. He tried to advance a watered-down counter-amendment and intervened in urging the white government of Alabama to defeat the proposed ratification. This, in turn, spurred other white supremacist governments in the former Confederate states to repudiate the Amendment. Those governments decided they were just going to wait and see what happened in the 1866 congressional elections.[57]

Despite Johnson's position, the Tennessee Unionist government, working hand-in-glove with moderate Republicans in the Congress like John Bingham, quickly ratified the Amendment. Governor Brownlow sent a telegram to the Clerk of the Senate which read, in part: "We have ratified the Constitutional Amendment in the House.... Give my respects to the dead dog of the White House."[58] Tennessee's representatives were quickly readmitted to the Congress.

The congressional elections of 1866 became a referendum on the 14th Amendment. It was the major issue of the campaign and resulted in a complete rout for the Democrats. Other state ratifications followed the election. On July 21, 1868, Congress declared the Amendment adopted.[59]

V. SECURING THE FUTURE

The story of Congress designing the 14th Amendment to secure the future peace was obscured by Professor Charles Fairman, who succeeded in setting the scholarly agenda on the Amendment from 1949 until the mid-1980s. Fairman wondered how the Amendment as drafted, particularly Section 1, could possibly have any effect on defending against a future war.

The answer is aptly summarized by an 1860 article in *Harper's Weekly*.

> The Republicans believed that white, slave-holding Southerners knew that if the right of free speech, guaranteed by the Constitution, were tolerated in the South, slavery would be destroyed by the common-sense of the Southern people ... [This] made [John] Calhoun and all his school insist upon suppressing it. Consequently, in its most important provision, the Constitution has been a dead letter in every slave State for more than thirty years.[60]

Republicans, Unionists and antislavery advocates, who started out as a minority, had used free speech, including freedom of the press and freedom in the pulpit, not only to establish the party, but to win the national election. These groups believed passionately in free discussion. They believed that had they been able to go into the South and campaign without being threatened, and had they been able to have free speech in the South and talk about slavery, there would never have been a Civil War. These advocates, therefore, believed that freedom of speech and other rights were going to protect the country from a future war.

Justice Swayne made an important point in his *Slaughter-House Cases* dissent: "By the Constitution, as it stood before the war, ample protection was given against oppression by the Union, but little was given against wrong and oppression by the States. That want was intended to be supplied by this amendment." Protecting against state oppression is what the 14th Amendment is supposed to do. Securing rights was an integral part of securing peace for the future.[61]

VI. SECURING RACIAL EQUALITY

Since its passage and ratification, legislators, courts and scholars have contested the extent of the commitment to rights and racial equality encompassed in the 14th Amendment. One argument advanced to limit the reach of the Amendment to secure rights is an argument that I have termed "racism trumps equality." The argument goes like this: The mid-1800s were terrible times, and even abolitionists were in some way racist and responsive to their racist constituents. Therefore, since everything was so racist in those days, one cannot interpret the words as written. Rather, one has to interpret the words in light of this racism and therefore one has to interpret them very narrowly.[62]

A fair reading of history supports a different thesis. There are strong counter-examples to institutionalizing endemic racism in the Equal Protection Clause from none other than 14th Amendment author John Bingham (a moderate and one of the leaders of the House). He is even called a man of "conservative tendency" by the editor of the *Journal of the Joint Committee of Fifteen on Reconstruction*. The sentiments recounted below, then, are not radical ideas out of the mainstream, but rather reflect the beliefs of the people in the middle.[63]

In 1862, during the debate over the abolition of slavery in the District of Columbia, Bingham committed to a very expansive definition of a person or mankind:

No matter upon what spot of the earth's surface they were born; no matter whether an Asiatic or African, a European or an American sun first burned upon them...no matter whether strong or weak, this new Magna Charta[64] to mankind declares the rights of all to life and liberty and property are equal before the law.[65]

In 1866 Bingham defended the efforts that African Americans made in the Civil War in response to the standard Democratic argument, in this instance advanced by an obscure Congressman, James W. Chanler (D-NY). Chanler claimed that the African race had never accomplished anything, had no prior history, and were not capable of voting, so they should not be involved in the government. This was, in Chanler's view, a white man's government.[66]

Bingham, the moderate, replied without the diplomacy of Lincoln. Bingham had very strong feelings about these issues. In this exchange, he said:

> I will bear witness now, by the authority of history, that this very race of which he speaks is the only race now existing upon this planet that ever hewed their way out of the prison-house of chattel slavery to the sunlight of personal liberty by their own unaided arm.

Speaking about the African American contributions to the War, Bingham continued:

> [T]hese people have borne themselves as bravely, as well, and, if I may add, as wisely during the great contest just closed, as any people to whom [Chanler] can point, situated in like circumstances, at any period of the world's history.

Bingham noted that even though slavery existed for two centuries

> ...the moment that the word 'Emancipation' was emblazoned upon your banners, those men who, with their ancestors, had been enslaved through five generations, rose as one man to stand by this republic.

In talking about the war effort itself (and I am trying to convey the zeal that Bingham had), he said that African Americans were

> ...doing firmly, unshrinkingly, and defiantly their full share in securing the final victory of our arms. I have said this much in defense of men who had the manhood, in the hour of the nation's trial, to strike for the flag and the unity of the republic in the tempest of the great conflict, and to stand, where brave men only could stand, on the field of poised battle, where the earthquake and the fire led the charge. Sir, I am not mistaken.[67]

At another point, Congressman S.S. Cox (D-OH) accused Bingham of being willing to have all actions taken as long as they would affect the Southern states, but that Bingham would take steps to try to stem the immigration of African Americans into Ohio. Bingham's reply was consistent with what he had previously argued with respect to Kansas and Oregon. "I desire to say to the gentleman that I have no idea myself that under any possible pressure I will ever consent that any man born upon the soil of this Republic, by any vote or any word of mine would ever be excluded from any state, my own included."[68]

There are thousands of examples of why this "racism trumps equality" theme just does not work. The consistently expressed sentiments and actions of the major drafter of Section 1 of the 14th Amendment belie them.

VII. CONCLUSION

The members of the 39th Congress were not perfect people. They talked about overcoming their own acknowledged prejudices. These Congressmen and state ratifiers did not write into the 14th Amendment their own worst practices and bad conduct. Instead, they wrote into the 14th Amendment their highest ideals and their best aspirations.

The congressmen who drafted and adopted the language of the 14th Amendment interpreted their own work. As John Bingham said, they were trying to "restore this Republic and perfect your Constitution."[69] They probably failed at perfecting the Constitution, but we honor them 140 years later for striving for those ideals, for making progress as imperfect as it may have been. Their efforts should inspire us to endeavor to make the Constitution, in interpretation and application as well as word, if not perfect, at least more perfect than the one we inherited.

An earlier version of this chapter was published in *Akron Law Review*, Vol. 42 No. 4, pp. 1019 Copyright © 2009, *Akron Law Review*, The University of Akron, School of Law.

This article is dedicated to the memory and accomplishments of the Honorable John F. Seiberling (1918–2008), a member of Congress for 16 years (1971–1987) who served on the House Judiciary Committee and made lasting contributions in many areas, including constitutional law and the protection of the environment. He served in World War II and for both his military record and his civic services, was referred to as an "American Hero" by the *Akron Beacon Journal* upon the occasion of his death.

4

The Union as It Wasn't and the Constitution as It Isn't

Section 5 and Altering the Balance of Powers

Elizabeth Reilly, The University of Akron School of Law

Much [has been] said about the Union as it was and the Constitution as it is. [I] want[] the Union as it wasn't and the Constitution as it isn't.
—Andrew Jackson Hamilton, urging ratification of the 14th Amendment

The original draft of Section 1 of the 14th Amendment, as introduced by its primary framer, John Bingham of Ohio, read: "The Congress shall have the power to make all laws which shall be necessary and proper to secure to the citizens of each State all privileges and immunities of citizens in the several States, and to all persons in the several States equal protection in the rights of life, liberty, and property."[1] These words signaled that enhancing Congress's power was central to remaking the Constitution and the Union. The prototype and the eventual Amendment staked out new ground: Congress became a direct and active protector of rights. That role was a marked departure from Congress's role in the Founders' Constitution.

The framers of the Amendment were well aware that they were granting a new and sweeping power that turned the relationship between Congress and individual rights on its head. They chose powerful language to embody that change. Thus, they purposely echoed the constitutional language in the initial grants of legislative power. Article 1, Section 8 begins: "The Congress shall have Power..."

which continues in Clause 18 "to make all Laws which shall be necessary and proper for carrying into Execution the foregoing Powers, and all other Powers vested by this Constitution in the Government of the United States." But even more evocative, as explored below, is the direct contrast drawn with how the 1st Amendment introduces the entire Bill of Rights: "Congress shall make no law...."

This second founding reallocated powers on all dimensions, restructuring the nation and the government to better guarantee fundamental rights and liberties. The 14th Amendment rebalanced national and state power. But critically, and less widely acknowledged and understood, the Amendment rebalanced the legislative and judicial powers with respect to individual rights. Before, the judiciary protected rights reactively by overriding invasive legislative and executive actions. The Reconstruction Amendments endowed the legislature with the power and responsibility to act systemically and pro-actively on behalf of guaranteeing rights and remedying violations of them.

Before the Reconstruction Amendments, there was no general understanding that Congress possessed power to legislate to secure individual rights and privileges, especially those framed as limitations upon governmental power. Rights were conceived as needing protection from, not by, Congress. This structure resulted, in practice, in Congress's role being to steer clear of violating rights, not to be the positive declarer and protector of rights.

The framers of the 14th Amendment interpreted their work as a fundamental rethinking of powers and rights. When Bingham introduced the prototype, he noted expressly that "save the words conferring the express grant of power to the Congress," the principles of the rights were already in the Constitution. The problem was that congressional power to enforce rights had been withheld "by every construction of the Constitution, its contemporaneous construction, its continued construction, legislative, executive, and judicial." Adherence to the "immortal bill of rights" had up to that point rested solely upon "the fidelity of the States." Had the power been given to Congress to enforce obedience to those principles, Bingham maintained that the "rebellion" would have been "an impossibility." In Bingham's mind, the congressional power to enforce rights was not only "the want of the Republic," but also "absolutely essential to American nationality." On behalf of the Joint Committee on Reconstruction, Bingham recommended the Amendment "for the purpose of giving to the whole people the care in future of the unity of the Government which constitutes us one people, and without which American nationality would cease to be."[2]

This grant of power to Congress ultimately became Section 5 when the multiple pending amendments were joined into a single amendment: "Congress shall have power to enforce, by appropriate legislation, the provisions of this article." But its critical relationship to effectuating rights remained. As explained by Senator Howard when introducing the full Amendment to the floor of the Senate, this "additional power ... to Congress" was "necessary" to "effectuate ... and enforce ... the great object of the first section of this amendment."[3] As interpreted by its framers, Section 5's grant of power to Congress profoundly reconceived the role of the national legislature. Its revolutionary nature is apparent if one considers the original theory of legislative power and its relationship to rights, and the antebellum Supreme Court precedents on the same subject. Section 5 was not merely a sharp departure from previous constitutional theory but also used the lessons of history to turn that theory on its head. Its "positive grant of legislative power ... to achieve civil and political equality for all citizens," did not exist in the Constitution until the Reconstruction Amendments.[4]

This chapter explores the differences between the Founders' 1787 Constitution and the Bill of Rights, and the new structure of the Union incorporated into the 14th Amendment. Part I details the political and legal philosophy of the Founders with respect to the relationship between legislative power and the protection of individual rights and liberties. This theoretical construct championed individual rights by cabining congressional power and granting the Court a primary role to protect liberties. Part II discusses the antebellum Court's interpretation of congressional powers with respect to rights.

Part III then contrasts those conceptions with the Republican ideology that undergirded the political philosophy of the framers of the 14th Amendment. Part III continues by demonstrating why the framers insisted upon an affirmative grant of power to Congress, and how the 39th Congress interpreted their proposed amendment as having accomplished their goals. Consistent with Republican legal and political ideology of the time,[5] the necessity both of congressional power and of an affirmative grant of that power infused the Amendment from its inception.

Part III also argues that in reconstituting the Union, the 39th Congress altered the original structural alignment of national powers and the boundaries of the respective spheres of judicial and legislative power with respect to rights. Part IV briefly examines the Supreme Court's initial interpretations of the new congressional power, which read Congress's ability to protect rights extremely narrowly, and its modern limiting interpretation of Section 5. At both times, the Court invoked understandings of federalism and separation of powers that harkened to the Founders' Constitution, rather than to the Constitution of the framers of the 14th Amendment. Part IV concludes by elucidating the contrast between the Court's initial and most recent interpretations, and those of the framers and their successors in later Reconstruction Congresses, who consistently interpreted the Amendment as expanding the power of Congress to enforce rights.

Throughout the debates during the framing and ratification of the 14th Amendment, the framers coupled an understanding of the need to recast the Union with the understanding that to do so, the Constitution itself needed to repudiate doctrines that had undermined both Union and liberty.[6] Following the ratification of the 14th Amendment in 1868, the Constitution newly empowered Congress as an essential protector of liberty, supplanting the 1787 conception of Congress as a potential threat to liberty.

I. CONGRESS AND THE RIGHTS IN THE FOUNDERS' CONSTITUTION

The "Constitution as it is" in 1866 was largely the Founders' Constitution. It protected rights negatively, by withholding congressional power over them. At the original framing, there was apparently no thought to accord the legislature a greater expanse of power to act positively on behalf of liberties. Rather, the legislature was a source of "interferences in cases affecting personal rights."[7] The resources of the framers were expended finding methods to cabin legislative power in order to protect rights.

The original theoretical underpinnings of the relationship of legislative power to preservation of rights restricted Congress rather than empowering it. Initially, the Federalists argued that the limited powers afforded through Article 1 to Congress, and to the national government generally, were sufficient to protect individual rights. They conceptualized the Article 1 enumerations and limitations as protecting rights from Congressional incursion by a withholding of power. The Founders' Constitution championed individual rights by relying on the Court and the states to protect them. The Court was a counterweight to prevent Congress from impinging upon rights in the exercise of its granted powers.

These theories are structurally embodied in the antebellum Constitution. The Article 1, Section 8 express "Powers of Congress" did not relate to rights, but to governing a nation. Article 1, Section 9 contained "Prohibited powers," a number of them designed to protect rights of individuals or prerogatives of states from Congressional encroachment.

Even the Bill of Rights, necessitated by demands for express written protections for fundamental liberties, was conceived as restricting the otherwise legitimate exercise of enumerated legislative and executive powers from encroaching on rights. There is great rhetorical power and meaning in the first words being *"Congress shall make no law."*

Broad legislative power was a necessary feature of the 1787 Constitution. Nonetheless, the Founders feared unchecked legislative power. *The Federalist Papers* addressed the concern that the legislative power was a potential source of danger to individuals and to states. In *Federalist 48*, James Madison characterized the legislative power as most dangerous to liberty, apt to draw "all power into its impetuous vortex" and able to usurp power and thus to interfere with rights. But in *Federalist 41*, Madison opined that the legislature would have no power to invade rights because of the limitations of enumeration. Thus, the Article 1 definition of legislative powers was portrayed as one method for protecting the Union from the danger of the legislative prerogative.[8] Adverting to Article 1, Section 9's express limits on legislative power, Madison in *Federalist 44* described them as a "constitutional bulwark in favor of personal security and private rights." Alexander Hamilton argued in *Federalist 84* that there was no need to excerpt rights from those "powers not granted" because the Constitution itself was a bill of rights. Congress, in theory, had no power over rights; the people retained those powers.

Acknowledging that the Necessary and Proper Clause had excited considerable opposition as the way to "exterminate liberties," Hamilton sought to explain the limits of the Clause in *Federalist 33*. He noted that all powers carry with them the means to effectuate their exercise, and that the people and the states would enforce appropriate boundaries. The Founders were also aware that majorities could override minority interests and rights, especially in legislatures. This potential outcome posed significant problems for structuring a government less likely to wield power to override individual rights. *Federalist 51*, drawing upon arguments first exposited in *Federalist 10*, noted that rights would be protected by the "extended republic" of the new nation, the power of the separate departments of government and the divisions of the legislative branch itself to "resist encroachments," and the multiplicity of interests represented in the "great variety of interests, parties, and sects" it would naturally possess.

The Founders knew it was hard to constitute limits to legislative power. Thus, they did not entrust Congress with defining and protecting individual liberties, nor did they rely upon textual limits alone. Rather, they formulated a governmental structure protective of liberty. Madison touted the structural protections curbing legislative power built into the Constitution in *Federalist 44*. These external limitations on Congress were designed to prevent it from exceeding its granted powers. The balance of powers struck enforced the internal limitations of Article 1 through empowering the "least dangerous" branch, the Court, to guard the Constitution and individual rights from legislative encroachment.[9] The judicial power would confine the legislature to exercising its own powers without invading rights as a purpose or by-product. Without that check, reserving rights would be meaningless.

The 1787 Constitution and the Bill of Rights also relied heavily upon the states and the people to act as guardians of liberty. The Founders' concept prevented legislative power from encroaching on states because they thought states were better designed to protect liberties, being closer to the people, and hence necessarily more responsive to their demands and needs. Madison explained that the powers delegated to Congress were "few and defined" with states retaining powers concerning the "lives, liberties and properties of the people" in *Federalist 45*, and that any infringement of liberties would be opposed by the states in *Federalist 46*. Therefore, "[p]rior to the Civil War, the states defined the status and enforced the rights of the individual . . . [and] functioned as the primary guarantors of the fundamental rights of American citizens."[10]

The Bill of Rights similarly entrusted the Court with the protection of those liberties. "A bill of rights . . . would give legitimacy to principles of liberty, help the people to internalize these values, and provide a basis for rallying against abuses of power. It would also give new power to the courts. Madison announced, with excessive optimism, that 'courts of justice' would form 'impenetrable barriers' against violations of the liberties in the Bill of Rights."[11]

II. ANTEBELLUM JUDICIAL INTERPRETATION OF CONGRESSIONAL POWER OVER RIGHTS

Judicial interpretations of Congress's power dovetailed with the political theory encapsulated in the constitutional structure. In 1803, the Supreme Court in *Marbury v. Madison* confirmed the role of the judiciary and its power to override legislative actions that exceeded legislative power.[12] In *Barron v. Baltimore*, the Court in 1833 forcefully interpreted the Bill of Rights as negating only federal and thus legislative power, making the rights unenforceable against the states:

> Serious fears were extensively entertained that those powers which the patriot statesmen . . . deemed essential to union, and to the attainment of those invalu-

able objects for which union was sought, might be exercised in a manner dangerous to liberty. In almost every convention by which the constitution was adopted, amendments to guard against the abuse of power were recommended. *These amendments demanded security against the apprehended encroachments of the general government*—not against those of the local governments.

Rather, the constitutional limits upon state actions were contained only in Article I, Section 10.[13]

There was one piece of antebellum legislation in which Congress purported to legislate on behalf of rights. It turned out badly for Congressional power. In the Missouri Compromise in 1820, Congress had exercised its power over the territories to prohibit slavery in the Louisiana territory north of the 36°30' north parallel, in an attempt to preserve a balance of power between free and slave states. The Compromise was drawn into issue in *Dred Scott v. Sanford*, when Scott claimed that his extended sojourn in free territory effected his freedom from slavery. Scott argued that Congress had plenary power over the territories; the Court agreed the power existed subject to all the limitations of the Constitution. Under the Court's theory, if the 5th Amendment's Due Process Clause was a source of Congressional power to legislate, then legislation to protect liberty should be authorized. But instead, despite a long history of great deference to Congress's exercises of Article 1 powers, the Supreme Court declared the Compromise an unconstitutional exercise of legislative power.

Chief Justice Taney's opinion for the Court found that the rights in slave property, enshrined in the body of the Constitution, were rights the federal government was bound to protect.

> [T]he right of property in a slave is distinctly and expressly affirmed in the Constitution. The right to traffic in it, like an ordinary article of merchandise and property, was guarantied [sic] to the citizens of the United States, in every State that might desire it, for twenty years. And the Government in express terms is pledged to protect it in all future time, if the slave escapes from his owner. This is done in plain words—too plain to be misunderstood. And no word can be found in the Constitution which gives Congress a greater power over slave property, or which entitles property of that kind to less protection than property of any other description. The only power conferred is the power coupled with the duty of guarding and protecting the owner in his rights. Upon these considerations, it is the opinion of the court that the act of Congress which prohibited a citizen from holding and owning property of this kind in the territory of the United States north of the line therein mentioned, is not warranted by the Constitution, and is therefore void.[14]

The 5th Amendment merely prohibited interference with property, including slave "property." Conversely, the Runaway Slave Clause and other protections bound Congress to protect slave "property." Taney noted neither the 5th Amendment, nor any of the Bill of Rights, was a source of legislative prerogative to make laws with respect to property and liberty. "The powers over person and property of which we speak are not only not granted to Congress, but are in express terms denied, and they are forbidden to exercise them. . . . It is a total absence of power everywhere," including within the federal sphere of the territories.[15]

The only legislative power "in favor of" rights that the Court had ever upheld was the power to legislate on fugitive slaves, in *Prigg v. Pennsylvania*. Congress had legislated with respect to the return of fugitives from justice and fugitive slaves in 1793. Several Northern states had passed laws to ensure that claims of fugitive slave status were fairly adjudicated and proven, before relinquishing blacks to purported masters. Pennsylvania authorized prosecutions for kidnapping if these procedures were not adhered to. When the state of Maryland objected to rendering a citizen charged with violating these laws in Pennsylvania, the question of state power to pass these laws came before the Court. *Prigg* held that Congress had the exclusive power to legislate with respect to fugitive slaves, because the Constitution had conferred a "power coupled with a duty" on the federal government, in the judgment of the Court.[16]

A close examination of the Court's analysis in *Prigg* reveals that Justice Story carefully tethered Congress's power to textually explicit affirmative statements in the body of the Constitution, such as those in the Runaway Slave Clause of Article 4, Section 2, Clause 3. "The clause manifestly contemplates the existence of a positive, unqualified right on the part of the owner of the slave." Congressional power required a constitutional mandate addressed to the national government—a positive right awarded to an individual—coupled with an affirmative duty imposed on the government to act on behalf of that right ("at once a guarantee and duty").[17]

Further limits were imposed by two phrases in the Runaway Slave Clause which the Court read as expressing positive sources of power. The Court found that the language "upon Claim of" vested national judicial power and that the Clause's phrase "shall be delivered" explicitly imposed the duty of return. Both phrases imposed national responsibility to protect the right in slave property. Story further tethered the sources of legislative power by noting that the Clause had been fundamental to creating the Union, which explained why it had to bestow power on the national government to enforce it as a positive right.[18]

The reasoning of *Prigg* is carefully constricted. Unless the Constitution explicitly grants a positive right, coupled with an explicit federal duty, there is no grant of affirmative power to legislate with respect to that right: "[T]he national government [must have legislative power to act] in cases where rights are intended to be absolutely secured, and duties are positively enjoined by the constitution." Limitations on power are not recognized as affirmative grants of power. There is language that arguably exceeds this boundary. However, it follows language coupling the right with a duty: "If, indeed, the constitution guaranties the right, and if it requires the delivery . . . the fundamental principle . . . would seem to be, that where the end is required . . . and where the duty is enjoined, the ability to perform it is contemplated to exist." Justice Story's other examples of constitutional grants of rights that also grant legislative power to fulfill them are notably limited to powers or duties imposed in the body of the Constitution.[19]

Prigg prevented the states from legislating to provide procedural protections to determine the status of an alleged fugitive slave, holding that such power was exclusive to Congress. But it also recognized the states did not have to aid the federal government in capturing or rendering fugitive slaves. The Fugitive Slave Act of 1850 mandated state assistance for slaveholder "rights." In 1860 in *Kentucky v. Dennison*, the Court held that the national government could not force the states to comply with that mandate; Congress had no power against the states in the absence of a direct grant of constitutional power both over the right and over the states. Coupled with the holding of *Barron*, the Court had made it clear: limitations upon the states were enforceable only if the Constitution both expressly limited the powers of the states and granted power to the branches of the federal government to enforce those limits. The Bill of Rights did not meet those standards.[20]

The combination of *Barron, Prigg, Dred Scott* and *Dennison* prohibited Congress from legislating to protect rights. The Bill of Rights merely encompassed limitations upon, not powers of, Congress. Congressional power in matters of rights was confined only to rights within the body of the Constitution accompanied by an expressly imposed duty upon Congress to protect them. In addition, the federal government, including the Court, was powerless to enforce the guarantees of the Bill of Rights and other rights against the states. This interpretation was so engrained that in 1876, the post-14th Amendment *Cruikshank* Court still declaimed: "Only such existing rights were committed by the people to the protection of Congress as came within the general scope of the authority granted to the national government.... [The Bill of Rights]... added nothing to the already existing powers of the United States."[21]

III. REPUBLICAN IDEOLOGY AND CONGRESSIONAL POWER

A. *Republican Ideology and the Importance of Congressional Primacy*

Republican ideology had been forged in the crucible of antislavery activism. Hence, the framers of the 14th Amendment were acutely aware of the impact of the decisions in *Barron, Prigg,* and *Dred Scott*. Contrary to the Court's interpretation, Republicans believed that the Bill of Rights did bind the states, at least morally, and even legally, through Article 4 privileges and immunities (as they interpreted it) and by virtue of the 13th Amendment. However, Republicans understood that Congress and the Court could not enforce those rights because of the Court's interpretations of the Constitution. Bingham expressed the upshot of this ideology when he opined that slavery, enshrined at the framing, had made it necessary to disable the federal government from enforcing rights. The framers were thus aware of the need to grant power to Congress and subject the states to the limitations of rights.[22]

The framers of the 14th Amendment were both thoughtful and wary. They had suffered repeated defeats during the antebellum period and in their own 39th Congress, as detailed in earlier chapters by Garrett Epps, Paul Finkelman and Richard Aynes. The framers also understood the power that the original constitutional framework gave the judicial and the executive branches to override their intentions, having suffered those defeats in the recent past. These experiences made clear to them the inadequacy of relying upon the Supreme Court and the President to achieve the framers' goals, especially of protections for rights, liberty, and citizenship. They were, therefore, thorough when they drafted the Amendment, and presciently—although less effectively than they had hoped—included Section 5 to alter the separation of powers.

Bingham thought ensuring that Congress had the power to enforce rights contained in the Constitution was "the most important issue that would come before the Congress." Consistent with Republican ideology, he believed that those rights bound the states, but that "every construction of the Constitution...legislative, executive and judicial," made them unenforceable. Changing that interpretation, by changing the Constitution and according power to Congress, was a great object of the Amendment. Bingham consistently argued that the proposed Amendment needed "to arm Congress with the power to compel obedience to the oath [to uphold the Constitution, including the guarantees of rights it contained]." He decried that "it has been the want of the Republic that there was not an express grant of power in the Constitution to enable the whole people of every State, by congressional enactment, to enforce obedience to these requirements [the Bill of Rights] of the Constitution."[23]

Had such a power to legislate affirmatively with respect to rights been well understood or accepted, Section 5 would have been unnecessary, or have drawn no comment. But the grant of that power remained clear, forceful and primary, even after the Amendment was restructured to address the additional concerns of Sections 2, 3, and 4. The congressional power ultimately located in Section 5 was in every draft of the Amendment. Nothing indicates that Bingham or Congress believed that the change from the prototype to the full amendment would diminish Congress's power to enforce the rights secured by the enhanced Section 1.

Indeed, when introducing the full version of the 14th Amendment onto the floor of the Senate, Senator Howard used similar arguments for the centrality of the grant of congressional power. He referenced the need for explicit congressional power over rights, noting the inadequacy of relying upon the Necessary and Proper Clause:

> Now, sir, there is no power given in the Constitution to enforce and to carry out any of these guarantees [of the Bill of Rights]. They are not powers granted by the Constitution to Congress, and of course do not come within the sweeping clause of the Constitution authorizing Congress to pass all laws necessary and proper for carrying out the foregoing or granted powers, but they stand simply as a bill of rights in the Constitution, without power on the part of Congress to give them full effect. . . . The great object of the first section of this amendment is, therefore, to restrain the power of the States and compel them at all times to respect these great fundamental guarantees. How will it be done under the present amendment? As I have remarked, they are not powers granted to Congress, and therefore it is necessary, if they are to be effectuated and enforced, as they assuredly ought to be, that additional power should be given to Congress to that end. This is done by the fifth section of this amendment."[24]

Both proponents and opponents of the Amendment were acutely aware that the Supreme Court had interpreted Congress's constitutional powers to preclude the ability to act affirmatively in defense of guaranteed rights. As William Rich has pointed out, Andrew Rogers, a member of the Joint Committee and an opponent of the Amendment, agreed with Bingham and Howard that "guarantees, privileges, and immunities are not powers, and when the Constitution authorized Congress to make all laws necessary and proper to carry into execution the powers vested in the Government, it meant powers strictly." Moderate Republican Congressman Hale agreed with "the broad consensus on this point, explaining that the constitutional text 'limited [congressional authority] directly to these [Article 1, Section 8,] powers; it is not a general power to enact all laws for carrying out the provisions of the Constitution.'" The grant of power mattered, and it mattered mightily.[25]

This belief system explains the framers' views about the role of the 14th Amendment with respect to the Civil Rights Act of 1866. The Act was passed after the ratification of the 13th Amendment, and before passage of the 14th. The 39th Congress believed the Act's provisions were necessary to secure the rights and protection for freedmen in the South. However, there was substantial doubt as to whether its provisions defining and protecting rights against states and private actors were authorized by—or would be held by the Court to be authorized by—the 13th Amendment, or needed additional constitutional sanction. On initial presentation, President Johnson vetoed the Act, citing a lack of congressional power to enact it. Although Congress overrode the veto easily, members understood that there was a need to secure the legislative power to enact it.[26]

The framers understood that the 14th Amendment would secure the ends and the constitutionality of the Civil Rights Act. Thaddeus Stevens noted the Amendment would prevent repeal of rights protected by the Civil Rights Act; Garfield stated the purpose was to fix the Act in the Constitution; Raymond, who had voted against the bill because of doubts as to its constitutionality, was satisfied that the bill now came "before us in the form of an amendment to the constitution which purports to give Congress the power to attain this precise result." In other words, to preserve the protections in the Act from being struck down by the Court, the framers incorporated them into an Amendment that explicitly granted Congress power to effectuate its guarantees, precisely what the Court had required in *Barron* and *Prigg*.[27]

Some of the members of the 39th Congress argued a possible exception to the antebellum Court's narrow reading of Congressional power with respect to rights. Representative Wilson of Iowa championed Congress's power to pass the Civil Rights Act of 1866 pursuant to the 13th Amendment. He used the theory from *Prigg* that Congress had power to enforce those rights because they were guaranteed by the 13th Amendment. Others, including the main proponent of the Congressional Power Clause, John Bingham, were not convinced that such a congressional power existed or had been recognized by *Prigg*. Nor were Republicans sanguine that the Court would find those rights encompassed in the abolition of slavery. The argument ultimately depended upon agreement from the Supreme Court, by no means a foregone conclusion and an unlikely sequel to *Prigg* and *Dred Scott.*[28]

As Richard Aynes pointedly notes: "Bingham's conviction that an express enforcement provision was required proved correct in *Ex parte Virginia*, where the Court stated, 'Were it not for the 5th Section of the 14th Amendment, there might be room for argument that the 1st Section is only declaratory of the moral duty of the State, as was said in *Commonwealth of Kentucky v. Dennison.*'"[29] The framers were quite cognizant—and according to the Supreme Court in 1879 quite correct—that they were inhabiting new territory when they empowered Congress to protect rights.

B. Reimagining the Legislative and Judicial Roles with Respect to Rights

The Founders' Constitution gave primacy to the judiciary as the protector of rights, and used this role to prevent the legislature from becoming a predator of rights. Section 5, conversely, accords Congress a primary role as a bulwark of, not a potential threat to, individual rights. It reconceived the legislature's role and power both with respect to the states and with respect to securing individual liberties. The 39th Congress and later Reconstruction Congresses reimagined their role pursuant to these powers.

To the framers of the 14th Amendment, the Court had failed in its role as a bulwark of individual liberties, especially in *Prigg* and *Dred Scott.* "[They] vividly remembered the capture of the judiciary by the Slave Power, and they feared it had not yet fully freed itself." During debate, Representative Kelly noted "all that has been done judicially in furtherance of this great wrong [slavery]." As noted earlier, the need for Congress to have a recognized and active role was so strongly perceived that the original draft of Section 1 focused on granting Congress the power to secure the necessary rights as a first matter.[30]

Even the strongest proponents of a then-existing constitutional power to protect rights understood that such a power needed to be implied, and hence depended upon Supreme Court agreement. Representative Wilson reflected the views of others when he urged that the *Prigg* precedent could be used to imply power: "The possession of the rights by the citizen raises by implication the power in Congress to provide appropriate means for their protection; in other words, to supply the needed remedy."[31]

Conversely, Democrat Andrew Rogers opposed the prototype amendment, arguing that Congress should be content to leave enforcement of the rights contained in the Constitution to the Court, as in the past. But the framers refused to leave protection for rights solely in the hands of the Court, even after strengthening the statement of rights in the ultimate Section 1 of the Amendment. As Michael McConnell argues, "They were not content to leave the specification of protected rights to judicial decision." And Garrett Epps contends: "[R]elegat[ing Congress] to an occasional role as an auxiliary enforcer of court decisions seems far from what the Slave Power-minded framers intended."[32]

Section 5 bears witness that the framers intended a new and unmistakable power and role for Congress, one not subject to the whims of the Court. Key framers repeatedly refer to the grant of legislative power to protect rights as essential to achieve the goals of the Amendment. Congress was not sanguine that the executive and the Court would recognize and enforce an exercise of that power. The recurrence of the grant of power in all three Reconstruction Amendments reinforces the inference that there was a felt need to make it abidingly clear that power existed, not to be denied by the President or the United States Supreme Court. When Section 5 prominently reconceived Congress's role with respect to liberty, it necessarily affected the Court's role as well, restriking the balance between the two branches.[33]

IV. JUDICIAL INTERPRETATION AND THE REFUSAL TO RECOGNIZE LEGISLATIVE POWER

Despite its high purpose and its structural changes to the constitutional framework, the 14th Amendment was not universally embraced as a vehicle for accomplishing its guarantees. The United States Supreme Court promptly eviscerated much of the meaning of Section 1 and cast doubt on Congress's Section 5 power in its first interpretation of the Amendment in the *Slaughter-House Cases*. Although the question of congressional power was inapplicable to the case facts, as the challenge was to local legislation, the Court intimated a restricted role for Congress, limiting its power to correcting state laws that discriminated on the basis of race. "If, however, the States did not conform their laws to [the] requirements [of the Equal Protection Clause], then by the fifth section of the article of amendment Congress was authorized to enforce it by suitable legislation. We doubt very much whether any action of a State not directed by way of discrimination against the negroes as a class, or on account of their race, will ever be held to come within the purview of this provision." The Court imposed restrictions on Congress only three years later in *United States v. Cruikshank*, finding that Congress did not have the power to protect rights to life, liberty or peaceable assembly from race-motivated mob violence. *Cruikshank* struck down convictions for violating the Enforcement Act of 1870, and introduced both the narrowing of congressional power to enforce rights and the state action limitation. "The 14th Amendment prohibits a State from depriving any person of life, liberty, or property, without due process of law; but this adds nothing to the rights of one citizen as against another. It simply furnishes an additional guaranty against any encroachment by the States."[34]

Cruikshank also signaled limitations on recognizing enhanced congressional prerogative to protect rights. In the *Civil Rights Cases*, the Court used the state action limitation to strike down significant provisions of the Civil Rights Act of 1875, which guaranteed equal access to public accommodations. Other cases completed the task of severely restricting the reach of the Section 5 power, striking down laws such as the Ku Klux Klan Act and others passed pursuant to that power. By 1883, the Amendment appeared to be all but impotent as a source of congressional power, federal power, and individual rights.[35]

In contrast to the Court's interpretation, the framers in the 39th Congress, and the Congresses immediately following them, interpreted the power conferred in Section 5 to encompass reenvisioned roles and boundaries for the judicial, executive and legislative power especially vis-à-vis individual rights. Congress enacted Reconstruction statutes pursuant to its interpretation of the power and in response to the morphing abuses of rights being practiced in the former slave states. Those measures identified rights as fundamental as access to the government and polls, to contract, and to the courts as well as those essential to social inclusion, such as access to public accommodations of all sorts, and provided protection for their exercise from invasions by both government and private actors. In addition to the Civil Rights Act of 1866, originally entitled "An Act to protect All Persons in the United States in Their Civil Rights, and furnish the Means of their Vindication," Congress passed The Enforcement Act of 1870 (originally entitled "An Act to enforce the rights of citizens of the United States"), the Ku Klux Klan Act of 1871 (originally entitled "An Act to enforce the Provisions of the 14th Amendment to the Constitution of the United States, and for other Purposes"), and the Civil Rights Act of 1875 (originally entitled "An act to protect all citizens in their civil and legal rights"). Bingham noted during debate in 1871 that Congress had the power to pass this extensive legislation, because the Amendment constituted an "express prohibition on every State of the Union, which may be enforced under existing laws of Congress, and such other laws for their better enforcement as Congress may make."[36]

Later Congresses were cognizant that the Court's misconstruction of their efforts in Section 5 had eviscerated their powers and the guarantees of the Amendment. During the debates on the Blaine Amendment in 1876, Senator Oliver Morton noted: "The fourteenth and fifteenth Amendments which we supposed broad, ample, and specific, have, I fear, been very much impaired by construction, and one of them in some respects, almost destroyed by construction. Therefore, I would leave as little as possible to construction. I would make [the proposed provisions] so specific and so strong that they cannot be construed away and destroyed by the courts."[37]

Congress resurrected the Amendment as a source of principles guaranteeing rights during the Civil Rights era of the 1960s. But the Supreme Court's early restrictive interpretations of legislative power led Congress to use the Commerce Power to support the legislation. A much-altered Supreme Court upheld those statutes, and began to articulate an interpretation of Section 5 (and its companion Section 2 of the 15th Amendment) that accorded power to Congress to resolve existing problems to the guarantees of rights through far-reaching legislation.[38]

But consistent with the interpretive limits imposed by the early Court decisions, the modern Court has reasserted significant restraints on Congressional power on federalism grounds. These current decisions also specifically raise separation of powers concerns to limit the reach of the congressional Section 5 power. The recent Supreme Court decisions limit congressional power to interpret, define, or create rights. Instead, the Court confines the Section 5 power to decreeing remedies for persistent state violations of Court-recognized constitutional rights. The cases taken together stand for the propositions that (1) Congress may only enact remedies to enforce a Court-understood violation of the 14th Amendment; (2) the prescribed remedy must be congruent with and proportionate to evidence-based findings of state violations, or be appropriate prophylaxis against such violations; (3) the legislation must operate against state action only; and (4) Congress must use statutory language that is unmistakably clear about the intent to explicitly override state sovereign immunity as embodied in the 11th Amendment. These decisions have revitalized scholarship on the original and historical meaning of the Section 5 grant of power.[39]

City of Boerne v. Flores heralded the modern Court's renewed restrictive reading of Congressional power, and invoked separation of powers as well as federalism in support of its limitations. The Supreme Court interpreted the deletion of Congressional power from Section 1 as a diminution of the power ultimately accorded in Section 5: the power granted was "no longer plenary but remedial." However, the history of the change does not indicate any substantive alterations. The placement and the language adopted in the 14th Amendment mirror both the 13th and 15th Amendments, and technical drafting for consistency might account for the change. Aside from the losing arguments of the opponents of the Amendment, objections to the grant of power did not seek to limit it. Rather, debate centered upon whether the Necessary and Proper Clause would give Congress sufficient power to restrict the States through legislation with respect to the matters contained in the Amendment, or if Congress needed a direct grant of power to ensure its power. Significant support for a strong congressional role continued throughout the adoption and ratification of the Amendment, from prototype to final version.[40]

The actual shift of the grant of power from the section guaranteeing rights to a separate, last section of the Amendment occurred in the Joint Committee on Reconstruction. The placement occurred as part of reconceptualizing the separate constitutional amendments the Committee proposed into a single, multi-subject amendment in which the goals of Congress coalesced into a unified whole. Before the restructuring, the separate component amendments bogged down the process of adopting them. Robert Dale Owen proposed the multi-section version to Thaddeus Stevens, who embraced it enthusiastically and took it to the Joint Committee, where it also received a favorable reception. Bingham's concerns and actions were confined to making sure the rights section was sufficiently broad and specific.[41]

In the Joint Committee, when fashioning the final version of the Amendment it would report out, the committee voted to approve the wording of Section 5 before considering Bingham's final version of Section 1. Thus, the grant of congressional power preceded the full definition of the rights Congress would receive the power to enforce.[42]

The drafters' interpretation of the reach of the power did not change. The 39th Congress perceived Johnson's actions with respect to the former confederate states as actively interfering with their process of reconstruction. He persisted in pardoning high-ranking confederates and in purporting to recognize unreconstructed state elections. Johnson's veto messages insisted that Congress had no power to enact the legislation. Interestingly, Bingham brought the proposed amendment to the floor of the House after each of President Johnson's serial vetoes of the civil rights and freedmen's bureau legislation.[43]

Before the redrafting, Bingham had repeatedly emphasized the need to correct Congress's lack of power to effectuate and enforce the rights in the Constitution. He attributed that lack of power to the original founders' decision to protect slavery, a protection inconsistent with effectuating the Bill of Rights, privileges and immunities, and due process against the states. After the redrafting, Bingham told the House the Amendment corrected the problem, giving Congress "power to do what hitherto it had possessed no power to accomplish. . . . to protect by national law the privileges and immunities of all the citizens of the republic and the inborn rights of every person within its jurisdiction whenever the same shall be abridged or denied by the unconstitutional acts of any State."[44]

A demotion of the importance of congressional power or its reach receives no support from the lack of a vote on the prototype. In December 1865, Congress referred the concept of Section 1 to the newly created Joint Committee. Bingham withdrew the prototype because the House failed to approve considering the prototype under a special order of business. Joseph James recounts that a shrewd Stevens counseled recommitment to committee so the Joint Committee could maintain control of the calendar when it was brought up. After Johnson vetoed the Freedmen's Bureau Bill, Bingham introduced the Amendment again. At that time, the Democrats and other opponents argued against it either as a superfluity or as a radical centralization of power in the national government, to the derogation of state authority, not because of the role it gave Congress. Bingham moved to table and it was returned to committee. This motion was Republican-led and passed, and James notes that some in favor of it wanted the Senate to handle first the representation issue of what is now Section 2.[45]

One comment that might lend credence to a desire to weaken the congressional power was made by a Democratic opponent to the Amendment. In earlier floor debates, Andrew Rogers of New Jersey, a member of the Joint Committee (who had voted against reporting out the proposal), attacked the prototype of Section 1 of the Amendment as a move to centralize power unduly. He argued that rather than increase public unrest by amending the Constitution, Congress should be content to leave enforcement of the rights contained in the Constitution to the Court. Bingham had already pointed out that the courts had denied to themselves the power to enforce those rights against the states, which is why Bingham emphasized the need for Congress to have power. Rogers repeated many of the same arguments on the last day of debate on the full multi-section Amendment. He decried the force of the Amendment to make the Civil Rights Act of 1866 constitutional; he objected to congressional power to define and enforce rights against the states. His objections support the conclusion that the Amendment indeed intended to vest the very power in Congress that he had earlier wished kept solely in the province of the courts. Although not exclusively based upon his objections to Sections 1 and 5, Rogers' vote against the Amendment indicates he did not see any sufficient weakening of the powers it contained.[46]

Skepticism among the framers about the Court's willingness to secure rights, coupled with the affirmation of congressional power to enact the Civil Rights Acts of 1866, makes it nonsensical that Section 5 truncated congressional powers to protect only those rights that Court interpretation made clear preexisted the legislation. Consistent with his declarations during the debates on the Amendment, Bingham recalled in 1871 that the final form of the Amendment embraced more, not less, than his original proposition, and followed the advice of *Barron* both to impose a specific limitation upon the states' powers and accord Congress the stated power.[47]

The alteration in Section 1, setting the rights out starkly, has great rhetorical power and strengthens the grant of rights. The change enhanced the status of the rights, rather than diminishing Congress's ability to recognize and enforce them. Representative Hotchkiss of New York had objected to the earlier version precisely because it left enforcement of the rights to the whim of future Congresses. The initial version depended upon Congress alone to give the rights meaning and protection. The change made the rights self-executing, requiring the states to respect them and empowering the Court to enforce them against the states. Making the Court responsible as well is hardly proof that Congress removed its own responsibility or intended to diminish it drastically. The entire design seems aimed at increasing the reach, meaning, and reality of the sweeping grant of rights that generated the Amendment itself.[48]

The modern balance of powers between Court and Congress differs from the antebellum concept and practice, even under the Court's current restrictive view of Section 5 powers; Section 5 authorizes Congress to enact active and prophylactic protections and enforcement of critical guaranteed rights and liberties formerly conceived as limitations on power. The power to legislate prophylactic remedies effectively permits Congress to go beyond current Court pronouncement when necessary. As *Boerne* notes, "All must acknowledge that § 5 is 'a positive grant of legislative power' to Congress," and that the "sweep of Congress's enforcement power" is wide, if not unlimited. Congress, because of the Section, has power, and hence "not just the right but the duty to make its own informed judgment on the meaning and force of the Constitution." Congress can emphasize noticing and correcting infringements when they are systemic. Systemic wrongs are the least likely to result in a blameworthy actor causing harm, and thus they are difficult to identify, fight, and correct through court action. Congress alone has the ability to respond with a method that can provide accessible enforcement mechanisms to prevent and remedy these wrongs.[49]

Because of the 14th Amendment, Congress occupies a place affirmatively designed to make it a protector of liberties, not simply their chief predator.

V. CONCLUSION

Legal and political theory about the appropriate role of Congress with respect to identifying, protecting and enforcing personal liberties changed significantly from the time of the original framing in 1787 to the time of the framing of the Reconstruction Amendments. Congress was originally conceived of as a predator on personal rights, leading to a legal regime where almost all rights provisions simply negated congressional power. By the time of the framing of the 14th Amendment, Republicans believed that Congress was necessary to recognizing and enforcing rights, and affirmatively granted Congress a positive power to do so through Section 5.

Legal and political realities of the time support this reconception of Congress and significant grant of additional powers. The framing of the 14th Amendment proceeded at a time when the executive was seen both as having too much power and as affirmatively interfering with the work and goals of Reconstruction, especially with respect to the rights of freedmen and the quashing of the Slave Power, which were deemed necessary to lasting peace, stability, and union. The Amendment was designed to and did shift power over Reconstruction to the Congress. One aspect of that shift was enshrined in the alteration of the pardoning power incorporated into Section 3. Hence, the Amendment effectuated a power shift between Congress and the executive that empowered Congress relative to the executive.

Similarly, the Amendment recast the powers of Congress and the Supreme Court. The framers squarely acknowledged that the failure of the original Constitution to maintain the Union and protect citizens and rights had deep roots in slavery. The 39th Congress perceived that the sway of the Slave Power had influenced the Supreme Court—that "slavery had 'polluted' and 'defiled' the judiciary." The Supreme Court's role in stripping Congress of any power to enforce rights was much on the minds of the framers. Their final amendment reversed the shame of *Dred Scott* with the Citizenship Clause of Section 1 and the Empowerment Clause of Section 5. The Court had also rendered states impotent to protect rights of alleged fugitive slaves by finding an exclusive congressional power coupled with a duty. The inconsistency of these two decisions, sharing in common only the effect of protecting slavery, made the framers at best skeptical of the Court's role in protecting liberties, and hence more determined to wrest power in that arena for the Congress as well.[50]

The framers of the 14th Amendment were exceedingly cautious because their deeply held values and views had been trampled consistently, their sources of power read out, and their power to protect liberty by statute rendered null. They knew from experience that "the great principles of individual freedom and civil liberty cannot be too often repeated," and that only great clarity and forceful grants of power, done redundantly to reinforce their purpose "beyond all doubt and misconstruction," would work.[51]

The Reconstruction Amendments drastically altered the Founders' division of powers through the positive and affirmative grant of power to Congress to ensure that rights were realized and enforced. The 39th Congress drafted Sections 1 and 5 cognizant of the Supreme Court pronouncements the Amendment needed to override and to follow in order to effectively guarantee both rights and the congressional role in protecting rights. Skeptical of the Court as a protector of rights, Congress provided to itself the constitutional power to protect rights and guard against misinterpretation. Section 5 of the 14th Amendment reimagined Congress's role. The framers were cognizant that they had claimed a new power for Congress and had thus altered its role vis-à-vis the Court as the protector of rights.

The 39th Congress, and succeeding Congresses that included many of the same members, interpreted their powers widely. They did not wait for the Court to interpret the meaning of privileges or immunities, citizenship, or equal protection of the laws before enacting laws to make those rights real and protect their exercise. Congress's repeated acts to curb the abuses of rights in the unreconstructed South empowered reconstruction governments as well as federal prosecutors, courts, and bureaucrats. Those statutes are the earliest and most direct interpretations of the reach of the power accorded in Section 5.[52]

In addition to its well-recognized changes to individual rights and federal–state powers, the 14th Amendment effectuated a change, practically and ideologically, in the former balance among the three branches of national power. The framers and ratifiers did indeed create both a Union as it wasn't and a Constitution that is dramatically different in where and how it strikes the balance of power on behalf of liberty.

An earlier version of this chapter was published in *Akron Law Review*, Vol. 42 No.4, pp. 1081–1109. Copyright © 2009 *Akron Law Review*. Used with permission.

I would like to thank Richard Aynes, Wilson Huhn, and Sarah Cravens for their comments and assistance on earlier drafts, and Ellen Lander for her editorial assistance. Despite their best efforts, if any historical or other errors appear, they are solely my responsibility.

II: Finite Disappointment

THE SUPREME COURT AS FIRST INTERPRETER

5

Justice Miller's Reconstruction

The *Slaughter-House Cases*, Health Codes, and Civil Rights in New Orleans,1861–1873

Michael A. Ross, University of Maryland at College Park

F ew decisions by the United States Supreme Court have been more criticized than the *Slaughter-House Cases*[1], the first case in which the Supreme Court interpreted the 14th Amendment. Of the Court's nineteenth-century opinions, only *Dred Scott v. Sandford* and *Plessy v. Ferguson* have been more vigorously attacked by historians and legal scholars. For over a century, both conservative and liberal historians have taken issue with the 1873 *Slaughter-House* decision. The majority opinion and its author, Justice Samuel Freeman Miller, have become lightning rods for censure in the tragic unraveling of Radical Reconstruction.

The main reason for this censure is that in the *Slaughter-House Cases* the Supreme Court began to limit the positive effects that the 14th Amendment might have had upon the lives of African Americans. Specifically, the Court narrowly interpreted the 14th Amendment's Privileges or Immunities Clause. Defined broadly, that Clause might have given the federal government greater powers to protect the civil and natural rights of African Americans from discriminatory and violent acts.

The Court had other interpretations open to it. It could have ruled that the 14th Amendment's Privileges or Immunities Clause meant that the federal government had the power to protect, from infringement by state governments, citizens' basic rights—those enumerated in the Bill of Rights, but also other fundamental rights such as the right to pursue an occupation. By declining to do so, the Court left to Southern state governments the responsibility of protecting the rights of African Americans. "By strangling the privileges or immunities clause in its crib," one scholar remarked, the Court either purposefully or negligently left the freed men and women at the mercy of their former masters.[2] A historian of the Supreme Court lamented in the 1960s that "the only thing slaughtered in the Slaughterhouse cases was the right of the Negro to equality."[3]

In debates over *Slaughter-House*, historians, jurists, and law professors have repeatedly raised two key questions. First, they have debated whether or not Justice Samuel Miller's interpretation of the 14th Amendment's Privileges or Immunities Clause is correct. The growing consensus on that issue is that Miller's opinion ignored the intention of some of the framers of the 14th Amendment that the Privileges or Immunities Clause should protect, against the actions and laws of the states, the guarantees contained in the Bill of Rights.[4]

A second significant question that has been raised by *Slaughter-House*—and the one that this chapter addresses—is what compelled the Supreme Court, which was dominated by Republicans, to reach a decision apparently so at odds with the Republicans' agenda for Reconstruction? Presidents Abraham Lincoln and Ulysses S. Grant had, after all, stacked the Court with members of their own party. Moreover, the author of the opinion, Samuel Miller, an 1862 Lincoln appointee from Iowa, is usually described as the leader of the Court's liberal wing and as one of the few justices during Reconstruction and the Gilded Age who defended America's economic underdogs. Before the Civil War, Miller had opposed slavery and had helped found the Republican Party in Iowa. Historians have asked what led Miller and the other members of the Court's Republican majority to reach a decision so adverse to the stated goals of Republican Reconstruction.[5]

The answer that many historians have offered to the second question is that *Slaughter-House* reflected a growing disgust among Northerners with Radical Reconstruction. These scholars have seen the 1873 *Slaughter-House* decision as a precursor to the Compromise of 1877 and a means of conferring second-class status on blacks while restoring control of the South to white conservatives.[6] Some have suggested that the Court deliberately selected a case that involved white plaintiffs (the civil rights in question in *Slaughter-House* were those of white butchers) so that it could gut the 14th Amendment and the rights of black people without causing widespread outrage in the North.[7] Another group of scholars, however, has suggested that the members of the Court, like many other Americans, were reluctant to overturn the system of federalism they had always known and that, while the justices shared some concern for the rights of African

Americans, they did not want the national government to become the primary defender of those rights. For scholars who hold this view, Miller's opinion in *Slaughter-House* represents not a conscious attempt to end Reconstruction and to undermine black freedom but rather a conservative response by justices who were unable to accept that the 14th Amendment's unadorned language had dramatically altered the federal system.[8]

This chapter considers anew the motives of Samuel Miller and the Court's majority in *Slaughter-House* and builds on the work of the second group of scholars, who have resisted the urge to blame the decision on racism, conservatism, and the forces of reaction. Although in hindsight, the *Slaughter-House* decision seems to be a portent of the social, legal, economic, and political ills that befell African Americans after 1877, those effects were not obvious at the time of the decision in 1873. Rather, when viewed within the social, economic, and political context of the early 1870s, the *Slaughter-House Cases* may be read as a progressive attempt to affirm the authority of the biracial government of Louisiana, to grapple with horrible sanitary conditions in New Orleans, and to thwart conservatives, such as Justice Stephen J. Field, who hoped to defeat state regulation of private property. The *Slaughter-House Cases* touched on so many crucial issues of American life that one-dimensional, monocausal explanations of the justices' motivations lead to flawed conclusions and induce historians to ignore, misinterpret, or discount the inspiring language about race that is contained in the majority opinion. In order to identify the forces that impelled Miller and the other Republicans in the Court's majority to reach their decision, one must view the case within the context of Louisiana, the South, and America in 1873, and one must understand the pragmatic worldview of the opinion's author.

I. THE PUBLIC HEALTH AND SOCIAL CONTEXT OF THE SLAUGHTER-HOUSE ACT OF 1869

Slaughter-House began in the noisome abattoirs of New Orleans. Though the case is notorious for its deleterious effects on American race relations, the case arose from a seemingly benign attempt by Louisiana's Reconstruction legislature to limit the filth, stench, and unsanitary conditions of New Orleans slaughterhouses. In March 1869, the Louisiana state legislature passed "An act to protect the health of the City of New Orleans," which required all of the city's butchers to slaughter their animals across the Mississippi River from the city in a new state-of-the-art "grand slaughterhouse." The act also required that all livestock arriving from the countryside and the West be landed and penned at this new site and that the meat produced there pass inspection by a public health official before heading to market. Angered by this law, hundreds of New Orleans butchers sued to enjoin the Crescent City Slaughterhouse—the "grand slaughterhouse" of the 1869 act—from asserting any of its rights under that act. The butchers claimed that their "right to pursue an occupation," a right that they argued was protected by the Privileges or Immunities Clause of the new 14th Amendment, had been violated.[9]

Stringent sanitary regulations were long overdue in a city nationally known for its squalor. The streets of New Orleans, most of them unpaved, were filthy. The city had no public sewer system and, therefore, toilets were emptied into open gutters, and garbage was tossed into the streets and vacant lots. When the sultry heat of midsummer descended on the city, the smell of waste, rot, and decay was overpowering. Travelers compared the streets of New Orleans unfavorably to those of Cairo and Constantinople. Naturalist John James Audubon called the Crescent City's French Market the "dirtiest place in all the cities of the United States."[10]

Of all the noxious nuisances in a city famous for its filth, the slaughterhouses and bone-boiling establishments were by far the worst. Scattered throughout the city's neighborhoods (though with a heavy concentration in an area known as Slaughterhouse Point upstream from the city), slaughterhouses operated side-by-side with hospitals, schools, businesses, and tenements. Simply driving animals from unloading points on the river to neighborhood slaughterhouses created a horrendous scene. In a raucous daily event, stock dealers landed hundreds of cattle, pigs, and sheep on the banks of the river and then drove them to various slaughterhouses. The terrified animals rushed "wildly and madly through the street, endangering the limbs and the lives of men, women and children." Butchers slaughtered over 300,000 animals in New Orleans each year, and the conditions surrounding their operations were ghastly.[11]

The abattoirs were bloody, filthy, and unregulated. Burly butchers killed the animals with hammers or knives, then skinned, gutted, and hung their fly-covered carcasses on hooks to dangle unrefrigerated for hours, even days. The mass of gory waste generated by these squalid businesses was then thrown directly into either the streets or the Mississippi River. A New Orleans doctor testified to a legislative committee: "Barrels filled with entrails, liver, blood, urine, dung, and other refuse, portions in an advanced stage of decomposition, are constantly being thrown into the river ... poisoning the air with offensive smells and necessarily contaminating the water near the bank for miles."[12] Much of the rotting refuse from the slaughterhouses and stock landings collected in the river around the giant suction pipes from which New Orleans drew its water supply. "When the river is low," the president of the New Orleans Board of Health testified, "it is not uncommon to see intestines and portions of putrified animal matter lodged immediately around the pipes. The liquid portion of this putrified matter is sucked into the reservoir."[13] Pilings designed to stop the bulk waste matter from entering the pipes proved inefficient, and the pumping system repeatedly clogged.[14]

New Orleans slaughterhouses had undermined the public's health for many years. Attempts to regulate them had begun as early as 1804, when the colonial government ordered all butchers to move their slaughtering operations out of the city and over to the west bank of the Mississippi River. However, as the city grew, the butchers' power increased and, after persistent complaints about the inconvenience of shuttling back and forth across the river, the butchers forced their way back to the right bank upstream from the city. As New Orleans' growth continued, housing and businesses quickly sprouted up alongside these new slaughterhouses. In 1866 over a thousand outraged New Orleans citizens petitioned the Louisiana legislature to move the slaughterhouses and stock landings across the river once again.[15]

Extending their concerns beyond foul odors and unhealthful meat, officials in New Orleans and other locations around the country blamed deadly diseases such as yellow fever and cholera on slaughterhouses. This pertained particularly to New Orleans, which had been repeatedly and ferociously plagued by these two scourges during the nineteenth century. Nearly every summer of the antebellum period epidemics of yellow fever or cholera closed businesses, forced quarantine of New Orleans shipping at other ports, and sent the rich to the countryside and the poor to their deaths. In 1853, yellow fever and cholera killed over 10,000 Crescent City residents.[16]

In 1869, the Louisiana legislature passed a law to regulate slaughtering operations in New Orleans. The legislature did not act in a vacuum; the 1869 slaughterhouse act followed the passage of similar laws that were part of the sanitary reform movement affecting the entire nation after the Civil War. By the time Louisiana lawmakers acted, San Francisco, Boston, Milwaukee, and Philadelphia had already passed slaughterhouse ordinances. New York City had set the example for these measures, as its dynamic Board of Health regulated slaughterhouses and other unhealthful nuisances, thereby contributing to the eradication of cholera. Among the New York Board's most effective laws was one passed in 1866 that required all butchers located below 40th Street to use a centralized slaughterhouse. The new facility operated away from the crowded downtown neighborhoods and allowed efficient inspection of the city's meat supply. The Board of Health's regulations were bitterly opposed by New York's butchers but were popular with most of the city's middle- and upper-class inhabitants.[17]

The Louisiana slaughterhouse law closely imitated its New York predecessor. However, despite the obvious benefits of the Louisiana law, white residents of New Orleans—unlike the citizens of New York—vehemently opposed slaughterhouse regulation. Their opposition was shared, of course, by the city's white butchers. The statute, after all, required that butchers stop slaughtering on their own property, move their operations across the Mississippi River, pay a fee to use the new slaughterhouse, and then consent for the meat to be inspected by government officials. For New Orleans tradesmen, used to a completely unregulated business, this statute was a bitter pill.[18] Moreover, the operation of the law permitted African Americans and others who had previously been excluded by a lack of capital to become butchers. In the past, anyone entering the trade usually had to raise enough money to build a small slaughterhouse. After the law was passed, one needed only enough capital to buy animals for slaughter. Numerous black residents of New Orleans after the war took advantage of the decreased requirements for capital and entered the trade.[19] This change undermined the control of the trade by the tightly knit community of Gascon butchers (immigrants and descendants of immigrants from southwestern France), who jealously guarded their monopoly.[20] Before the 1869 law was passed, the Gascon butchers had forcibly driven off black competitors, just as the white stevedores of New Orleans did in 1880. After the slaughterhouse regulation was passed, financial barriers to entering the trade fell away.[21]

The butchers' self-interest explains their strong opposition to the slaughterhouse law, but why did the rest of white New Orleans rally around them? Before 1869, the butchers had never been well liked as a group. They had conspired for years to keep prices high and had assaulted the senses and health of the city's residents. The municipal government had, at the urging of the citizenry, tried many times in the past (albeit unsuccessfully) to force the butchers to clean up their operations.[22] The answer that most historians and legal scholars have offered to this question is that many residents resented the "grand slaughterhouse" being built by a private corporation. The corporation, in return for constructing the edifice that butchers would be required to use, was allowed to collect fees from butchers. The opposition, some historians suggest, was a traditional Jacksonian response to a monopoly.[23] Furthermore, the political timing of the slaughterhouse investors was unfortunate; one historian has argued that "they had obtained their franchise at a time when the public was beginning to have serious second thoughts about the subsidies and franchises...lavished on corporations in the past as a means of stimulating growth."[24] Political opposition to the investors was intensified because many of them were from the North, and, as "carpetbaggers," they were accused of bribing the legislature in return for the monopoly.[25] White newspaper editors repeatedly raised unproven charges of corruption, alleging that the legislature passed the slaughterhouse law for the benefit of a few businessmen.[26]

Both explanations, however, are incomplete and overlook the context of contemporary Louisiana politics and society. No hard evidence has ever surfaced that there was bribery involved in the law's enactment. Those charges originated with white editors of New Orleans newspapers searching for arguments against the law.[27] Surprisingly, most historians have accepted at face value the unproven allegations of these editors.[28] Furthermore, even if there had been bribery, legislative corruption was common in Louisiana and usually stimulated little public outrage.[29] Why would the slaughterhouse bill—which achieved long-standing objectives of both Democrats and Republicans—be the one to cause a furor?

To be sure, ever since the Civil War, the whole idea of enforced health codes had taken on the appearance of a Yankee-directed enterprise. General Benjamin F. "Beast" Butler, who commanded the Union occupation of New Orleans, had forced the city to undergo a rigorous wartime sanitation effort. In order to protect the health of his troops, the much-despised Butler had organized an extensive clean-up of the city and the river bank. Locals had expected Butler's troops to drop dead during their first seasoning summer in the Crescent City. Instead, the epidemics of cholera and yellow fever ceased, largely because Butler put "thousands of unemployed Louisianans to work removing garbage, patrolling the river, and closing the slaughterhouses north of the city."[30] New Orleanians refused to grant the hated Butler any credit for the improvements in public health. They characterized the break from yellow fever and cholera as purely coincidental, even though the epidemics ceased during the occupation and resumed after Butler and his troops left the city and the sanitation program ended. In 1867, yellow fever alone killed approximately 3,000 New Orleans residents.[31]

It was also true that the slaughterhouse bill had been pushed, in part, by transplanted Northerners. The law was part of a broader effort by "carpetbaggers" in the Louisiana legislature to reshape and modernize the state's economic and social life. Many Yankee legislators were shocked and disgusted by the backwardness of

New Orleans and Louisiana as a whole. While conceding that New Orleans had enjoyed economic success in the antebellum period, they attributed the city's good fortune to its position on the Mississippi River rather than to the acumen or enterprise of its residents. Northerners saw a decaying, primitive, reactionary city that had succeeded in spite of itself. Sporting little Yankee-style prosperity, it was served by few railroads and a single, six-mile canal. There were only four paved streets and a small number of covered warehouses and wharves, and the city was almost completely surrounded by marshy, unnavigable swamps and bayous. To many Northerners, New Orleans seemed a rotting Gomorrah run by corrupt and ignorant officials and filled with gamblers, prostitutes, drunkards, duelists, and thugs. Henry Clay Warmoth, Louisiana's Illinois-born Reconstruction governor, summed up these negative impressions when he called New Orleans "a dirty, impoverished, and hopeless place." As if to support the impression of general backwardness and disregard for public health, the malodorous, polluting, pathogenic slaughterhouses sat squarely within New Orleans's most populous areas and each summer the city's businesses ground to a halt as businessmen and their families fled the "necropolis" of America for the countryside in order to avoid epidemics.[32]

As part of the plan to reshape New Orleans and Louisiana in the Northern image, the Republican legislature authorized an aggressive plan of internal improvements. The legislature chartered railroad and canal companies and other corporations charged with repairing the dilapidated levees along the Mississippi. A private company, much like the one authorized in the slaughterhouse bill, was given the task of building a modern facility for the Crescent City Water Works. Another company acquired the monopoly for cleaning the city's privies. The legislature also created steamboat companies and enterprises to build warehouses and docks. There were plans to make nearby bayous navigable. "There was a conscious purpose," wrote one Dunning-school historian, "to introduce in the South the energy and methods of the North and West in the hope of similar economic results." Carpetbaggers in the Louisiana legislature envisioned a new South with railroads, canals, schools, and free labor, all modeled on those of the North. Eventually, they hoped white Southerners would see the benefits of these changes and join the Republican crusade.[33] However, when the Republican legislators turned to bonds and exclusive private charters to fund their improvement plans, they armed their white opponents with ammunition for potent charges of corruption and monopoly.

Because of the lack of capital in Louisiana after the war and the dire financial circumstances of the Reconstruction government, however, legislators had

little choice but to turn to creative methods of funding their Whiggish development program. At the end of the war, Louisiana's economy lay in shambles. The
plantations had been decimated by war. Trade had dropped to a fraction of
prewar levels as had sugar production. Wharves, steamboats, and cotton warehouses had been torched by fleeing Confederate troops. Severe crop failures and
cotton blights in 1866 and 1867 compounded these problems. Most ominously,
the river trade, lifeblood of the New Orleans economy, steadily continued to lose
business to Northern railroads. Midwestern crops that had previously been
shipped south on the river began to move east on iron rails.[34]

With the economy prostrate and many whites simply refusing to pay taxes
to the Reconstruction government, tax revenues slowed to a trickle, and legislators opted for issuing bonds to pay for their ambitious modernization plans.
However, as Louisiana's credit plummeted, state bonds became hard to sell, and
in order to achieve its public goals, the legislature granted exclusive privileges
to private corporations like the Crescent City Livestock Landing and Slaughtering Company. The plan worked. Sensing a sound venture, investors—who
included former officers of the Union and Confederate armies, brokers, ship-
pers, and merchants—bought the company's publicly traded stock beginning
in 1869, and the new slaughterhouse was constructed. The founding of the Crescent City Slaughterhouse appears to have been a rational response to the city's
sanitation needs and the state's shortage of capital. It hardly amounted to the
"monopoly" decried by New Orleans's white press.[35]

II. THE POLITICAL CONTEXT OF THE RECONSTRUCTION
LEGISLATURE AND THE SLAUGHTER-HOUSE ACT
OF 1869

In the end, the real reason for resistance by the white residents of New
Orleans to the slaughterhouse bill was their opposition to the biracial Reconstruction legislature that had enacted it—not to monopoly and corruption. The
charges of monopoly and corruption served as useful rhetorical devices for white
editors and lawyers intent on thwarting every effort, beneficial or otherwise, of
a legislature that contained black elected officials. This context, and the circumstances leading to the passage of the law, must be examined in order to understand white opposition to the slaughterhouse bill and how the controversy
reached the United States Supreme Court.

White New Orleans had never acquiesced to a biracial state government. In
July 1866, Governor J. Madison Wells, a Republican, called for the election of addi-

tional delegates to a reconvened state convention authorized to draft a new constitution that would enfranchise blacks and prohibit many former Confederates from voting. When the convention met in New Orleans, an armed white mob, which included New Orleans police officers, surrounded the hall, broke down the doors, and killed those inside—delegates and blacks hiding from the mob. In what General Philip H. Sheridan labeled "an absolute massacre," white terrorists killed 34 blacks and 3 whites. The New Orleans riot, which followed a similar riot in Memphis twelve weeks earlier, helped to galvanize the North against Andrew Johnson's presidential Reconstruction and brought about military Reconstruction directed by Congress. The reaction of Justice Samuel Miller to the New Orleans riot mirrored that of many other Northerners. In his private correspondence, he noted that the violence had confirmed for him that Southern whites, with "their peculiar hatred . . . for the negro," were "men who seem incapable of forgiving or learning."[36]

It seemed that changes in the South could be brought about only by force. Under the aegis of federal troops, state constitutional conventions charged with reshaping the legal, political, social, and economic order were called throughout the South in 1867 and 1868. Before the election of convention delegates in Louisiana, General Sheridan enforced Reconstruction laws that disfranchised many former rebels and allowed 83,000 black men to register to vote. As a result, "the Louisiana convention was the first major elective body in Southern history dominated by a black majority," and it produced a constitution that seemed to promise a new day in the state.[37]

"The Constitution of Louisiana drawn up by the convention of 1867–1868," one historian has noted, "was probably the most radical of any of the constitutions which resulted from the Reconstruction Acts." The new document desegregated education, prohibited racial discrimination in public places, and denied many former Confederates the right to vote. It also included a bill of rights—the first in Louisiana's history—that voided the Black Codes, outlawed slavery, and guaranteed trial by jury, the right to peaceful assembly, and freedom of religion and the press. Most white Louisianans reacted with hostility. Editors of the *New Orleans Bee* reflected white sentiment by calling the new constitution "the work of a few white men who were elected to the convention by the votes of ignorant negroes, and by means of disenfranchising those who by their ownership of the soil, their birthright as free men, and their education as citizens ought to be [Louisiana's] masters and its law givers."[38]

The new Louisiana legislature, charged with enacting measures that would support the new constitution, included black men. Although not a majority by any means (35 out of 101 members in the House and 7 out of 30 in the Senate), blacks joined with white Republicans to form Republican pluralities in both branches. The election of black men to the legislature, combined with the presence of carpetbaggers, enraged many New Orleans whites. Opponents labeled the new legislature a horde "of ignorant negroes cooperating with a gang of white adventurers."[39]

Louisiana newspapers issued a racial call to arms, urging citizens to fight any and all acts passed by this new legislature, and New Orleans papers branded laws passed by that body "a parody of legislation." "We are now laboring under the evils brought upon us by ignorance, the incapacity, and the notorious corruption of our so-called representatives in the General Assembly," the *New Orleans Bee* charged in January 1869. Using the rallying cry "that the 'white man's flag' shall be upheld," editors claimed in December of the same year that the laws being passed "by the Legislature are of no more binding force than if they bore the stamp and seal of a Haytian[sic] Congress of human apes instead of the once honored seal of the state." In February 1869, the *Bee* called one African American state senator "a coal black negro with kinky hair, thick lips, and feet the size of a sauce pan," and in July asserted that "no true citizen of Louisiana can ever coalesce with such men."[40]

Louisiana whites were most opposed to those laws that attacked racial segregation. In February 1869, the biracial legislature passed what its opponents derisively called the "Social Equality Bill." This enactment made it a criminal offense to deny African Americans entry to hotels, steamboats, railroad cars, barrooms, and other public accommodations.[41] The *Daily Picayune*, opposing the bill's passage, called it the work of "misguided black men and very worthless and wicked white ones, the object of all being strife and consequent bloodshed." "It will be defied and condemned," the *Bee* predicted in February 1869, "by every white man who has any sense of dignity and superiority of his race over that of the negro."[42] In the following month, the legislature passed a law to enforce the article in the 1868 constitution that required public schools in Louisiana to be open to all races. This law, too, enraged whites, who labeled the enactment the "School Integration Bill." "The white people of the city and the state," warned the *Bee*, "will not consent to the commingling of their children with the children of negroes in any school whatever." The newspaper urged that whites resist the law, stating that the legislature wants to "drive us as equals into association with a servile race. Let us show them that laws are helpless to enforce such a commixture."[43] White men reacted to such editorial calls for resistance by joining terrorist organizations—the Knights of the White Camelia and the Ku Klux Klan—and, in doing so, indicated their intent to destroy the biracial Republican government. By the early 1870s, nearly half the white men in New Orleans were members of such groups.[44]

In March 1869, less than a month after the passage of the "Social Equality Bill," and within weeks of the adoption of the "School Integration Bill," the biracial Louisiana legislature approved the slaughterhouse law. Given this context, white New Orleanians opposed the legislation even though it finally ameliorated the terrible conditions in the slaughterhouses. The white residents of New Orleans and the editors of its newspapers responded as if all acts of the legislature had to be opposed regardless of their merit. The *Bee* called the bill "a monstrous perversion of law." It was "no law, although a law," a "wicked imposition which deserves the respect of nobody." Saying that the statute was the work of "ignorant and corrupt, not enlightened and virtuous lawmakers," a white editor asked "Why is it that legislation since the adoption of the Constitution of 1868 has been uninterruptedly for plunder and oppression?"[45]

Louisiana Republicans did not hesitate to point out the disingenuous nature of the conservatives' charges against the legislature and the slaughterhouse law. "In an effort to keep up the old prejudice against the new order of things," the editor of the *New Orleans Republican* wrote in March 1870, "the opposition have failed to see any good in the work of those who have been called upon to take part in the state government under the new constitution." Because the Republican party had had the temerity to pass laws protecting blacks' civil rights, conservatives felt obligated to attack all Republicans in, and acts of, the legislature. "Everybody has been proclaimed infamous, vile, ignorant and corrupt, that had had anything to do with a state government that recognized the civil and political equality of the colored man."[46]

In different times the community would not have rallied around the butchers, who were, at best, unsympathetic protagonists. In addition to operating businesses that produced filth and stench, they had also conspired for many years to keep meat prices high. New Orleans papers conceded as much. "But admitting the butchers may have practiced a monopoly," the *Bee* argued on June 22, "you do not destroy a monopoly by setting up another as bad or worse." In the racially charged atmosphere of 1869, white New Orleans residents formed an alliance of convenience with the Gascon butchers and stock dealers in order to fight what they saw as oppression by the biracial state government. "We make common cause with the butchers and stock dealers," wrote the *Bee*, "because their interests just now happen to be our interests." "The butchers are not only fighting their own battle," went the argument, "they are fighting the battle of the community." As a result, perceptions of the once-troublesome butchers had changed, "and public opinion is unmistakably with them." The butchers' legal challenge to the slaughterhouse law thus became a New Orleans cause célèbre, which the newspapers and populace closely followed.[47]

III. THE CONTEXT OF THE LEGAL CHALLENGE TO THE SLAUGHTERHOUSE ACT OF 1869

Because the butchers' legal challenges to the law became intertwined with Louisiana whites' opposition to the Reconstruction government, the butchers had the best legal representation that the old order could offer. The lead attorney in most of the hundreds of cases that individual butchers brought against the state was John A. Campbell, the former U.S. Supreme Court justice who resigned from the Court at the start of the Civil War to join the Confederacy. While on the Supreme Court, Campbell had concurred with the majority in the infamous *Dred Scott* decision.[48] During the war, he served as the Confederacy's assistant secretary of war and was a leading theorist for the secessionist slaveholders. After being imprisoned for four months by Northern troops at the end of the war, Campbell moved to New Orleans where he developed a successful legal practice, much of which was devoted to fighting the Reconstruction government and returning the planter class to power. Beginning in 1868, Campbell and his law partner Henry Spofford flooded the courts with lawsuits obstructing Warmoth's development projects, the integration of the schools, and the biracial legislature's power to tax. "At the very moment Campbell was contending in the Louisiana courts that the 14th Amendment had the broadest possible meaning and hence protected the [rights of the butchers]," one historian noted, "he was also defending the right of a New Orleans theatre to segregate Negro opera-goers, despite a statute of Louisiana which then forbade that form of discrimination."[49]

Campbell ardently believed that the Reconstruction regimes in the South had to be destroyed at all costs. "The Southern communities will be a desolation until there is a thorough change of affairs in all the departments of government," Campbell wrote in 1871, and continued in the same vein, "Discontent, dissatisfaction, murmurings, complaints, even insurrection would be better than the insensibility that seems to prevail." Defenders of the old political, economic, and racial order placed so much faith in his legal maneuverings that a saying developed in New Orleans: "Leave it to God and Mr. Campbell." In Campbell, they had found a true believer in the Old South who would not rest until the social equality law, the school integration law, and the slaughterhouse statute were overturned. Campbell became the Old South's champion, the lawyer who would take the *Slaughter-House Cases* to the Supreme Court.[50]

In February 1873, after four years of pleading for New Orleans butchers in state and federal courts, Campbell finally challenged the slaughterhouse law before the U.S. Supreme Court. In his written brief and oral argument, Campbell ladled out a thick soup of rhetorical excess. Quoting from Turgot, de Tocqueville, and Leiber, Campbell portrayed the butchers as patriot citizens and lovers of liberty oppressed by a heavy-handed legislature. He likened the slaughterhouse legislation to the onerous regulations of seventeenth-century European monarchies, imposed at a time when "the peasant could not cross a river without paying to some nobleman a toll, nor take the produce which he raised to market until he had bought leave to do so; nor consume what remained of his grain till he had sent it to the lord's mill to be ground." Escape from such petty tyrannies, Campbell added, was "exactly what the colonists sought for and obtained by their settlement here, their long contest with physical evils that attended the colonial condition, their struggle for independence, and their efforts, exertions, and sacrifices since." The "right to exercise their trade" unfettered by government intrusion, Campbell argued, was one of the fundamental rights that the founding fathers had fought and died for. Now, he asserted, the new 14th Amendment's Privileges or Immunities Clause definitively protected this fundamental right from autocratic "state" statutes like the slaughterhouse law.[51]

Amidst all his bluster about liberty, however, Campbell inadvertently revealed his true fears and base motivations. He dreaded, not the rise of a new monarchy, but, instead, the development of a democratic system in which blacks and Catholic immigrants could participate. The 14th Amendment, Campbell claimed, was framed at a moment when "[m]ore than three millions of a population lately servile, were liberated without preparation for any political or civil [life]. Besides this population of emancipated slaves, there was a large and growing population who came to this country without education in the laws and constitution of the country, and who had begun to exert a perceptible influence over our government." Campbell argued that the amendment had been framed to keep a democracy composed partly of blacks and immigrants from running amok. Hence, he asserted, the duty of the Supreme Court was to declare unconstitutional laws like the slaughterhouse statute that were based in black ignorance and Yankee greed.[52]

Campbell tried to stand the 14th Amendment on its head: an unrepentant rebel, he attempted to use the amendment to undermine the biracial government of Louisiana, which had passed legislation reflecting the ideology and public policy positions of the Republican Party.

In writing the majority opinion for the Supreme Court, Justice Samuel Miller opposed Campbell's argument and sided with the attorneys for the Slaughterhouse Corporation.[53] In his majority opinion which was joined by Justices Nathan Clifford, David Davis, Ward Hunt, and William Strong, Miller concluded that the 14th Amendment's Privileges or Immunities Clause did not make the federal government the protector of all civil rights, such as the right to exercise one's trade. While the federal government could protect a more narrow list of rights—those traditionally associated with national citizenship such as the right to assemble peaceably and the privilege of writ of habeas corpus—citizens still had to seek protection for most of their civil rights from state governments and state courts.[54]

When placed within the context of Louisiana politics, Justice Miller's majority opinion in *Slaughter-House* hardly seems like a racist attempt to retreat from Reconstruction. Instead, it can be seen as a vote of confidence for a biracial Reconstruction government then struggling to overcome the forces of reaction. Justice Miller found it inexplicable that the 14th Amendment, which he considered a means of protecting African Americans in the South, might be used to strike down a sanitation law with such obvious social benefits. Even with "the most casual examination," Miller argued, "no one can fail to be impressed with the one pervading purpose" of the 14th and 15th Amendments. "[W]e mean the freedom of the slave race, the security and firm establishment of that freedom, and the protection of the newly-made freeman and citizen from the oppressions of those who had formerly exercised unlimited dominion over him."[55] The 14th Amendment was not designed to thwart a valuable health measure that removed slaughterhouses from a crowded city.

Justice Miller's support for the slaughterhouse law also reflected his deep interest in the sanitation movement.[56] His interest was rooted in personal experience and medical expertise. During the 1840s, Miller had been a doctor and earlier had written his medical school dissertation on the causes and treatment of cholera. He eventually left the profession out of frustration that the only available remedies, such as purgatives and bleedings, had failed to cure the disease. Miller had been ahead of his time in recognizing the connection between cholera and fouled water. While many experts in the 1840s blamed the disease on "the free use of vegetables, of an indigestible nature," or on "the intemperate, the imprudent, the filthy" habits of the urban poor, Miller realized that cholera struck city dwellers and rural farmers, rich and poor, indiscriminately. In Barbourville, the small southeastern Kentucky hill town where he practiced, Miller linked cholera to the Cumberland River, which ran near the town. Cholera, Miller noted, was "to be found along the course of the Cumberland, and on every realm which pays tribute to that river."[57]

Not only was Miller familiar with the dangers of cholera, he also had a detailed knowledge of pigs and slaughtering arising from his experiences in Barbourville, a trading town on the old Wilderness Road. Before the rise of steamboats and railroads, drovers guided their herds through Barbourville to the Cumberland Gap on the long trek to markets in Baltimore and Philadelphia. During peak travel seasons, the town's narrow main streets were overrun with cows and pigs heading east and the wagons, horses, and mules of emigrants heading west; and no one in town could avoid the attendant filth and dangers. Miller noted that Barbourville was "remarkable as being the most unhealthy place in the mountains or probably Kentucky, in proportion to its population."[58]

Miller left Kentucky in 1849, largely because of his opposition to slavery, and moved to the Mississippi River town of Keokuk, Iowa. Though in Barbourville he had seen firsthand what hordes of pigs and cows could do to a town, in Keokuk he witnessed on a massive scale the full impact of the slaughtering trade. In the 1850s and early 1860s, despite a population of only 15,000 inhabitants, Keokuk became the nation's sixth largest hog slaughtering center, ranking behind only Chicago, Cincinnati, Louisville, St. Louis, and Milwaukee. By the early 1860s, Keokuk butchers killed over 110,000 hogs a year. Given the high pig-to-human ratio, the swine-killing industry dominated the town. Keokuk's streets echoed with the "shrill and piercing" cries of tens of thousands "kicking, squirming, agonizing" pigs.[59] Despite the significant amount of money that slaughtering pumped into Keokuk's economy, the industry had numerous local critics. During Miller's years in the "porkopolis" of Iowa, residents mounted a successful campaign to regulate the industry. Fearing cholera, city officials passed ordinances to control the driving of hogs through the streets, to keep them from running wild, and to stop the "perfidious traffic" in unwholesome meats.[60]

These experiences had a lasting impact on Miller's views, and, by the time the *Slaughter-House Cases* reached the Supreme Court, Miller had long since recognized the need to regulate the slaughtering industry. He was uniquely knowledgeable among the Court's justices about cholera, medicine, hogs, and slaughterhouses, was sympathetic to the efforts of the Louisiana legislature to regulate New Orleans' abattoirs, and would resist interpretations of the 14th Amendment that would undermine those efforts. "The regulation of the place and manner of conducting the slaughtering of animals, and the business of butchering within a city," Miller wrote, "and the inspection of the animals to be killed for meat, and of the meat afterwards, are among the most necessary and frequent exercises of [a state's police] power."[61]

Just as he recognized the need to regulate the slaughterhouses in order to thwart deadly epidemics, Justice Miller shared the Republican legislators' dynamic economic vision for the postwar South. Even in his antebellum years, Miller had championed such efforts. In trying to reshape the South in the image of the North, Louisiana legislators were doing exactly what Miller had advocated in Kentucky years earlier. In Barbourville, Miller had been an ardent follower of Kentucky's antislavery leader, Cassius M. Clay, who believed that slavery degraded labor and that Kentucky's tobacco monoculture stifled the sort of varied, vigorous growth then occurring in the North. Clay promoted a plan to replace Kentucky's plantations with food-producing farms and, with the aid of government-funded internal improvements, to turn Kentucky's water-rich mountain region into a manufacturing paradise modeled on New England mill towns.[62] Persuaded by Clay's economic ideology, Miller joined his crusade, campaigning actively against slavery and in favor of government-directed economic modernization of the state. But when the Kentucky Constitutional Convention of 1849 enhanced the protections that earlier constitutions had provided to slaveholders and to the institution of slavery, Miller left the state for the free soil of Iowa. However, Miller took with him Clay's message that the South would always lag economically unless Yankee-style enterprise was imposed upon it. In 1869, Miller still longed for the day when the South would "forget the past" and, instead, "the great interests of finance, currency, internal improvements ... shall absorb us all." This was also the message of Louisiana's Republican legislators in the 1860s.[63] Critics of Miller's opinion in *Slaughter-House* have either ignored or downplayed Miller's commitment to Northern-style economic development in the South, his interest in the sanitation movement, his knowledge of slaughtering and cholera, and the volatile context of Louisiana politics.

Instead, it has been suggested that Miller and the majority could have upheld the slaughterhouse law and still allowed the federal judiciary to accept a new role as the defender of civil rights. The Court could have ruled that the 14th Amendment allowed the Supreme Court to scrutinize and strike down state laws

that interfered with fundamental rights, but that the right to operate a slaughterhouse in the midst of a crowded city was not one of the fundamental rights
protected by the amendment. "But Justice Miller," historian Loren Beth has
written, "went far beyond the needs of the case before him in an obvious attempt
to destroy, as far as possible, any affirmative reading of the 14th Amendment."[64]
Such criticism misses the nuance of Miller's views. Miller's goal wasn't merely
to uphold the validity of the slaughterhouse law nor was it to destroy the 14th
Amendment. He simply did not believe that the 14th Amendment gave the
federal judiciary the power to strike down state regulatory laws. "Such a construction" of the Amendment, Miller wrote, "would constitute this court a perpetual censor upon all legislation of the States, on the civil rights of their own
citizens, with authority to nullify such as it did not approve as consistent with
those rights."[65] To confirm his fears about the intentions of the notoriously conservative federal judiciary, Miller needed only to look to his right, figuratively
speaking, at the arch-conservative Justice Stephen J. Field, eager to strike down
state regulations from the bench.

Miller preferred to rely on the states and their constitutions to protect civil
rights. Most state constitutions contained provisions that, if vigorously enforced,
would protect those rights. Louisiana's Constitution, for instance, had strong language barring discrimination in public accommodations, businesses, and schools.
Additionally, in early 1873, it was by no means clear that congressional Reconstruction would fail or that the old economic and racial order of the South would return.
Although ex-Confederates had regained power in some Southern states, in others
biracial Reconstruction governments remained firmly in control. Congressional
Republicans, moreover, had not given up the fight. To shore up Republican governments in the South, Congress had just passed the powerful Ku Klux Klan Act.
Furthermore, the passage of Senator Charles Sumner's potent Civil Rights Act was
two years in the future. Even as late as 1877, Louisiana Republicans still believed
that their Reconstruction government would endure, and they reacted with utter
disbelief when President Rutherford B. Hayes agreed to remove the federal troops
from the South. In 1873, Miller's opinion in *Slaughter-House* affirmed the validity
of a biracial legislature that many expected to survive. Had the Court ruled against
the slaughterhouse law, it would have supported the Reconstruction legislature's
critics who alleged that blacks and Yankees were either too ignorant or too corrupt
to adopt legislation that could pass constitutional muster.[66]

Miller did not pin all his hopes on the survival of the Reconstruction governments. He also had great regard for the power of the 14th Amendment's Equal

Protection Clause to achieve the Amendment's objective of protecting black rights. Rather than a radical transformation of the federal system that would have resulted from a broad reading of the Privileges or Immunities Clause, the Equal Protection Clause held out the promise of a powerful enforcement mechanism requiring minimal federal interference in most state activities. The Equal Protection Clause, Miller argued, allowed the Supreme Court to strike down any state law "which discriminated with gross injustice and hardship against [blacks] as a class." If "States did not conform their laws to its requirements," Congress could also pass suitable legislation to bring the offending states into line. For Miller, this was the perfect balance, offering powerful assurances that, even if the Reconstruction state governments faltered, the onerous black codes would not be restored because the federal government would intervene on the behalf of black Southerners. Most important, by relying on the Equal Protection Clause, the federal judiciary could protect the rights of black citizens without assuming the power to overturn valuable state health and economic measures that affected groups like white butchers. "We doubt very much," Miller wrote of the Equal Protection Clause, "whether any action of a State not directed by way of discrimination against the negroes as a class, or on account of their race, will ever be held to come within the purview of this provision. It is so clearly a provision for that race and that emergency, that a strong case would be necessary for its application to any other."[67]

Though a number of Republicans criticized Miller's *Slaughter-House* opinion for not incorporating the Bill of Rights into the 14th Amendment, others embraced the decision as a powerful affirmation that the overriding purpose of the 14th Amendment was to protect the rights of African Americans. Republican supporters of Miller's decision used *Slaughter-House* to defend the constitutionality of the Civil Rights Act of 1875. Miller's opinion, Senator Oliver P. Morton of Indiana argued, "shows that the very history and purpose that called the 14th Amendment into existence was to protect the colored race from all unjust discriminations in the law, of whatsoever kind," which included even discrimination by owners of private businesses and public accommodations if licensed by the state. "Rights are of no avail unless they are enforced," Morton said, adding that *Slaughter-House* confirmed that "Congress has the power to protect rights if states won't." "The States have the same right they always had to make police regulations," he concluded, "with this single difference, that whatever regulations they may make must operate equally upon men of all colors coming within the same conditions." "Judge Miller, then, is of the opinion that under the [Equal

Protection] clause no State can oppress a colored citizen by virtue of its laws,"
Senator Timothy O. Howe of Wisconsin proclaimed during the Civil Rights Act
debates. He went on to state, "The very object of the bill now before us is therefore sanctioned by the opinion of that one judge."[68]

IV. CONCLUSION

Despite much evidence to the contrary, historians continue to charge that
Miller's *Slaughter-House* opinion revealed a Court tired of what it saw as the
excesses of Radical Reconstruction and motivated by a racist desire to restore
stability in the South by returning the old racial and economic order to power.[69]
To be sure, the decision's critics can accurately make the point that Miller and
the other members of the Court's majority had never been truly radical Republicans like Charles Sumner and Thaddeus Stevens. Instead, they were Republican
moderates who often lagged behind other members of their party who were
more progressive on race issues. During his antebellum years, for example, Miller
had opposed slavery, but viewed immediate abolition in the South as too radical.
He favored Lincoln's goal of containing slavery in the South in hopes that the
institution would ultimately become extinct. What Miller's critics ignore,
however, is how much his racial views, like those of many thousands of other
white Americans, had changed as a result of the sweeping events of the Civil War
and Reconstruction.

In this regard, Miller's opinion in *Slaughter-House* reads almost as an auto-
biographical piece on the transformative power of the 1860s on his views about
race. In the *Slaughter-House* opinion, Miller unambiguously stated that the cause
of the recent Civil War had been slavery:

> The institution of African slavery, as it existed in about half the States of the
> Union, and the contests pervading the public mind for many years, between
> those who desired its curtailment and ultimate extinction and those who
> desired additional safeguards for its security and perpetuation, culminated in
> the effort, on the part of most of the states in which slavery existed, to separate
> from the Federal government, and to resist its authority. This constituted the
> war of the rebellion, and whatever auxiliary causes may have contributed to
> bring about this war, undoubtedly the overshadowing and efficient cause was
> African slavery.[70]

Moreover, after the war began and its casualties mounted, Miller and many
other Americans recognized that destroying slavery had become the objective of
the war and was a desirable and necessary result. Slavery, Miller wrote, "perished

as a necessity of the bitterness and force of the conflict. When the armies of freedom found themselves upon the soil of slavery they could do nothing less than free the poor victims whose enforced servitude was the foundation of the quarrel." In addition, the courage of black troops in Union armies deeply impressed Miller. "[W]hen hard pressed in the contest," Miller said of black troops, "these men (for they proved themselves men in that terrible crisis) offered their services and were accepted by [the] thousands to aid in suppressing the unlawful rebellion."[71]

At the end of the war, Miller, like many Republicans, held high hopes for President Johnson's Reconstruction policy. But these hopes quickly faded with the rise of the notorious black codes. The Southern states, Miller lamented in *Slaughter-House*, had quickly "imposed upon the colored race onerous disabilities and burdens, and curtailed their rights in the pursuit of life, liberty, and property to such an extent that their freedom was of little value ... They were in some States forbidden to appear in the towns in any other character than menial servants. They were required to reside on and cultivate the soil without the right to purchase or own it. They were excluded from many occupations of gain, and were not permitted to give testimony in the courts in any case where a white man was a party."[72] At the time of the passage of the black codes, Southerners justified many of these laws by saying that blacks needed to be forced to work, to which Miller retorted, "This pretense is made in a country ... where the negro has done all the work for generations, and where the white man makes a boast of the fact that he will not labour."[73]

Miller soon recognized that "without further protection of the Federal government," the freed slaves' plight would "be almost as bad as it was before."[74] According to Miller, the Southern states should, and would, be compelled "to place the negro on an equality with the white man in all his civil rights." As Miller chided a Southern relative in 1866, "The power to make laws, which are to operate on the black man and not on the white, will be taken from these states. ... This may be relied on."[75] The Privileges or Immunities and the Equal Protection Clauses of the 14th Amendment, Miller accurately noted in *Slaughter-House*, were the direct and necessary response to the black codes. Never again could a state enact laws specifically designed to degrade a particular race. Those two clauses thus served an important and virtuous purpose. That purpose, however, was not to prevent states from passing health regulations that had nothing to do with race.

In the end, Miller's critics are placed in the paradoxical position of arguing that the *Slaughter-House Cases*, an opinion full of rich language emphasizing the need to protect black civil rights, was actually an attempt to undermine those very rights. It is a charge that simply does not ring true. While admitting that the Reconstruction governments in the South had their flaws and had made some mistakes, Miller did not want to see those governments destroyed. He simply did not trust Southern whites, "men who seem incapable of forgiving or learning," when left to their own devices, to protect the rights of blacks.[76]

Miller's opinion in the *Slaughter-House Cases* failed to achieve its goals. This failure reflected the difficulties that Miller and the other justices faced when trying to grapple with the extraordinary changes that had taken place in American life during the 1860s. With one opinion, Miller hoped to preserve the federal system while providing protection for black civil rights. He wanted to support the biracial Reconstruction government in Louisiana, and uphold the ability of states to adopt economic and health regulations that affected private property. And he wanted to prevent the Supreme Court, with its conservative justices like Stephen J. Field, from becoming the perpetual censors of state regulations. Tragically, the opinion failed on all counts. Four years after *Slaughter-House*, the "Compromise of 1877" brought Reconstruction to an end and restored racist Southern Democrats to power. These new, but reactionary, governments turned the *Slaughter-House* opinion against itself by using it as a defense of states' rights and Jim Crow. Stephen J. Field, moreover, eventually carried the day on the Supreme Court, convincing his brethren to use the 14th Amendment's Due Process Clause to strike down reformist state regulations.

Miller had lost and lost badly. But, clearly, the ultimate victory of virulent racism and laissez-faire jurisprudence is not what Miller and the Court's majority in the *Slaughter-House Cases* intended.

An earlier version of this chapter was published in the *Journal of Southern History*, Vol. 64, No. 4 (Nov., 1998), pp. 649–676. Copyright 1998 by the Southern Historical Association; Michael A. Ross. Reprinted, with changes, by permission of the Editor.

The author would like to thank William Barney, Peter Coclanis, Paul Finkelman, Paul Kens, Michael Les Benedict, William Leuchtenburg, Roger Lotchin, and John Semonche for their comments on this essay.

6

Rebuilding the Slaughter-House
The Cases' Support for Civil Rights
David S. Bogen, University of Maryland School of Law

The *Slaughter-House Cases*[1] have a bad reputation for good reason. Justice Miller's narrow reading of the Privileges or Immunities Clause was used to prevent the federal government from adequately protecting African Americans after the Civil War. Further, his opinion for the Court significantly delayed the application of the Bill of Rights to the states.[2] But no one knows whether the world would be better with a different decision, because counterfactuals are never certain. The case did not involve either racial discrimination or incorporation. Total condemnation of the opinion for weakening civil rights overlooks its context, misreads its design, and misses the opportunities within its interpretation of the Amendment.[3]

This chapter sets forth how the *Slaughter-House Cases* support civil rights. Justice Miller used federalism in order to protect Reconstruction legislatures where significant numbers of African Americans participated fully for the first time. His recital of the history and purpose of the Civil War Amendments centered on the Amendments' design to protect African Americans, and suggested sweeping federal power to accomplish that end. Gutting the Privileges and Immunities Clause compelled the Court to read the Equal Protection Clause broadly; that interpretive stance was indirectly responsible for the reapportionment decisions of the Warren Court. The *Slaughter-House* Court's structural analysis and its view of federal protective power provide a basis for congressional power to protect citizens from any interference with their participation in the federal political process (voting and discussion of and access to the federal government). Justice Miller's analysis also supports federal power to protect citizens from race-based obstruction to their participation in state elections.[4]

The difficulties of proving racial motivation introduced by later Court decisions do not justify blaming Miller's *Slaughter-House* opinion for the end of Reconstruction and the rise of segregation. It is the later cases—*United States v. Harris, United States v. Cruikshank,* and *The Civil Rights Cases*—that mark the Supreme Court's retreat from the federal power to deal with race proclaimed by *Slaughter-House.* Although *United States v. Guest* revived the analysis in 1966, more recently, *United States v. Morrison* cast doubt on *Guest's* statements of federal power to reach private action.[5]

This chapter argues the Court should return to the *Slaughter-House* interpretation and resolve that doubt in favor of the constitutionality of laws to prevent discriminatory interference with access to state elections or other facilities. As I will discuss further, Article 4's guarantee of a republican form of government reinforces that result and provides an alternative path for returning to the vision of the *Slaughter-House Cases.*

I. SLAUGHTER-HOUSE CASES

The 14th Amendment[6] and the federal government's measures to reconstruct governments in the old Confederacy produced state legislatures with significant numbers of African Americans, as well as newcomers from the Northern states and Southerners who had not played any leading role in the War.[7] Opponents condemned the Reconstruction legislatures with epithets both racial and non-racial, for example, "carpetbaggers"[8] and "scalawags."[9] However, these legislatures brought civil rights to the states. For example, Louisiana enacted a public accommodations law in February 1869 that prohibited the exclusion of persons of color from places of public conveyances and accommodation. The state also enacted further civil rights statutes.[10]

Along with its civil rights statutes, the Louisiana legislature also adopted a measure to restrict the slaughtering of meat in New Orleans to a single location, a slaughterhouse owned by a group of investors known as the Crescent City Slaughter-House Company. The opposition to the monopoly was high: the butchers, of course, opposed limits on their practice; the old Southern Democrats opposed anything done by the Republican legislature; and accusations of bribery and monopoly filled the air. A series of suits and countersuits, as well as political and pragmatic twists and turns, took place before the group of cases known as the *Slaughter-House Cases* reached the Supreme Court.[11]

The butchers hired former Supreme Court Justice John Campbell, a member of the *Dred Scott* majority who had resigned from the Court and served in the Confederate government. Campbell sought to use the new Amendments to foil the laws of the Reconstruction legislature. He claimed the monopoly violated the 13th Amendment ban on involuntary servitude and the 14th Amendment's restrictions on state violations of due process, equal protection, and the privileges or immunities of citizens of the United States. Campbell and his co-counsel emphasized the generality of the language of the 14th Amendment and urged that it apply to all restrictive legislation.[12]

Justice Miller's opinion for the majority began with a straightforward public health analysis of the statute: confining the operation of slaughterhouses to a single location below the city and regulating its operation served the public health. The limited monopoly served the interests of the city by encouraging private enterprise to finance the slaughterhouse and assuring enforcement of restrictions. This was within the police power of the state.[13]

Responding to the butchers' linguistic argument, Miller said that the new amendments must be interpreted in light of the purpose of ending racial discrimination. In that perspective, the 13th Amendment did not apply to a monopoly for a slaughterhouse location. The Amendment forbade personal servitude, not limitations on the use of property.[14]

Justice Miller distinguished the privileges and immunities of citizens of a state from those of citizens of the United States. The fundamental rights of "protection by the government, with the right to acquire and possess property of every kind, and to pursue and obtain happiness and safety" were privileges of citizens of a state. Thus, slaughterhouse ownership and freedom to butcher in other places were matters for state concern, not privileges or immunities within the scope of the 14th Amendment Clause. The Clause itself created no privileges or immunities of citizens of the United States, but only referred to those derived from the "[f]ederal government, its [n]ational character, its [c]onstitution, or its laws."[15]

Justice Miller dismissed arguments based on the Due Process Clause as beyond any previously accepted. He also rejected the butchers' equal protection claim because it was not comparable to the race-based denials that gave rise to the Clause.[16]

II. THE *SLAUGHTER-HOUSE CASES*' BARRIER TO CIVIL RIGHTS

Justice Miller's opinion contradicted the framers' vision of the Privileges or Immunities Clause. The drafters believed that citizens were entitled to the same privileges and immunities that are in Article 4, and that the Privileges or Immunities Clause of the 14th Amendment made the Civil Rights Act of 1866 constitutionally unassailable and converted it from a statutory to a constitutional command.[17] Miller's historical analysis of the new amendments supported Reconstruction, but his concern for federalism led him to view the Privileges and Immunities Clause warily. He feared the expansive nationalizing effect of privileges and immunities if the 14th Amendment Clause referred to the fundamental rights that Justice Washington identified in *Corfield v. Coryell* as the privileges and immunities of citizens in Article 4. Miller's rejection of the fundamental rights analysis contributed to a judicial retreat from Reconstruction. On the other hand, he recognized racial civil rights as the core of the Civil War Amendments.[18]

The *Slaughter-House Cases* dissenters identified the privileges and immunities of citizens of the United States as fundamental rights, such as those articulated by Justice Washington in *Corfield v. Coryell*. The dissent focused on the negative rights that restrict the power of government to interfere with the enjoyment of life, liberty, and property: "Clearly among these must be placed the right to pursue a lawful employment in a lawful manner, without other restraint than such as equally affects all persons." Miller surely recognized the dangers to civil rights in this argument. (Campbell had used a very similar analysis to argue in Louisiana that the state's public accommodations law violated the Privileges or Immunities Clause.[19])

More importantly, *Coryell*'s fundamental rights included positive rights, specifically the right to protection by the government. Justice Miller understood that the federal government had the responsibility and power to secure all the privileges or immunities of citizens of the United States. If they included the protection of life, liberty, and property, then the security and protection of fundamental civil rights would be transferred from the states to the federal government. The federal government could not only remedy state failures to secure and protect such rights, but it could also protect them regardless of state actions. In Miller's view, if the federal government had plenary power to enact such laws, federalism would be at an end. Government would change to a national form. Insisting that the 14th Amendment's framers did not intend such a result, Miller said that privileges and immunities of citizens of the United States refer to their rights as federal citizens, that privileges or immunities relate to the function of the government, and that the scope of federal power had not been significantly altered except by the other Amendments and other Clauses of the 14th Amendment itself.[20]

After *Slaughter-House*, courts throughout the legal system used the limited version of privileges or immunities to deny the Amendment's application to state licenses, including bar membership. Worse, the Court consistently cited

Slaughter-House in decisions finding that the federal government lacked power to protect citizens against violence directed at preventing their voting. The decision's rationale precluded the use of the Privileges or Immunities Clause as a source for congressional regulation of contract and property rights. Thus, Congress had to use other powers to protect individuals from private acts of discrimination, and even today, the Court holds that some attempts by Congress to protect citizens from violent acts and discrimination are beyond its power.[21]

Further, pursuant to Miller's reasoning, the Clause could not be used in any argument for fundamental rights not derived from the functions of the federal government. His insistence that the Privileges or Immunities Clause did not create any new constitutional rights precluded the use of that Clause to incorporate the individual rights guarantees.[22] Thus, the Court for many years refused to apply the Bill of Rights against the states, citing the *Slaughter-House Cases* as support for that position.[23]

Nevertheless, in context, Miller's interpretation of the Privileges or Immunities Clause protected the civil rights legislation of reconstructed legislatures through a strong version of federalism. The misuse of the case to impair federal power ignored the opinion's design to shift protection of the civil rights of African Americans to other Clauses.

III. *SLAUGHTER-HOUSE* DETOURS: NEUTRAL ANALYSIS PERMITTING EXPANSIVE INTERPRETATION

Although Justice Miller's opinion foreclosed use of the Privileges or Immunities Clause to enforce the fundamental rights of citizens, the opinion left the door open for the use of other Clauses to accomplish many of the same ends. With respect to several of these Clauses, the *Slaughter-House Cases* did not support civil rights, but it offered them no barrier. The Court and Congress eventually moved into the openings to accomplish through the Commerce Clause, the 13th Amendment, and the Due Process Clause much of what might have been accomplished by a broad interpretation of the Privileges or Immunities Clause.

A. *Commerce Clause*

The federal government did not regulate expansively during the nineteenth century. The states' powers to enact laws affecting commerce posed the main Commerce Clause issue. The Court's analysis of the problem distinguished commercial regulation from exercises of the police power.[24] The *Slaughter-House Cases* noted that regulation of slaughtering was within the police power of the states, citing *Gibbons v. Ogden* for the proposition that health laws were matters subject to state legislation. Justice Miller referred to "the exclusive authority of State legislation over this subject," citing several cases to show that health regulation was a matter for the states and not for Congress. Most of the cited cases upheld state laws against dormant Commerce Clause challenges and did not focus on the federal power to enact laws regulating commerce.[25]

The categorical distinction between police and commerce regulations reflected in the *Slaughter-House Cases* was a weak barrier to congressional power. As long as Congress regulates interstate commerce, it preempts state law, even exercises of state police power.[26] The key question was how far the federal power to regulate commerce extended. The *Slaughter-House Cases* did not discuss the question, because no relevant federal statute applied. Thus, the decision posed no obstacle to the broad interpretation of the commerce power in the twentieth century, a power that has become the primary source for the exercise of federal power, including the exercise of power to promote civil rights.[27]

B. The 13th Amendment

Campbell argued for the butchers that the slaughterhouse monopoly was an involuntary servitude in violation of the 13th Amendment because it prohibited men and women from using their own property as they wished. Miller responded that the 13th Amendment referred to personal servitude and not to limitations on the use of property, and he gave some examples of involuntary servitude. His brief analysis did not touch on Congressional power to assure that slavery would not exist.[28]

Justice Miller's history of the adoption of the Amendments noted that the Black Codes were "almost as bad" as slavery, and that the 14th Amendment was adopted because the 13th Amendment had not secured all the framers supposed they had secured. Even if each law individually did not create slavery, the total had that effect. Miller wrote his brother-in-law, William Ballinger, that the Black Codes "do but change the form of slavery." Miller's comment suggested that cumulative acts that imposed personal servitude would be fodder for Congress. Even if statesmen believed "something more was necessary in the way of constitutional protection," Section 2 of the 13th Amendment might still grant Congress power to enact statutes like the Civil Rights Act of 1866. Republicans passed the Civil Rights Act and the 14th Amendment in the same session, arguing just that position. Thus, the Supreme Court acted consistently with the *Slaughter-House* interpretation in 1968, when it held in *Jones v. Alfred H. Mayer Co.* that

Congress could prohibit private persons from racially discriminating in the sale or lease of property.[29]

C. Due Process

Campbell and co-counsel Fellows also argued for the butchers that the monopoly violated the Due Process Clause, claiming that "it deprives them of their property without due process of law." They contended that "[t]he right to labor, the right to one's self physically and intellectually, and to the product of one's own faculties, is past doubt property, and property of a sacred kind." And they concluded that the grant of privilege was improper and not due process of law.[30]

Miller's response to the due process argument focused on Campbell's contention that the right to labor was a property right. He pointed to past interpretations of due process and noted that prior courts had never found restraints of trade to be deprivations of property subject to the prohibition of the Clause. Campbell had not argued that the butchers were denied liberty without due process. Therefore, Miller's rejection of the property argument did not address whether government was substantively limited when it attempted to regulate liberty. Campbell made no argument under the Due Process Clause for application of individual rights provisions of the Constitution against the states, and Miller's opinion thus did not comment on whether that Clause could be a vehicle for incorporation of the Bill of Rights.[31]

Justice Bradley's dissent in *Slaughter-House* noted that the Due Process Clause swept in almost all of the individual rights mentioned in the Constitution. Because Justice Miller made no comment on this, later courts could pick up the Clause and run with it. And that is what the Court has done, incorporating almost all of the guarantees of the Bill of Rights to apply to the states through the Due Process Clause.[32]

Once the Court accepted the incorporation of freedom of speech and other substantive individual rights through the Due Process Clause, the Court could extend the Clause to unenumerated substantive rights.[33] The noncommittal approach of the *Slaughter-House Cases* left the due process door ajar for the Court to walk through.

IV. THE *SLAUGHTER-HOUSE CASES'* SUPPORT FOR CIVIL RIGHTS

Justice Miller rooted his opinion in a vision of the Civil War Amendments as a series of attempts to accomplish the basic purpose of ending racial oppression:

[T]he one pervading purpose found in them all, lying at the foundation of each, and without which none of them would have been even suggested; we mean the freedom of the slave race, the security and firm establishment of that freedom, and the protection of the newly-made freeman and citizen from the oppressions of those who had formerly exercised unlimited dominion over him.

He said that purpose must be considered in any interpretation of the Amendments:

[I]n any fair and just construction of any section or phrase of these amendments, it is necessary to look to the purpose which we have said was the pervading spirit of them all, the evil which they were designed to remedy, and the process of continued addition to the Constitution, until that purpose was supposed to be accomplished, as far as constitutional law can accomplish it.

The Court's rejection of the butchers' involuntary servitude and due process claims reflected this view, but its federalism-focused privileges or immunities discussion seemed to conflict. In order to reconcile federalism with racial equality, the Court relied on the Equal Protection Clause. To reconcile federalism with the need to protect citizens from racial intimidation, it stressed implied structural rights and federal protective power over affirmative rights.[34]

A. Equal Protection

The butchers' counsel attacked the monopoly as an act of "legislative partiality" in violation of the Equal Protection Clause. Miller responded that equal protection was concerned with racial discrimination, and the monopoly was not a similar oppression:

We doubt very much whether any action of a State not directed by way of discrimination against the negroes as a class, or on account of their race, will ever be held to come within the purview of this provision. It is so clearly a provision for that race and that emergency, that a strong case would be necessary for its application to any other.[35]

Taken alone, the Equal Protection Clause offers no guidance for application. All classes are distinguishable by reason of the criteria used to define the class. The only issue is whether that criterion is a permissible one, and that is a substantive decision. Without context, a court could find that nothing violates the Clause or that anything it disliked violates the Clause. Miller's racial focus provided a guideline to determining appropriate criteria without opening the door to ad hoc judicial invalidation. Since *Slaughter-House*, the Court has expanded the Clause beyond race, but the underlying purpose of the Clause and the relationship of forbidden categories to the reasons for outlawing racial discrimination remain relevant.[36]

The butchers' argument assumed that laws regulating the use of property were subject to equal protection,[37] but that was questionable. Operating a slaughterhouse could be characterized as a privilege rather than a property right. "Protection" could be limited to securing life, liberty, or property "against injury or wrong or outrage or violence." However, Miller did not envision any such limitation on the application of the Equal Protection Clause. If the Privileges or Immunities Clause did not secure racial equality, the Equal Protection Clause must be the source for fulfilling the purpose of the Amendment. Thus, Miller characterized the equal protection of the laws in terms that could apply to all discriminatory laws.[38]

Miller's *Slaughter-House* opinion undergirded the Supreme Court's civil rights decision in *Strauder v. West Virginia* that defendants were entitled to a jury selected without racial discrimination. The *Strauder* dissenters (Justices Field and Clifford) argued that all defendants received equal treatment since they faced the same jury, and various groups, such as nonresidents, might be excluded from jury membership. The majority, however, insisted that equal protection applied to jury membership and, at a minimum, should preclude racial discrimination. Quoting Miller's *Slaughter-House* opinion, the Court said, "The existence of laws in the States where the newly emancipated negroes resided, which discriminated with gross injustice and hardship against them as a class, was the evil to be remedied, and by [the 14th Amendment] such laws were forbidden." Equal protection should not be limited to laws that exclude one race from the protections of tort, contract, property, and criminal law, but should reach all laws that discriminate racially:

> What is this but declaring that the law in the States shall be the same for the black as for the white; that all persons, whether colored or white, shall stand equal before the laws of the States, and, in regard to the colored race, for whose protection the amendment was primarily designed, that no discrimination shall be made against them by law because of their color? The words of the amendment, it is true, are prohibitory, but they contain a necessary implication of a positive immunity, or right, most valuable to the colored race,—the right to exemption from unfriendly legislation against them distinctively as colored,—exemption from legal discriminations, implying inferiority in civil society, lessening the security of their enjoyment of the rights which others enjoy, and discriminations which are steps towards reducing them to the condition of a subject race.[39]

Justice Holmes cited the *Slaughter-House Cases'* statement of the purpose of the 14th Amendment when he applied the 14th Amendment to primary elections in *Nixon v. Herndon*.[40] *Slaughter-House* itself had noted that suffrage was essential to fully secure the person and property of the freed slave, suggesting that equal protection could not be achieved without the vote.[41] Holmes' decision in *Herndon* that racial discrimination in primaries violated equal protection led to the application of the 14th Amendment in voting rights cases. That progression enabled the Court to examine under equal protection claims of legislative malapportionment that it had rejected as political questions when argued as violations of the guarantee of a republican form of government.[42] Thus, by focusing on the touchstone for interpreting the Clause and intimating a general application, Miller's *Slaughter-House* opinion supported the growth of equal protection that has occurred in the twentieth and twenty-first centuries.

B. Privileges or Immunities Implied from the Federal Government's National Character

Miller's interpretation of the Privileges or Immunities Clause rendered the Clause ineffective, but not the privileges or immunities themselves. His structural reading encouraged courts to find implied rights that relate to the function of the federal government. Thus, Miller's *Slaughter-House Cases* opinion reinforced his opinion in *Crandall v. Nevada*, which discovered a right to travel interstate implicit in national citizenship. *United States v. Guest* upheld the power of the federal government to protect the exercise of that privilege against private as well as government obstruction. Moreover, the right of access to federal offices underlying the right to travel supported federal power to protect citizens of the United States against private interference with their relationship to the federal government, including voting in federal elections, access to federal facilities, and petition and assembly on federal matters.[43]

i. Right to Travel. The road the Court took encouraged recognition of a right to travel, including the freedom from discrimination against new residents. Today, the best known citation of *Slaughter-House Cases* to support civil rights is the use made in *Saenz v. Roe*:

> [I]t has always been common ground that this Clause protects the third component of the right to travel [the right of the newly arrived citizen to the same privileges and immunities enjoyed by other citizens of the same State]. Writing for the majority in the *Slaughter-House Cases*, Justice Miller explained that one of the privileges conferred by this Clause "is that a citizen of the United States

can, of his own volition, become a citizen of any State of the Union by a bona
fide residence therein, with the same rights as other citizens of that State."[44]

Justice Stevens used the *Slaughter-House Cases* to support a decision that
found a federal law unconstitutional because it distinguished between newly-
arrived citizens and established citizens in the receipt of TANF (Temporary
Assistance for Needy Families) benefits. Stevens also noted the right to travel
interstate.[45] Although Stevens did not cite *Slaughter-House* for this right, Miller's
Slaughter-House Cases opinion, quoting from *Crandall v. Nevada*, asserts it:

> [A privilege or immunity of citizenship in the United States is] the right of the
> citizen of this great country, protected by implied guarantees of its Constitu-
> tion, "to come to the seat of government to assert any claim he may have upon
> that government, to transact any business he may have with it, to seek its pro-
> tection, to share its offices, to engage in administering its functions. He has the
> right of free access to its seaports, through which all operations of foreign
> commerce are conducted, to the subtreasuries, land offices, and courts of
> justice in the several States."[46]

The security and protection of national privileges or immunities rests with
the federal government. Thus, the federal government can assure its citizens they
can travel to its facilities. In *United States v. Guest*, the Court held that private
citizens who acted with the intent of interfering with interstate travel could be
indicted under 18 U.S.C. § 241 for conspiracy to injure a citizen in the free exercise
of a "right or privilege secured to him by the Constitution or laws of the United
States." Although Justice Harlan argued that the constitutional right to travel was
only a right to be free of state interference, the majority found that the right
included freedom from private interference, citing *Crandall*. Congress could have
enacted a specific statute to punish such interference using its power to regulate
interstate commerce, but *Guest* shows that the privilege is applicable against
private citizens and serves as an independent source of congressional power.[47]

In short, Miller's *Slaughter-House* opinion recognized that a right to interstate
travel and to reside in other states is a privilege or immunity of citizens of the United
States inferred from the nature of the union, and that recognition supports federal
legislation to protect travelers from private acts of violence aimed at them.

ii. Federal Political and Civil Rights. The Court has used the structural analysis
exemplified by *Slaughter-House* to find additional privileges or immunities
derived from the nature of the federal government. These decisions are rooted
in an understanding of government by the people: voting in federal elections,

access to the federal government, and discussion of federal affairs. Congress can protect all of these privileges from interference, whether the interference comes from government or from private individuals.[48]

Even before the *Slaughter-House Cases* decision, Judge Hugh Lennox Bond of the Fourth Circuit upheld the Enforcement Act of 1870 in the trial of members of the Ku Klux Klan in South Carolina for interference with voting in federal elections. He said that Congress had power to protect the integrity of federal elections.[49] The Supreme Court agreed with that position in *Ex parte Siebold*, noting congressional power to regulate time, place, and manner of federal elections, and asserting that this includes power to protect the vote from private injury and from state misfeasance.[50] Similarly, writing for the Court in *Ex parte Yarbrough*, Justice Miller upheld the convictions of private individuals for injuring a person in the exercise of his right to vote in a federal election. The defendants argued that states could provide the necessary laws, but Miller responded that state action was irrelevant to the federal power to protect federal operations, and that voting was a critical federal operation: "It is as essential to the successful working of this government that the great organisms of its executive and legislative branches should be the free choice of the people, as that the original form of it should be so." It did not matter that the voter was not a federal official, since the voter was acting in the exercise of a federal right:

> The power in either case [protecting federal officials or protecting voters in federal elections] arises out of the circumstance that the function in which the party is engaged or the right which he is about to exercise is dependent on the laws of the United States. In both cases it is the duty of that government to see that he may exercise this right freely, and to protect him from violence while so doing, or on account of so doing. This duty does not arise solely from the interest of the party concerned, but from the necessity of the government itself that its service shall be free from the adverse influence of force and fraud practiced on its agents, and that the votes by which its members of Congress and its President are elected shall be the free votes of the electors, and the officers thus chosen the free and uncorrupted choice of those who have the right to take part in that choice.[51]

Federal law can also protect access to federal offices. Miller's opinion in *Crandall v. Nevada* based the citizen's right to travel on an assumption that citizens had a right of access to federal offices and agencies.[52] Pursuant to that reasoning, interference with a citizen's access to federal offices and agencies interferes with the exercise of a federal right, even if the individual sought access in his or her home state.[53]

Another structural right implied from the nature of government is the right to assemble and petition the federal government for redress of grievances. After listing travel and protection abroad as privileges of citizens of the United States in the *Slaughter-House Cases*, Miller said that "[t]he right to peaceably assemble and petition for redress of grievances, the privilege of the writ of habeas corpus, are rights of the citizen guaranteed by the Federal Constitution."[54] Less than four years after *Slaughter-House*, the Court noted in *Cruikshank* that the 1st Amendment prohibited "Congress from abridging 'the right of the people to assemble and to petition the government for a redress of grievances.'" The Court asserted that the right preexisted the Constitution; it was essentially a natural right for the states to protect. The Amendment only prevented Congress from abridging it. Thus, the Court, with Miller's support, repudiated incorporation of the Bill of Rights through the Privileges or Immunities Clause. But the Court added:

> The right of the people peaceably to assemble for the purpose of petitioning Congress for a redress of grievances, or for any thing else connected with the powers or the duties of the national government, is an attribute of national citizenship, and, as such, under the protection of, and guaranteed by, the United States. The very idea of a government, republican in form, implies a right on the part of its citizens to meet peaceably for consultation in respect to public affairs and to petition for a redress of grievances.

The Court went on to say that if it had been alleged that the "object of the defendants [had been] to prevent a meeting for such a purpose, [then] the case would have been within the [Enforcement Act] statute, and within the . . . sovereignty of the United States."[55] Thus, Congress may protect people who are petitioning or attempting to transact business with the federal government, or even meeting among themselves to discuss federal affairs.

The *Cruikshank* dicta revealed the dual nature of the *Slaughter-House* reference to peaceable assembly. Because there have been few cases of federal legislation protecting speakers from private interference, later cases have focused on the limits on government contained in the Free Speech Clause and its incorporation through due process. However, the implied structural privilege to discuss federal laws enables Congress to protect citizens engaged in that activity from private interference.[56]

iii. State Political and Civil Rights. Critics of *Slaughter-House* often focus on its use in subsequent cases that struck down indictments and convictions for horrendous assaults, including killing African Americans who dared to act politically.[57] The murderers escaped punishment for unspeakably outrageous acts because the Court either construed the statute or the indictment to broadly apply to any voter interference without regard to racial motivation. The Court held that rights such as voting in state elections are not privileges or immunities of citizens of the United States, but only privileges of state citizenship. The Court reasoned that, unlike voting in national elections, the state elective office was not constitutionally based, and the only federal privilege was to be free of racial discrimination. Thus, violent but non-racially based assaults on state voters were like assaults on anyone else. The Court feared the danger to federalism if the federal government could punish these acts. Their decisions overlooked paths that would have upheld federalism and the indictments; but, even as it released the perpetrators, the Court traced out a theory of federal power to punish the acts that took place.[58]

The search for federal power to reach perpetrators of violence on African Americans begins with Miller's analysis of the purpose of the Civil War Amendments. Miller's reference to Clauses of the Civil War Amendments as new privileges or immunities of citizens of the United States signaled an expansion of congressional power to protect citizens from private interference with the exercise of those rights. Miller said they called for protecting the new citizen "from the oppressions of those who had formerly exercised unlimited dominion over him." But the Court has held that the 14th and 15th Amendments created rights primarily against the state. Where the right is only against the state, only the state can violate the Amendment. Yet, unless the federal government could deal with private acts of terrorism and the destruction of the African Americans' civil and political rights by violence, new citizens would not be protected from the oppressions of their former masters. Miller believed that Congress could prohibit racially motivated political violence, as he wrote in *Ex parte Yarbrough*. Of course, Congress has power to prohibit interference with constitutional rights, since Congress has power to enforce those rights.[59] The problem was how private behavior could constitute interference with a right that existed solely against the state. Miller's subsequent decisions show how Congress was authorized by the Reconstruction Amendments to protect citizens from private as well as governmental interference.

Circuit Court Judge Bond's opinion in *Crosby* offered one explanation to sustain the application of the Enforcement Act against private citizens. He argued that Congress was the sole judge of the appropriateness of legislation to enforce the Amendment and that it could find that the best way to protect against state discrimination was to punish all persons who acted to prevent the vote on a racial basis.[60]

Justice Bradley's opinion on circuit in *Cruikshank* gave another explanation. He distinguished between the fundamental rights that exist independently of

the Constitution and those created by the Constitution and federal law. With
respect to natural rights, Bradley said the Constitution does not create the rights
but only limits government interference with them, and congressional power
must be directed to government action. The right to vote, he contended, was
different in nature, because it conferred a positive right that did not exist before.
On this basis, Bradley argued that a right created by the Constitution may be
protected by the federal government:

> [T]he amendment . . . substantially guaranties the equal right to vote to citizens
> of every race and color, I am inclined to the opinion that congress has the power
> to secure that right not only as against the unfriendly operation of state laws,
> but against outrage, violence, and combinations on the part of individuals,
> irrespective of the state laws. Such was the opinion of congress itself in passing
> the law at a time when many of its members were the same who had consulted
> upon the original form of the amendment in proposing it to the states.[61]

Both Bradley and Bond saw the protection of voting without racial discrimination as the aim of the 15th Amendment, and found Congress has power to
achieve that end by prohibiting private race-based conspiracies to prevent
persons from voting in state elections. Both explanations had difficulty with the
Amendment's references to state action, but the Court soon indicated its agreement with these views. The Court said in *United States v. Reese* that the 15th
Amendment gave citizens a new constitutional right to be exempt from racial
discrimination. In *Cruikshank*, the Court said that the 15th Amendment provides
the right to vote where state law discriminates, and that Congress can therefore
protect that right. Both opinions spoke of exemption from discrimination rather
than exemption from state acts that discriminate.[62]

Justice Miller's subsequent opinion in *Ex parte Yarbrough* provided a better
basis for reconciling the language of the Amendment with the power to forbid
private racially-motivated attacks on voters in state elections. After holding that
the federal government could protect the right to vote in federal elections because
it was a federal privilege, he argued that the right to vote in a state election
without being subject to discrimination was also a federal privilege. The source
of the right to vote where the state excluded African Americans would be the
provisions of the 15th Amendment. Thus, the person exercising that vote would
be exercising a federal constitutional right, and the federal government can
protect the exercise of federal rights:

> [The 15th Amendment] did, in effect, confer on [blacks] the right to vote,
> because, being paramount to the State law, and a part of the State law, it
> annulled the discriminating word white, and thus left him in the enjoyment of

the same right as white persons. . . . In such cases this fifteenth article of amendment does, proprio vigore, substantially confer on the negro the right to vote, and Congress has the power to protect and enforce that right.[63]

This analysis focused on the constitutional obligation of the state to provide the opportunity to vote without racial discrimination. Federal law may prohibit interference with the state's performance of that obligation. Even if state law is racially neutral, private violence by groups like the Ku Klux Klan could exclude a race from the opportunity to vote provided by the state. The result would be ballots handed out by the state to one race only. The citizen has a right to obtain the vote from the state without racial discrimination, and private acts on a racial basis could exclude the voter from a benefit that the state was constitutionally bound to provide. Thus, Congress should have power to prohibit interference with the right of the citizen to vote without being subjected to racial discrimination.[64]

This analysis empowers Congress to assist states in fulfilling their constitutional duties; it does not preempt them. Where the constitutional duty of the state is negative (for example, "do not interfere with someone's natural rights"), private interference with those rights does not interfere with the state's constitutional obligation. Where the state has an obligation to provide individuals with something, private acts may interfere with the state's performance of its obligation. However, even if the duty is the positive one of protecting another individual from harm, infliction of the harm does not interfere with the state performing its duty. Thus, the analysis does not threaten federalism because it does not authorize the federal government to enact civil laws of contract and property, or criminal law.

Given the purpose analysis of *Slaughter-House*, the dicta in the cases following it correctly found congressional power to ban election interference based on race. *Reese, Cruikshank,* and *Yarbrough* discussed the right to vote in state elections entirely in terms of the 15th Amendment, because the Court had not yet found that the Equal Protection Clause applied to voting. Although the state determines what state offices are elective, as well as defining eligibility to vote for them, equal protection developments that describe voting as a fundamental interest suggest it may be time to reexamine the scope of privileges and immunities of United States citizens in state elections.

Today, the Court has recognized a much broader scope for federal privileges in state elections. In making these decisions, the Court has said that "the right of suffrage is a fundamental matter in a free and democratic society."[65] The right to vote without invidious discrimination by the state is a privilege of citizens of the United States because the privilege is derived from the Constitution. Under the reasoning used in *Slaughter-House, Cruikshank, Reese,* and *Yarbrough,* all owing to Miller's first interpretations of the scope of the 14th Amendment, Congress should have power under Section 5 of the Amendment to prohibit private interference with voting in state elections based on invidious discrimination.

James v. Bowman stands as an obstacle to this analysis. The case was decided at the turn of the century and, to some degree, put a nail in the coffin of Reconstruction. In *James,* the Court stated that a statute that purports to punish individual action could not be sustained under the 15th Amendment. In reaching its decision, the Court relied on 14th Amendment cases that held state action is necessary—the *Civil Rights Cases* and *Harris.*[66] A majority of the Supreme Court rejected this analysis in a fractured opinion in *United States v. Guest.* Three justices in the plurality agreed with the three dissenting justices that Congress could reach private action under its power to enforce the 14th Amendment's Equal Protection Clause. Justice Brennan wrote in dissent:

> Viewed in its proper perspective, § 5 of the 14th Amendment appears as a positive grant of legislative power, authorizing Congress to exercise its discretion in fashioning remedies to achieve civil and political equality for all citizens. No one would deny that Congress could enact legislation directing state officials to provide Negroes with equal access to state schools, parks and other facilities owned or operated by the State. Nor could it be denied that Congress has the power to punish state officers who, in excess of their authority and in violation of state law, conspire to threaten, harass and murder Negroes for attempting to use these facilities. And I can find no principle of federalism nor word of the Constitution that denies Congress power to determine that in order adequately to protect the right to equal utilization of state facilities, it is also appropriate to punish other individuals—not state officers themselves and not acting in concert with state officers—who engage in the same brutal conduct for the same misguided purpose.[67]

In other words, where the Constitution requires a state to furnish something on a nondiscriminatory basis, Congress has power to vindicate that right by punishing anyone who interferes with access to that good or service. Section 5 of the 14th Amendment, like Section 2 of the 15th Amendment, empowers Congress to protect the states from acts that would interfere with fulfilling their constitutional obligation.

This is the reasoning of *Yarbrough.*[68] Consistent with Miller's early interpretation, Congress should have power to protect the state in fulfilling its constitutional obligations—that is a method of enforcing the obligation itself.

For example, Congress should be able to protect state officials from rioters who attempt to compel them to segregate.[69] The federal government must have power to protect any person carrying out a federal obligation. Violence generally does not interfere with the ability of the state to protect its citizens equally, because the state satisfies its obligation by punishing the offender through its civil and criminal laws; however, where private persons interfere with access to the state so that the state provides its benefits to only one group (the ones who were able to appear), the private action creates discrimination. In that context, the federal government should be able to protect the state from private interference with its federal obligation.

V. THE GUARANTEE CLAUSE

The Guarantee Clause recognizes the importance of governance by the people of a state as a privilege of citizens of the United States. Article 4, Section 4 of the Constitution provides that the "United States shall guarantee to every State in this Union a Republican Form of Government, and shall protect each of them against Invasion; and on Application of the Legislature, or of the Executive (when the Legislature cannot be convened) against domestic Violence." The Court, without overriding the interpretation of Miller in *Slaughter-House* and its progeny, could use the Guarantee Clause to avoid the state action limits of its equal protection precedents.

The Court has treated the Guarantee Clause as raising a political question inappropriate for judicial review.[70] However, the Necessary and Proper Clause in Article 1, Section 8 grants Congress the power "[t]o make all Laws which shall be necessary and proper for carrying into Execution . . . all other Powers vested by this Constitution in the Government of the United States." Thus, Congress has power to enact a law necessary to guarantee every state a republican form of government. Some Republicans used the Guarantee Clause to justify Reconstruction measures after the Civil War.[71] As early as 1868, in *Texas v. White*, Chief Justice Waite said that "the power to carry into effect the clause of guaranty is primarily a legislative power, and resides in Congress."[72]

If the core meaning of republican government is control by the people over their rulers, the guarantee may protect the choices that the state makes from federal interference. Professor Merritt has argued powerfully that the Clause "prohibits the states from adopting nonrepublican forms of government [and] forbids the federal government from interfering with state governments in a way that would destroy their republican character."[73]

But the guarantee of a republican form of government should also empower the federal government to assist the existing state government in maintaining its republican character. Rather than interfere with state choices, the federal government could protect those choices. Thus, the federal government should have the power to assure that persons are able to vote when they are properly constituted as voters by the state or by the constitutional prohibition against invidious discrimination. Any attempt by persons to prevent others from voting for reasons that would be invidious discrimination should be within the power of Congress to regulate to protect access to something that the Constitution requires the state to afford without such discrimination. As a majority of justices suggested in *Guest*, this should be a basis for the exercise of congressional enforcement power under Section 5 of the 14th Amendment.

A. Voting

According to the reasoning in the *Slaughter-House Cases* and its progeny, the federal government can protect individuals from interference with their exercise of federal rights. If a republican form of government is guaranteed to the states by the Constitution, the federal government should have power to protect the states from threats to their form of government. Several Supreme Court cases have denied federal power to protect voting in state elections, either on the ground that voting in state elections is not a federal right, or that the constitutional limits apply only to state and not individual actions. However, none of these cases squarely addressed the federal power to act under the Guarantee Clause.[74]

The Court did mention the Guarantee Clause in *United States v. Cruikshank*, but it did not directly confront the argument that the Clause supported voting rights legislation. In *Cruikshank*, the Court dismissed an indictment that charged defendants with injuring parties because they had voted in a state election. The Court said that the "right of suffrage is not a necessary attribute of national citizenship," citing *Reese*. However, the indictment was based on the Enforcement Act of 1870, which made it a crime to conspire to injure a person "with intent to prevent or hinder his free exercise and enjoyment of any right or privilege granted or secured to him by the Constitution or laws of the United States." In order to find a violation of the Enforcement Act, the Court would have to hold that voting in states was a right or privilege secured by the Constitution or laws of the United States. It did not do so. The Court could not rely on the Guarantee Clause to establish the right because its precedents held that the Clause was non-justiciable. The Court indicated that the Guarantee Clause was relevant, but did not apply in this case, noting the need for the state to call for assistance. The Court did not examine whether the Clause empowered Congress to enact a statute that spe-

cifically prohibited interference with the vote. Thus, *Cruikshank* also sets no precedent with respect to congressional Guarantee Clause power.[75]

B. Other Aspects of a Republican Form of Government

    The Guarantee Clause should also extend to empower Congress to protect
individuals in obtaining access to state government, as *Guest* suggested.[76] Interaction of government with the people is an essential part of the republican form
of government, and the federal government should be able to guarantee it.

    In addition, the federal government should be able to protect speech on local
and state political affairs. As the Court said in *Cruikshank*, "The very idea of a
government, republican in form, implies a right on the part of its citizens to
meet peaceably for consultation in respect to public affairs and to petition for a
redress of grievances."[77] If Congress has power to guarantee to the states a
republican form of government, it must be able to protect the political speech
of its citizens on local matters. Such freedom of speech is derived from the function of speech in the operations of government.

VI. CONCLUSION

    The *Slaughter-House Cases* have been used by opponents of civil rights because
Justice Miller limited the impact of one Clause of the 14th Amendment. The opinion
itself was designed to protect Reconstruction legislatures in the hope that they could
secure civil rights on a state level. A number of aspects of the opinion do promote
the protection of civil rights. Much of the negative effect of Miller's opinion on the
use of the Privileges or Immunities Clause has been overcome by using other Clauses
of the Amendment in ways that his opinion left open. The historical analysis in the
opinion has been used to support broader federal power to deal with racial discrimination, and its reference to the right to travel has been cited to support such a
federal right. Finally, the opinion's support for federal protection of political speech
has been overlooked, but the analysis of privileges of federal citizenship, in conjunction with the often neglected Guarantee Clause, warrants federal protection of
individual access to state government in voting, facilities, and political discussion.

An earlier version of this chapter was published in *Akron Law Review*, Vol. 42 No.4, pp. 1129–1164.
Copyright © 2009 *Akron Law Review*. Used with permission.
    I would like to thank Patrick Tyler and Alice Johnson for their research assistance, my colleague
Taunya Banks, and especially The University of Akron School of Law, its Constitutional Law Center,
Professor Richard Aynes, and *Akron Law Review*.

7 Why "Privileges or Immunities"?
An Explanation of the Framers' Interpretation and the Supreme Court's Misinterpretation

William J. Rich, The University of Akron School of Law

In the *Slaughter-House Cases*, Justice Field accused the majority of turning the 14th Amendment's Privileges or Immunities Clause into a "vain and idle enactment which accomplished nothing," and Justice Swayne argued that the majority "turn[ed]...what was meant for bread into a stone." Most contemporary commentators appear to agree. Robert Bork went so far as to compare that Clause to a provision "written in Sanskrit" or "obliterated past deciphering by an ink blot."[1] Did the framers of the 14th Amendment make a colossal mistake? Or were Justices Field and Swayne correct when they blamed Justice Miller's majority opinion in *Slaughter-House* for leading the nation astray? The answer to the first question is "no," and the answer to the second question is a qualified "no." The phrase "privileges or immunities" made sense at the time when Congressman Bingham and his colleagues inserted it into the 14th Amendment. They, therefore, properly interpreted their work as encapsulating a substantive, and significant, change into the Constitution. Yet, a sympathetic reading of *Slaughter-House* reveals that Justice Miller also interpreted the Clause to have meaning. This chapter argues that our contemporary misunderstanding of the Privileges or Immunities Clause reflects continuing failure to appreciate positive aspects of the interpretive framework offered by Justice Miller in 1873.

I. FEDERALISM (NOT JUST THE BILL OF RIGHTS)

In the 140 years following ratification of the 14th Amendment, much of the debate has focused upon incorporation of the Bill of Rights. Many commentators argue that the framers of the Amendment intended to incorporate the Bill of Rights when they drafted the Privileges or Immunities Clause. Detractors who argue against incorporation ask, among other things, why the framers did not simply use that language if their intent was to make states subject to the Bill of Rights. The Supreme Court muddled these issues, rejecting the Privileges or Immunities Clause as a basis for incorporation in the *Slaughter-House Cases* and then using the Due Process Clause to accomplish virtually all of the same goals. Because the Supreme Court used the "wrong clause," however, academic debate continues unabated.[2]

The central thesis of the following discussion is that this debate has been too narrow. The framers interpreted the phrase "privileges or immunities" as including *more* than the Bill of Rights. When they promulgated the 14th Amendment, they understood that incorporation of the Bill of Rights would only accomplish a portion of their objectives. In addition, they wanted to assure state compliance with rights derived from federal law in a broad sense. And they chose the phrase "privileges or immunities of citizens of the United States" specifically to meet this objective.

For an illustration of this point, consider the case of Samuel Hoar. In 1844, Massachusetts sent Hoar as an emissary to South Carolina to protest that state's imprisonment of British and American seamen with African ancestry who arrived in the port of Charleston. The South Carolina legislature denounced Hoar, claiming the state's right to exclude "free negroes and persons of color" who could not be United States citizens and therefore were not protected by "the privileges and immunities of citizens in the several States." Hoar hastily retreated, fearing for his life. The Hoar affair became a cause célèbre, with Southern states rallying to the support of South Carolina, while the Massachusetts legislature invoked the need for congressional action to protect the citizens of that state.[3]

Rather than dying a quiet death, the controversy sparked debate in Congress both before and after the Civil War. From the beginning, references to the Hoar affair implicated not only the substantive rights of a black seaman and the Massachusetts judge who traveled to defend him, but also the underlying issue of national government authority to protect those rights. In his first speech on the floor of Congress supporting what became the 14th Amendment, Congressman John Bingham decried the lack of safety for a Massachusetts citizen in the streets of Charleston, and denounced South Carolina for "utterly disregard[ing]...the privileges and immunities" of Samuel Hoar. In a debate that took place on February 26, 1866, Congressman Bingham argued that the Privileges or Immunities Clause of the proposed 14th Amendment that he had authored protected the same rights found in the text of Article 4, other existing Constitutional provisions, and the Supremacy Clause. The only new ingredient was congressional power to enforce those provisions. Two days later, as part of the same debate, Bingham again emphasized the defiance of federal law that had taken place in Oregon and throughout the Southern states.[4]

While the reference to Hoar could be characterized as an example of the need to incorporate the Bill of Rights, protecting the right of all Americans to exercise freedom of speech and to petition state governments, that depiction misses a larger point. Hoar had traveled to South Carolina to denounce that state's defiance of Commerce Clause and Treaty Clause protection for the right of free navigation. He planned to argue that the South Carolina law conflicted with "the express provisions or fundamental principles of the national compact." The 14th Amendment Privileges or Immunities Clause was drafted for the broad purpose of assuring that individuals would be able to enforce federal law against state authorities.[5]

The framers of the 14th Amendment aptly chose the phrase "privileges or immunities" to reflect this combination of interests. Although the terms were familiar enough to lawmakers, having already appeared in the text of the Constitution with respect to rights of state citizens, the phrase's meaning had only been discussed at length in one prior federal court opinion. In *Corfield v. Coryell*, Justice Bushrod Washington devoted a page of text to the meaning of the phrase, but did little to provide clarity beyond holding that it did not prohibit all state laws according different treatment to citizens and non-citizens. He did include within its ambit "the enjoyment of life and liberty, with the right to acquire and possess property of every kind, and to pursue and obtain happiness and safety" subject to "such restraints as the government may justly prescribe for the general good of the whole."[6]

In the years leading up to the Civil War, courts had seized upon the Article 4 Privileges and Immunities Clause as a tool for the enforcement of slavery. White slaveholders were generally entitled to the protection of the Privileges and Immunities Clause; blacks were not. Despite notable exceptions, the dominant question in cases like *Dred Scott* was not "substantive," but rather whether blacks were entitled to the same privileges or immunities as whites.[7]

During the debates on the 14th Amendment, the framers articulated a range of views regarding the Privileges or Immunities Clause, including references to fundamental rights and to solidification of federal supremacy. They viewed the Privileges or Immunities Clause as an important protection of national authority with respect to issues beyond those that the first eight amendments controlled. Some members of Congress were less concerned about the power to establish the substance of privileges or immunities than with ensuring that the federal government had the authority to enforce the equality component of Article 4. Nothing in the text of the Constitution gives Congress the authority to impose the Constitution's textual constraints on states. Without that authority, Congress could not provide relief for those whose rights to privileges and immunities had been violated, nor could it impose liability on those who interfered with such rights.[8]

The importance of this issue of federal power to those who framed the 14th Amendment merits elaboration. Members of Congress made repeated references to this concern for federal supremacy during the course of debates over the 14th Amendment. For example, in addressing questions about enforcement of the Privileges or Immunities Clause, Congressman Baker quoted the text of that provision and asked:

> What business is it of any State to do things here forbidden? To rob the American citizen of rights thrown around him by the supreme law of the land? When we remember to what an extent this has been done in the past, we can appreciate the need of putting a stop to it in the future.[9]

In historical context, Baker's reference would have been understood as an appeal to reinforce federal supremacy. That element of the debate was rarely extended because it was never seriously challenged. The issue remained important enough, however, for Congressman Bingham to emphasize it in his final speech before the House of Representatives supporting promulgation of the 14th Amendment. Bingham again referred to South Carolina's interference with enforcement of national law. When that event took place, a "body of great and patriotic men looked in vain for any grant of power in the Constitution" that would protect South Carolina residents who sought to "bear true allegiance to the Constitution and laws of the United States." He argued that states should never again be allowed to "abjure their allegiance" to the United States by attempting to "nullify" federal law. In Bingham's view, adopting the Privileges or Immunities Clause meant, at a minimum, that questions about federal supremacy had been put to rest.[10]

Three categories of "rights" within the scope of privileges or immunities emerge from an assessment of Congressional debates and subsequent treatment of these issues.[11] The first category includes rights directly defined in the text of the Constitution and determined to be applicable to the states. The Bill of Rights as currently incorporated into the Due Process Clause fits within this definition. So do rights found in Article 1, Sections 9 and 10 of the Constitution (such as habeas corpus and protections against ex post facto laws) and those within the Privileges and Immunities Clause of Article 4, Section 2.

A second category involves rights derived from acts of Congress specifically authorized by the Constitution. This category includes Commerce Clause and Treaty Clause rights such as those that should have protected the seamen who entered Charleston Harbor. Rights of this category would also include patent rights or bankruptcy rights as defined by Congressional legislation.[12]

The third category includes those interstitial rights which may be fairly inferred from the Constitution. The "right to travel," fits within this definition. Interestingly, this right was first identified by the Supreme Court in *Crandall v. State of Nevada*[13] by Justice Miller in 1867—during the passage and ratification of the 14th Amendment.

The rights encompassed in "privileges or immunities" of "citizens of the United States" as defined above do not include what the dissenters in the *Slaughter-House Cases* argued: that the 14th Amendment gave Congress control over substantive rights that fall within the scope of *state* privileges and immunities.[14] But the majority justices did recognize federal supremacy, concluding that the privileges or immunities protected by the 14th Amendment were those rights that "owe their existence to the Federal government, its National character, its Constitution, or its laws." Congress, they recognized, had gained authority to enforce the Article 4 Privileges and Immunities Clause when non-residents of a state were discriminated against, but not to rewrite the laws encompassed by that Clause. Apparently focusing on the federal supremacy concerns, the Court read the drafting and ratification debates to mean that the 14th Amendment Privileges or Immunities Clause only extended federal authority to rights directly linked, either explicitly or implicitly, to the national government.[15]

II. CONGRESS (NOT THE SUPREME COURT)

During the ratification debates, critics of the phrase "privileges or immunities" voiced concerns that the text swept too broadly and enlarged federal power without providing clear guidance regarding the boundaries of that power. Reassurance by advocates of the 14th Amendment consisted in significant part of expressions that the Privileges or Immunities Clause did not expand the substantive scope of existing protection. Some have taken such statements as implied rejections of incorporation, in spite of repeated favorable references to the Bill of Rights. This focus upon the Bill of Rights debate has side-tracked contemporary scholars from a primary reason for choosing the phrase "privileges or immunities." The framers were more likely to have been concerned about enforceability of rights and protections, and about the role of Congress in defining those rights that would be enforceable against the states.[16]

Origins of the 14th Amendment began with fears that the 13th Amendment failed to give Congress adequate authority to enact early civil rights legislation.[17] The framers therefore focused on expanding that power, and it is reasonable to believe that they foresaw a predominant role for Congress in defining the scope of the Amendment. The Privileges or Immunities Clause corresponds to that focus, especially when judged in light of the broad definition of that phrase extant at the time. Given that the framers of the 14th Amendment were focusing on federalism issues, there are good reasons to believe that members of Congress were chiefly concerned about their own legislative authority as distinct from the authority of the courts.

Admittedly, the framers were aware of problems associated with judicial interpretation of the text of the Constitution, especially as visited upon the nation in the case of *Dred Scott v. Sandford*.[18] The framers crafted the 14th Amendment in part to overrule the racist assumptions upon which that case was based,[19] thereby sending a message to the Supreme Court to avoid such debacles in the future. "*All persons born or naturalized in the United States*" were given citizenship status and protected from discriminatory treatment. But Congress was emphatically given the "power to enforce" the provisions of the 14th Amendment, in Section 5.

Congress accepted that challenge with enactment of the Ku Klux Klan Act of 1871 (also known as the Civil Rights Act of 1871), which imposed liability on persons who "under color of any law . . . cause . . . the deprivation of any rights, privileges, or immunities secured by the Constitution of the United States." The purpose of this law was explained by Congressman Bingham, primary sponsor of the 14th Amendment, as to "provide by law for the better enforcement of the Constitution and laws of the United States." In 1874, a Committee on Revision of the Laws, charged with the responsibility to "amend the imperfections of the original text" without altering meaning, revised language from the Ku Klux Klan Act to develop what we now find in 42 U.S.C. § 1983, protecting "any rights, privileges, or immu-

[handwritten annotation: How is this consistent with, eg., Bingham saying P & I clause adds nothing new to obligating states?]

nities secured by the Constitution *and laws*" of the federal government. With this language, Congress communicated the broadly accepted understanding that the Privileges or Immunities Clause was to be co-extensive with rights found within the text of the Constitution as well as rights defined by Congress exercising its authority as defined by Article 1 of the Constitution. Today, federal statutory rights may be enforced by invoking § 1983, but few appear to remember that authority for doing so may be traced to the Privileges or Immunities Clause.[20]

III. JUSTICE MILLER WAS NOT THE ENEMY

Few Supreme Court justices have been more savagely attacked than Justice Samuel Miller, and few opinions have been subject to such prolonged criticism as Justice Miller's opinion in the *Slaughter-House Cases*. The criticism looks good in hindsight; subsequent Supreme Court decisions rejected incorporation of the Bill of Rights into the Privileges or Immunities Clause, and *Slaughter-House* opened the door for those decisions. Casting blame in that manner, however, distracts from a more charitable view of the *Slaughter-House* framework which retains contemporary significance.[21]

Misunderstanding of *Slaughter-House* begins with a failure to appreciate the competing ideologies of the litigants in that case. John A. Campbell, who represented the plaintiffs, was a former U.S. Supreme Court Justice who shared responsibility for the *Dred Scott* decision as a member of that Court, and who resigned from that office to join the Confederacy. He was also a disciple of John C. Calhoun. Attorneys on the other side of the argument were followers of Daniel Webster, who had opposed secession and organized an army to support President Jackson's battle against nullification. After reviewing this alignment of counsel, some may argue that the plaintiffs' attorneys were abandoning their historical ideological commitments by challenging state authority to regulate the butchers of New Orleans and advocating national oversight. An alternative perspective suggests that Chief Justice Miller and others in the majority understood that the plaintiffs were attempting to promote individual property rights, and in that sense the plaintiffs' arguments remained in line with their prior commitment to the owners of slaves. Calhoun's arguments for states' rights were based upon an assumption that South Carolina would retain the institution of slavery, and his conservative ideology had as much to do with preserving individual property rights as with restraining the national government.[22]

Justice Miller's opinion in *Slaughter-House* took a decidedly cautious approach toward striking down state measures designed to protect public health. While there are phrases in his opinion which, with the benefit of hindsight, suggest an unduly limited scope for the 14th Amendment, the basic framework that he described for interpreting the Privileges or Immunities Clause parallels major components of the approach described in this chapter. Miller explicitly referred to both navigation rights and the interstitial right to freedom of travel as examples of privileges or immunities.[23] He rejected a meaning that would have incorporated the writings of Adam Smith (or Herbert Spencer) into the Constitution, and history demonstrates the wisdom of that response. On the latter issue, the *Slaughter-House* dissenters surely do not offer much in the way of a positive alternative.

A primary focus of Justice Miller's interpretation of the Privileges or Immunities Clause was his effort to dispel belief that *new* substantive rights were to be identified and defined by the courts, without having an independent basis in the Constitution or laws of the United States government. Instead, the Clause protected those rights that "owe their existence to the Federal government, its National character, its Constitution, or its laws." The first example he gave was the case of *Crandall v. Nevada*, a case from 1867 in which Justice Miller had established the right of United States citizens to travel freely from one state to another. The right to travel falls within a more general category of rights derived from the "national character" of the government.[24]

Justice Miller illustrated a second category of protections embodied by the Privileges or Immunities Clause by reference to the "right to peaceably assemble and petition for redress of grievances" and the "privilege of the writ of habeas corpus," both of which were identified as "rights of the citizen guaranteed by the Federal Constitution."[25] With this language, Justice Miller incorporated individual rights which the text of the Constitution identified only in relation to Congress. One may argue that he referred to the right of petition, rather than to other provisions embodied in the Bill of Rights, because of the drama associated with Samuel Hoar, which remained on the minds of those who understood the purpose of the 14th Amendment. Several authors have noted that Miller's reference to the right of petition is consistent with broader arguments for incorporation. On balance, Professor David Bogen makes a stronger argument that Miller's reference to a "right to petition," although ambiguous, was intended only to limit state interference with the right to petition the national government;[26] that interpretation became manifest two years later with Chief Justice Waite's decision in *United States v. Cruikshank.*[27]

A final category of protections identified by Justice Miller was derived from federal law, and illustrated by reference to both navigation and treaty rights. Again, the use of illustrations that were of central concern to Samuel Hoar seems

[handwritten annotation: Reads Miller to say Cong. can enact laws that → P + I's & natural citizenship.]

more than merely coincidental. More important than the specific context, however, was the embrace of laws derived from the powers assigned to Congress and the national government as a source of privileges or immunities.[28]

Some have questioned the importance of this implied restatement of federal supremacy.[29] Justice Miller downplays the significance of this third category through his broad description of state police powers, which he viewed as outside of the ambit of federal privileges or immunities.[30] His relatively limited conception of federal power was consistent with the understanding of congressional authority in the late nineteenth century. Since that time, however, dimensions of federal power have expanded dramatically, as illustrated by contemporary interpretations of the Commerce Clause.[31]

Subsequent generations accepted the link that Justice Miller drew between the Privileges or Immunities Clause and the Supremacy Clause, beginning with congressional enactment of what we now know as 42 U.S.C. § 1983. Thomas Cooley's 1880 treatise explained that the Privileges or Immunities Clause protected rights to participate in foreign or domestic commerce, benefits of postal laws, and navigation and travel rights because "over all of these subjects the jurisdiction of the United States extends, and they are covered by its laws." A widely recognized article from 1918 by Professor D. O. McGovney explained that, to understand the Privileges or Immunities Clause, counsel must simply ask "what provision or text of Federal law creates or grants this alleged privilege or immunity." More contemporary commentators reinforced this understanding, although doing so in disparaging terms, expressing the lack of any "independent function [of the Privileges or Immunities Clause], except as an alternative to using the Supremacy Clause." Both the history leading up to the Civil War and contemporary experience, however, demonstrate the importance of this element of the framework described by Justice Miller.[32]

IV. CONTEMPORARY IMPLICATIONS

The Supreme Court got it right in *Saenz v. Roe*, when the justices decided in 1999 that the right of new state residents to enjoy the same privileges as those accorded to long-term residents is derived from the 14th Amendment Privileges or Immunities Clause. Justice Stevens' opinion for the Court cites Justice Miller's *Slaughter-House* opinion as authority for that conclusion, and by doing so revives the first component of the constitutional framework derived from that text.[33]

Although the second segment of Justice Miller's framework could have been expanded to incorporate provisions of the Bill of Rights, conceptions of sovereignty accepted by Miller, and at least some of his colleagues, constrained that development.[34] The significance of that loss, however, should not be overstated. The "Incorporation Doctrine" should now be treated as settled law; contemporary battles over that issue sustain interesting academic squabbles, but have little likelihood of changing judicial treatment of the rights of American citizens. Thus, although the second component of Justice Miller's framework may not be linked to the Privileges or Immunities Clause, analogous protection extends from contemporary due process analysis. While perhaps unsatisfactory to constitutional purists, this solution meets the needs of those victimized by state abuse.

It is the third component of the *Slaughter-House* framework which appears to have been lost in the shadow of recent ideological battles within the Supreme Court. In a series of opinions from *Seminole Tribe* in 1996 to *Garrett* in 2001, five Supreme Court justices decided that rights derived from federal law stemming from congressional exercise of its power pursuant to Article 1, Section 8 of the Constitution are constrained by the 11th Amendment. Those justices substituted their own conventional wisdom for the actual text and history of the 11th Amendment and for the conceptions of sovereignty existing at the time the 11th Amendment was promulgated. They conceded the fact that the Due Process and Equal Protection provisions of the 14th Amendment override the 11th Amendment, but then circumscribed congressional authority to interpret those Clauses. To date, they have totally ignored the Privileges or Immunities Clause.[35]

The result of recent Supreme Court decisions limiting congressional authority to abrogate the 11th Amendment is a fundamentally incoherent conception of federalism generally, and of the Privileges or Immunities Clause in particular. The Supreme Court interpretation of the 11th Amendment is at odds with the framers' conceptions of sovereignty that gave rise to the language in that text. In more particular terms, the justices acknowledge that language in 42 U.S.C. § 1983 provides for enforcement of federal statutes, but have never addressed the relationship between § 1983's language and the Privileges or Immunities Clause. By ignoring this relationship, the Court is left with untenable conclusions, such as the decision that states may freely violate federal patent law with impunity. Bankruptcy law has become similarly twisted in order to avoid the unworkable implication that states are immune from judgments deriving their authority from federal statutes.[36]

Why is this so important? In a broader context, scholars categorize rights in both "negative" and "positive" terms. Negative rights impose constraints on government, and, to the regret of some, the Bill of Rights, the Due Process

Clause and the Equal Protection Clause have all been limited to that category. Those who believe in the importance of positive rights, however, may see the Privileges or Immunities Clause as a repository of such rights. By their nature, positive rights lend themselves to legislative control, and, properly understood, the Privileges or Immunities Clause recognizes such Congressional action. Authority to establish positive rights that states must adhere to or face consequential damages should follow from contemporary recognition of the Privileges or Immunities Clause.[37]

In practical terms, this means that Congress should have authority to create statutory rights consistent with constitutional (especially Article 1) grants of Congressional power and to enforce them against state abridgement. This would mean that Congress has the power to protect state workers from age discrimination or from discrimination based upon disabilities by abrogating state immunity from such actions. It also means that the door should be reopened for enforcement of fair labor standards against state employers, and calls for elimination of the unworkable proposition that Congress lacks power to provide for enforcement of patent rights against state governments. All responsibilities assigned to Congress under Article 1 of the Constitution should once again include the power to ensure state compliance with federal law.[38]

V. CONCLUSION

Returning to the question of what the framers of the 14th Amendment could have been thinking when they chose the phrase "privileges or immunities," a transparent purpose emerges. They cared about incorporation of the Bill of Rights, but that was only one element of their quest. They also cared about rights derived from the national character of the government. Assuring the supremacy of federal statutory rights had major significance at that point in history. "Privileges or immunities of citizens of the United States" embraced all of these sources of law. This conclusion is consistent with Congressman Bingham's assurance at the time that the central purpose of this provision was simply to "bear true allegiance to the Constitution and laws of the United States." It is also consistent with Justice Miller's understanding that "privileges" and "immunities" include "nearly every civil right for the establishment and protection of which organized government is instituted," but that only those aspects that fall within the scope of federal authority are protected by the 14th Amendment.[39]

It is time to breathe new life into the historical narrative that accompanies our understanding of the Privileges or Immunities Clause of the 14th Amendment. To do so requires reconsideration of Justice Miller's *Slaughter-House* opinion and resuscitation of the missing piece of the framework established by that opinion. In this respect, the view of its first interpreters in the Congress would be recognized as consonant with the first interpretation of the Clause given by the Supreme Court. Restoration of federal statutory rights will result.

I appreciate assistance from my colleagues, Jeff Jackson and Bill Merkel, who provided helpful feedback during the preparation of this article. I am also grateful for the support from Richard Aynes and participants in The University of Akron's 14th Amendment Symposium, with particular thanks to David Bogen for his insight and guidance.

An earlier version of this chapter was published in *Akron Law Review*, Vol. 42 No.4, pp. 1111–27. Copyright © 2009 *Akron Law Review*. Used with permission.

8 The Legacy of *Slaughter-House, Bradwell,* and *Cruikshank* in Constitutional Interpretation

Wilson R. Huhn, The University of Akron School of Law

The *Slaughter-House Cases, Bradwell v. Illinois,* and *Cruikshank v. United States,* all decided between 1873 and 1876, were the first cases in which the Supreme Court interpreted the 14th Amendment. The reasoning and holdings of the Supreme Court in those cases have affected constitutional interpretation in ways which are both profound and unfortunate. The conclusions that the Court drew about the meaning of the 14th Amendment shortly after its adoption were contrary to the intent of the framers of that Amendment and a betrayal of the sacrifices which had been made by the people of that period. In each case, the Court perverted the meaning of the Constitution in ways that reverberate down to the present day.[1]

In these cases the Court ruled on several critical aspects of 14th Amendment jurisprudence, including (1) whether the 14th Amendment prohibits the States from interfering with fundamental rights; (2) how the equality of different groups should be determined; and (3) how much power Congress has to protect the civil and political rights of American citizens—in particular, whether the 14th Amendment authorizes Congress to enact legislation to prevent mobs or other private individuals from violating people's fundamental rights. In each instance, the Court narrowly construed the Amendment's constitutional principles of liberty, equality, and the power of Congress to protect civil rights.

I. *SLAUGHTER-HOUSE CASES*

In the *Slaughter-House Cases* the Supreme Court came to a commonsense result—the Court upheld a law that concentrated all of the butchering business in the city of New Orleans to a location south of the city limits in an area controlled by a state-created monopoly. The Court found the law to be a constitutional exercise of the police power of the state, a reasonable regulation protecting the public health. The Court could have rested its opinion solely upon this finding, as even the *Lochner* Court would likely have upheld the law on those grounds. But the *Slaughter-House* Court went much further, venturing into wide interpretation of the 14th Amendment, its Clauses, and its effects. In doing so, the Court practically eviscerated the Privileges or Immunities Clause of the 14th Amendment.[2]

The Supreme Court ruled in *Slaughter-House* that the butchers had no constitutional claim under the 14th Amendment because the constitutional right that they were asserting—the right to earn a living at an honest occupation—although a fundamental right, was not a "privilege or immunity of national citizenship" within the meaning of the 14th Amendment. The key to the reasoning of the Court on this point was that there is a distinction between state citizenship and national citizenship. The Court stated, "It is quite clear, then, that there is a citizenship of the United States, and a citizenship of a State, which are distinct from each other, and which depend upon different characteristics or circumstances in the individual." The Court then reasoned that fundamental rights do not arise from the fact of American citizenship; rather they arise from people's status as citizens of the several states. In reaching this conclusion, the Court relied on a pre-14th Amendment case, *Corfield v. Coryell,* in which Judge Bushrod Washington had defined the privileges and immunities of citizens of the several states as being

> ... those privileges and immunities which are, in their nature, fundamental; which belong, of right, to the citizens of all free governments; and which have, at all times, been enjoyed by citizens of the several States which compose this Union, from the time of their becoming free, independent, and sovereign, [and as including at least the following:] Protection by the government; the enjoyment of life and liberty, with the right to acquire and possess property of every kind, and to pursue and obtain happiness and safety.[3]

Relying on *Corfield,* the *Slaughter-House* Court identified our "fundamental" rights in the following terms, and placed their protection within the sole ambit of the states:

Th[is] description, when taken to include others not named, but which are of the same general character, embraces nearly every civil right for the establishment and protection of which organized government is instituted. They are, in the language of Judge Washington, those rights which the [sic] fundamental. Throughout his opinion, they are spoken of as rights belonging to the individual as a citizen of a State. They are so spoken of in the constitutional provision which he was construing. And they have always been held to be the class of rights which the State governments were created to establish and secure.[4]

The *Slaughter-House* Court asked rhetorically, "[w]as it the purpose of the 14th Amendment, by the simple declaration that no State should make or enforce any law which shall abridge the privileges and immunities of citizens of the United States, to transfer the security and protection of all the civil rights which we have mentioned, from the States to the Federal government?" To the majority of the Court, the answer was "no," but legal scholars almost unanimously agree with the four dissenters that the Court answered that question incorrectly.[5]

In reaching this result the Court ignored the straightforward language of the 14th Amendment. The first words of the Amendment state:

All persons born or naturalized in the United States and subject to the jurisdiction thereof, are citizens of the United States and of the State wherein they reside. No State shall make or enforce any law which shall abridge the privileges or immunities of citizens of the United States...

The framers of the 14th Amendment made state citizenship secondary to national citizenship. They provided that all persons born in the United States are American citizens, and that Americans are citizens of whatever state they happen to reside in. Yet in *Slaughter-House*, the Supreme Court turned that unmistakable hierarchy on its head, and as a result they consigned the fundamental freedoms that Americans rightfully regard as their birthright to the dubious protection of the states. After the *Slaughter-House* interpretation, our fundamental rights—freedom of speech, freedom of the press, freedom of religion, freedom of assembly, and all of the other privileges and immunities set forth in the Bill of Rights, as well as all of our unenumerated rights—were returned to the whims and prejudices of state constitutions, state laws, state and local police, state courts, and state juries for their protection.

In placing state citizenship over national citizenship, the *Slaughter-House* Court reflected the view of John C. Calhoun. In 1833, Calhoun had equated the idea of a citizen of the United States to a "citizen of the world...a perfect nondescript," and stated that people's rights depend upon being the citizen of a state or territory. Dissenting in *Slaughter-House,* Justice Stephen J. Field excoriated the majority for adopting Calhoun's view of the relative importance of state and national citizenship. In the words of Charles L. Black, Jr., the *Slaughter-House* Court "surrendered to Calhoun . . . the great heresiarch on the relative importance and worth of *national* citizenship (not very much) and state citizenship (nearly everything)."[6]

Even more seriously, the reasoning of the Court in *Slaughter-House* making a person's fundamental rights dependent on state citizenship and state institutions allowed future segregationists to base their political philosophy upon the theory of "states' rights." George Wallace could not have argued, in his January 1963 inauguration address as Governor of Alabama, that he had the power to protect and defend "segregation today . . . segregation tomorrow . . . segregation forever" unless he believed that such a question was a matter of state citizenship. Similarly, three months later, those who denounced the civil rights activities of Martin Luther King, Jr., and other members of the Southern Christian Leadership Conference in Birmingham, Alabama, as the work of "outsiders," relied upon the implicit belief that only Alabama institutions had the right and the power to address matters of constitutional importance in the State of Alabama.[7]

King responded accordingly:

> I am cognizant of the interrelatedness of all communities and states. I cannot sit idly by in Atlanta and not be concerned about what happens in Birmingham. Injustice anywhere is a threat to justice everywhere. We are caught in an inescapable network of mutuality, tied in a single garment of destiny. Whatever affects one directly, affects all indirectly. Never again can we afford to live with the narrow, provincial "outside agitator" idea. Anyone who lives inside the United States can never be considered an outsider anywhere within its bounds.[8]

Yet even today, the misconception that the States should have the final word in defining our fundamental rights holds influence in some quarters. During the 2008 presidential campaign, in an interview with veteran television journalist, Katie Couric, Republican Vice-Presidential candidate, Governor Sarah Palin expresses both her belief in the right to privacy and her understanding that the parameters of that right should be determined by the individual states. "I believe that individual states can best handle what the people within the different constituencies in the 50 states would like to see their will ushered in an issue [*Roe v. Wade*] like that."[9]

These beliefs and their tenacity in constitutional and popular interpretation may be traced to the Court's decision in *Slaughter-House* assigning responsibility to the states for the protection of a person's fundamental rights.

The immediate and principal consequence of the Court's ruling in *Slaughter-House* was to remove the Privileges or Immunities Clause as the safe harbor of people's fundamental rights. However, Americans proved reluctant to believe that the Constitution afforded no remedy when the states violated fundamental rights. Later in the nineteenth century, the Supreme Court turned to the Due Process Clause of the 14th Amendment as the textual home of our fundamental rights against state injustice. As semantically awkward and historically inaccurate as the choice of the Due Process Clause was, the word "liberty" nevertheless shone brightly there, and the Court began the long, slow process of "incorporating" people's substantive fundamental rights into the 14th Amendment—defining the nature and the scope of the rights that are "implicit in the concept of ordered liberty."[10]

But that victory is not without costs. Supreme Court justices have rightfully, and continuously to this day, objected that neither the text nor the history of the Due Process Clause justifies the theory of "substantive due process." For example, Justice Antonin Scalia has stated his belief that the Due Process Clause protects only procedural, not substantive rights: "The text of the Due Process Clause does not protect individuals against deprivations of liberty *simpliciter*. It protects them against deprivations of liberty 'without due process of law.'"[11]

In hindsight, it should not be surprising that the first substantive due process right recognized by the Supreme Court a century ago was "liberty of contract." In an individualistic nation of self-sufficient farmers and tradesmen, where government regulation was largely unknown, with a frontier that took three centuries to move from the beachheads along the Atlantic coast to the interior of Alaska— a frontier where the existence of government itself was barely felt—in this country of small farmers, ranchers, small businessmen, and adventurers, we might rationally expect an economic philosophy of *laissez faire* to arise.[12]

What is surprising—what should be surprising—is that the Supreme Court took so long to recognize and protect the non-economic political and social rights of American citizens. Even the specific provisions of the Bill of Rights listing the privileges and immunities of criminal defendants were not automatically applied against the States by the Court, as the framers of the 14th Amendment so clearly intended. Instead, the Court took decades to decide whether each of those specific guarantees should be considered inherent to 14th Amendment Due Process.[13]

The Court labored even longer to begin defining the enumerated and unenumerated substantive rights of personal autonomy, what the Declaration of Independence calls "the pursuit of happiness," that is protected by the word "liberty" in the Constitution. The Supreme Court first struck down a law because it interfered with the rights of parents to raise their children in 1923. The Court first enforced the 1st Amendment's prohibition on laws abridging freedom of speech and freedom of the press in 1931. The Supreme Court first upheld a person's right to freedom of religion in 1940. It took until 2003 for a majority of the Supreme Court to announce the simple, straightforward principle that people have the right to make "intimate and personal choices" involving sex, marriage, raising children, and living arrangements.[14]

Why did it take so long for the Court to recognize these rights? The answer to that question depends not only upon an understanding of *Slaughter-House*, but an understanding of *Bradwell* as well. I now turn to that case.

II. *BRADWELL V. ILLINOIS*

The Court decided *Bradwell* the same day as *Slaughter-House,* and the reasoning in *Bradwell* relied upon and reinforced the legal theories developed in *Slaughter-House.* But unlike *Slaughter-House,* in *Bradwell* the Supreme Court came to an unjust result.

Myra Bradwell was an accomplished legal publisher who stood for the bar in the State of Illinois. The Illinois Supreme Court rejected her application on the ground that she was a woman even though the state statute governing admission to the bar referred to "persons" and made no distinction upon gender lines. The Illinois Supreme Court ruled that the law had been intended to permit only men, and not women, to enter the legal profession, and it turned down Bradwell's application to be a lawyer.[15]

On appeal, the majority of the United States Supreme Court noted that Bradwell had no claim under the Privileges or Immunities Clause because, as the Court had just ruled in *Slaughter-House,* her right to earn a living was a fundamental right under *state* law, not *national* law, and accordingly she must look to the State of Illinois for redress of that right.[16]

It may be surprising to modern readers that the Court did not specifically discuss Bradwell's rights under the Equal Protection Clause. However, the Court had discussed Equal Protection in *Slaughter-House,* and it incorporated its reasoning into its opinion in *Bradwell.* In *Slaughter-House* the Court found "the one pervading purpose" of the 14th Amendment to be the protection of "the freedom of the slave race." The Court expressed the opinion that the framers intended the Equal Protection Clause to protect African Americans—but no other groups—from discrimination:

> We doubt very much whether any action of a State not directed by way of discrimination against the negroes as a class, or on account of their race, will ever be held to come within the purview of this provision. It is so clearly a provision for that race and that emergency, that a strong case would be necessary for its application to any other.[17]

Accordingly, the majority in *Bradwell* rejected Bradwell's 14th Amendment claim.

Justice Joseph P. Bradley's concurring opinion in *Bradwell*, however, articulated a different legal theory which has affected constitutional analysis ever since. Bradley concluded that the inequality of women is not simply a matter of the law of Illinois or even the law of man—it is the law of God. In a passage from his opinion which deserves to be repeated in full because it represents a prejudice that we must be vigilant against, Bradley stated:

> [T]he civil law, as well as nature herself, has always recognized a wide difference in the respective spheres and destinies of man and woman. Man is, or should be, woman's protector and defender. The natural and proper timidity and delicacy which belongs to the female sex evidently unfits it for many of the occupations of civil life. The constitution of the family organization, which is founded in the divine ordinance, as well as in the nature of things, indicates the domestic sphere as that which properly belongs to the domain and functions of womanhood. The harmony, not to say identity, of interest and views which belong, or should belong, to the family institution is repugnant to the idea of a woman adopting a distinct and independent career from that of her husband. So firmly fixed was this sentiment in the founders of the common law that it became a maxim of that system of jurisprudence that a woman had no legal existence separate from her husband, who was regarded as her head and representative in the social state; and, notwithstanding some recent modifications of this civil status, many of the special rules of law flowing from and dependent upon this cardinal principle still exist in full force in most States. One of these is, that a married woman is incapable, without her husband's consent, of making contracts which shall be binding on her or him. This very incapacity was one circumstance which the Supreme Court of Illinois deemed important in rendering a married woman incompetent fully to perform the duties and trusts that belong to the office of an attorney and counsellor....
>
> The humane movements of modern society, which have for their object the multiplication of avenues for woman's advancement, and of occupations

adapted to her condition and sex, have my heartiest concurrence. But I am not prepared to say that it is one of her fundamental rights and privileges to be admitted into every office and position, including those which require highly special qualifications and demanding special responsibilities. In the nature of things it is not every citizen of every age, sex, and condition that is qualified for every calling and position. It is the prerogative of the legislator to prescribe regulations founded on nature, reason, and experience for the due admission of qualified persons to professions and callings demanding special skill and confidence. This fairly belongs to the police power of the State; and, in my opinion, in view of the peculiar characteristics, destiny, and mission of woman, it is within the province of the legislature to ordain what offices, positions, and callings shall be filled and discharged by men, and shall receive the benefit of those energies and responsibilities, and that decision and firmness which are presumed to predominate in the sterner sex.[18]

Justice Bradley's reasoning relies primarily upon tradition ("the civil law has always recognized a wide difference in the respective spheres and destinies of man and woman") and religious doctrine ("founded in the divine ordinance") in concluding that women should not be permitted to serve as lawyers. It is this general interpretive strategy which continues to hamper and constrain analysis of the Equal Protection Clause. Compare Justice Bradley's reasoning in *Bradwell* with that of Chief Justice Warren Burger a century later in *Bowers v. Hardwick*, a gay rights case:

As the Court notes, the proscriptions against sodomy have very "ancient roots." Decisions of individuals relating to homosexual conduct have been subject to state intervention throughout the history of Western civilization. Condemnation of those practices is firmly rooted in Judeao-Christian moral and ethical standards. Homosexual sodomy was a capital crime under Roman law. See *Code Theod.* 9.7.6; *Code Just.* 9.9.31. See also D. Bailey, *Homosexuality and the Western Christian Tradition* 70–81 (1975). During the English Reformation when powers of the ecclesiastical courts were transferred to the King's Courts, the first English statute criminalizing sodomy was passed. 25 Hen. VIII, ch. 6. Blackstone described "the infamous crime against nature" as an offense of "deeper malignity" than rape, a heinous act "the very mention of which is a disgrace to human nature," and "a crime not fit to be named." The common law of England, including its prohibition of sodomy, became the received law of Georgia and the other Colonies. In 1816 the Georgia Legislature passed the statute at issue here, and that statute has been continuously in force in one form or another since that time. To hold that the act of homosexual sodomy is somehow protected as a fundamental right would be to cast aside millennia of moral teaching.[19]

Compare, as well, Justice Scalia's reasoning from his dissenting opinion in
United States v. Virginia (VMI), where he argued that the Commonwealth of Virginia had the right to exclude women from attending a prestigious state university.
Justice Scalia commenced his opinion with an inaccurate charge and an appeal to
history: "Today the Court shuts down an institution that has served the people of
the Commonwealth of Virginia with pride and distinction for over a century and
a half." The Supreme Court, of course, did not "shut down" the Virginia Military
Institute, it merely ordered the Commonwealth of Virginia to admit women to the
Institute. Justice Scalia repeatedly invoked "tradition" as justifying the state's egre-
gious gender discrimination, for example stating, "[the Court] counts for nothing
the long tradition, enduring down to the present, of men's military colleges supported by both States and the Federal Government." Justice Scalia closed his
opinion with a long quotation from "The Code of the Gentleman," a booklet that
VMI students had been required to keep in their possession at all times. This
booklet, which Justice Scalia apparently found reflected a tradition of "manly
honor," was filled with romanticized notions of etiquette towards women:

> A Gentleman ... Does not speak more than casually about his girl friend. Does
> not go to a lady's house if he is affected by alcohol. ... Does not hail a lady from
> a club window. ... [N]ever discusses the merits or demerits of a lady. ... Does
> not ... so much as lay a finger on a lady. ..."

Justice Scalia concluded:

> I do not know whether the men of VMI lived by this code; perhaps not. But it
> is powerfully impressive that a public institution of higher education still in
> existence sought to have them do so. I do not think any of us, women included,
> will be better off for its destruction."[20]

In his opinion in the *VMI* case, Justice Scalia summarized his approach to
constitutional analysis in this brief statement: "It is my position that the term
'fundamental rights' should be limited to 'interest[s] traditionally protected by
our society.'" More specifically, Justice Scalia explained:

> [I]n my view the function of this Court is to *preserve* our society's values regard-
> ing (among other things) equal protection, not to *revise* them; to prevent back-
> sliding from the degree of restriction the Constitution imposed upon demo-
> cratic government, not to prescribe, on our own authority, progressively higher
> degrees. For that reason it is my view that, whatever abstract tests we may
> choose to devise, they cannot supersede—and indeed ought to be crafted *so as
> to reflect*—those constant and unbroken national traditions that embody the

people's understanding of ambiguous constitutional texts. More specifically, it is my view that "when a practice not expressly prohibited by the text of the Bill of Rights bears the endorsement of a long tradition of open, widespread, and unchallenged use that dates back to the beginning of the Republic, we have no proper basis for striking it down."[21]

The "tradition" approach favored by Chief Justice Burger and Justice Scalia is entirely consistent with Justice Bradley's reasoning in *Bradwell.* Traditional understandings of liberty and equality effectively strangle emerging constitutional claims by groups which have been traditionally discriminated against such as gays and women. Similarly, tradition was also used to justify racial segregation in *Plessy v. Ferguson,* where the Court stated that in determining whether or not people could be segregated by race on trains, the State of Louisiana was entitled to act in accordance with "the established usages, customs, and traditions of the people."[22]

It took ninety-eight years for the Supreme Court to rectify its decision in *Bradwell.* As late as 1948, the Court sustained a state law that prohibited a woman from working in a tavern unless the tavern was owned by her husband or her father. The first time that the Supreme Court found any law to be in violation of the Equal Protection Clause because it discriminated on the basis of gender was 1971, in the case of *Reed v. Reed.* Other groups who have been traditionally discriminated against waited even longer for the Court to acknowledge their equality. Not until 1996 did the Court for the first time strike down a law because it discriminated against people on the basis of sexual orientation, and not until 2003 did the Court finally invalidate state laws making homosexuality a crime.[23]

A majority of the Supreme Court has now rejected the "tradition" approach to defining constitutional rights advocated by Justice Bradley in *Bradwell,* Justice Brown in *Plessy,* Chief Justice Burger in *Bowers,* and Justice Scalia in *VMI.* Justice Anthony Kennedy has stated, "[H]istory and tradition are the starting point but not in all cases the ending point of the substantive due process inquiry." In *Lawrence v. Texas,* the Court expressly adopted the language proposed by Justice Stevens from his *Bowers* dissent, stating:

> [T]he fact that the governing majority in a State has traditionally viewed a particular practice as immoral is not a sufficient reason for upholding a law prohibiting the practice; neither history nor tradition could save a law prohibiting miscegenation from constitutional attack.[24]

In place of tradition the Supreme Court has adopted a realistic standard for defining the concepts of "liberty" and "equality" under the Constitution. In defining "liberty," the Court now takes two factors into account: (1) How important is this behavior in the life of the individual—how "intimate and personal" is that choice? and (2) How much harm is this behavior likely to cause?[25]

Similarly, constitutional standards regarding equality are no longer based primarily upon tradition and certainly not upon religious teachings. The legal standard that comes closest to a realistic definition of equality was first announced in 1885 in the case of *Barbier v. Connelly*, in which the Court stated:

> Class legislation, discriminating against some and favoring others, is prohibited; but legislation which, in carrying out a public purpose, is limited in its application, if within the sphere of its operation it affects alike all persons similarly situated, is not within the amendment.[26]

The "similarly situated test" from this case has been widely quoted and used in Equal Protection cases. In his concurring opinion in *Railway Express Agency v. New York*, Justice Robert Jackson illustrated how to apply this realistic approach to Equal Protection questions. Groups of persons who are similarly situated must be treated similarly. Groups of persons may be treated differently only if there are "real differences" between them, and only if those differences "have an appropriate relation to the object of the legislation or ordinance."[27]

In the interpretation of the Constitution, we now stand on firmer ground than did the Court in *Slaughter-House, Bradwell, Plessy,* and *Bowers.* Tradition is still an important consideration in constitutional analysis, but it is not the only determinant, nor is it controlling. In assessing our constitutionally protected sphere of liberty to engage in certain activity, in addition to tradition, we look to the importance of the activity to the individual as well as to the harm that may result from the individual's actions. In defining equality, we consider not only tradition but also whether the group of people whom the law is treating differently is similar to or different from other groups in the context of the law being challenged. Most importantly, we no longer regard fundamental rights to liberty and equality as aspects of state citizenship rather than national citizenship. No longer are the States considered to be the repositories, and more frequently the graveyards, of human rights.

III. *UNITED STATES V. CRUIKSHANK*

In the third case, *Cruikshank*, the Supreme Court inflicted even more damage to the Constitution and to the cause of human rights than it had in *Slaughter-House* and *Bradwell.* The Court reached an even more unjust result, and its reasoning was even more twisted. This case weighed an appeal from the conviction of three individuals on federal charges resulting from the mass murder known as the Colfax Massacre. The underlying facts of the case and the miscarriage of

justice that the Supreme Court authored in their opinion reversing the defendants' convictions are ably set forth in Charles Lane's *The Day Freedom Died: The
Colfax Massacre, The Supreme Court and the Betrayal of Reconstruction.*[28]

Briefly, following the election of 1872, the Democratic Party of Louisiana
attempted to steal the election by means of fraud and intimidation. The Republican Party—African Americans and their supporters—resisted these efforts in
one parish by occupying the courthouse in Colfax. On April 13, 1873, a large mob
of whites attacked the courthouse and killed over 60 persons, mostly African
Americans, in cold blood, most of them after they surrendered. Only three of
the attackers were convicted,[29] and these three were not convicted of murder
but rather for violating a statute which Congress had enacted in 1870 that made
it a crime for individuals to conspire to interfere with any rights of American
citizens under the Constitution or under federal laws. The Supreme Court
reversed the defendants' convictions under this statute because the indictments
failed to sufficiently allege that the defendants violated rights protected under
the Constitution or laws of the United States.[30]

The Court began its consideration of the legality of the indictments and
resulting convictions with an extended discussion of the principal theory that
it had announced in *Slaughter-House* and applied in *Bradwell*—the distinction
between state and national citizenship. The Court stated:

> We have in our political system a government of the United States and a gov-
> ernment of each of the several States. Each one of these governments is distinct
> from the others, and each has citizens of its own who owe it allegiance, and
> whose rights, within its jurisdiction, it must protect. The same person may be
> at the same time a citizen of the United States and a citizen of a State, but his
> rights of citizenship under one of these governments will be different from
> those he has under the other.[31]

The Court elaborated upon this theory and concluded that citizens might
seek the federal government's protection from encroachments on their national
rights, but they must seek the state government's protection from violations of
their rights derived from state citizenship.[32]

The trial court had convicted the defendants on sixteen counts of the indictment which consisted of eight different charges relating to two victims of the
massacre. The first and ninth counts of the indictment charged the defendants
with interfering with the victims' right to peaceably assemble. The Supreme
Court concluded that Congress lacked the authority to protect this particular
right because it was a matter which was committed to the States:

The first amendment to the Constitution prohibits Congress from abridging 'the right of the people to assemble and to petition the government for a redress of grievances.' This, like the other amendments proposed and adopted at the same time, was not intended to limit the powers of the State governments in respect to their own citizens, but to operate upon the National government alone. . . . They left the authority of the States just where they found it, and added nothing to the already existing powers of the United States.

The particular amendment now under consideration assumes the existence of the right of the people to assemble for lawful purposes, and protects it against encroachment by Congress. The right was not created by the amendment; neither was its continuance guaranteed, except as against congressional interference. For their protection in its enjoyment, therefore, the people must look to the States. The power for that purpose was originally placed there, and it has never been surrendered to the United States.[33]

The third and eleventh counts of the indictment alleged that the defendants conspired to deprive the victims of life and liberty without due process of law. At this point, the Court, for the first time in constitutional history, invoked what has become known as the "state action" doctrine. The Court based this theory upon the previous distinction it constructed between state and national citizenship. The Court stated:

The very highest duty of the States, when they entered into the Union under the Constitution, was to protect all persons within their boundaries in the enjoyment of these 'unalienable rights with which they were endowed by their Creator.' Sovereignty, for this purpose, rests alone with the States. It is no more the duty or within the power of the United States to punish for a conspiracy to falsely imprison or murder within a State, than it would be to punish for false imprisonment or murder itself.

The fourteenth amendment (sic) prohibits a State from depriving any person of life, liberty, or property, without due process of law; but this *adds nothing to the rights of one citizen as against another.* It simply furnishes an additional guaranty against any encroachment by the States upon the fundamental rights which belong to every citizen as a member of society.[34]

In essence, the Court ruled that the defendants' convictions had to be reversed because the conduct of the defendants constituted *private action* and not *state action.* Accordingly, it was for the States, and not the federal government, to punish their behavior.

Other scholars and I have written about how the framers of the 14th Amendment were, in fact, primarily concerned with addressing the practices of racial discrimination by private parties and the many acts of private violence being visited upon blacks and their white allies in the South[35]—how Congress enacted statute after statute prohibiting that discrimination and punishing that violence[36]—and how Congress adopted the 14th Amendment with the avowed purpose of making that legislation constitutional. After all of their efforts—after the terrible struggle of the Civil War and the immense suffering their generation endured to bring a new birth of freedom to America[37]—the Supreme Court struck down the Civil Rights Acts adopted by the Reconstruction Congress on the ground that the Amendment had failed to give Congress authority to punish the acts of private parties.

The Court's interpretation interposing the state action requirement in *Cruikshank* certainly did not accord with the understanding of the framers of the 14th Amendment. The Republican members of Congress had articulated this principal theory: "Allegiance and protection are reciprocal rights." They believed that citizens owe allegiance to their government because (and to the extent that) the government affords them protection.[38] The framers enacted legislation to protect American citizens in their fundamental rights from interference either by the states or by private parties, and they adopted Section 5 of the 14th Amendment to remove any possible doubts about the constitutionality of that legislation.[39] The Supreme Court rejected the framers' political philosophy and interpretation of their handiwork when they ruled that the States, and not the national government, had responsibility for protecting citizens in their fundamental rights. The Court betrayed the intent of the framers when they declared the civil rights laws enacted by the Reconstruction Congress unconstitutional.[40]

The *Cruikshank* Court found that other counts of the indictment similarly failed to allege that the defendants deprived the victims of any federal rights. For example, the Court ruled that separate charges of the indictment were insufficient because they neglected to specify whether the defendants assaulted the victims because they voted in elections for national office as opposed to elections for state office, or because the indictments failed to allege that the defendants assaulted the victims "because of the race or color of the persons conspired against." The Court also found that some charges of the indictment were unconstitutionally vague.[41]

The cruel and heedless result reached by the Court in *Cruikshank* signaled open season on blacks and other racial minorities.[42] The decision in *Cruikshank* prevented the federal government from protecting black voters from violence. This initiated a shameful period in American history—the Jim Crow era—in which the Court was fully complicit. In numerous decisions between 1873 and 1927, the Court narrowly construed the constitutional rights of African Americans and other racial and ethnic minorities, upholding state laws that fostered racial segregation and other discriminatory policies. Not only did the Court refuse to enforce the principle of equality implicit in the Equal Protection Clause of the 14th Amendment, but it also refused to let Congress enforce this principle. In some cases the Court misconstrued federal civil rights legislation as it had in *Cruikshank.* In other cases the Court simply declared federal civil rights laws unconstitutional, usually invoking the state action doctrine it had formulated in *Cruikshank.* By this series of decisions the Court enabled state-sponsored segregation, inferior educational programs, "anti-miscegenation" statutes, lynching, and loss of the right to vote for African Americans.[43]

Not until 1938 did the Supreme Court, fortified with two justices newly appointed by Franklin Delano Roosevelt, begin to strike down the system of state-sponsored segregation that the Court had helped to erect. Not until 1954 did the Supreme Court, with five members appointed by Roosevelt, declare "separate but equal" to be inherently unequal and unconstitutional. And not until 1964 did Congress enact and the Supreme Court uphold major civil rights legislation, this time under the Commerce Clause.[44] And the legacy of the restrictions on Congressional action in behalf of fundamental rights continues to haunt constitutional law, with the Court now limiting Congress's ability to enforce fundamental and statutory rights against the states by relying on amendments that predate the changes made by the 14th Amendment.[45]

IV. CONCLUSION

The Supreme Court's decisions in *Slaughter-House, Bradwell,* and *Cruikshank* had a devastating effect on human rights under the Constitution. Our basic liberties were placed at the mercy of state laws and state officials. Equality was defined primarily by reference to tradition, a tradition which was all too often intolerant. And Congress was prevented from enacting legislation that would have protected people in their basic rights.

Thank goodness the reasoning of those cases has largely been circumvented or overruled. Even though *Slaughter-House* emasculated the Privileges and Immunities Clause, the evolving doctrine of Substantive Due Process has served to make both the Bill of Rights and the Right to Privacy effective against the States. Furthermore, our right to liberty is also no longer limited by tradition but rather depends upon how important an activity is to an individual and whether that activity is causing harm. Even though *Slaughter-House* and *Bradwell* eviscerated the Equal Protection Clause, limiting its application to race alone and defining equality as no more than traditional conceptions of human potential, today Equal Protection applies to all classes of persons and equality is measured realistically by reference to how similar or how different groups of people really are. As Thurgood Marshall admonished in *United States v. Kras,* "[i]t is perfectly proper for judges to disagree about what the Constitution requires. But it is disgraceful for an interpretation of the Constitution to be premised upon unfounded assumptions about how people live."[46] Finally, although the Supreme Court in *Cruikshank* commenced its practice of narrowly interpreting and striking down civil rights acts as unauthorized under Section 5 of the 14th Amendment, Congress has found other constitutional sources of authority besides the 14th Amendment which authorize it to adopt civil rights legislation, although the Court continues to seek ways to limit that power. The baneful legacy of *Slaughter-House, Bradwell,* and *Cruikshank* has nearly run its course.

An earlier version of this chapter was published in *Akron Law Review,* Vol. 42 No. 4, pp. 1051. Copyright © 2009, *Akron Law Review,* The University of Akron, School of Law; Wilson R. Huhn.

III. Never Losing Infinite Hope
THE PEOPLE AS FIRST INTERPRETERS

9 The Use of the 14th Amendment by Salmon P. Chase in the Trial of Jefferson Davis

C. Ellen Connally, The University of Akron

The 14th Amendment to the United States Constitution has been, since its inception in post Civil War America, the subject of controversy and debate. To legal scholars it is a "second American Constitution," the Amendment that altered the fundamental nature of federalism.

Although freed slaves were the ostensible beneficiaries of the Amendment, the first time the Amendment came before the Supreme Court, the parties seeking its benefits were not freedmen, but butchers in the City of New Orleans.[1] The resulting decision in the *Slaughter-House Cases* is one that is still debated and stands as a primary example of an unintended consequence of a constitutional amendment. Although historians and legal scholars have considered a number of the unintended consequences of the 14th Amendment,[2] one result, unforeseen by its proponents, has been totally overlooked.

While Sections 1 and 5 of the Amendment have been the subject of much litigation, Section 3 has been generally ignored as a remnant of the Civil War. On its face, Section 3 was enacted to disqualify from public office those who had taken an oath to support the Constitution and then joined the rebellion; a provision which was bitterly resented in the former Confederacy. In the minds of the framers of the 14th Amendment, it was in the best interest of the nation to place its administration, both state and national, in the hands of those who had never been in insurrection against it. If former Confederates were sent back to public office, they could arguably do by legal means that which they did not succeed in doing by virtue of the Civil War.[3]

Section 3 can be interpreted as a criminal sanction for engaging in rebellion; that is, the inability to hold public office can arguably be seen as a penal sanction imposed by the government for the act of insurrection. The section can also be seen as a disability imposed on those who had taken an oath and then violated the oath.[4] If found to be a punishment as opposed to a mere disqualification, similar to disqualifications such as age and foreign birth, Section 3 of the 14th Amendment would bar any criminal prosecution for rebellion by virtue of the Double Jeopardy Clause of the United States Constitution.

In the proceedings that came to be known as *United States v. Jefferson Davis*, a legal determination was required to establish whether or not Section 3 imposed a simple disqualification or an actual punishment. In 1868, a preliminary ruling in favor of the criminal sanction argument was utilized for the benefit of a most unlikely party—namely, Jefferson Davis, the former president of the Confederacy.[5] Could those who pushed for the adoption of the 14th Amendment, those who some historians consider the last vestiges of the abolitionist movement, have foreseen that the Amendment enacted to guarantee the rights of freed blacks would be used to free the man who symbolized the slaveocracy that the Amendment's framers so despised? And moreover, could they have foreseen that the person who utilized this unintended consequence would be Salmon P. Chase, one of the primary architects of antislavery litigation?

This chapter tells the unusual story of how Salmon P. Chase used the 14th Amendment, in particular Section 3, to obtain a result that was politically correct for himself and ultimately saved the nation from a trial that would have litigated the difficult legal problems that were at issue in the Civil War.

In the waning days of the Civil War, Salmon P. Chase, Chief Justice of the United States Supreme Court, began planning an inspection tour of the South. The exact reason for the trip has been a matter of conjecture, but it apparently stemmed from Chase's desire to learn as much as possible about conditions in that part of the country. This knowledge was pertinent to Chase since his judicial circuit included rebel territory. Of particular concern to the Chief Justice were the condition of the freedmen and the prospects of universal manhood suffrage, which Chase saw as a cornerstone of Reconstruction. The death of President Abraham Lincoln did not alter his plans. Before broaching the subject of his trip with President Andrew Johnson, Chase, a man noted for his organizational skills, learned that the U.S. Revenue Cutter Service *Wayanda* would shortly make a trip to New Orleans and was available to the Chief Justice and his entourage. With the blessing of President Johnson, Chase left Washington on May 1, 1865. During the course of the trip he wrote seven letters to Johnson describing conditions and making recommendations.[6]

Meanwhile, since the fall of Richmond in early April, Jefferson Davis, the erstwhile president of the Confederate States, had been heading west to continue the Confederate fight. His arrest was authorized under the military powers of the president in the form of an executive proclamation dated May 2, 1865 charging Davis as an accomplice in the murder of Abraham Lincoln and offering a reward of $100,000. Except for the proclamation arising from the assassination, there was no order to pursue or capture the Confederate president. General William T. Sherman wrote Chase on May 6, 1865 that "[t]o this hour the War Dept has sent me no orders to hunt for, arrest, or capture Jeff Davis."[7]

On May 10, 1865, Davis was arrested by Lieutenant-Colonel Benjamin Pritchard of the Fourth Michigan Cavalry in Irwinsville, Georgia. From Irwinsville, Davis was transported to Savannah, Georgia, and then to Hilton Head, South Carolina, where he was placed aboard the steamer, *William P. Clyde,* for the ocean voyage to Fortress Monroe, Virginia, a United States military installation. The United States government would hold him there pending the disposition of the immediate charge relating to the murder of Lincoln. While the steamer, *Clyde,* was in Hilton Head Harbor, it came alongside the ship carrying Chase and was "made fast" to his vessel. In a letter the following day to the president, Chase reported, "Gen[eral] Gillmore asked me if I wished to see [Davis]; but I said 'No, I would not let any of our party see him. I would not make a show of a fallen enemy.'"[8]

On that day in May 1865, Chase and Davis were literally "ships passing in the night," a happenstance of fate that caused the two of them to be at the same place at the same time. The two men could not have been more divergent in thinking and philosophy. Salmon Portland Chase was the architect of antislavery litigation in America, the so-called attorney general of the fugitive slave, sole voice of the Radical Republicans in Lincoln's cabinet, and now Chief Justice of the Supreme Court of the United States.[9] Jefferson Davis was the president of the Confederate States of America, champion of states' rights, the very icon of the institution of slavery in America, and now a defeated warrior.[10] It would be more than three and one-half years before the two men would meet face to face—in a courtroom in Richmond, Virginia.

Long before the conclusion of the Civil War, Chief Justice Chase, like countless others, had pondered the question of whether or not Jefferson Davis and other rebel leaders should be placed on trial for treason. General Ulysses S. Grant set the tone for leniency at Appomattox when he said, "The rebels are now our fellow countrymen!" Robert E. Lee was not imprisoned and his officers and men "were allowed to go free under parole by Grant's easy and generous terms of surrender, in which, as one knows by a careful study of the sources, Lincoln had a prior hand." Some Confederate leaders fled the country in what has been called the "flight into oblivion" and some few were imprisoned for brief periods of time; all went free without standing trial. The one great exception was the case of Jefferson Davis.[11]

Early on, Chase "foresaw constitutional and legal problems of a formidable nature that would hamper if not foreclose a trial" for Davis. Aside from the legal and constitutional implications, Chase undoubtedly considered the impact of his participation in any litigation in light of his own political ambitions, which were always uppermost in his mind. The White House always loomed on the horizon for Chase, and he never rejected the possibility of leaving the bench for higher office. Chase was a viable candidate for the presidency in 1860 and had allowed a committee to be formed to promote a bid to unseat Lincoln in 1864, even though he was serving as a member of Lincoln's cabinet.[12] Critics allege that even the Southern tour was designed to seek support for the 1868 Republican nomination.[13] When, early in 1868, Chase recognized the futility of his attempts at gaining the Republican nomination because of the growing strength of Grant, he strongly considered and sought the Democratic nomination for the presidency.[14]

Had Lincoln lived, it is likely that Davis would not have been pursued nor would he have likely faced prosecution.[15] Although there were public debates throughout the war regarding the possibility of charging Davis with treason,[16] from the early stages of the conflict Lincoln's attitude was that of sympathetic understanding toward the South, in general, and individual Southerners. In his last cabinet meeting, Lincoln voiced a desire to act kindly toward the enemy, and hoped that Davis would escape the country "unbeknown" to him.[17]

Originally, Johnson did not share Lincoln's compassion. From the earliest days of secession he voiced a desire to have at least the leaders of the rebellion punished. When he assumed the presidency, he maintained his vindictive attitude toward the South, commenting to a New Hampshire delegation that "Treason is a crime and must be punished as a crime ... It must not be excused as an unsuccessful rebellion." Johnson, however, gradually became more sympathetic and within months of becoming president adopted Lincoln's fundamental policy toward former Confederates.[18]

But the question was whether or not his newfound leniency would extend to Jefferson Davis, the former president of the Confederate States of America. Since their days together in the House of Representatives in the early 1840s, friction existed between Andrew Johnson and Jefferson Davis. Several Davis biographers attribute the animosity to a remark made by Davis on the floor of the House in 1846 in which he seemingly demeaned and held in ridicule the position of tailors. Since Johnson was a tailor early in his life, he was personally offended by what he thought was a disparaging remark about the working class. "[A]ll his life Johnson would be ultrasensitive about his humble origins and resentful of the planter aristocrats," symbolized by Davis.[19] Whether this personal dislike rose to a level of vindictiveness that would cause Johnson to treat Davis differently from other Confederates is open to debate. Historians continue to speculate as to

> whether Andrew Johnson truly changed during the spring and summer of 1865, moving from his angry denunciation of Southern aristocrats into an alliance with them against the antislavery people of the North, or whether his Reconstruction policies were simply a continuation of his old-style Jacksonian unionism. Johnson did not perceive himself as changing, though to the outside world he seemed to veer 180 degrees.[20]

The prospect of the victorious North bringing criminal charges against Davis or other rebel leaders was fraught with political and legal pitfalls. Prosecution of former rebels would go to the very heart of the constitutional question raised by the departure of the Southern states; that is, could states secede from the Union, and if they did secede, was secession treason? The Constitution is silent on the question of secession. Therefore, only the Supreme Court could give a definitive and final answer—an answer that has never been delivered by the Court. Supporters of Davis argued that Davis and other leading secessionists applied the "compact theory" of the federal government, a theory advocated by Thomas Jefferson and James Madison and their successors who saw the American government as a confederation of states.[21] If the question of secession came before the high court, Chase as Chief Justice would be compelled to take a position on the issue, a prospect not necessarily advantageous to any future presidential candidate.

Chase could hardly forget that the Court's 1857 decision in *Dred Scott*[22] laid the groundwork for the legal issues that fueled the Civil War and caused irreparable damage to the reputation and standing of the court and particularly Chief Justice Roger Taney. The Supreme Court was so widely distrusted by the moderate Republicans in the 40th Congress of 1867–1868 that the Court could easily have been the object of destruction rather than Andrew Johnson. Even with the four Lincoln appointments to the court, not even Chase could predict the outcome of a case that would force a ruling on the issue of secession. A decision that states could secede would mean that the 625,000 persons who lost their lives in the recent conflict died in vain. A trial of Jefferson Davis for treason would bring all of these issues to the fore, a fact that fueled Davis's desire to have a trial.[23]

Six weeks after the surrender of Lee, Davis remained at Fortress Monroe, Virginia, a prisoner of the military.[24] Northern newspapers bragged that "Davis can never escape" and compared his imprisonment to that of Napoleon at Elba and St. Helena.[25] In the early weeks of his detention, Charles O'Conor, a prominent New York lawyer, attempted to contact Davis to offer his legal services.[26] O'Conor, a "Democrat of pronounced states-rights and Southern sympathies,"[27] was "the acknowledged head of his profession in the United States."[28] The Governor of Mississippi offered to pay a fee of $20,000, but O'Conor declined the fee declaring "he desired to serve America by furthering prompt justice and would accept no financial remuneration whatever."[29] The Johnson administration, however, refused Davis the right to confer with counsel, even by letter. On June 15, 1865, O'Conor complained to Secretary of War, Edwin Stanton, regarding his inability to confer with his prospective client. In response, Attorney General James Speed indicated that the permission to have a personal interview with the accused was refused on the ground that "Davis was 'not in civil custody.'"[30]

While Davis's confinement was the talk of Northern and Southern newspapers during the months of May and June 1865, the nation's attention in terms of legal proceedings was focused on the trials of the Lincoln conspirators. With assassin, John Wilkes Booth, already dead, the Johnson administration proceeded to try the conspirators before a military commission, a procedure about which Chase voiced misgivings. Chase consistently stated that military commissions should not function as courts. The assassination had taken place in the District of Columbia where civilian courts were open and functioning and should be utilized. A year later, Chase, along with a majority of the Supreme Court would rule that when the civilian courts were open and functioning, civilians should not be tried by military commission.[31]

In the case of the Lincoln conspirators, the military court rendered speedy justice finding all parties guilty.[32] However, there was no evidence that Davis was involved in the conspiracy. At the conclusion of the proceedings, the proclamation accusing Davis was not withdrawn; he was not brought to trial on the murder charges nor was he set free. The Johnson administration intended to leave Davis in military custody with the intention of proceeding on the basis of treason. His continued presence in military custody, and a desire to have him tried before a military tribunal was at the urging of Secretary of State, William Seward and Secretary of War, Edwin Stanton. Attorney Speed and others in the administration had serious reservations on both the charge of treason and venue. These men thought Davis should be brought before a civil court if he were to be tried.[33]

Treason, the only crime defined by the United States Constitution, is enumerated in Article 3, Section 3:

> Treason against the United States, shall consist only in levying War against them, or, in adhering to their Enemies, giving them Aid and Comfort. No Person shall be convicted of Treason unless on the Testimony of two Witnesses to the same overt Act, or on Confession in open Court.... Congress shall have Power to declare the Punishment of Treason.

In 1790, Congress passed a statute providing for the death penalty upon a conviction for treason, and this law was in effect at the time of the Civil War.[34] But the acts of disloyal Northerners or adherents to the Confederacy did not seem to fit within the definition of "levying war" or "giving aid to the enemy" that was envisioned by the original statute. If insurrection amounted to levying war and was accepted as treason, hundreds of thousands of men, most of them youths, were guilty of an offense that carried a mandatory sentence of death by hanging. To the Congress, the old law was unworkable for the emergency.[35]

On July 31, 1861, Congress passed a law which provided that anyone found guilty of conspiracy to overthrow the United States government or to interfere with the operation of its law "shall be guilty of a high crime." The punishment was set at a fine not less than $500 and not more than $5000; or by imprisonment for not more than six years. This legislation provided the courts with alternatives to execution in case of conviction for conduct that some would argue to be treason and others would assert was insurrection and/or rebellion. The purpose of this measure was to deal with offenses involving defiance of the government, offenses which needed punishment, but for which the treason law would have been unsuitable.[36] Under an 1862 law—commonly known as the "Second Confiscation Law"—upon conviction for treason, courts were given an alternative to a mandatory sentence of execution and could, within their discretion, impose a sentence of up to five years in jail and a fine not less than $10,000. This statute also granted freedom to those enslaved by persons convicted under the act.[37] The purpose of the law was to bring the statutory provisions concerning treason into harmony with the existing emergency and to soften the penalty for the offense.[38] In the bond hearing for Jefferson Davis, the District Court Judge, John C. Underwood, observed:

> It is a little remarkable that in the midst of a gigantic civil war, the congress of the United States changed the punishment of an offense from death, to fine and imprisonment [Act July 17, 1862]; but under the circumstances it was very honorable to the government of the United States, and exhibited clemency and moderation.[39]

Shortly after Davis's arrest, an indictment for treason under the 1862 law was brought against him in the District of Columbia court, but no action was ever taken on these charges.[40] A trial in Washington would have had to rely on a theory of constructive treason since Davis was not actually present in the nation's capital during the war. Supporters of this position argued that the commander-in-chief of the rebel army was constructively present with all the insurgents who waged war in the Northern states and the District of Columbia. But "the government abandoned the doctrine of constructive presence as unconstitutional and advised that the proper place for a trial was in [Richmond,] Virginia," the capital of the Confederacy.[41]

The prospects of a trial in Richmond gave rise to concerns as to whether it was possible to secure a fair and impartial jury in the former capital of the Confederacy. The *Philadelphia Inquirer* was typical of many Northern newspapers that commented that a trial "in the hotbed of treason by a jury of sympathizing traitors would be a transparent farce." Questions about the potential pro-defense jurors in the South failed to consider the ability to obtain a fair and impartial jury in a Northern city, which would have a jury equally as biased for the prosecution. In the North, Davis was regarded as the arch traitor and demands for his head were widespread, far in excess of any other rebel leader.[42]

No matter what the outcome of a trial, the proceedings could prove problematic. A "not guilty" verdict would embarrass the government. A finding that Davis was not guilty of treason would imply that the Civil War was fought in vain. A "guilty" verdict of course would be attacked by Southern loyalists, and, if rendered by a jury with black members, would be condemned as a mockery, particularly in the South, and make the imprisoned Davis more of a martyr than he already was. These political realities, aside from the fact that Davis wanted to be vindicated in the courts, were the basis of Davis's persistent demands to be placed on trial. "Davis wanted his day in court so that he could broadcast to the country the legitimacy and virtue of his cause. As [he] saw it, any fair trial had to result in his vindication."[43]

A trial in Richmond did, however, provide one benefit to the Johnson administration, and that was the fact that Chief Justice Salmon P. Chase was the Justice of the Supreme Court assigned to Virginia. Under the system existing at that time, each justice of the United States Supreme Court, in addition to duties on the high Court, sat in a circuit court as a trial judge along with the local district judge. The presence of Chase as the trial judge, even in spite of his known reservations about the case, would surely add credibility to any findings on the guilt or innocence of Davis. But the unknown factor was the presence of Judge John C. Underwood, federal district judge for the Eastern District of Virginia, which included Richmond. Attorney General Speed did not think that Underwood was a suitable judge before whom to try Davis because of his temperamental partisanship.[44]

In August 1865, President Johnson notified Chase that he wished to meet regarding initiation of legal proceedings against the leaders of the Confederacy. Chase immediately came to Washington and met with the president.[45] However, Chase was deeply concerned about the propriety of the president talking to him about the case. "Chase heard [the president] out and then proceeded to deliver a short lecture on the impropriety of the executive discussing such an important matter of state as a treason trial with the chief of the judicial branch." Aside from the ethical questions of a judge discussing the merits of a case with one side of the litigation, Chase was plagued with the problem that he had no heart for the prosecution. He had never been a supporter of the Republican desire to render harsh treatment to Confederate leaders and hoped that the administration and Northerners would see the disadvantage of making a martyr of the president of the Confederacy through prosecution.[46]

Prior to a meeting with Johnson, Judge Underwood seemingly agreed with both Chase and Lincoln relative to avoiding any prosecution of Davis. Underwood "had previously taken the position that the great conflict had outgrown the character of a rebellion, and had assumed the dimensions of a civil war, and that sound policy and humanity demanded that the technical treason of its beginning should be ignored." But after a meeting with the president, Underwood reversed his position. He reasoned that his previous position was based on "overwhelming excitement of the times . . . thinking, perhaps, that his education in the principles of the Society of Friends and his former hostility to capital punishment had misled him."[47] Immediately after the interview with the president, Underwood proceeded to Norfolk, Virginia and gave the district attorney a mere three hours to prepare an indictment against Davis. The charges returned by the grand jury were made "in the precise language suggested by the President... with the limitation" that other influential Confederates were dropped from the indictment on the basis that it would be "improper to include... any but the most influential and guilty," namely, Jefferson Davis. This indictment was rendered under the Second Confiscation Act that provided only for imprisonment and fines and not the death penalty.[48]

While the government prepared its case, Davis remained in military custody at Fortress Monroe. On September 21, 1865, five months into Davis's incarceration, the Senate called on the president for information on the subject of a trial for the prisoner, but Johnson did not reply. On October 2, 1865, Johnson addressed a second formal letter to Chase relative to the prospective prosecution. Contrary to their earlier discussions, this time Johnson did not mention Davis specifically, but indicated that it may become necessary for the government to prosecute some high crimes and misdemeanors committed against the United States within the district of Virginia, and inquired whether the "district is so far organized and in condition to exercise its functions that yourself, or either of the associate justices of the Supreme Court, will hold a term of the Circuit Court there during the autumn or early winter, for the trial of causes."[49] This letter was the first formal indication that the government wished to proceed with a trial in civil court as opposed to a military court, even though the prisoner remained in military custody.

Chase replied that he was not prepared to hold court. By way of explanation, he pointed out that there was insufficient time between the opening of the Supreme Court term for the fall of 1865, when all judges were required to be in attendance, and the date proscribed for the opening of the district court, November 27, "for the transaction of any very important business." He further explained that a civil court could not function while martial law existed. Although Chase had a well-known distaste for military government, the basis of his refusal to hold court while military rule persisted was the provision in the Constitution regarding separation of powers; each branch of government is separate and cannot overlap in its functions.[50]

Indicative of the desire in the North to pursue charges against Davis, on December 21, 1865, the Senate made another request of the president to be "informed upon what charges, or for what reasons, Jefferson Davis is still held in confinement, and why he has not been put upon his trial." Attorney General Speed replied that during the crisis of the war, Davis, like any other insurgent, was taken into custody as a prisoner of war. "Though active hostilities have ceased, a state of war still exists over the territory in rebellion. Until peace shall come in fact and in law, they can rightfully be held as prisoners of war."[51]

On April 2, 1866, President Johnson issued a proclamation of peace declaring "that the insurrection which had existed in the States of Georgia, South Carolina, North Carolina, Virginia, Tennessee, Alabama, Louisiana, Arkansas, Mississippi, and Florida was at an end." Such a proclamation would have initially appeared to have ended military control, restored civilian government, and complied with the requirements set forth by Chase for the opening of the district court, but Chase was not satisfied that military rule had ended. He wrote a friend on May 15 that the proclamation "might be fairly construed as abrogating martial law, and restoring the writ of habeas corpus; but subsequent orders from the War Department have put a different construction upon it."[52]

On May 8, 1866, the circuit court of the United States of Virginia met at Norfolk with Judge Underwood presiding and a grand jury was impaneled and sworn for the purpose of bringing charges against Davis. This grand jury returned yet a third indictment against Davis stating the date of the offense as June 15, 1864. The earlier indictment that was returned the previous summer was "lost from the records of the court." This new indictment was again under the 1862 law, which provided only for a fine and imprisonment if convicted, and set forth traitorous intents and purposes on the part of Davis alleging that "with force and arms, unlawfully, falsely, maliciously, and traitorously did...levy, and carry on war, insurrection, and rebellion against the said United States of America."[53] The grand jury, presided over by Judge Underwood, allegedly included black and white illiterates. This fact alone was sufficient to enrage white Southerners, already sympathetic to the cause of Davis, and in their minds raise further questions about the propriety of Underwood acting as the trial judge.[54]

In response to this indictment, Davis's team of lawyers appeared in court in Richmond on June 5, 1866 on behalf of their client. They inquired when the case would be tried and asserted that their client's right to a speedy trial was being denied. By then, Davis had been in custody for 13 months. Once again, counsel for Davis indicated their willingness and readiness to go to trial.[55]

But the district attorney, Lucius H. Chandler was not present even when the case was continued to the following day in anticipation of his arrival. The prosecution was represented by an assistant U.S. Attorney, Major J. S. Hennessey who said that "in the absence of the district attorney, Mr. Chandler, the question could not be answered at once." The following day Hennessey stated that the government did in fact wish to proceed with the prosecution but they were not prepared to go forward on that date. His reasons were as follows: first, Davis was still in military custody; second, the attorney general was engaged in other business and not available; and finally, Davis was not physically strong enough to withstand a lengthy trial. Underwood, after making a statement regarding the defendant's improved living conditions, granted the request of the assistant district attorney for a delay and continued the case until the first Tuesday in October, when he believed that the Chief Justice and the attorney general would be available.[56]

Two days later, other counsel for Davis, Charles O'Conor and Thomas G. Pratt, ex-governor of Maryland, accompanied Attorney General Speed to Chase's residence in Washington to ascertain if he would consider bond for the accused. Chase reiterated that he would not act until the writ of habeas corpus was restored and military law had ceased in the South. A request to Judge Underwood for bond met with a similar response for essentially the same reasons; Underwood also stressed that he could not allow for the posting of bond because Davis was in military custody and had never been in the custody of the district court.[57]

By September of 1866, Chase was able to raise another legal roadblock to Davis's trial. Through a clerical error, the Judiciary Act of July 23, 1866 failed to set new circuit boundaries for the district courts.[58] Chase questioned whether the old allotments gave jurisdiction and concluded: "It is very doubtful, therefore, whether the Chief-Justice can hold any court in Virginia till after some further legislation by Congress, making or authorizing allotment to the new circuits."[59]

While Salmon Chase and John Underwood were both members of the Republican Party, their respective positions on Davis were symbolic of the split in the Republican Party relative to the treatment of former Confederates. Chase, considered a radical while in Lincoln's cabinet, now wanted to avoid the trial, extend mercy, and put the issue of the Civil War in the past. The War was over. The secession movement had been defeated. So why rule on the question of whether or not secession is treason? Underwood, formerly a moderate, now wanted to proceed with a trial and extract some form of punishment. Seen in light of today's standards, his partisan activities on behalf of the Republican Party would raise serious questions as to his ability to be fair and impartial in the *Davis* case. However, as will be demonstrated, the harsh treatment received by Underwood at the hands of historians with Southern leanings may be reflective of their impression of him as a Republican partisan and most likely colored their interpretation of his actions. Underwood also engaged in a number of questionable decisions that did little to endear him to the judicial district that he served.[60]

Born in Litchfield, New York in 1809, Underwood attended Hamilton College (Clinton, New York) and then went to Virginia to serve as a tutor for two years. He returned to New York to become a lawyer and later briefly returned to marry a former student, Maria Gloria Jackson of Clarksburg, Virginia (now West Virginia). Underwood was considered a Tammany Hall politician and practiced Free-Soil Politics. While living in Virginia before the war, Underwood made himself unpopular by attempting to preach abolitionist doctrines. In 1856, Underwood offered his assistance to William H. Seward for a possible presidential bid. He and Seward would become lifelong friends. With one or two other Republicans in the State of Virginia, Underwood attended the 1856 Republican Convention where he made antislavery remarks that further inflamed his fellow Virginians and caused him to be exiled from the state.[61]

Unable to return to his adopted state, Underwood remained in New York where newspapers "hailed him as the 'exile from Virginia,' a 'martyr to free speech'" and the "hero of Virginia Republicanism." As a result he enjoyed sudden fame in the North where he became a frequent and popular speaker on behalf of John Charles Fremont, the Republican presidential nominee in 1856. Speaking to large audiences, Underwood often appeared on the same platform as such major figures as Horace Greeley, and sometimes as the main speaker for the evening.[62]

"Shuttling between New York and Virginia in the late 1850s, [Underwood] had helped to organize the Virginia Republican party and had worked to provide northern funds for the establishment of Republican newspapers in western Virginia." He was among a small group of Virginia Republicans who attempted to host the 1860 Republican national convention in Wheeling, Virginia. Plans were proceeding in a very hopeful manner until John Brown staged his famous raid in 1859, causing the convention to be shifted to Chicago to avoid Southern hostilities. Underwood attended the 1860 Republican convention, once again as a supporter of Seward. When the bandwagon shifted to Lincoln, Underwood threw his full support to the nominee. This support and his active participation in Republican politics paid off. It was even suggested that he might receive a cabinet post. Instead, he was nominated to the office of United States Counsel in Peru.[63] Unwilling to accept the post and perhaps through the influence of Chase, Underwood was confirmed as Fifth Auditor to the United States Treasury on August 1, 1861.[64]

As a leader of the Virginia Republican Party, Underwood played a major role in the formation of the "restored government" of Virginia formed by the Union loyalists after secession, which led to the creation of the state of West Virginia.[65] In 1864, Underwood was rewarded for his service to the Republican Party by an appointment as District Court Judge in Richmond, Virginia. "First among many Federal judges that the South would learn to hate," Chase biographer Frederick Blue calls Underwood an "undisguised partisan Republican." Another Chase biographer and Civil War historian, John Niven, is equally as harsh when he comments that "Chase came in conflict with the corrupt and vengeful district court judge, John Underwood."[66]

Underwood's status as a Northerner, an abolitionist, and a Republican was sufficient to cause an immediate dislike among the residents of Virginia.[67] His disparaging remarks about the city of Richmond to a grand jury on May 7, 1867 did further damage to his reputation,[68] and his legal maneuvering gave his critics ample ammunition. In a case involving the confiscation of the home of Dr. William McVeigh, a popular doctor of Richmond who was the owner of a large and well-placed residence in the city of Alexandria, Underwood's actions do come into question. Under the 1862 Confiscation Act, Underwood, on the motion of the district attorney, struck the answer of the defendant McVeigh as "irregular and improperly admitted." He reasoned that McVeigh, as a Confederate, had no standing to file an answer or assert any claims and recorded that McVeigh was in default. The property was condemned and the federal marshal carried out the sale to the highest bidder and sold the real estate. "The transcript does not name the purchaser: but it soon appears that a title in fee was vested in Mrs. Maria J. Underwood, wife of the Judge." In November of 1864, Chase (acting as a circuit court judge with appellate jurisdiction over Underwood) affirmed Underwood's decree, allowing the case to proceed to the Supreme Court. A unanimous Supreme Court reversed the ruling, reasoning that allowing the order to stand "would be a blot upon our jurisprudence and civilization."[69]

The other matter that raised questions in the minds of former Confederates about the propriety of Underwood's rulings involved criminal cases and the use of the writ of habeas corpus, a legal remedy that was at the heart of Chase's antislavery litigation.[70] Underwood's rulings also involved the newly adopted 14th Amendment and specifically Section 3. Between the time of the adoption of the Amendment in July 1868 and the final hearing of the *Davis* case in December of the same year, Underwood heard three cases invoking the writ. The facts were essentially the same. Each of the defendants, all of whom happened to be black, were found guilty of various capital offenses in Virginia state courts and sentenced to be hanged. Once the 14th Amendment was ratified, the defendants alleged that their convictions were invalid as a result of Section 3 of the Amendment. It was their position that the judges who conducted their trials were former Confederates who fell within the disqualified class set forth in the Amendment, making their actions a nullity and the resultant convictions void. Underwood, acting alone and without the knowledge of Chase, ruled that "Section Three of the Amendment operated of its own force, at once, to remove every disqualified person from office; accordingly the trial had been invalid and the petitioner could not be held." Underwood granted the defendants' request for writs of habeas corpus and released the defendants.[71]

Upon learning of this ruling, Chase addressed a letter to Underwood on November 19, 1868, just prior to the final hearing on the *Davis* case, a hearing in which Chase would make a ruling involving the same section of the 14th Amendment. Chase admonished Underwood to cease such rulings until the two could confer on the subject. Apparently, Underwood took no heed. On January 14, 1869, Chase addressed another letter to Underwood questioning his conduct. Newspapers and the organized bar attacked the finding of the judge.[72] Based on Underwood's premise, every case tried by a state court judge, or for that matter any decision made by a public official who had been a part of the rebellion in any way, was deemed to be a nullity as a result of the disqualification section of Section 3 of the 14th Amendment, something the opponents of Underwood propounded was clearly outside the intent of the framers of the Amendment.[73] Here were black defendants that the white population of Virginia saw as convicted by a duly elected Virginia state court judge, whose convictions were set aside by a Northern Republican federal judge by virtue of his interpretation of the 14th Amendment. This intervention by the federal courts in state court matters was at the core of the arguments that caused the Civil War.

But yet, the disparaging remarks about Underwood and views of his decisions must be considered in light of the sources from which they were drawn. The report of the *Davis* case which appears in the *Federal Reports* was, according to the footnote "Reported by Bradley T. Johnson, Esq., and here reprinted by permission." Dunbar Rowland reprints the identical report in volume 8 of his work on the *Davis* trial. Rowland points out that Bradley was a member of the Virginia Bar and dates the report to 1876. It is unclear as to whether or not Bradley relied on a verbatim transcript of the proceedings to create his report. But as a member of the Virginia Bar, it must be assumed that he was a Southerner who would be more than likely to write with a Southern bias. 1876 was the year of the disputed election of Hayes and Tilden that resulted in the restoration of Southern control in the South. Is it possible that, after the election, the Republicans lost control of the official Federal Reports and suddenly a Southerner gives a "fair and impartial" report of the *Davis* proceedings and/or the decisions of Judge Underwood? In contrast, Albert Bushnell Hart, who wrote his original biography of Chase in 1899, is not critical of Underwood, nor is Schuckers, whose work on Chase was released in 1874. So any view of Underwood's actions in the *Davis* proceedings must be assessed in light of the available sources.[74]

In March 1867, Congress passed the corrective legislation that solved the problem Chase presented regarding the allotment of justices to the judicial circuits. With its passage, a major obstacle to the trial of Davis was overcome and counsel for Davis decided to force the issue of Davis's confinement by bringing their client to court on a writ of *habeas corpus* and compelling the government to either try him or allow him to post bond.[75]

But the government's case against Davis was in shambles. Attorney General Speed resigned from the Johnson administration in the summer of 1866. He was replaced by Henry Stanbery who refused to become personally involved in the prosecution. Stanbery had made no preparation of the case against Davis and had no plans of doing so. By taking the position that the Attorney General was only required to represent the government in cases before the Supreme Court, he avoided involvement in the *Davis* case and placed sole responsibility of its trial on special counsel, William Evarts. To strengthen the prosecution, Evarts secured the services of H. H. Wells, an expert criminal lawyer, and Richard Henry Dana. However, Evarts, like Stanbery, had little interest in the prosecution. Speaking to Dana, he said "It may be that the trial will take place at the end of November, more likely in May next, as likely as either, not at all."[76]

In a conference with Davis's lawyers in May of 1867, the government's lawyers "intimated to O'Conor that there would be no trial that term and that bail would be accepted." Probably recognizing the weakness of their case and the lack of public interest in continuing the prosecution, the prosecutors indicated a willingness to grant Davis his freedom, at least temporarily.[77] The fact that Evarts found that he alone was responsible for the prosecution and that he had only two weeks to prepare for a bond hearing may have contributed to this decision.[78] One also speculates as to whether or not the government lawyers hoped that Davis would leave the country. His wife and children were residing in Canada. Other former Confederates were living in England.[79] Allowing Davis's release on bond, with the hope that he would place himself outside the jurisdiction of American courts, would provide an easy solution to all concerned. This speculation becomes more plausible when the amount of the bond is considered.

Later that month, Davis was brought to court. The military transferred his custody to the court marshals and bond was posted in the amount of $100,000, one-tenth of the original amount offered by the same Northerners, led by Horace Greeley, who had lobbied so long to obtain the release of Davis. On May 13, 1867, after 720 days in custody, Jefferson Davis was released to the cheers of sympathetic Southerners.[80] The case was set for trial in the fall session.

But the case did not go forward in the fall. Just prior to the opening of the regular Richmond district court session in November of 1867, Chase notified Underwood by letter that the press of business in Washington prevented him from attending court. Fortunately for the prosecution, who was still attempting to prepare a case, the matter was postponed until the following March to suit the convenience of the Chief Justice.[81]

In March 1868, events in Washington further hampered the prosecution of Jefferson Davis. The impeachment trial of President Andrew Johnson was held between March and May 1868, and this trial required the attendance of the Chief Justice. In addition, Stanbery resigned from the position of Attorney General to represent Johnson in the impeachment trial. When Stanberry was reappointed by the president, Congress refused to confirm the reappointment and William Evarts became attorney general. But Evarts had also been an integral part of the defense team in the Johnson impeachment trial, so in the spring of 1868 he was hardly ready to proceed with the prosecution of Davis, even with the assistance of Wells and Dana.[82]

Unbeknownst to the defense, in early 1868 Evarts and newly appointed special counsel, Richard Henry Dana concluded that "before a trial could be brought, a new indictment must be found and that no trial should take place except before Chase." Dana was also convinced that the prosecution of Jefferson Davis should be abandoned. In a letter to Evarts dated January 25, 1868, he "urge[d] that the prosecution be abandoned.... Why should the U[nited] States voluntarily assume the risk of a failure, by putting the question of the treason of Jefferson Davis to a petit jury of the rebel vicinage?" In addition to legal problems that Dana had already pointed out with the indictments, time was running out on the indictments. The case had to be tried within three years of the offense. This meant that the government only had until April of 1868 to bring the case to trial. As a result, a Richmond grand jury brought a new indictment against Davis on March 26, 1868.[83]

This new indictment accused Davis of treason in the form of levying war against the United States for a period beginning May 2, 1861 to May 10, 1865 and was brought under the 1790 law that called for execution upon a finding of guilt. The less stringent laws dealing with treason and rebellion, that had been enacted during the war and that had been used in the earlier indictments, were ignored. By indicting Davis under the 1790 law that required execution, the prosecution may have been intentionally setting themselves up for defeat. Perhaps, they brought an indictment on a charge that they knew they could not win. Dana was doing his best to see that Davis never came to trial at all.[84]

On June 3, 1868, Chase arrived in Richmond prepared to commence the trial but, probably to his relief, no one else was ready. Not even the district attorney was in attendance. "[A] Mississippi lawyer read the agreement between Evarts and O'Conor postponing the case and there was nothing for the court to do but to concur." Since this date was just a month before the Democratic convention, in preparation of which Chase's daughter, Kate Chase Sprague, and friends were actively seeking to garner the nomination for Chase, it is probable that Chase would have rather been elsewhere. But neither would he have wanted to be forced into a ruling on the *Davis* case that would alienate Southern Democrats. In a letter dated June 3, 1868 from Richmond to Judge Milton Sutliff, Chase remarked that if he were president, he would "proclaim a general amnesty to every body of all political offences committed during the late rebellion.... I can see no good to come, at this late day, from trials for treason."[85]

While the prosecutors were manipulating the indictment, in July, the Democrats nominated Horatio Seymour for president, handing Chase another defeat in his bid for the White House. The Republicans nominated Grant whose prospects for victory were strong. Chase had alienated himself from the Republicans as a result of the impeachment, differing views on Reconstruction and his attempt to gain the Democratic nomination. If Chase wanted to have any influence on Reconstruction, he must do it from the Supreme Court. His former influence with the executive branch was now gone.[86] His prospects of ever reaching the office he so desired must have seemed remote.

Chase, who had stood on ethical principles early in the proceedings against Davis when he refused to talk to Johnson about the proceedings and made a wasted trip to Richmond, now engaged in his own manipulations. Just after the adoption of the 14th Amendment in July 1868, an associate of Charles O'Conor, counsel for Davis, had a conversation with Chase. Chase made it clear that he took the position that the disability imposed by Section 3 of the 14th Amendment constituted a punishment within the meaning of the law. If Davis were subjected to a punishment as a result of the 14th Amendment, no further punishment could be imposed by virtue of the Double Jeopardy Clause of the Constitution. According to Chase, the defense could anticipate a favorable ruling on a motion to quash the indictment, thereby disposing of the case on a procedural technicality. The merits of the case would not be reached. Section 3 of the 14th Amendment would save Chase from making a decision on the question of whether or not secession is treason.[87]

To add to the irony of Chase's interpretation of the Amendment and revelation of his prejudgment of the case, Chase biographer John Niven asserts that during the period between the adoption of the Amendment by Congress and its ratification by the states, Chase had attempted to have the Disqualification Clause of the 14th Amendment dropped on the basis that it was too harsh on former Confederate officials. This deletion, which would seemingly make the Amendment more palatable to the South, required a quid pro quo. Namely, Chase would require acceptance of impartial suffrage with property and literary requirements. This suggestion was not acceptable to the South and the suggested deletion was not pursued.[88]

On December 3, 1868, the Davis matter was finally ready to proceed to trial.[89] Ironically, the United States District Court now used the building that two years before housed the Treasury and Confederate executive offices. Whether the two judges, Chase and Underwood, were at odds as some authors suggest is difficult to ascertain, particularly in light of the harsh treatment that Underwood has received at the hands of Southern historians. The first order of business was a ruling on the motion to quash the indictment, the motion that Chase had suggested to defense counsel some months earlier.[90] It is possible, as was often the practice in circuit courts of the time, that the judges agreed to disagree for purposes of sending the case to the Supreme Court, which is what Chase biographer Hart suggests.[91] Is it possible that Chase anticipated an amnesty from the outgoing president?

The facts were not in issue. Davis provided an affidavit that he had taken an oath to support the Constitution in 1845 when he was elected to Congress. The Court took judicial notice of the fact that Davis had engaged in insurrection by virtue of his service as an official of the Confederate States of America, placing him clearly within the class of those disqualified by the Amendment. The sole question before the court was whether or not the disqualification was a punishment within the meaning of the law. If the disqualification was found to be a punishment, then any further punishment inflicted against Davis would be a violation of the Double Jeopardy Clause of the Constitution and he must go free.[92]

The courtroom was filled with people. All counsels were present and prepared to go forward. At the commencement of the case, the district attorney read a statement that the press of business in Washington kept William Evarts, the attorney general, from attending. During the course of the arguments, available accounts assert that Chase seemed to have forgotten Underwood was at his side. According to Davis biographer McElroy, "Underwood was so detested among Mr. Davis' counsel that O'Conor ignored his very existence, and addressed himself exclusively to the Chief Justice." However, McElroy gives no authority for his statement. The arguments continued for two days, with Chase denying several requests for recesses during the course of the arguments.[93]

The legal proceedings that commenced in a burst of retribution for the horrors of the war and the assassination of Lincoln had now dragged on too long. Former Confederates now served in the Congress. A new president had been elected. Chase likely understood that his chances of going to the White House were now behind him. It was time to close the judicial chapter on the Civil War. "To Chase, Johnson, and an increasing number of Northerners, punishing Jefferson Davis no longer seemed as important as it had in 1865."[94]

After completion of two days of oral arguments, Chief Justice Chase opened court for the purpose of rendering a decision on the motion to quash. He announced to no one's surprise that the Court could not agree. Chase voted to quash the indictment. Underwood voted to deny the motion. Since the two judges could not agree, the matter was certified to the Supreme Court.[95]

On December 25, 1868, President Johnson, with the impeachment behind him and the end of his term close at hand, issued a proclamation of general amnesty, which granted a full pardon for the offense of treason to all participants in the rebellion, which included Davis. "The outraged Senate demanded that he explain by what authority he acted, and he responded with a recital of the history of presidential amnesties from Washington to Lincoln." The amnesty proclamation declared "unconditionally and without reservation . . . a full pardon and amnesty for the offence of treason against the United States, or of adhering to their enemies during the late civil war, with restoration of all rights, privileges, and immunities under the Constitution and the laws."[96]

This effectively disposed of the criminal prosecution. On February 26, 1869, the Attorney General wrote to Davis's legal counsel that instructions had been given to enter a *nolle prosequi* as to all indictments "for treason alleged to have been committed during the late war and that his office had 'no information of any such prosecution' pending anywhere against Jefferson Davis." An unknown clerk made an entry in the journals of the Supreme Court in February, 1869 dismissing the request to certify the question of the motion to quash.[97]

Jefferson Davis was a free man. He lived until 1889 always wearing grey suits in honor of his beloved Confederacy. He never sought a pardon and persisted to his death that he would have preferred a trial which he felt would have vindicated him. In 1881, he published his memoirs in the form of his two volume work, *The Rise and Fall of the Confederate Government.*[98] Many Southerners, to Davis's chagrin, paid little attention to the book and in the North it was dismissed as the "ravings of an unrepentant traitor."[99] In 1978 at the instigation of then-Mississippi Senator Trent Lott, Congress passed a bill restoring the full rights of citizenship to Jefferson Davis. The bill was signed on October 17, 1978 by President Jimmy Carter.[100]

Chase continued as Chief Justice of the Supreme Court until his death in 1873. In the years following the *Davis* ruling, Chase steered the Supreme Court on a prudent and realistic course. He was well aware that the Republican-dominated Congress would take any opportunity to threaten the independence of the Court. Chase was a major figure in Civil War America. First and foremost, he was the architect of antislavery litigation. He is recalled as the governor of Ohio, Secretary of the Treasury, presidential contender, and Chief Justice of the United States. But it should not be forgotten that through a novel and ingenious use of Section 3 of the 14th Amendment, Chase saved the Supreme Court from having to make the ultimate legal decision regarding the American Civil War. He also denied Jefferson Davis the trial that he always wanted, a trial that Davis felt would vindicate him and his cause. Chase, through the use of Section 3 of the 14th Amendment, saved the nation the pain of making a decision on whether or not secession is treason. It is unlikely that any of the framers of the Amendment would have anticipated this result, but such is the nature of constitutional law.

An earlier version of this chapter was published in *Akron Law Review,* Vol. 42 No. 4, pp. 1165. Copyright © 2009, *Akron Law Review,* The University of Akron, School of Law; C. Ellen Connally

10 "Horror of a Woman"
Myra Bradwell, the 14th Amendment, and the Gendered Origins of Sociological Jurisprudence

Gwen Hoerr Jordan, University of Illinois-Springfield

On June 14, 1873, Myra Bradwell reprinted a short article from the *St. Louis Republican* in the *Chicago Legal News* announcing the U.S. Supreme Court's decision in her case. The article glossed over the import of the Supreme Court's interpretation of the new 14th Amendment and focused instead on the Illinois court's underlying decision to deny women the right to practice law. The piece had a pejorative tone because, three years earlier when Bradwell filed her appeal to the U.S. Supreme Court, Missouri had become the second state to grant a woman a license to practice law. By the time the Supreme Court rendered its decision in April 1873, five states and the District of Columbia had admitted women to their bars. The *St. Louis Republican*, a Democratic newspaper, readily chided its Northern neighbor:

> It seems very hard for some of the Republican States to learn a simple lesson in that liberality which they pretend to teach to others. Women, qualified for the vocation, are admitted to the bar in Missouri, without let or hindrance, and no shock to our social system has come of the practice. But the Republicans of Illinois appear to have the same horror of a woman that an old-fashioned Democrat once had of a negro.[1]

This short article reveals an important insight that challenges some contemporary interpretations of *Bradwell v. Illinois*. First, it points out what we know, but sometimes overlook, that the Supreme Court holding in *Bradwell* did not prevent women from becoming lawyers or practicing law. More importantly, however, it suggests that Justice Bradley's oft-cited concurrence–where he reveals his horror of a woman, writing that "[t]he harmony, not to say identity, of interest and views which belong, or should belong, to the family institution is repugnant to the idea of a woman adopting a distinct and independent career from that of her husband"[2]–perhaps did not reflect the dominant ideology of the day. Looking beyond the Supreme Court opinions, this chapter attempts to assess what *Bradwell v. Illinois* meant to Myra Bradwell and the women's rights movement.

Many scholars have well and thoroughly analyzed both Justice Miller's majority opinion and Justice Bradley's concurring opinion in *Bradwell*. Richard Aynes even crafted a hypothetical opinion for Chief Justice Chase, the sole dissenter in the case, as Chase died before he was able to write his own opinion. Almost every constitutional law casebook describes *Bradwell* as the second nail in the coffin of the 14th Amendment's Privileges or Immunities Clause. The casebooks explain that in *Bradwell*, Justice Miller reiterated the majority's holding in *Slaughter-House Cases* that the Clause only protected the privileges and immunities of national citizenship and that the right to work in one's chosen profession was not one of those privileges.[3]

Most casebooks also include *Bradwell* as representative of the Court's support for the ideology of separate spheres, citing Justice Bradley's infamous concurrence where he, perhaps too vociferously, espoused support for the "wide difference in the respective spheres and destinies of man and woman," and revealed his horror of a woman who acted outside of her sphere. This concept divided social roles based on gender, preserving the public domain for men and relegating women to the private, domestic sphere. These casebooks suggest, I believe mistakenly, that Bradley's perspective represented the dominant gender ideology that endured into the twentieth century.[4]

The most progressive casebooks and a number of additional legal scholars place *Bradwell v. Illinois*, I believe correctly, within the women's rights movement. Myra Bradwell was among the women's rights activists who immediately perceived the potential of the new 14th Amendment to emancipate women. She used her case to make a claim on the Amendment, hoping to secure an interpretation that its provisions granted women full citizenship rights, privileges, and obligations and ensured them due process and equal protection of the law.[5] By contextualizing the case within the women's rights movement, these progressive accounts suggest that Bradwell and other women's rights activists were involved in an assault on the separate spheres doctrine that was gaining some support. This context also allows us to see the connection between Myra Bradwell, Elizabeth Cady Stanton, Susan B. Anthony, and Virginia Minor and the strategy they pursued to use the 14th Amendment to bring women into the public sphere as full and equal citizens.[6]

Bradwell was a leader in the Illinois women's rights movement. She initiated her case at a time when the women's rights movement was beginning to divide over the issue of woman suffrage and the 15th Amendment. I contend that Bradwell was not part of that divide, but rather represented a third faction of the women's rights movement that pursued a comprehensive strategy of securing women's legal equality through affirmative rights claims. Bradwell and her followers maintained this strategy—even as the splintering factions narrowed their focus to securing woman suffrage and later abandoned what Ellen Carol DuBois described as their original "democratic vision."[7]

Bradwell never chose sides in the fight between the National Woman Suffrage Association, led by Susan B. Anthony and Elizabeth Cady Stanton, and the American Woman Suffrage Association, led by Lucy Stone and Julia Ward Howe.[8] Instead, Bradwell held fast to her democratic vision, maintained relationships with both groups, and developed her arguments in concert with those activists who were intent on establishing that the 14th Amendment granted women full and equal citizenship rights, privileges, and obligations.

I argue that, through her case, Myra Bradwell developed two legal innovations that would be invoked by other rights activists through the remainder of the nineteenth century and throughout much of the twentieth century, albeit sometimes in opposition to each other. The first was an argument that the Equal Protection Clause of the 14th Amendment should be applied to women.[9] The second was the introduction of a new form of legal interpretation that set forth the foundations of what would later be called sociological jurisprudence. As elite lawyers and justices were advocating an ideology that William Wiecek has labeled "legal classicism," which was based on the notion that the legal order was an "autonomous, determinate, natural, neutral, necessary, objective, and apolitical structure of principles and norms,"[10] Bradwell was adapting the ideology of instrumentalism to the cause of women's rights, crafting what I will call presociological jurisprudence arguments.[11]

To support these claims, this chapter is divided into three parts. Part 1 situates Bradwell firmly within the women's rights movement and asserts that she intended her case to advance women's rights beyond opening the legal profession to women. Part 2 sets forth the arguments Bradwell presented in support of her application for a law license to the Illinois Supreme Court. It demonstrates how Bradwell developed a line of legal reasoning that drew on the principles of instrumentalism but transformed its goal to one of social justice. Part 2 also describes how Bradwell asked the court to view the law within a broad social context, to consider the changing social and economic circumstances when interpreting the law, and to apply the law in a manner that would secure social justice. Part 2 further asserts that Bradwell's claim of sex discrimination was based, in part, on the Equal Protection Clause of the new 14th Amendment.

Part 3 sets forth some of the responses by the public and those in the legal community that supported Bradwell and other women's rights activists making similar claims. These popular responses were critical of the majority opinion and the endorsement of separate spheres articulated in Justice Bradley's concurrence. Part 3 argues that these criticisms cast doubt on the notion that the separate spheres doctrine was as widely and uncritically accepted as Justice Bradley implied. The chapter concludes with an assessment that this is neither a story of great defeat, nor one of grand victory.[12] Rather, this chapter suggests that Myra Bradwell's interpretation of the 14th Amendment and the tools she crafted in concert with other mid-nineteenth century women activists served as an important foundation for the incremental advances women secured over the subsequent 150 years.

I. MYRA BRADWELL AS A LEADER IN THE WOMEN'S RIGHTS MOVEMENT

Myra Colby Bradwell was a rights activist her entire life. Like many of the women activists of her generation, she was raised as an abolitionist. She was also among the first cohort of women who were able to take advantage of the opportunity to study in the seminaries and colleges that were newly opened to women. In 1852, at the age of twenty-one, she married fellow abolitionist and lawyer James Bradwell. When her husband opened his first law office in Chicago in 1855, Myra Bradwell assisted him in his practice. Within a few years, she determined to become a lawyer herself: "I came to find out that a woman could accomplish as much labor in the same lines as a man, and therefore, I concluded to read law."[13]

Bradwell interrupted her studies during the Civil War to join other Northern reform women in active support of the Union Army. She was president of the Soldiers' Aid Society, one of the organizations that provided medical services and supplies to wounded soldiers and relief to their families. She also was an officer in the Northwestern Sanitary Commission, established to assist in maintaining hygienic field hospitals and camps. Through these activities Bradwell and the other Commission activists learned how to establish and lead organizations to advance a cause.[14]

After the war, she began her fight for women's rights in earnest. Bradwell's first step was to establish a legal newspaper for lawyers and judges that prominently featured legal issues relating to women. Because some of the laws of coverture still applied, Bradwell petitioned the Illinois legislature for a special charter that allowed her to enter into contracts necessary for her to own and operate her own business. In October 1868, Bradwell founded the *Chicago Legal News*, the city's only weekly legal newspaper. Within five months, the Illinois legislature granted the paper a special charter to immediately publish all new laws passed at the end of each legislative session. It also deemed that the paper's publication of those laws was proper evidence of their content in court and that the paper was a sufficient method of publication of legal notices. The paper quickly became an important resource for lawyers and earned praise from lawyers and judges in Chicago and across the country.[15]

Bradwell published the *Chicago Legal News* for a year before she applied for her law license. During that year she became one of the leaders of the women's rights movement in Illinois and utilized her paper, with its large male readership, as one of her primary tools to advance the movement. Bradwell filled the *Legal News* with articles on the professional and political activities of women, prominently chronicling women's participation in the legal profession.[16] She also advocated for a number of women's rights law reforms, including woman suffrage and property rights.[17] One of her first successful legislative campaigns, which she conducted largely within the pages of the *Chicago Legal News*, was to secure the enactment of Illinois' second Married Woman's Property Act.

In 1865, the Illinois Supreme Court, like other states, ruled that the state's first Married Women's Property Act, passed in 1861, failed to grant women the right to own and control their own wages because they were not her separate property. Women's rights activists were engaged in a campaign to change these laws, and Bradwell led the charge in Illinois. During the paper's first year, Bradwell flooded the *News* with articles imploring the Illinois legislature to pass a second act that would deem women's wages to be their sole and separate property and even travelled to Springfield to lobby for the bill in person. She relentlessly pursued the matter until the legislature finally acquiesced with a second act in March 1869.[18]

During this time, Bradwell also participated in organizing the Illinois Woman's Suffrage Association (IWSA) and found herself in the middle of a fight among the leaders of the national suffrage movement. The IWSA was one of two woman suffrage organizations established in Illinois in February 1869. Bradwell was elected an officer in the IWSA, and her position brought her into contact with Susan B. Anthony and Elizabeth Cady Stanton, two of the national leaders who both attended and addressed the IWSA's founding convention. Bradwell and her husband were among those elected as representatives of the IWSA to attend the National Equal Rights Association Convention held three months later in May 1869. Bradwell again interacted with Stanton and Anthony at the Equal Rights convention, but like many of the attendees, disagreed with their decision to oppose the 15th Amendment if women were not included. This disagreement led to a well-studied split among the woman suffrage activists. Susan B. Anthony and Elizabeth Cady Stanton led the dissenting faction and established the National Woman Suffrage Association (NWSA) as an independent woman suffrage organization. Lucy Stone, her husband Henry Blackwell, and Julia Ward Howe responded by establishing the American Woman Suffrage Association (AWSA).[19]

Bradwell refused to take sides in the split. She was part of the coalition in the IWSA that kept the Illinois association neutral in the national fight during its first two years. Bradwell served on the executive committee of the IWSA and hosted its meetings in the *Chicago Legal News* offices. Bradwell was elected, along with her husband, and a number of others, to attend the AWSA's first convention in Cleveland in November 1869. However, the delegates' relationship with the AWSA was qualified. They were bound by a resolution, adopted unanimously by the IWSA executive committee, which required them to maintain a neutral position in the fight between the national suffrage factions:

> *Resolved,* That the delegates elected to the National Convention be requested not to identify themselves with any division that may exist among prominent workers in the cause in other parts of the country, or to participate in any action intended as antagonistic to any existing Woman's Suffrage organization.[20]

The delegates abided by their resolution. When Susan B. Anthony appeared at the hall in Cleveland, James Bradwell urged the leaders of the AWSA to allow her to sit on the platform and address the convention. Myra Bradwell was elected one of two Secretaries for the AWSA, but the IWSA did not affiliate with the association, and Bradwell did not agree to exclusive membership. At the first meeting of the IWSA executive committee after the convention, the delegates acknowledged the animosity that existed between the leaders of the two national organizations and expressed their desire to "promote harmony in the further-ance of the great object sought to be attached by both sections." They discussed the possibility of forming a Northwestern Suffrage Association as a means of bringing the other two factions together and then passed a second resolution that reiterated the IWSA's neutrality:

> *Resolved,* That while we sympathize with the objects had in view in the forma-tion of the National Woman Suffrage Associations formed in Cleveland and New York, we will not become auxiliary to either, until the difficulties between the two are settled.[21]

The IWSA preserved its middle position for another fifteen months. During that time, the IWSA steadfastly urged the two national associations to merge. It even persuaded both Susan B. Anthony and Lucy Stone to come to a meeting in Chicago in November 1870 to "review the contest." But the IWSA suffered its own division six months later that caused the Bradwells and five other officers to withdraw from the association and allowed Stanton and Anthony sympathiz-ers to take over the IWSA in April 1871.[22] The Bradwells, nonetheless, maintained their neutral position.

The fracture in the IWSA occurred over issues of religion and divorce. Bradwell and those who withdrew opposed the practice of "free divorce"[23] and were offended by a pamphlet written by Alonzo J. Grover and published by the Executive Committee of the Cook County Woman's Suffrage Association (CCWSA) that challenged the authority of the Bible.[24] Catharine Waite and Jane Graham Jones, the primary leaders of the CCWSA during its first years, both sympathized with Susan B. Anthony.[25] In 1871, just before the division occurred, and perhaps one of the acts that precipitated it, Catharine Waite was elected the new president of the IWSA.[26]

The defection was well orchestrated and dramatic. James Bradwell, as chair of the IWSA executive committee, called a meeting of the committee for April 18, 1871. Neither he nor his wife attended the meeting, but Elizabeth Babbit did. Babbit read a paper signed by the dissenters, declaring their withdrawal from the organization and explaining that their decision was based on principle. They cited Grover's pamphlet and the CCWSA's advocacy of free divorce, and accused Waite and others of attempting to "force us into a union with" the CCWSA. Bradwell, who at this point was already being accused of trying to destroy the family because of her attempts to become a lawyer, could not be associated with this publication or position. She and the others left and the IWSA fell firmly in the hands of NWSA supporters.[27]

Myra Bradwell remained committed to securing women's legal equality, including woman suffrage, and therefore maintained a relationship with both factions of the fighting national leaders. It appears that she and her husband had true affection for Lucy Stone.[28] Bradwell's relationship with Catharine Waite, Susan B. Anthony, and Elizabeth Cady Stanton was less personal, but, nonetheless, respectful.[29] Like Anthony and Stanton, Bradwell was fighting for more than suffrage. In a poem she read to the Illinois Press Association shortly after she left the IWSA, Bradwell outlined her law reform agenda. It included securing and advancing women's right to education, work, contract, guardianship, property, inheritance, and physical protection from a drunken or violent husband.[30] Bradwell was in the middle of her fight to secure her law license and open the professions to women when she delivered this poem—a fight she waged with the assistance of Waite, Stanton, Anthony, and a number of other women's rights activists.

The fight began just after Bradwell had secured the second Illinois Married Women's Property Act and in the midst of her suffrage activism with the IWSA (before the dissension). She closely followed the events in the neighboring state of Iowa where, in June 1869, Arabella Mansfield had become the first woman to secure a state license to practice law. Mansfield had studied law for two years in her brother's law office. Judge Francis Springer, known for his support of the woman's rights movement, had encouraged Mansfield to apply for her license. Although the Iowa law regulating the licensing of attorneys to the bar restricted admission to "white male persons," Springer admitted Mansfield to the bar, making her the first licensed woman lawyer in the country.[31] Bradwell prominently celebrated Mansfield's admission in the *Chicago Legal News*.[32] Myra Bradwell applied for her Illinois law license three months later, in September 1869. She applied in part because she wanted to practice law, but Bradwell also applied to advance the broader cause of women's rights.[33]

II. BRADWELL'S CASE AS A STRATEGY IN THE WOMEN'S RIGHTS MOVEMENT

Bradwell's application and subsequent lawsuit were part of her lifelong fight to secure women's legal equality. Bradwell was not a radical. She believed in liberal individualism, Christianity, and marriage. What she denounced was the concept of separate spheres and the laws, doctrines, and social practices that limited women's citizenship rights. Twenty years after she first filed her application, she was still angry at those who had openly questioned her ability to be a lawyer because she was a woman and chastised her for attempting to leave her rightful place as wife and mother. "All the wiseacres of the land," she explained, "made doleful prophecies concerning the end of my career ... [and] predicted that I'd wreck my family and break my hearthstone to smithereens." Two decades later it was still important to her to prove them wrong: "I often wish all those excellent folk who used to picture me as a fanatic destroyer of domesticity and the sweetness of true womanhood could see my two daughters and our home-life." Bradwell had never fought against marriage or motherhood, but she had always argued that being a wife and mother should not limit a woman's citizenship status or be a barrier to a woman working in her chosen profession. Bradwell wanted equal rights, not revolution.[34]

A. Bradwell's Equal Protection Argument and Her Contribution Toward the Development of Sociological Jurisprudence

Bradwell ultimately lost her case, but by her own assessment, her efforts helped to dismantle the doctrine of separate spheres and her legal arguments were an important contribution to the women's rights movement.[35] These arguments and her innovation in jurisprudence were all set forth in her case at the state level.[36] She developed the arguments in concert with other women's rights activists as the case progressed. Bradwell filed three briefs to the Illinois Supreme Court in support of her application for a license to practice law. Each one offered increasingly sophisticated arguments that incorporated and developed the contemporaneous events and arguments set forth by other women's rights activists.

The first brief accompanied her initial application. The brief was not required by statute but Bradwell submitted it along with the required documents, a certificate of legal study and proof of successful completion of the state bar examination. Because she was the first woman to apply for a license in the state, Bradwell wanted to reassure the justices that her application was legally proper. She stated simply that she met the statutory requirements and therefore her sex should not prohibit her from entering her chosen profession. She acknowledged that the governing statute used the male pronoun in its recitation of requirements to enter the bar, but argued that it was not an explicit requirement that the applicant be male. She cited as evidence the Illinois statute that specified "[w]hen any party or person is described or referred to by words importing the masculine gender, females as well as males shall be deemed to be included." Bradwell also cited other examples in the statutes where the court would have to interpret the male pronoun "he" to include women to avoid an absurd result.[37]

It was in Bradwell's second brief that she began to invoke arguments that included what would become tenets of sociological jurisprudence.[38] She wrote this brief in response to the Illinois court's initial denial of her application. The decision came in a short letter sent by the court reporter, stating that the court denied her application based on the laws of coverture. She used new statutes, other court decisions, examples of women's social progress, and her own special situation to argue that the laws of coverture no longer applied. She asserted that in light of these changes the court must reconsider and grant her application.[39]

Bradwell first asked the judges to consider the new laws and court decisions that granted women property rights as a changed circumstance that should affect their interpretation of the statute governing law licenses. Bradwell insisted that the two Illinois Married Women's Property Acts, passed in 1861 and 1869 that allowed women to enter into contracts and control their own wages, invalidated the rule of coverture. She also cited a number of court decisions in Illinois, other states, and in England, which she contended were precedents that supported the changed legal and social position of married women, specifically the condition that women could contract and engage in business dealing. Bradwell also reminded the court that the Illinois legislature had granted her a special charter to own and operate the *Chicago Legal News*. These arguments, using new statutes and court decisions as persuasive precedents to illustrate changed social and legal circumstances, became a common strategy of sociological jurisprudence in the twentieth century.[40]

Bradwell next asked the justices to consider the current social conditions when interpreting the Illinois licensing statute. She set forth these changes by describing the many advances women had made in public life:

> The doors of many of our universities and law schools are now open to women upon an equality with men. The Government of the United States has employed women in many of its departments, and appointed many, both single and married, to office. Almost every large city in the Union has its regularly admitted female physicians.... The bar itself is not without its women lawyers, both single and married.

Bradwell then described the details of Arabella Mansfield's law license application and Judge Springer's interpretation that the use of the word "male" in the Iowa statute was "not an implied denial of the right to females." Bradwell offered both Mansfield's admission and Springer's interpretation of the Iowa statute as precedent-setting changes in the social and legal position of women and asked the court to interpret and apply the Illinois law to her case in line with these changes.[41]

Bradwell developed her argument by drawing on the strategies of instrumentalism that had developed during the antebellum period and were being challenged by legal classicists. Legal classicism was the form of judicial interpretation that believed the Constitution was based on "concepts and principles [that] were static and unchanging" and required judges to interpret the Constitution based on the original intent of those who drafted and enacted it. Legal classicism opposed the early nineteenth century practice of some state court judges who had used the law to advance economic policies that supported entrepreneurial growth and expansion, interpreting the laws in light of the current social and economic circumstances.[42] In opposition to legal classicism, Bradwell invoked the strategy of the instrumentalists, but transformed their ends to advance a nascent notion of social justice. She urged the court to interpret the law in light of the changed social conditions of women and grant her a license to practice law "as a matter of right and justice."[43]

The connection between Bradwell's arguments and instrumentalism is explicit in her brief. She specifically invoked the words of the instrumentalist English jurist, Lord Mansfield, citing a case where Mansfield had ruled that regardless of the prescriptions of common law there were exceptions when a married woman could contract and be sued. Lord Mansfield intended his decision to advance the free market, not woman's rights, but Bradwell contended that his decision also supported the contention that the law must adapt to the changing social circumstances of women's position. She quoted Mansfield's assessment that when "the reason of the law [ceased], the law itself must cease; and that, as the usages of society alter, the law must adapt itself to the various situations of mankind." Bradwell merely changed the goal of the instrumentalist approach from economic expansion to gendered justice.[44]

These presociological jurisprudence arguments are echoed in the arguments of justices and legal scholars credited with developing concepts of sociological jurisprudence, legal realism, and living constitutionalism. In the last two decades of the nineteenth century, Oliver Wendell Holmes, (who some call the father of legal realism) published treatises challenging the notion of legal interpretation as objective and detached from social realities. In the first decade of the twentieth century, Roscoe Pound conceived the term "sociological jurisprudence," issued a call for "pragmatism as a philosophy of law," and advocated the concept that the law should be used to achieve social justice. In the 1920s, Benjamin Cardozo advocated living constitutionalism, explaining that the "content of constitutional immunities is not constant, but varies from age to age."[45] Although none of these men referenced Bradwell, their writings developed the arguments she set forth in November 1869.

Bradwell did not cultivate this reasoning on her own. She worked in consultation with other women's rights activists who were also employing this approach in attempts to influence the interpretation of various state laws and the new U.S. Constitutional amendments. Adam Winkler has identified that the New Departure strategy of women suffragists included arguments that the Constitution was a living document and that it be interpreted in light of the changed social and political circumstances. According to Winkler, Elizabeth Cady Stanton publicly articulated this position in January 1870 while testifying before the Senate Committee on the District of Columbia. She was arguing in favor of a petition to grant women suffrage.[46]

Stanton's arguments, like Bradwell's, described democracy and law as evolutionary. She first claimed that the underlying principles of the Constitution required that its provisions apply to all its citizens. She then offered examples of the changed social and legal circumstances of women and argued that these changes required that the legislature grant women the right to vote. Specifically, she cited the recent Supreme Court decision that held that when a foreign born woman married a man born in the United States, she became a citizen. Stanton reasoned that this means a woman born in the United State is already a citizen and therefore entitled to all the privileges and immunities of citizenship.[47] Although, like Bradwell, her arguments did not persuade her audience to grant the demand she sought, her arguments were important to the movement.

Both Bradwell and Stanton also supplemented their presociological arguments with a textual interpretation argument that Stanton described as the New Departure, which asserted that women were already enfranchised because the right to vote was one of the privileges and immunities of U.S. citizens protected by the 14th Amendment. Ellen Carol DuBois credits Frances and Virginia Minor with the origins of the New Departure argument, first publicly articulated in six resolutions at a state suffrage convention in Missouri. On October 28, 1869, Anthony published their resolutions in *The Revolution* and delivered ten thousand copies to activists and politicians throughout the country.[48]

Myra Bradwell drew on their argument and adapted it for use in her own case. On December 31, 1869 she submitted her third and final brief to the Illinois

Supreme Court, this time resting a woman's right to practice law on the Privileges and Immunities Clause of Article 4 and the Civil Rights Act of 1866. Unlike the Minors, and the argument her attorney would make on her appeal, Bradwell did not make a claim based on the Privileges or Immunities Clause of the 14th Amendment. Rather, she asserted that the denial of her application on the basis of her status as a married woman violated her United States citizenship rights established by the Equal Protection Clause of the 14th Amendment and the 1866 Civil Rights Act. Like Minor, she argued that the court should employ a broad interpretation of the new laws.[49]

In her brief, Bradwell drew heavily on both the Equal Protection Clause and the Civil Rights Act. She argued that the Act guaranteed all United States citizens the "full and equal benefit of all laws and proceedings for the security of persons and property." Bradwell asserted both the Act and the Equal Protection Clause granted her "the right to exercise and follow the profession of an attorney-at-law upon the same terms, conditions and restrictions as are applied to and imposed upon every other citizen of the State of Illinois and none other." Bradwell reasoned that because she complied with all of the state requirements for admission to the bar, "it is contrary to the true intent and meaning of said amendment and said 'Civil Rights Bill,' for your petitioner to be refused a license to practice law, upon the sole ground of her 'married condition.'" Although she rested her case on alternate constitutional and legal provisions, her argument followed the New Departure reasoning.[50]

She also made a claim based on the Privileges and Immunities Clause of the 4th Article of the Constitution, again asking the court to employ a broad interpretation of that Clause. She submitted an affidavit attesting that she was born in Vermont and argued she was therefore a citizen of that state and the United States. She asserted that under this Article as a citizen of another state, Illinois was required to grant her all the privileges and immunities of a United States citizen. She then listed her assessment of what rights were included in the privileges and immunities of citizenship, a list dramatically different from the one the U.S. Supreme Court would construct in its interpretation of the Privileges and Immunities Clause of the 14th Amendment on her appeal. Bradwell's list included general rights, like "the protection of the Government, the right to the enjoyment of life and liberty, [and] to reside in the State." It also included rights that she had spent much of her adult life fighting to ensure were extended to women, including the right "to acquire and possess property," "to carry on trade," and her immediate fight "to follow any professional pursuit under the laws of the State." She demanded that these rights "must work equally upon all citizens of the State," concluding that "under this section of the Constitution she has a right to receive a license to practice law upon the same terms and conditions as the most favored citizen of the State of Illinois."[51]

Three weeks later, Elizabeth Cady Stanton made similar arguments in her appeal for woman suffrage. In her address to the Senate Committee on the District of Columbia on January 22, 1870, she employed Francis Minor's resolutions and argued that the right to vote was one of the privileges and immunities protected by the 14th Amendment. Like Bradwell, she used the changed social and legal circumstance of women and the evolution of the Constitution to support her call for this broad interpretation. Although both women lost their immediate appeals, their efforts introduced these new legal arguments into the public discourse. Other women's rights activists drew on their innovations in their continued fight for women's civil and political rights.[52]

An example that garnered significant public attention occurred one year later, when Victoria Woodhull employed these two innovations in her argument to the United States Congress in support of woman suffrage. Woodhull also introduced the concept of justice as both evidence of social change and as a legitimate legislative goal, claiming that "the principle of justice and moral right ha[d] gained sway" and demanding the Congress interpret the existing Constitutional provisions in light of these advances and pass a declaratory act acknowledging women's enfranchisement.[53]

Anthony used these arguments in her defense in the case of the *United States v. Susan B. Anthony*. Anthony had been charged with voting illegally. The judge presiding over Anthony's case deemed her incompetent to testify because she was a woman. Anthony, therefore, had her attorney, Henry Selden, speak for her. He set forth both the New Departure argument that called for a broad textual interpretation, and the presociological jurisprudence argument that demanded that the court consider the changed social and legal circumstances in interpreting the law. He challenged the ideals of legal classicism and the use of originalism that required judges to discern the intent of the framers and apply the law as if it were static. Like the others before him, Selden lost his case, but his arguments advanced the new methods of interpretation, which had for the first time been set forth by a man.[54]

Bradwell's direct influence is most visible in the arguments offered by other women lawyers who invoked her words in support of their own law license applications.[55] In the neighboring state of Wisconsin, Lavinia Goodell applied for a license to practice law before the Wisconsin Supreme Court in 1875. She offered a plethora of arguments invoking notions of equality as well as gender difference (that she asserted would enhance women's ability to practice law) and interwove arguments that employed classical legal reasoning, the New Departure, and presociological jurisprudence arguments. She asserted that the Wisconsin legislature had not intended to exclude women when it enacted the state's licensing regulations just five years earlier. She explained that the laws were passed "when progressive ideas concerning the enlargement of the sphere of woman's industries were more widely known and adopted" and reasoned that therefore it "may reasonably be presumed to have been within the minds of the legislators" that women would be admitted. She also cited recently enacted laws that advanced the legal position of women. Goodell lost her initial suit, but the case received considerable attention, primarily because Chief Justice Ryan's opinion articulated his horror of a woman in the same terms Justice Bradley had used two years earlier.[56]

The following year, Belva Lockwood took women's fight to practice law, and Bradwell's arguments, back to the United States Supreme Court and to Congress. She worked closely with Bradwell, who documented the events in the *Chicago Legal News.* Lockwood, who was already licensed to practice law in the District of Columbia, sought to be admitted to practice law before the United States Supreme Court. Chief Justice Morrison R. Waite rejected her application, noting that only men had ever been admitted to the Supreme Court bar and therefore precedent barred her admission. Using the new method of interpretation, Lockwood rejected his reasoning, asserting that "it was the glory of each generation to make its own precedents." She then took her appeal to Congress.[57]

Lockwood drafted a bill that granted women the right to be admitted to practice law on the same grounds as men and argued that the changed social conditions and the current position of woman required its passage. In 1878, the House of Representatives passed the bill but it stalled in the Senate. She submitted a brief to the Senate encouraging it to act in accordance with the demands of the age: "This country is one that has not hesitated when the necessity has arisen to make precedents" she wrote, "the more extended practice and the more extended public opinion [supporting women lawyers] . . . has already been accomplished." California Senator Aaron Sargent, a longtime supporter of woman's rights and a close friend of Susan B. Anthony's, took up Lockwood's fight.[58]

Sargent followed Bradwell's lead in his arguments to his fellow senators. He claimed that women were citizens and then listed the social and legal evolutions that had advanced their condition. He invoked the names of accomplished women from a diversity of occupations and professions, including women lawyers. He cited the state laws that had advanced women's legal rights, including the many states that already admitted women to their bars. He also submitted petitions signed by lawyers in both New York and the District of Columbia that supported women's admission to the Supreme Court bar, which supported Lockwood's claim that there was popular support for the bill. The Senate acquiesced and enacted the law in February 1879.[59] In a moment of great triumph, Lockwood was admitted to the Supreme Court bar on March 3, 1879.[60]

B. The Illinois and United States Supreme Court Decisions in Bradwell's Case

Bradwell lost her case at both the state and federal level. The Illinois Supreme Court rejected the arguments she set forth in her three briefs. The U.S. Supreme Court never even heard her arguments. Although Bradwell keenly suffered the defeat, these decisions did not dissuade the continued use and development of either the presociological arguments or the New Departure. They were not even definitive on the issue of women securing their law licenses. Rather, they represent both courts' attempts to stay the evolution of democracy that was moving toward the demise of the ideology and practice of separate spheres.

The Illinois Supreme Court discussed its fear of women's progress in its opinion. It first stated definitively that married or not, no woman could be admitted to the Illinois bar and summarily dismissed Bradwell's constitutional claims. Then, it rested the decision on its horror of a woman. The court was acutely aware and openly afraid of the woman's rights movement's quest for legal equality and the social upheaval that it believed would follow if the movement succeeded. Chief Justice Charles B. Lawrence explained that "this step [admitting Bradwell to the bar], if taken by us, would mean that, in the opinion of this tribunal, every civil office in this State may be filled by women; that it is in harmony with the spirit of our constitution and laws that women should be made governors, judges and sheriffs. This we are not yet prepared to hold."[61]

But there was growing support for women holding political office and working in the profession. Within two years, the Illinois legislature removed its barriers. The tide was turning and the justices felt it. Their pronouncements were defensive attempts to hold off the tide, rather than reflections of the general consensus. But the Illinois court dealt a significant blow to the movement and Bradwell understood this. She described the court's decision as a denial of women's citizenship. She charged, "what the decision of the Supreme Court of the United States in the *Dred Scott* case was to the rights of negroes as citizens of the United States, this decision is to the political rights of women in Illinois— annihilation."[62] Bradwell then took her case to the U.S. Supreme Court.

Bradwell did not represent herself in her appeal. Instead, she hired Matthew Carpenter, a well-known attorney, U.S. Senator, and woman suffrage supporter to argue her case to the United States Supreme Court. Bradwell wanted her case cast as a woman's rights case and framed in the broadest terms. She wanted the Supreme Court to rule that the 14th Amendment and the Civil Rights Act established women as full citizens entitled to all rights, privileges, and obligations of citizenship and to the equal protection of the law. But Carpenter did not comply with Bradwell's intentions. He did not consult with Bradwell prior to submitting his brief or presenting his oral argument before the Court.[63]

Carpenter was also the attorney for the Crescent City Slaughter-House company in *Slaughter-House Cases*. He argued in the *Slaughter-House Cases* that the law granting the monopoly was proper under the state police power. In Bradwell's case, he followed the argument of his opponent in the *Slaughter-House Cases*, former Supreme Court Justice John Campbell, and argued that the right to work, which he labeled the liberty of pursuit, was one of the fundamental rights included in the Privileges or Immunities Clause of the 14th Amendment. He did not present *Bradwell*'s argument that the Illinois court's denial of her law license violated the Equal Protection Clause of the 14th Amendment or the 1866 Civil Rights Act. Carpenter determined not to make any arguments based on gender equality and went so far as to differentiate the right to work from the right to vote. He blatantly argued against the New Departure and claimed that the right to vote was a political right, not a privilege or immunity protected by the 14th Amendment.[64]

Bradwell never commented publicly on Carpenter's concession that the right to vote was not included in the privileges and immunities of citizenship. She instead published Carpenter's argument in full in the *Chicago Legal News* and described it generally as an "able, concise, and unanswerable argument."[65] Leaders of the suffrage movement, were not so cavalier. Matilda Joslyn Gage wrote an editorial to the *Chicago Tribune* and described as "inconsistent" and "befogging" Carpenter's argument that the 14th Amendment granted women civil equality but not political equality.[66] Anthony wrote a personal letter to Bradwell describing Carpenter's arguments as "such a school boy pettifogging speech . . . wholly without basic principle," but she conceded "still the courts are so entirely controlled by prejudice and precedent we have nothing to hope from them but endorsement of dead men's actions."[67] Perhaps Bradwell remained silent on the point because she understood the difficulties of crafting an argument that would persuade the justices.

The U.S. Supreme Court took three years to render its ruling in Bradwell's case. When it did, it ruled against Bradwell, basing its opinion on the Privileges or Immunities Clause of the 14th Amendment. The Court made its decision in *Slaughter-House Cases* first, and then applied its reasoning to *Bradwell*. When the majority opinion by Justice Miller was read in open court—a decision which discussed its constitutional grounds but abstained from any comment of the issue of women's rights—there was no notable reaction by the audience in the courtroom. In contrast, when Justice Bradley's concurring opinion was read, with its emphasis on separate spheres and women's place, one reporter described that "it seemed to cause no little amusement upon the bench and the bar."[68] The implication is that Justice Bradley's horror of a woman was so out of step with the current sentiment that the audience considered it comical.

Bradwell offered her own assessment of the Court's decision in the *Chicago Legal News*. She respectfully disagreed with the majority's interpretation of the 14th Amendment—both in determining its construction and in its definition of the privileges and immunities of citizens—but she was livid at Bradley's concurrence. She pointed out the inconsistency between his dissent in *Slaughter-House Cases* and his concurrence in her case. "If, as Justice Bradley says, the liberty of pursuit is one of the fundamental privileges of an American citizen," she asked, "how can he then, and be consistent, deprive an American citizen of the right to follow any calling or profession under laws, rules and regulations that shall operate equally upon all, simply because such citizen is a woman?" She posited that he "lower[ed] the dignity" of his office "by traveling out of the record to give his individual views upon what we commonly term 'Woman's Rights.'"[69] The public response to Bradwell's case and to other women lawyers suggests that Bradwell was not alone in her assessment.

III. POPULAR SUPPORT FOR CHALLENGES TO THE DOCTRINE OF SEPARATE SPHERES

The Supreme Court and a number of state courts resisted various women's claims for legal equality and, specifically, their attempts to become licensed attorneys. But Supreme Court decisions do not always or necessarily represent public sentiment on the specific issue in dispute or those underlying it. In the case of women's fight for legal equality, and specifically women's right to practice law, the Supreme Court lagged behind a more progressive public sentiment. There were some state courts and legislatures that granted women rights, including the right to practice law, even as Justice Bradley pronounced that it was a violation of divine and natural law.[70] And there was evidence of significant public support for the women who sought to enter the profession.

The first evidence of public support for women's foray into the legal profession accompanied Arabella Mansfield's admission, the first woman who secured a state law license. Mansfield had the support of a number of members of the Iowa bar, including the male lawyers who administered her bar examination. They passed her with high honors and lauded her skill, noting that "in her examination, she has given the very best rebuke possible to the imputation that ladies can not qualify for the practice of law." They further remarked on the changed social circumstances that, they asserted, required her admission. They explained that they construed the Iowa statute controlling the admission of attorneys to include women despite its use of the word "male" as a response to "the demands and necessities of the present time and occasion."[71]

Support for Mansfield also appeared to extend beyond the activists that enabled her admission. The lawyers who examined her claimed that the committee's support for Mansfield was representative of all the lawyers in the state. "[W]e feel confident . . . ," they explained, "that we speak not only the sentiments of the court and of your committee, but the entire members of the bar, when we say that we heartily welcome Mrs. Mansfield as one of our members, and most cordially recommend her admission."[72] Further evidence of public support was set forth in the local newspaper, which asserted that Mansfield is a "lady of strong mind. That she has the brain and the necessary ability to make a good record for herself no one will dispute."[73] As the number of women lawyers grew, so it appears did the public's approval of their endeavors.

Those who supported women lawyers attempted to answer the two greatest concerns expressed by those, like Justice Bradley, who championed the doctrine of separate spheres. They argued that women were intellectually capable of professional pursuits. Simultaneously, they insisted that working outside of the domestic sphere would neither make the women unfeminine nor destroy the family. Therefore, a number of papers that reported on Mansfield's admission described her as "the grace and beauty of the Iowa bar."[74]

Alta Hulett had similar public support in Illinois in the early 1870s. A local paper described her in a way that was supportive of her ambitions and reassuring to those who feared women's rights would upset the social order. It observed she was "a charming young lady ... of more than ordinary personal attractions bright and prepossessing in appearance, and evidently in earnest in her purpose to acquire a profession," as she "was watching the progress of a case with as much interest as any of the legal gentlemen present."[75]

After Hulett passed the bar but was denied a license, newspapers around the country covered her story with an undertone of support.[76] A New Hampshire paper described the Illinois court as out of step with the modern times, noting "[t]he 'old fogy' Judges of the Illinois Supreme Court have [now] refused two applications of females [Bradwell and Hulett] to be admitted to the bar of that State."[77] Local newspapers increased their support for Hulett when she, with the assistance of Myra Bradwell and others, drafted a state law that would open all professions to women.[78] Hulett increased her popular support by lecturing throughout the state in support of the bill. She debuted her lecture "Justice versus the Supreme Court" in her hometown in northern Illinois where the crowds were overflowing and cheered often throughout her speech.[79]

These displays of support for the early women lawyers by members of their local communities and some members of the bar are not evidence that the ideology of separate spheres had been overthrown, but they do suggest that there was growing opposition to its constraints. As one newspaper described, women's efforts to practice law were "a new and most interesting phase of the great battle now raging along the entire of society between Progress and Prescription." There were those that would never change their minds. Bradwell herself acknowledged that "[n]othing save a blast from Gabriel's trumpet can dispel these lifelong prejudices."[80] But the naysayers, rather than representing the dominant sentiment, were speaking out against the changes that were taking place.

Reactions to Myra Bradwell's case by the press and members of the bar offered additional support for the changing public sentiment on the condition of women. First, as Nancy Gilliam has noted, the State of Illinois did not present any case in opposition to Bradwell's appeal. It did not submit a brief to the Supreme Court supporting the Illinois Supreme Court's decision nor did it send a representative to the oral arguments. Although Gilliam claims there is some precedent for this, "it was not customary for a state to treat a suit so cavalierly."[81]

Editorial comments in a number of newspapers offer further evidence that there was a growing sector that disagreed with Bradley. The *Chicago Tribune* claimed that Bradwell had the skills and intellect to be an attorney and described Bradley as "cling[ing] to the old idea of woman's sphere in life ...." Another report, written while the case was on appeal before Bradley rendered his concurrence, praised Bradwell for her efforts and expressed its opinion that public sentiment was on her side: "Mrs. Bradwell has done well to push her claims... [and w]e have not the least doubt that the next legislature of Illinois will remove the grievance under which this accomplished woman, and all her sisters in that state, now suffer."[82]

Lavinia Goodell, like the other women lawyers, also received significant support for her professional efforts in local and national newspapers. When she was first admitted to practice law in Janesville, Wisconsin, a Milwaukee paper noted the occasion and offered its support. It attempted to calm any horror of a woman fears its readers might have by editorializing that Goodell "possesses a pleasing and modest address." It also affirmed that she had sufficient "intellectual vigor to rank among the foremost of her profession." Other newspapers across the country noted the event without editorial, but without any negative undercurrent.[83]

Goodell also received broad public support after Chief Justice Ryan denied her application in an opinion that closely followed Justice Bradley's position.[84] Wisconsin attorney Ole Mosness published an editorial in the *Wisconsin State Journal* criticizing the court's decision. The Wisconsin press called the decision unjust and predicted that, "[t]here will be very decided dissenting opinions expressed by members of the bar and by the people...." A Milwaukee paper explained that Ryan denied Goodell's application based on a "law that is about a thousand years old." And finally, the *Journal* contended that if practicing law would place women's purity in danger, "it would be better to reconstruct the court and the bar, than to exclude the women."[85] On the occasion of her reapplication, one editorial despaired at the lingering prejudices that existed within the judiciary: "The prejudice of sex is the most imbecile, the least excusable, of all prejudices—and yet it is one of the strongest."[86] But the Wisconsin Supreme Court's subsequent admission of Goodell (Ryan was the sole dissenter) suggests that the prejudice had lessened.

Public support for women lawyers increased throughout the decade. By 1877 the *New York World* published an article encouraging women to practice law, especially in the Federal Courts. It cited Alta Hulett and Phoebe Couzins, a lawyer practicing in St. Louis, as examples of women "who have succeeded fairly, as well as men of equal mental caliber would have done, and this without ceasing to be womanly." "There can be no earthly reason," it continued "why women should not be admitted to compete with men in any occupation for which they are fitted...."[87]

Add to
Wiebe

By the 1890s, papers throughout the country commented on the increase in the number of women lawyers. They particularly noted that there were several women practicing who were members of the Supreme Court Bar. A newspaper in Bismark, North Dakota described these accomplishments and then editorialized, "[i]n a single decade the number of women lawyers increased from one to seventy-five."[88] None of the papers expressed any opposition or even discussed the issue of separate spheres; rather, there was a suggestion of pride in the way society had progressed.

IV. CONCLUSION

The evolution of Bradwell's early sociological jurisprudence arguments is complicated. Many scholars have identified Florence Kelley's work at Hull House in Chicago and as the executive director of the National Consumers League in New York to advance protective labor legislation as a significant contribution to the development of sociological jurisprudence.[89] Kelley first initiated these reforms for women and children with the intention of then expanding their protections to male laborers. As Rogers Smith explains, efforts to secure "protection for all and [maintain] a consistent, egalitarian liberal feminism, [had] proved to be inadequate, but there [was] no doubt that conditions of working women did urgently demand improvement."[90] Kelley and her colleague Josephine Goldmark developed the idea of using current economic and sociological evidence to enact laws that would limit the hours women laborers could be required to work, establish a minimum wage, and establish health and safety requirements for conditions in the workplace. Together they gathered the evidence and drafted the document that became known as the Brandeis brief. They convinced Louis Brandeis to argue their case before the U.S. Supreme Court and won a victory when the Court upheld Oregon's ten-hour work day law in *Muller v. Oregon*.[91] Roscoe Pound later labeled this strategy as sociological jurisprudence.

Part of this strategy initially required arguing that laboring women needed special protections, drawing on the old notions of women's delicacy. This appeared to be inconsistent with women's rights activists' demands for legal equality. Scholars continue to debate the cost and effectiveness of these reforms and the damage they did to the women's rights campaign.[92] These laws were at the heart of the second major split in the women's movement in the 1920s when protective legislation proponents bitterly fought with Alice Paul and the proponents of her proposed Equal Rights Amendment. They were also in conflict with women who brought claims of sex discrimination based on the Equal Protection Clause.[93]

But there were others who followed Bradwell's example and used evidence of women's social advances to support arguments for sex equality. In the 1880s and 1890s other women lawyers used Bradwell's argument about the changing social circumstances and position of women to secure entrance to other state bars and, as discussed, Belva Lockwood and her supporters used the argument to secure the 1879 federal law that allowed women lawyers to practice in the federal courts. Additionally, some women activists employed the strategy to fight for criminal laws and procedures that would protect women's bodies from physical and sexual abuse. In the twentieth century, women lawyers including Catharine Waugh McCulloch and Dorothy Kenyon used these arguments in their campaigns for women jury service.[94]

The Supreme Court considered only a very few cases in which women made a claim of sex discrimination based on the Equal Protection Clause in the century after *Bradwell*.[95] The Supreme Court's decision in *Slaughter-House Cases* that the Equal Protection Clause was limited to ensuring the rights of African Americans stunted women's initial invocation of the Clause. But the Court abandoned that distinction in its decisions on sex discrimination claims in the twentieth century. During the first half of the century, the Court rejected claims of sex discrimination based on the Equal Protection Clause by claiming that discrimination based on sex was not arbitrary, but rational, because men and women weren't equal. As Justice Holmes explained in *Quong Wing v. Kirkendall*, "the 14th Amendment does not interfere [with a law that makes a distinction in sex by placing a lighter burden on women than men] by creating a fictitious equality where there is a real difference."[96]

But there were those who disagreed, including women lawyers and an occasional dissenting Supreme Court Justice. In his dissent in *Quong Wing*, Justice Joseph Lamar argued that the Montana law that imposed a tax on men that did hand laundry work but exempted women, was an arbitrary distinction. He wrote, "[t]he individual characteristics of the owner do not furnish a basis on which to make a classification for purposes of taxation."[97] Justice Rutledge made a similar argument in his dissent in *Goesaert v. Cleary* in 1948, asserting that since the Michigan law "arbitrarily discriminate[d] between male and female owners of liquor establishments," it was a denial of equal protection.[98]

The sex equality decisions by Congress and the Supreme Court during the second half of the twentieth century are well-studied.[99] In 1963, Congress passed the Equal Pay Act that prohibited sex discrimination in federal salaries.[100] In 1964, Congress enacted Title VII of the Civil Rights Act that made it illegal for an employer to discriminate on the basis of sex. In 1972, Congress passed Title IX of the Education Amendments, which prohibited sex discrimination in education programs that received federal funds, and the Equal Rights Amendment, although it failed ratification. In 1971, the Supreme Court began to apply the Equal Protection Clause to overturn legislation that arbitrarily discriminated on the basis of sex, although it continues to debate what level of scrutiny to use in evaluating such laws.[101] Many scholars argue that despite these decisions, sex inequality persists.[102]

Myra Bradwell lost her appeal, but the Supreme Court decision in *Bradwell v. Illinois* should not historically negate the innovations she forged through her case. Her interpretations, encapsulated in each act she took in the process—from her initial application, her briefs to the Illinois Supreme Court, her appeal to the U.S. Supreme Court, and her prolific editorials on every aspect of her case and the cases of others—brought attention to the legal issues, garnered significant popular support for the cause, and advanced the women's rights movement. Through her legal arguments, she also initiated two legal innovations that became important tools in the fight for rights: crafting the foundations of sociological jurisprudence and forging the argument that the Equal Protection Clause should be applied to women. She drew on the ideas and assistance of other women's rights activists, men and women, to develop these innovations, and encouraged others to continue the fight. Over the subsequent century, the women's rights movement developed and implemented the arguments Bradwell initiated in her case. Their legacy, however, (and perhaps, of course) was mixed. Myra Bradwell's case and legacy is not a story of great victory, but neither is it one of great defeat.

An earlier version of this chapter was published in *Akron Law Review*, Vol. 42 No.4, pp. 1201–1244. Copyright © 2009 *Akron Law Review*. Used with permission.

This article draws on concepts the author presents in *Agents of (Incremental) Change: From Myra Bradwell to Hillary Clinton*, 9 Nev. L.J. 580 (2009), which details the development of a women's law reform faction within the women's rights movement beginning in the mid-nineteenth century and continuing to the turn of the 21st century.

The author wishes to thank Arthur McEvoy, Jane Larson, Eric Arnesen, David Kyvig, James Schmidt, Susan Levine, Katrin Schultheiss, Felice Batlan, Barbara Babcock, Barbara Welke, Dan Hamilton, Elizabeth Mertz, Stuart Macaulay, Mitra Sharfi, Laura Singleton, Risa L. Lieberwitz, Marianne Constable, Rima Schultz, the participants of the Northern Illinois University History Brownbag Series, the University of Wisconsin Socio-Legal Studies Brownbag, the UW Institute for Legal Studies Fellows Colloquium, and the Chicago Bar Association Alliance for Women.

11 14th Amendment Citizenship and the Reconstruction-Era Black Public Sphere

James W. Fox, Jr., Stetson University College of Law

All persons born or naturalized in the United States, and subject to the jurisdiction thereof, are citizens of the United States and of the State wherein they reside. No State shall make or enforce any law which shall abridge the privileges or immunities of citizens of the United States; nor shall any State deprive any person of life, liberty, or property, without due process of law; nor deny to any person within its jurisdiction the equal protection of the laws.[1]

Consider the first sentence of Section 1 of the 14th Amendment. The non-legal reader might quite reasonably say that such an introductory and framing sentence indicates that the Amendment is about citizenship. Such a reading would be reinforced by moving to the second sentence, which gives lexical priority to the concepts of citizenship privileges and immunities in its list of protected areas. And the reader who bothered to go deeper into the Amendment—indeed, deeper than many lawyers and law professors ever do—would surely find confirmation of the importance of citizenship in Section 2 (addressing citizenship in its somewhat convoluted linkage between congressional apportionment and the voting rights of black male citizens),[2] and Section 3 (enforcing a form of citizenship allegiance by barring members of the confederacy who had previously served in the government of the United States or any state from serving in any state or federal position after the war).[3] The reader might even note that citizenship continues to be the topic of the ensuing 15th Amendment, ratified only two years later, which more directly prohibited abridgment on the basis of race of "[t]he right of citizens" to vote.

But constitutional law is not a normal interpretive enterprise. Sections 2 and 3 of the 14th Amendment, being more political than legal enactments, have had essentially no judicial or legal development. Even the first sentence of Section 1 and the ensuing Privileges or Immunities Clause have had relatively little play in the courts. With the single exception of the 1999 case of *Saenz v. Roe*,[4] the citizenship language of the 14th Amendment has practically no legal significance.

A few scholars have suggested ways of building some meaning around the citizenship ideas. Akhil Amar, for instance, has argued that the Citizenship Clause establishes that everyone born in the United States is "a free and equal citizen," and that the Clause helps empower the federal government "to dismantle the various nongovernmental structures of inequality that threatened the amendment's vision of equal citizenship." Rebecca Zietlow, carefully developing an idea first explored by Kenneth Karst, has argued that equal citizenship under the reconstruction amendments carries with it "rights of belonging." Such rights, Zietlow contends, are "more encompassing than the term 'civil rights,' [and] includ[e] rights that historically were not considered to be civil rights such as economic and social rights[.]" This idea of belonging is meant to capture and help "ensure inclusion, participation, and equal membership in our diverse national community."[5]

These ways of thinking about 14th Amendment citizenship do much to expand our understanding of the Amendment and the potential for governmental action at all levels. For example, a right of belonging arguably supports government programs that seek to develop and enforce a robust understanding of welfare rights, something that the more circumscribed view of traditional individual rights under due process or equal protection rubrics have failed to do. It also refocuses constitutional thinking away from rights that are primarily individualist toward a contextualization of individual rights with a focus on inclusion in a self-defining community in which the very act of inclusion enhances rights both communal and individual.[6]

Still, these approaches to equal or constitutional citizenship represent a starting point, not a conclusion. Taking up the invitations of these scholars, I will delve more deeply into the possible meanings of constitutional citizenship, but from a different angle.

I propose that the best source for meanings of constitutional citizenship will come not from traditionally originalist sources but from those who attempted to redefine citizenship in a more egalitarian and democratic manner and who established, both in word and in practice, meanings for citizenship on the ground. Although the analysis is somewhat in the tradition of the popular constitutionalism scholars,[7] I will borrow a framework from political and social theory: the theories of civil society and the public sphere. I do so because I think these theories capture—in ways often missed by both legal scholars and historians—the structure of nineteenth century social experience while at the same time connecting this experience to modern notions of politics and society.

After explicating some of the main principles of civil society and public sphere theory, I will analyze a particular form of civil society and the public sphere that I think reveals important aspects of democratic citizenship—the black convention movement. As we will see, this movement both enacted citizenship on the ground and engaged in a discourse about citizenship in the public sphere that presented alternative visions of citizenship. Ultimately, this experience shows how one essential aspect of citizenship is the creation of spaces for citizenship activities and engagement with the democratic public sphere.

I. CIVIL SOCIETY, THE PUBLIC SPHERE, AND COUNTERSPHERES

Originating simultaneously in Tocquevillian ideas of voluntary associations and Hegelian critiques of market capitalism, modern ideas of civil society stress the public yet non-governmental character of civil society.[8] Robert Post and Nancy Rosenblum, in an analysis of modern ideas of civil society, have defined it as the realm of social life characterized by "plural and particularistic identities"—"a zone of freedom for individuals to associate with others and for groups to shape their norms" and determine their own goals and operations.[9] The core idea is that civil society provides an activity-based, non-governmental arena for citizenship and provides "seedbeds" for a fully engaged citizenship.[10]

Civil society theory—even in its very divergent manifestations[11]—provides important insight on how democratic citizenship can exist and develop outside the immediate relations to the state. Civil society theory thus permits us to see the overlapping nature of the different aspects of citizenship, whether they be legal status (e.g., a person is a citizen of the United States), political activity (e.g., a person acts as a citizen when voting), or social (e.g., being a "good citizen" by contributing to the common good in a tolerant and civil manner).

Civil society theory is based on a concept reasonably well known at the time of the initial implementation of the Reconstruction Amendments—de Tocqueville's *Democracy in America* was one of the more popular works of the

1850s.[12] Civil society theory thus helps frame a better understanding of how citizenship was thought to exist contextually in the nineteenth century. The history of civil society, therefore, provides some opportunity to think more fully about democratic citizenship in law and culture and to investigate the ways in which freedom and equality can, and cannot, develop outside and alongside relations to the state.

Yet the theory's strength is also its weakness: the concept of civil society often bends too far away from the state, becoming seemingly oblivious to the government's role as a representative and agent of the citizenry. It is therefore also important to attend to the intersections between state and civil society, for it is here, most of all, where people are *citizens*.

Just as civil society theory provides a necessary corrective to ideas of citizenship by orienting us away from the thin conceptualization of citizenship currently associated with constitutional law, public sphere theory provides an essential perspective to civil society theory by orienting us back to the relationship both civil society and the citizen necessarily have with the state.[13] Theories of the public sphere center themselves on precisely the points where government and civic life intersect. As described by Jürgen Habermas, the public sphere consists of all places in our society where "something approaching public opinion can be formed," whether in the media, through elections, or in public fora,[14] and many of the actors are themselves organizations and structures of civil society.

Claims for citizenship, especially by the excluded, are made in the public sphere. In the battles over freedom and citizenship in the South after the Civil War, and in the women's suffrage movement, blacks and women sought to implement and redefine Reconstruction, often using the structures of civil society. The public sphere is where individuals come together in groups seeking recognition and rights as citizens, where the democratic benefits of civil society can be articulated to the legal and political spheres, where democratic critique can be maintained, and where political, economic, and social transformations can take place. While it may be civil society that provides the seedbeds for citizenship, citizenship qua citizenship can only bloom in the public sphere, for it is there that people assert their inherent equality and their status as full citizens, engaged in commerce, entertainment, and public activity on par with all others. This is why, in the decades after the Civil War, the public sphere was so hotly contested—defended by whites against claims of equal access by blacks, delimited by men against the incursions of women—and was generally the site of battle for equal and free citizenship.

Still, despite its more democratizing character, the concept of the public sphere, itself, has been shown to be problematic. Habermas' early construction of a bourgeois public sphere, which prized open debate among social equals, was a form of public sphere that is elitist and exclusionary and certainly not an adequate site for democratic critique of governmental, economic, or social subordinations. Nancy Fraser and others have pointed to the need to account for oppositional discourse and activity in the public spheres constructed within excluded or subordinated communities. With more historical attention to the development of social movements and subordinated groups, these scholars have identified "counterpublics" or "enclaves." This approach suggests the possibility of a plural public sphere, or what Robert Asen has described as a multiplicity of public spheres. Under this vision, counterpublics are sites where excluded or subordinated groups can develop and refine counterdiscourses, both to maintain and develop their own meanings and identities and, importantly, to reengage the dominant "public" sphere in a critical discourse. Within these counterpublics the democratizing value of the public sphere is imagined, and out of them come claims to citizenship and equality that in fact reform or transform the concepts themselves.[15]

The move to recognize multiple publics and to validate the publics and discourses developed in reaction to exclusionary, dominant publics is critical to being able to understand discourses about democratic citizenship during and after Reconstruction. As we will see, the dominant public discourse about citizenship failed to address many of the fundamental experiences and problems of black citizens, and the need for black citizens to engage in both public sphere discourse and alternative public discourses was essential.

Yet even the refinement of public sphere theory to include an essential pluralism needs to be reoriented back toward civil society and democratic citizenship. As Jeffrey Alexander argues, counterpublics, in their most important manifestations as vibrant social movements, "are oriented not simply toward gaining resources and power vis-à-vis the civil sphere but to securing a respected place within it." The universalizing rhetoric of democratic citizenship and democratic civil society retain an important critique that is lost in an excessive focus on counterpublics as purely sites of identity and community formation for the purpose of seeking power. Alexander sees a danger of reducing counterpublics to countercultures and falling into the trap of instrumentalism—of seeing political discourse as a battle of interests to obtain power rather than as a dynamic process of realizing, albeit necessarily imperfectly, a universalizing potential that is democratic civil society. We need to examine the ebbs and flows of this dynamic between the universalizing character of civil society and citizenship and the particularizing aspects of the essential formations of multiple publics and multiple civil spheres.[16]

Theories of civil society and the public sphere, therefore, offer a promising language for understanding the experience of constitutional citizenship in the years of and following Reconstruction, and these theories can themselves be rethought or refined by studying the experiences of claiming and implementing citizenship on the ground. I take up this period not because of some originalist desire to divine the understandings or intent of the framers and ratifiers of the Reconstruction Amendments (although African American understandings of citizenship are essential to any originalist project since the 14th and 15th Amendments were only ratified with the political participation of black Americans[17]). Rather, to give depth to the meanings of general political and cultural concepts such as citizenship, one needs, I think, to explore the lived experiences of the concept. In ways that can only happen on the ground, the battles over citizenship in the assertions of citizenship by African Americans and in the denials of that citizenship by white Democrats identified the key sites and experiences of citizenship. African Americans' experiences of trying to claim, define, and implement a free and equal citizenship after the war led them and some white Republicans to enact citizenship on the ground, and gave detail and meaning to vague constitutional language.

II. CITIZENSHIP CREATION DURING RECONSTRUCTION: THE LEGAL RIGHTS OF FREE LABOR

Many scholars follow historian Eric Foner's lead in arguing that Reconstruction Republicans adhered to a free labor ideology that identified freedom primarily with the right to earn wages. Thus in the Civil Rights Act of 1866, Republicans linked citizenship with the rights to contract and own property, and they repeatedly proclaimed the value of contract labor arrangements as the apotheosis of the new freedom and citizenship that they saw themselves granting to blacks. While there may have been a variety of Republican views on how expansive such rights would be, the basic thrust of congressional ideas of citizenship was that (male) citizens should have governmental protection of rights to contract, to buy, sell, and hold property, and to gain access to courts to protect those rights, all of which implemented the right of citizens to earn and support themselves with their own labor.[18]

In its specific listing of rights and privileges, the Act asserted and protected a collection of citizenship rights, including rights of contract, property, and access to the courts. To the modern ear, these are rather routine; but in the context of postbellum, post-slavery America, their centrality to creating a fully vibrant free, civil society was more directly evident. Take, for example, the right to contract. On one level it secured simply the legal right to transact and enforce agreements. Yet, in the context of the 1860s, this freedom to contract was fundamental. The country was developing into a modern force of industrial capitalism, and contract was one of the legal engines driving this transformation. Indeed, as Morton Horwitz argued in his classic discussion of the issue, "[t]he triumph of a contractarian ideology by the middle of the nineteenth century enabled mercantile and entrepreneurial groups to broadly advance their own interests through a transformed system of private law."[19]

Access to contract rights was the ticket to citizenship in the new capitalist economy. Congressional Republicans, by the very act of equating basic legal rights with freedom and racial equality, were redefining legal citizenship in a way that incorporated some aspects of the citizenship of belonging. They were in fact recreating a political society in which commercial norms such as free labor and free contract were the inheritance of each male citizen regardless of race, and in opening citizenship across race, Republicans were redefining citizenship to mean inclusion in civil society.

The Civil Rights Act of 1866 also secured property rights. Property was integral to self-sufficiency, and the goal of free labor, ultimately, was some ownership of property, both personal and real. Yet property, as Eric Foner has observed, represented a key ambiguity during Reconstruction. For white Republicans, property rights provided a means for securing productive, free-labor agriculture; while blacks might develop ownership of farms and plantations, the land itself was seen as primarily a productive resource that would replicate, in agricultural form, Northern capitalism. For the former slaves, on the other hand, land ownership created a zone of independence and privacy, a place where they need not work for former masters at depressed wages but could instead become self-sufficient, secure in their homes and their families, while also providing a means to bargain up wages for the labor they chose to sell.[20]

These differing views of property also reflected fundamental differences regarding civil society. For Northern Republicans, civil society focused significantly on the steering of labor toward economic productivity. This vision and commitment would be sorely tested in the coming decades as labor developed

Arguably the amendment didn't deal w/ these different concepts & allowed

its own views of civil society through labor unions and battled with many in the Republican Party, who shifted toward a predominantly industry- and business-oriented idea of civil society. But in the 1860s, it was still possible to maintain an egalitarian vision of free labor in which civil society and industrial labor were seen as unified.

For Southern blacks, however, wage labor seemed anathema to democratic civil society. The civil rights of contract and property were instead means of protecting and developing counterweights in civil society to the oppressions of post-slavery economic and political structures. Through the ownership of land and protections of access to the courts and enforcement of contracts, blacks could, it was thought, carve out spheres for families and churches, benevolent and economic associations, schools and newspapers, and could generally build community supports for their newly acquired legal citizenship.[21]

While the visions of civil society imagined by Northern whites and Southern blacks varied substantially, both understood that legal rights and legal citizenship helped create the possibility of black participation in civil society. It is important to see both the transformative and the restrictive aspects of the dominant citizenship discourse of Reconstruction. On one level Reconstruction really did present a radical transformation to ideas and realities of citizenship. The democratizing ideals of the Jacksonian era, in which white laborers had become full citizens and the right to labor, contract, and property were claimed to be open to all classes, merged with abolitionist ideals of racial equality. Legal rights were the site of communal transformation that had not been possible before 1865 in either the slaveholding South or in the Jim Crow North.[22]

Yet, this transformation only occurred with the assurances of limitations. In 1866, there was no place for black suffrage in the claim to full citizenship, and certainly no space for "social" citizenship, for equal access to public spaces in a way that would accord full civil status to black citizens. For these claims to break into citizenship discourse, the dominant public sphere would need a new discourse constructed in other public spaces, spaces where subordinated black voices could use the freedoms and rights of their newly acquired first-level citizenship to press for the continued transformation of citizenship and civil society.

III. CREATING A BLACK CIVIL SOCIETY AND PUBLIC SPHERE: THE BLACK CONVENTION MOVEMENT

Free labor citizenship was one of the dominant ideas of free citizenship present during Reconstruction, but it was predominantly an ideal advanced by

Northern elites (white and black) and was not necessarily the ideal for all freed blacks.[23] This is evident from the very start of the post-war period.

African American men had been meeting in national conventions since before the Civil War, and many black men, from both the North and the South, met at national and state conventions after the war.[24] These conventions were significant civic and citizenship acts on a number of levels. First, they demonstrated the remarkable commitment to active engagement with civil society in just the way that de Tocqueville had identified as a crucial aspect of the American brand of democratic citizenship. By engaging in this culturally valorized means of association and expression, black Americans enacted political citizenship through the public sphere despite their disenfranchisement throughout most of the country. Through the type of group activity common to large associations—committee work, drafting resolutions, debating proposals, compromising, balancing competing interests, building coalitions—participants in these conventions could engage in the activities of democratic citizenship, and often the conventions produced formal political activity by sending petitions to Congress, the president, or to the general citizen.[25] These conventions reveal how important the overlapping nature of citizenship can be, and how important the public sphere and civil society are for the engagement in and claim for full citizenship status. The very act of claiming citizenship through public discourse in voluntary associations itself defined the nature of that citizenship and helped eventually to transform that citizenship into a fuller political citizenship more broadly recognized by the dominant society.

This final point bears emphasis. When the citizenship activity of Reconstruction is viewed primarily as that of congressional actions, as the writing of legislation or the drafting of constitutional amendments, then citizenship remains passive. Citizenship is a thing granted, not claimed or asserted. While the egalitarian nature of this grant was indeed radical for the time and essential to any future development of full democratic citizenship, it was the claiming of citizenship by African Americans that reveals the full potential of citizenship activity.[26] The state and national conventions of African Americans thus represent a crucial and defining aspect of a more vibrant, active, and realizable citizenship.

African American conventions also defined citizenship through their specific articulations of the meaning of citizenship and freedom. In numerous meetings and conventions of freedmen meeting at the end of the Civil War, black Americans expressed their own understandings of freedom and full citizenship by stating their expectations and demands of whites in what would be, they hoped, a new country. Full access to American citizenship meant something very real. Freed blacks certainly wanted access to the basic legal rights such as contract and property ownership; the free labor ideal of legal citizenship held a prominent place in African American articulations of citizenship, especially in the earlier conventions of 1865 and 1866, which were dominated by men who had been free before the war and possessed some property. Yet even in the early conventions, the citizenship claims were more encompassing and fuller.[27]

Just as critical to the claim of citizenship through civil rights of contract and property were the uniform arguments of black conventions to assert a right to the franchise as fundamental to any meaningful citizenship or freedom. Congress had famously temporized on black suffrage in the debates over the 14th Amendment, as Radical Republicans did not appear to have the votes to achieve suffrage. In response, black conventions called for Congress to grant and protect the right of black citizens to vote, often pointing out that their "citizenship" claim to suffrage, as loyal citizens who fought for the Union, was plainly greater than those of the former Confederate soldiers. It was also clear to these convention members that other rights could be rendered meaningless without access to political powers. For black Americans during Reconstruction, access to civil society and political activity went hand in hand, and unlike the progression in Congress where civil rights came first, for African Americans the ballot was seen as the more important right on which all others would depend. As John Mercer Langston, one of the leading African American legal and political thinkers and activists, stated, suffrage was more fundamental than even the basic civil rights of property and contract because it was central to self-government and free institutions, and was "a constituent element of manhood . . . it stands prominent among the chief duties of civil society to sustain and guard it."[28]

However, just as political rights were critical for the protection of civil society, so too was civil society critical in the claim for political rights. Eric Foner has observed that one of the main reasons that black suffrage was on the national agenda after the war—given that Northern whites had not previously seen black suffrage as important—was the persistence and skill of blacks from New Orleans in petitioning Congress to address the issue. In particular, the Creole community had a history of developed civil society in an enclave of freedom before the war. New Orleans' black community had established a wide range of civil activities, from schools to orphanages to a free press to successful businesses, all of which supported a vocal and active political community. This enabled representatives of the community to present, in person, forceful arguments on behalf of black suffrage in ways that Northern whites were compelled to take seriously.[29]

Another striking example of the importance of the black public sphere in reframing Reconstruction citizenship came from the South Carolina Freedmen's Convention, meeting in Charleston at the Zion Presbyterian Church in November 1865. First, the participants recognized the full breadth of the communal and personal experiences at issue when they stated that they gathered "to deliberate upon our intellectual, moral, industrial, civil, and political condition." Importantly, the attendees were not isolating civil rights from political rights, or civil and political from economic, educational, or moral rights and duties; the isolated parsing of layers of citizenship by Congress in early 1866 made little sense to the men who were claiming freedom and citizenship from a history of bondage.

This point was reinforced through the language the convention used to describe what had been denied in slavery and what was required in freedom: "Heretofore we have had no avenues opened to us or our children—we have had no firesides that we could call our own; none of those incentives to work hard for the development of our minds and the aggrandizement of our race in common with other people." This statement describes not just a desire to have access to property and contract rights, but a fuller context in which those rights are implemented or denied. The conventioneers' wording is a claim not for rights in and of themselves so much as for rights as opportunities ("avenues"); not to the right of free labor for individual economic benefit but for intellectual and communal development ("development of our minds and the aggrandizement of our race"). This latter point in particular shows how individual and communal were understood together, how they were more integrated than classical liberal ideology and free labor ideology would indicate. The desire of freed blacks to be free of white control meant that "autonomy" for blacks consisted of "autonomy both as individuals and as members of a community." Whereas whites often talked of autonomy or freedom in more individualized terms, there was a clear communal consciousness in claims of autonomy and freedom by blacks. In this respect, civil society and citizenship claims by blacks should be seen as much more able to unify individualistic and communal concepts.[30]

Yet, it would be a mistake to see in the communal conceptions of Reconstruction-Era blacks a rigid separatism along racial lines that inhibited understandings of broader democratic community and citizenship. In several of the black conventions, delegates debated issues of race consciousness and separatism. For example, in Pennsylvania the delegates debated whether to condemn black merchants who did not treat black customers equally to white customers, ultimately deciding that preferential treatment of white customers was against their principle of equality, even if opposing such preferences entailed some economic sacrifice by black merchants.[31] Black delegates were beginning to work out an issue that they could only address fully in the black public sphere: the relative role and value of race-based community building versus race-neutral claims of individualized equality. These debates helped build a base for how biracial legislatures during Reconstruction would approach issues of social equality. Separate schools were often supported by black communities and Reconstruction legislatures in states that had substantial black legislative participation during Reconstruction, such as South Carolina and Mississippi. Nonetheless, these legislatures also advocated and passed laws desegregating public accommodations, and objected to laws *requiring* segregated schools.[32]

For black leaders during Reconstruction, racial separation and race-based social communities were part of a pluralistic, as opposed to a racialized, conception of American democracy. Race mattered, and racial improvement and consciousness could be harnessed in a positive way. Yet the *public* and *legal* understanding of persons, that is, *citizenship* was itself not racialized. As Eric Foner has written, "While most blacks valued [their] autonomous institutions and did not object to voluntary racial separation, they insisted the state must remain color-blind."[33] This was a conception of citizenship at once aspirational about the promise of deracialized equality and grounded in a recognition of the reality of racialized communities.

The South Carolina convention went on to frame their rights of citizenship in a larger context of civil society. In a statement to the United States Senate and House, the South Carolina convention listed the rights and privileges that they expected the federal government to secure, including: a right to receive protection of law and government ("the strong arm of law and order"), a right to protect laborers' ability to sell labor just as merchants sell their goods, a right to fair consideration of their claims on the "land question" (a reference, no doubt, to General Sherman's forty-acre-and-a-mule land grant, reversed by President Johnson), and a right to bear arms on a basis equal to whites. These rights seem consistent with rights recognized by congressional Republicans, even if Republicans failed to secure the land grants. But the members of the convention also claimed more than these basic legal rights. Like all other black conventions of the period, they asserted a right to suffrage, citing the injustice of being taxed without representation and the need to have suffrage to protect against unjust laws, reflecting a view consistent with John Mercer Langston's articulation of suffrage as a threshold right. Thus in South Carolina, as in Louisiana and elsewhere, blacks participating in a black public sphere responded to congressional hesitancy with their own redefinition of basic citizenship rights.[34]

The South Carolina convention went beyond this, however, and began developing an exploration of citizenship rights even broader than one connecting suffrage and basic civil rights. In their statement to Congress, the delegates also asserted a right to secure "the three great agents of civilized society—the school, the pulpit, the press[.]" Here we see most plainly a claim to civil society—or what delegates refer to as civilized society—in which education, religion, and the press are as fundamental to basic citizenship and freedom as first order legal rights and suffrage. This statement echoes Tocquevillian ideas that civil society in a democracy is composed of a range of activities (rather than merely voluntary associations). The delegates to the South Carolina convention evidently understood that they were situated within a legal, political, and civil society and that access to all spheres of social and political engagement were important to a broad nexus of activities of civil society. This view is further evident in the delegates' assertion of a right to engage in political discourse in open-access political conventions in which all citizens could debate the fulfillment of what they describe as basic rights "to enter upon all avenues of agriculture, commerce, [and] trade; to amass wealth by thrift and industry; [and] the right to develop our whole being by all the appliances that belong to civilized society[.]"[35]

This final phrase, "develop our whole being by all the appliances that belong to civilized society," aptly characterizes how the convention understood the "situatedness" of the individual rights. The phrase connects self-realization ("develop our whole being") with the structures of civil society ("the appliances that belong to civilized society"). It also employs a double meaning that unites individual African Americans to the African American community by referring to "our whole being." This message to Congress reflects a radical joining of traditionally liberal ideas of legal rights, emerging ideas of suffrage rights, and an as yet underdeveloped idea of the spheres of civil society—including education, commerce, labor, religion, and the press, among others—as necessary components to full development of citizenship and personhood.

In conjunction with many of the black state and national conventions, black Southerners were also forming local and state Equal Rights Associations. Several of the state conventions specifically referred to the associations as the organizational arms to carry out the proposals and projects discussed and supported by the convention delegates.[36] Equal Rights Associations and Union Leagues took the ideals of the black conventions—the claims for equal legal rights, political

activity, education, labor rights, and public welfare—to the local level. Equal
Rights Associations and Union Leagues actively sought to implement black citizenship through a number of activities, ranging from advocating suffrage, to
leading protests against segregated street cars, to organizing state black conventions, to assisting the poor and helping establish schools. The Georgia Equal
Rights Association had been established by the Georgia Freedmen's Convention
with the purposes of securing equal rights, aiding the poor, and promoting education for African Americans throughout Georgia. These associations often had
close ties with the Freedmen's Bureau; Georgia's association was headed by a
former officer of the Georgia division of the Freedmen's Bureau.[37]

Equal Rights Associations thus combined the ideals and personnel from the
black conventions with the support and personnel of the federal government.
Such organizations, while partly political, were also general social service operations designed to implement more fully freedom and citizenship within the
black communities of the South. This combination was, quite simply, civil
society writ small, a localized and focused effort to bring political claims to citizenship down to the personal, local, and immediate level for many blacks
throughout the South. What is particularly impressive about this movement is
the combination of speed and breadth by which the movement made its way
from national conventioneering to local political and social organizing, a movement that could only happen if it was coming from the ground up as well as the
top down and by a combination of political and social service activity. The activities of Union Leagues, Equal Rights Associations, and numerous other black
social groups were as much civic duties—burial of the dead, education and literacy, coordination of religious services—as they were political.[38]

The activities of the associations and leagues also achieved another function:
they were a means of the type of dignity-claiming activity essential to democratic
citizenship. As Michael Fitzgerald has argued, Union League activity and other
mass actions by black citizens "were . . . assertions of self-respect," public statements of dignity, equality, and citizenship. When blacks acted collectively
throughout the urban centers of the South to challenge segregation in 1867—
longshoremen's strikes in the port cities, other strikes in Richmond and Selma,
streetcar boycotts in Mobile—there was a fundamental claim of full citizenship
being made. And for black citizens who were both claiming and redefining citizenship, civil, political, and social equality were part of this citizenship package.[39]

It should not be surprising that a more radical engagement with civil society
took place through the Equal Rights Associations and Union Leagues than had

been expressed at the black conventions of 1865 and 1866. The conventions largely advocated a moderate form of civil society and civil and political rights. While the grass-roots conventioneers understood the combination of rights more organically than did congressional leaders, blacks at the conventions often echoed the free labor ideals being articulated by white Republicans in the North.[40]

What developed more fully in the ensuing years of Reconstruction was a recognition of the active aspects of politically engaged citizenship and the need for federal and other governmental protections for the free exercise of citizenship.[41] That this realization took place *on the ground* indicates just how complicated and embedded the resistance to equal citizenship was; it also shows exactly why it is critical for civil society to be grounded locally as well as organized nationally. Moreover, the experiences of the associations and leagues in working with the federal government through the Freedmen's Bureau left African Americans and some local white Republicans with a firmer understanding of the importance of governmental supports for the activities of civil society and its nongovernmental associations.

The more politicized and statist understanding of civil society that arose in the black public sphere also came about because of the remarkable participation of black citizens in local, state, and federal governments in the years of congressional Reconstruction, beginning in what Eric Foner has described as the *annus mirabilis* of 1867. As African Americans gained more power, they learned the importance of governmental action and, in the face of increased white hostility, they also recognized the essential nature of governmental power in combating racial oppression in civil society. That is, blacks learned that the state itself was an essential instrument of equal citizenship because civil society itself allowed for the perpetuation of racial norms.[42]

The importance of the state in black republican views of civil society was reflected in the actual activities pursued by Reconstruction legislators and governments of Southern states with substantial black participation. During the brief period from 1867 through 1874, several Southern legislatures adopted desegregation laws, asserting a right to open and equal access to public accommodations. The effort to desegregate streetcars and public events began with black and white civil rights protests, including boycotts and sit-ins, in the antebellum North. This movement continued in the postbellum South, with streetcar lines in New Orleans and Charleston changing segregationist policies in the face of these protests. In combination with the more radical white and black Republicans of the North, particularly centered in Massachusetts, Southern state legislatures followed with new laws desegregating public accommodations. As Eric Foner observes, the effort to pass laws desegregating public accommodations, including common carriers, places of amusement, and even businesses licensed by the state, at first met with overwhelming opposition from white Republicans and failed to pass. But as blacks gained more political power and prowess, they were able to persuade enough whites to achieve passage of the laws in several Southern states.[43]

Legislatures with substantial black participation also produced an activist state in terms of the range of services provided, particularly to the poor. Legislatures funded medical care, legal assistance, orphanages, and schools. Reconstruction legislatures also enacted some laws protecting laborers, including laws giving workers a first lien on an employer's property.[44] Government, under this vision, worked to produce equal citizenship both by pursuing desegregation of basic governmental functions and by providing governmental services to all races, even if in a de facto segregated manner, in a way that began to look like the provision of social rights and privileges that would not be more fully developed, in practice and in political theory, until the twentieth century.

IV. IMPORTANCE OF THE STATE AND PROBLEMS OF A BIFURCATED CIVIL SOCIETY

Even if we can find in the Reconstruction era evidence of a black civil society and public sphere that developed citizenship ideas and practices and moved the concept of citizenship beyond the more narrow confines articulated by congressional Republicans in 1865 and 1866, the fact remains that the ideal of democratic citizenship only appeared fleetingly during that period and was violently and systematically suppressed thereafter. What are we to make, therefore, of the historical denial of equal, democratic citizenship from about 1876 through at least the 1970s, the effects of which are still felt very profoundly?

On one level, we can see, in the loss of the possibilities that began budding during Reconstruction, the critical importance of federal supports for citizenship. The Supreme Court played its part in the demise of federal support for federal citizenship, with decisions such as the *Slaughter-House Cases*[45] and the *Civil Rights Cases*,[46] which converted federal citizenship into a legal chimera and incapacitated congressional authority to define and implement citizenship through very narrow and formalistic readings of the 14th Amendment. Whereas occasional political will at the federal level had led to the federal suppression of the Ku Klux Klan in the early 1870s—largely through the coordinated efforts of the newly minted Department of Justice and the military—the loss of that will and the eventual acceptance by the Republican party of an accommodation with the white South effectively eliminated the main means of opposing a violent overthrow of democratic government.[47] The "Redemption" of the South by white Democrats shows how fragile civil and political citizenship can be when it is confronted with persistent violent opposition without the protection of the government. One of the most important basic rights cited by the South Carolina black convention was the protection by the government, both by law and by force.[48] Absent such protection, absent the countervailing force represented by the state, civil society simply cannot develop, at least not in an integrative and open manner. While more recent analyses of civil society in the context of twentieth century totalitarian and authoritarian states highlights the problem of the overly repressive state,[49] the creation of the rigid Jim Crow South reveals how the removal of state power can also destroy the freedom and other benefits of civil society, especially when practices of subordination are allowed to operate on civil society.[50]

However, it must also be noted that the eventual dominance of Jim Crow occurred *through* the state, that is, through the instrumentality of state and local governments. It was most clearly the desire of white Democrats to control the state apparatus; the point was to control state government and to keep the federal government from interfering on behalf of black citizens.[51] That this means of control could only be effectuated through the combined use of private violence and a cover of state legitimacy did not change the fact that the state was a significant player. Thus, the critical problem, in the context of postwar white supremacy, was the loss of *competing* state organizations. As would be the case in the modern civil rights movement, implementation of citizenship and the reconstruction of American civil society required a vibrant, active, and competitive federal structure.

What happened to civil society during this period is also instructive. With the loss of state protection for black participation in and constructions of civil society, black citizens had to create more defined and cohesive enclaves of oppositional civil society. White supremacists still strove to attack instantiations of successful black civil society—Jim Crow violence was often directed against black businesses, black property owners, black civil associations, black schools, etc. But the ability of black communities to sustain themselves, to educate their youth, to acquire some level of financial support, and to sustain voluntary and religious organizational structures that could support resistance is a remarkable testament to the capacity of enclaves or counterspheres to exist and develop.[52]

The problem, however, was that such enclaves were forced to develop in a *closed* civil society that was rigidly bifurcated and insufficiently porous. The ideals of democratic citizenship expressed, albeit differently, in both white Republican and black ideology from Reconstruction, were ideals of a more universal citizenship that allowed for open access to all the "appliances" of civil society. The closed civil society of Jim Crow prevented those ideals of universal citizenship from being realized. Instead, what developed was, on the one hand, a false universal—the conversion of free labor ideology to a freedom-of-contract regime that privileged a white supremacist, male-centered version of capitalism as itself a universalized reality in the public sphere. On the other hand there arose an aggressively exclusionary public sphere and uncivil society, in which violence patrolled the borderlands against the incursion of labor, nonwhites, and women. Jeffrey Alexander, analyzing how Jim Crowism affected and infected the promise of civil society, argues (based in part on Houston Baker's analysis) that white America's creation of itself as a rational and "civil" or "civilized" society depended in fundamental ways on the simultaneous subordination of blacks and the imagining of blacks as inherently uncivil and uncivilized. Thus, white civil society itself became a distorted inversion, at once proclaiming its own universality while also depicting this universal as set against racial inclusion.[53]

Black citizens responded by creating a countersphere through black civil society. The discourses and institutions and cultural reproductions within black civil society produced many of the possibilities of a unifying civil society, or what Alexander calls civil repair. Once civil society was firmly divided with the ending of Reconstruction and creation of Jim Crow by about 1900, it would be primarily counterpublics—spheres in the black community, the women's suffrage movement, immigrant communities, and the labor movement—that fueled a reconstruction of civil society. As it had during the period of Reconstruction, black civil society throughout Jim Crow contained and nurtured a discourse of civil society that was both universalizing and critical of the dominant, uncivil white society. It is a remarkable feature of black civil society from Reconstruction through the Civil Rights Movement that it continued to develop, as one of its multiple discourses, a surprisingly hopeful view of citizenship as a promise realizable through the rule of law.[54]

V. LESSONS AND CAUTIONS

The initial experiences of African Americans in claiming and creating citizenship after the establishment of formal citizenship under the 14th Amendment reveal some important aspects of citizenship, civil society, and the public sphere. First, it seems clear from the experiences of black political discourse and the communal engagement of the convention movement that an alternative public sphere, one dedicated to the participation of African Americans and to the expression and development of issues and ideas concerning black Americans, was critical to the creation of some level of democratic and equal citizenship during Reconstruction. The efforts to include suffrage within a basic definition of citizenship would have been far less effective, and far easier for whites to sidestep, were it not for the persistent emphasis of blacks enacting their citizenship claims.

Furthermore, the ability of African Americans to engage in their own public spheres to develop discourse—an ability made possible by the first-order legal rights of free assembly and free speech that had been denied in the antebellum South—made the discourse that took place in the authoritative public sphere, the one in which legal and policy changes are made, that much richer. These benefits were seen in the biracial legislatures of Reconstruction, where the discourses of multiple public spheres could engage each other in a larger public sphere, helping to produce a range of governmental programs and laws which accounted for a richer, more varied type of citizenship than one finds in earlier, uniracial debates even within the Republican Party. This history indicates that some version of multiple spheres or counterspheres can be important to enriching democratic citizenship and democratic decision making in a pluralist society. The history is also important to any understanding of how people can claim and define their own citizenship, and thus convert mere citizenship into *democratic* citizenship.

Second, black citizens' engagement with these political issues was done initially as an act of political citizenship *prior* to the formal grant of political citizenship through suffrage. Legal or civil citizenship rights, like rights to assembly and speech, may well have been necessary for the development of the black public sphere. The right to suffrage was not. Indeed, the opposite may have been true: actions within the black public sphere and civil society may themselves have been fundamental to the establishment of suffrage, even if temporarily. The discourse developed in the black public sphere insisted on suffrage and helped prepare African Americans for effective political activity once suffrage came. Ultimately, the relationship between the black civil society/public sphere and ideas of political citizenship was symbiotic. Citizenship was not a steady progress through economic, political and social stages with entrance granted

from above by white legislators or constitution drafters. Rather, it was an
ongoing, organic development (that included long periods of retrenchment and
denials) in which the actions and ideas of African Americans, expressed within
and enabled by an alternative civil society and countersphere, played a significant role in recreating the nature and contours of citizenship, and in which
access to even partial citizenship in turn helped enable and foster the black
public sphere itself. This point is evident, for example, in the legislative agendas
of the Reconstruction legislatures, where even social rights, the rights to education and public services, developed at a very early stage.[55] Reconstruction reveals
that full citizenship develops in a more organic and less legalistic way than is
conceived in common constitutional understandings of citizenship.

Third, it is important to recognize how delegates to black conventions talked
about civil society in a way at once embracing individualized rights to labor,
contract, and property consistent with white Republican ideals, *and* asserting a
communal character to the establishment and development of the citizens for
whom these rights were to operate. Theorists of civil society often claim as one
of its virtues that it bridges the individual and communal theories of democratic
society; historically, it was in the counterspheres or alternate civil societies of
the nineteenth century in which such claims were most seriously and consistently developed, as evident in the black convention movement. Contrary to
some civil society revivalists who jump directly from de Tocqueville and the Age
of Jackson to late-twentieth century neighborhood associations with a curious
inattentiveness to what happened between,[56] the most instructive and constructive source for how civil society can build citizenship and engage social-moral
issues comes from the social movements that sought to realize the democratic
citizenship promise of the Reconstruction Amendments.

Fourth, the broader social and cultural experiences of black citizens after the
war reveal aspects of civil society that are essential to account for in any decent
conception of democratic citizenship. In thinking about what democratic citizenship can mean, and in thinking about how efforts were made to try to achieve
citizenship in the past, it should be remembered that full citizenship implies
access to a range of social and cultural activities and communities. The statements from the South Carolina convention about needing access to all avenues
and appliances of citizenship reflect an important indication of how civil society
in its broadest form, from voluntary associations to families to religious communities to economic organizations, would be necessary for developing citizenship,
both individually and communally.[57] Citizenship, as a concept, should allow for

consideration of these aspects of civil society, for it is in the nongovernmental spheres of civil society where the citizen can be made and supported.

Fifth, it should not be forgotten that civil society and government are best seen as a two-way street. Just as black civil society fed into governmental activities and conceptions of citizenship, the state was also a necessary part of securing the vibrancy of civil society. It was, finally, the loss of governmental support, in the form of federal troops and legal actions, that made possible the end of Reconstruction and the rise of a fully bifurcated and subordinated civil society.[58] While the church, family, and other aspects of black civil society could serve as sites and sources for resistance to Jim Crow, it was the absence of state support that made this enclave resistance necessary.

So what are the answers to my initial questions about defining democratic citizenship and the possible ways of thinking about constitutional citizenship? One answer surely is that it is deeply problematic to think of citizenship in a restricted, legalistic manner which would search for formal definitions and content in antebellum case law and attorney general opinions. If the experiences of the postbellum period tell us anything, they tell us that citizenship was being claimed at least as much as it was being granted. More importantly, the people claiming citizenship were not bound by classical liberal ideas of legal citizenship and legal status for individuals, although those ideas were important. Rather, people saw citizenship as a process of engagement by individuals with a variety of social, political, and legal groups or communities. The development of citizenship through the "appliances" of civilized society came to be seen as an engagement with many spheres of civil society itself, spheres ranging from legal to political to voluntary organizations to economic enterprises to education to religion, and to family and kinship.

Legal and legislative actions supporting citizenship were critical, but as the failures of Reconstruction showed, they were plainly insufficient. Voluntary and community associations provided critical loci for protest and organization, but they too were insufficient on their own. Similarly, access to education, enjoyment of religious association and exercise, and a variety of political engagements were also necessary, but not sufficient, in forming successful resistance to denials of citizenship and in efforts to claim at least some degree of full citizenship. Only through a complex engagement across all of these spheres would full democratic citizenship have had a chance to flourish; and primarily through the combined effort to destroy or constrain African Americans' freedom across all these spheres white supremacy retained power throughout the South.

The citizenship of inclusion and equality being explored during the initial implementations of the 14th Amendment teaches us that truly democratic citizenship must contain some degree of recognition of, access to, and support for the variety of spheres of civil society. To the extent that citizenship is a developmental concept—and certainly in the transition from bondsmen to freedmen this was true—it must incorporate some ideas and policies for helping to create and sustain full citizens. The experiences of Reconstruction also reveal that this process requires both state-based supports and programs, *and* extensive networks of private communal supports. Indeed, the effective practices of civil society in this period itself indicate the porous boundaries between state and private spheres.[59] The advantage of civil society and public sphere theory is precisely its ability to bridge this intersection of state and private in a way that more accurately captures what happened on the ground during and after Reconstruction and also permits us to see ways of reconciling and repairing the contradictions of equal citizenship ideas.

An earlier version of this chapter was published in *Akron Law Review*, Vol. 42 No. 4, pp. 1245–1275. Copyright © 2009 *Akron Law Review*. Used with permission.

I am grateful for the feedback I received from and interaction with the other participants at a symposium on the 140th Anniversary of the 14th Amendment sponsored by the Center for Constitutional Law at the University of Akron School of Law, including David Bogen, Ellen Connally, Gwen Jordan, William Rich, Michael Ross, and William Wiecek. I am particularly grateful for the guidance and encouragement of Dick Aynes and the advice and editing skill of Elizabeth Reilly. I also am grateful to my colleague, Kirsten Davis, for helping my exploration of public sphere theory and opening me to new ways of thinking about these topics. In addition, related aspects of this project have benefited from the feedback of participants at forums and presentations at the 2008 Midwest Political Science Association, the William S. Boyd School of Law (UNLV), and the Midwest Law & Society Retreat held by the Institute for Legal Studies at the University of Wisconsin Law School. This project was generously supported by a research grant from the Stetson University College of Law.

Endnotes

INTRODUCTION

1. *See* Bruce Ackerman, We The People 1: Foundations (1991); Bruce Ackerman, We The People 2: Transformations (1998); Garrett Epps, Democracy Reborn (2006). U.S. Const., Preamble (quotation).

2. Charles Fairman, *What Makes A Great Justice?*, 30 B.U. L. Rev. 49, 50 (1950) (the 14th Amendment and the Commerce Clause "the two most important passages in the entire Constitution"). Garrett Epps, *Second Founding: The Story of the Fourteenth Amendment*, 85 Or. L. Rev. 895 (2006); *Symposium on America's Constitution: A Biography*, 59 Syracuse L. Rev. 31, 41 (2008) (comments of Akhil Amar) (because of the proslavery original Constitution, we have had "two Constitutions," the second beginning with the 13th, 14th, and 15th Amendments); Felix Frankfurter, *John Marshall and the Judicial Function*, 69 Harv. L. Rev. 229 (1964) ("The 14th Amendment is probably the largest source of the Court's business."). A Westlaw search performed on March 26, 2009, requesting United States Supreme Court cases that included the terms "14th Amendment" and "Constitution" returned 3,833 documents.

3. Slaughter-House Cases, 83 U.S. 36 (1873); Bradwell v. Illinois, 83 U.S. 130 (1873); Minor v. Happersett, 88 U.S. 162 (1875); United States v. Cruikshank, 92 U.S. 542 (1876); United States v. Reese, 92 U.S. 214 (1876); Harris v. United States, 106 U.S. 629 (1883); The Civil Rights Cases, 109 U.S. 3 (1883). Michael Kent Curtis, *Resurrecting the Privileges or Immunities Clause and Revising the* Slaughter-House Cases *Without Exhuming* Lochner: *Individual Rights and the Fourteenth Amendment*, 38 B.C. L. Rev. 1, 4 (1996) ("The destruction of the Privileges or Immunities Clause and the development of an excessively broad state action doctrine had a profound impact on American history. They represented a one-two punch that did much to eliminate the 14th Amendment as an effective protector of individual rights and democracy.").

4. Rebecca E. Zeitlow, *Belonging, Protection and Equality: The Neglected Citizenship Clause and the Limits of Federalism*, 62 U. Pitt. L. Rev. 281, 293–94 (2000); Katzenbach v. Morgan, 384 U.S. 641, 650–51 (1966); South Carolina v. Katzenbach, 383 U.S. 301, 326–27 (1966).

5. William H. Seward, United States Secretary of State, Proclamation, 15 Stat. 708 (1868); Richard Aynes, *The 39th Congress (1865–1867) and the Fourteenth Amendment: Some Preliminary Perspectives*, 42 Akron L. Rev. 1019 (2009).

6. *E.g.*, Civil Rights Act of 1866, ch. 31, 14 Stat. 27 (1866) (originally entitled "An Act to protect All Persons in the United States in Their Civil Rights, and furnish the Means of their Vindication"); The Enforcement Act of 1870 (The Act of May 31, 1870), ch. 114, § 18, 16 Stat. 140 (1870) (originally entitled "An Act to enforce the rights of citizens of the United States"); Ku

Klux Klan Act of 1871, ch. 22, §2, 17 Stat. 13 (1871) (originally entitled "An Act to enforce the Provisions of the 14th Amendment to the Constitution of the United States, and for other Purposes"); Civil Rights Act of 1875, ch. 114, §§3–5, 18 Stat. 336, 337 (1875) (originally entitled "An act to protect all citizens in their civil and legal rights").

7. Robert J. Kaczorowski, The Politics of Judicial Interpretation: The Federal Courts, Department of Justice and Civil Rights, 1866–1876 (1985).

8. Slaughter-House Cases, 83 U.S. 36 (1873); Bradwell v. Illinois, 83 U.S. 130 (1873).

9. *Slaughter-House* at 82. The Court continued: "Under pressure of all the excited feeling growing out of the war, our statesmen still believed that the existence of the States with powers for domestic and local government, including regulation of civil rights—the rights of person and of property—was essential to the perfect working of our complex form of government, though they have thought proper to impose additional limitations on the States, and to confer additional power on that of the Nation." Earlier, the Court expressed fear of interpreting the Amendment more broadly, because the "consequences [would be] so serious, so far-reaching and pervading, so great a departure from the structure and spirit of our institutions . . . radically chang[ing] the whole theory of the relations of the State and Federal governments to each other and of both these governments to the people," and declined an interpretation "in the absence of language which expresses such a purpose too clearly to admit of doubt." *Id.* at 78.

10. Webster's Third New International Dictionary of the English Language (Philip B. Gove ed. 1993): "intend" at 1175, "interpret" at 1182.

11. *Slaughter-House* at 54 (summary of John Campbell's argument for the plaintiff-in-error). As Michael Ross has pointed out, this lofty assessment is hardly without irony, as counsel for the plaintiffs was in fact a staunch opponent of the 14th Amendment. Michael A. Ross, *Obstructing Reconstruction: John Archibald Campbell and the Legal Campaign Against Louisiana's Republican Government, 1868–1873*, 49 Civ. War Hist. 235, 235–53 (2003).

CHAPTER 1

1. *See* William E. Nelson, The Fourteenth Amendment: From Political Principle to Judicial Doctrine 1 (1988); *see also* Michael Kent Curtis, "No State Shall Abridge": The Fourteenth Amendment and the Bill of Rights (1986); Earl M. Maltz, Civil Rights, the Constitution, and Congress, 1863–1869 (1990); Bruce Ackerman, We The People 2: Transformations (1998); Akhil Reed Amar, The Bill of Rights: Creation and Reconstruction (1998); Jacobus tenBroek, Equal Under Law (enl. ed 1965).

2. No substantial school of constitutional thought holds that the intent of the drafters of a constitutional provision is irrelevant to the contemporary process of applying it. In the particular case of the 14th Amendment, it is sensible to give primacy to the intent of the drafters. Unlike the original Constitution, the 14th Amendment was drafted by Congress over a relatively short period of time to deal with particular problems. In addition, ratification of the Amendment was more or less explicitly demanded of the Southern states as a condition of their return to full political participation in the Union; the Southern states thus had no representation at the time the Amendment was framed. *See* David A. Strauss, *The Irrelevance of Constitutional Amendments*, 114 Harv. L. Rev. 1457, 1479 (arguing that the "Civil War Amendments" should be regarded as "something in the nature of a treaty, reflecting the outcome of the war").

3. U.S. Const. amend. XIV, § 5 (granting Congress the power to enforce provisions of the Amendment by enacting "appropriate legislation"); § 2 (imposing penalties in congressional representation on states denying the vote to "male inhabitants" who have not participated in rebellion or committed crimes); § 3 (barring from office former State and federal officials who participate in rebellion) (cf. art. II, § 1, cl. 8); § 4 (constitutionalizing United States public debt and forbidding states or the federal government from repaying or assuming any debt incurred in support of rebellion).

4. *Cf.* Christopher L. Eisgruber, *The Fourteenth Amendment's Constitution*, 69 S. Cal. L. Rev. 47, 80 (1995) (characterizing the Court's interpretive posture as one of "peculiar[] reluctan[ce] to recognize [proper constitutional interpretation's] dependence upon the 14th Amendment").

5. Slaughter-House Cases, 83 U.S. (16 Wall.) 36, 78 (1872).

6. City of Boerne v. Flores, 521 U.S. 507, 520 (1997).

7. United States v. Morrison, 529 U.S. 598, 620 (2000).

8. Nelson, The Fourteenth Amendment, at 4–5.

9. Slaughter-House Cases, 83 U.S. 125 (Swayne, J., dissenting).

10. Leonard L. Richards, The Slave Power: The Free North and Southern Domination, 1780–1860, at 1–2, 21–27 (2000); "By Blue Ontario's Shore:" "Slavery—the murderous, treacherous conspiracy to raise it upon the ruins of all the rest." Walt Whitman, Complete Poetry and Selected Prose 468, 473 (Justin Kaplan ed., 1982).

11. Richard Hofstadter, The Paranoid Style in American Politics (1965).

12. Abraham Lincoln, Draft of a Speech, *in* 1 Abraham Lincoln, Speeches and Writings, 1832–1858, at 487–88 (Don E. Fehrenbacher ed., 1989); Lincoln, First Debate: Lincoln's Reply, *in* 1 Speeches and Writings, at 508–16.

13. Richards, The Slave Power, at 13–14, 16; David Herbert Donald, Lincoln 208 (1995).

14. Horace Greeley, The American Conflict: A History of the Great Rebellion in the United States of America, 1860–64 (1864–1866); Hermann von Holst, The Constitutional and Political History of the United States (1881–1892) (eight volumes); 1 von Holst at 300; 2 von Holst at 171; 6 von Holst at 21; 7 von Holst at 458–59.

15. David Brion Davis, *Free at Last; The Enduring Legacy of the South's Civil War Victory*, N.Y. Times, Aug. 26, 2001, § 4, p. 1; J. G. Randall, *The Blundering Generation*, 27 Miss. Valley Hist. Rev. 3, 7–8 (1940).

16. Richards, The Slave Power, at 20.

17. *See, e.g.,* Burnham v. Superior Court, 495 U.S. 604, 611 (1990) (Scalia, J., concurring) ("Accurate or not, however, judging by the evidence of contemporaneous or near-contemporaneous decisions, one must conclude that Story's understanding was shared by American courts at the crucial time for present purposes: 1868, when the 14th Amendment was adopted.").

18. Richards, The Slave Power, at 2.

19. Lincoln, Speech at Chi., Ill., *in* 1 Speeches and Writings, at 442–43; Richards, The Slave Power, at 2–3; William E. Forbath, *The Ambiguities of Free Labor: Labor and Law in the Gilded Age*, 1985 Wis. L. Rev. 767, 774, 783.

20. James McPherson, The Struggle for Equality: Abolitionists and the Negro in the Civil War and Reconstruction (1964); Lincoln, 1 Speeches and Writings, at 478; Don E. Fehrenbacher, The Dred Scott Case 190–91 (1978).

21. David Herbert Donald, Liberty and Union 38 (1978); Don E. Fehrenbacher, The Slaveholding Republic: An Account of the United States Government's Relations to Slavery (Ward M. McAfee ed., 2001); Eric Foner, Free Soil, Free Labor, Free Men: The Ideology of the Republican Party Before the Civil War 99–102 (2d ed. 1995); William Gienapp, The Origins of the Republican Party 1852–1856, at 357–65 (1978); Michael Holt, The Political Crisis of the 1850s (1978); Michael Holt, The Rise and Fall of the American Whig Party: Jacksonian Politics and the Onset of the Civil War (1999); Richard H. Sewell, Ballots for Freedom: Antislavery Politics in the United States, 1837–1860 (1976); Larry Gara, *Slavery and the Slave Power: A Crucial Distinction*, 15 Civ. War Hist. 15–18 (1969). An early and sophisticated discussion of the legal and constitutional implications of the Slave Power hypothesis underlies much of Paul Finkelman, An Imperfect Union: Slavery, Federalism and Comity (1981).

22. Richards, The Slave Power, at 1–2 (first quotations), 9–10 (second quotation), 2–4 (third quotation).

23. U.S. Const. art. I, § 2, cl. 3; Richards, The Slave Power, at 42.

24. U.S. Const. art. IV, § 2, cl. 2

25. U.S. Const. art. IV, § 4

26. Wendell Phillips, The Constitution; A Pro-Slavery Compact, *in* The Anti-Slavery Examiner; No. 11 (1844), *reprinted in* The Anti-Slavery Examiner; Nos. 7–14 (1970); William M. Wiecek, The Sources of Antislavery Constitutionalism in America, 1760–1848, at 228 (1977); *see, e.g.,* Lincoln, Speech at New Haven, Connecticut, *in* 2 Speeches and Writings, at 132, 141–42.

27. Michael Vorenberg, Final Freedom 14–15 (2001).

28. Richards, The Slave Power, at 57.

29. William Lee Miller, Arguing About Slavery: The Great Battle in the United States Congress 49 (1996).

30. U.S. Const. art. IV, § 4.

31. Leonard L. Richards, "Gentlemen of Property and Standing" 14–15, 156 (1970); Russel Nye, Fettered Freedom: Civil Liberties and the Slavery Controversy, 1830–1860, at 54–69 (1949); Clement Eaton, Freedom of Thought in the Old South 331 (1940) (quotation).

32. Miller, Arguing About Slavery; Leonard L. Richards, The Life and Times of Congressman John Quincy Adams 152–60 (1986).

33. Michael Kent Curtis, Free Speech, "The People's Darling Privilege" 202–04, 227–31 (2000).

34. Lincoln, 2 Speeches and Writings, at 128.

35. David M. Potter, Impending Crisis 477 (Don E. Fehrenbacher ed., 1976); William W. Freehling, The Reintegration of American History: Slavery and the Civil War 197–98 (1994).

36. 1 History of American Presidential Elections, 1789–1844, at 501 (Arthur M. Schlesinger, Jr. & Fred L. Israel eds., 1972).

37. Prigg v. Pennsylvania, 41 U.S. (16 Pet.) 539, 612 (1842). *See generally* Fehrenbacher, The Slaveholding Republic, at 219–25; Finkelman, An Imperfect Union, at 132–34.

38. Fehrenbacher, The Slaveholding Republic, at 223; Richards, The Slave Power, at 95–96.

39. Holt, Political Crisis, at 39–40; Miller, Arguing About Slavery, at 284; *see* Potter, Impending Crisis, at 24. Iowa was admitted to statehood in 1846 as part of a compromise intended to offset this imbalance. J. Res. 8, 28th Cong., 5 Stat. 797 (1845) required any states formed north of the Missouri Compromise line to be free states—but this problem could be avoided by simply forming the new states from territory in which slavery was permitted.

40. Fugitive Slave Law, ch. 60, 9 Stat. 462 (1850); Finkelman, An Imperfect Union; Fehrenbacher, The Slaveholding Republic at 232, 251 ("[T]he Fugitive Slave Law of 1850 was the most intrusive action ever taken by the federal government on behalf of slavery."); Freehling, Reintegration, at 202; Holt, Political Crisis, at 89; Holt, The Rise and Fall, at 554; Bruce Levine, Half Slave and Half Free: The Roots of Civil War 186–87 (1992); Leon F. Litwack, North of Slavery: The Negro in the Free States, 1790–1860, at 248 (1961); James M. McPherson, Battle Cry of Freedom 80 (1988); Potter, Impending Crisis, at 131.

41. Fehrenbacher, The Slaveholding Republic, at 90; Richards, The Slave Power, at 198; John Hope Franklin, The Militant South: 1800–1861, at 105–19 (1956).

42. Kansas–Nebraska Act, 10 Stat. 277 (1854); Potter, Impending Crisis, at 160; McPherson, Battle Cry, at 147–49.

43. Dred Scott v. Sandford, 60 U.S. (19 How.) 393 (1856); Fehrenbacher, Dred Scott, at 418 (quoting Augusta Constitutionalist, Mar. 15, 1857); William E. Gienapp, The Republican Party and the Slave Power, *in* New Perspectives on Race and Slavery in America 51, 67 (Robert H. Abzug & Stephen E. Maizlish eds., 1986).

44. Fehrenbacher, Dred Scott, at 435 (quoting Platform of Ohio Republican Party, 1857).

45. 26 Barb. 277 (1857); Finkelman, An Imperfect Union, at 313

46. William E. Gienapp, The Origins of the Republican Party, 1852–1866, at 301–03 (1987); David Herbert Donald, Charles Sumner and the Coming of the Civil War 290–92 (1960); McPherson, Battle Cry, at 150 (quoting N.Y. Evening Post, May 23, 1856).

47. Cong. Globe, 36th Cong., 1st Sess. 1840 (1860).

48. Forrest G. McDonald, States' Rights and the Union: Imperium in Imperio, 1776–1876 (2000). At pages 165–66, McDonald argues that "everything the federal authority did" during the 1850s was favorable to the South and that many Southerners approved of the "constitutional views of John Marshall," "while northerners were adopting a Jeffersonian and Jacksonian suspicion of the federal government and the Supreme Court."

49. Lincoln, First Debate, Mr. Lincoln's Reply, *in* 2 Speeches and Writings, at 508, 524.

50. National Republican Platform, Adopted by the Chicago Convention (May 17, 1860), *in* 2 The American Party Battle, Election Campaign Pamphlets, 1828–1876, at 121–22 (Joel H. Silbey ed., 1999).

51. Chief Justice Taney's opinion in Ableman v. Booth, 62 U.S. (1 How.) 506, 507 (1858) sternly denied the power of state courts to interfere with a federal prosecution of a free-state citizen who "aided and abetted . . . the escape of a fugitive slave" from a U.S. marshal seeking to return him to slavery. Some free-state politicians must surely have noted the irony that

Notes

Taney, a faithful Jacksonian advocate of states' rights, took a narrow view of Congress's power to limit slavery in Dred Scott, but insisted on the widest possible scope for its power to restore fugitive slaves to their masters.

52. Sewell, Ballots for Freedom, at 294–94

53. Lincoln, Speech on Kansas-Nebraska Act, *in* 1 Speeches and Writings, at 316; Lincoln, Message to Congress, *in* 2 Speeches and Writings, at 307; Michael Vorenberg, Final Freedom 30 (2001).

54. Dan T. Carter, When the War Was Over: The Failure of Self-Reconstruction in the South, 1865–1827, at 32–33 (1985).

55. Schlesinger and Israel, ed., 2 History of Elections, at 1117, 1163; Gabor S. Boritt, Why the Civil War Came 87 (1996); LaWanda Cox & John H. Cox, Politics, Principle, and Prejudice, 1865–1866: Dilemma of Reconstruction America 32, 66 (1963); McPherson, The Struggle for Equality, at 314–18.

56. Cox & Cox, Politics, Principle, at 65; Eric L. McKitrick, Andrew Johnson and Reconstruction 49–50 (1960). For the party affiliation and biography of each member, *see* William H. Barnes, History of the Thirty-Ninth Congress of the United States 577–624 (1868).

57. Edward McPherson, The Political History of the United States of America During the Period of Reconstruction, 1865–1870, at 107–09 (1972) (1871)

58. *Id.* at 107.

59. *News from Washington*, Richmond Exam., Jan. 9, 1866, at 1 (dateline Jan. 7, 1866).

60. Theodore Brantner Wilson, The Black Codes of the South 67–68, 72, 98 (1965).

61. *Id.* at 105 and at 101 (quoting General Alfred Terry).

62. Cong. Globe, 39th Cong., 1st Sess. 74 (1866) (remarks of Representative Stevens).

63. Eric Foner, Reconstruction: America's Unfinished Revolution, 1863–1877, at 252 (1988).

64. Cong. Globe, 39th Cong., 1st Sess. 3–5 (1866).

65. McPherson, The Struggle for Equality, at 333.

66. Foner, Reconstruction, at 256–57 (quotation); *see generally* Foner, Free Soil; Michael Les Benedict, *Preserving the Constitution: The Conservative Basis of Radical Reconstruction*, 61 J. Am. Hist. 65, 67 (1974); Michael Les Benedict, *Preserving Federalism: Reconstruction and the Waite Court*, 1978 Sup. Ct. Rev. 39.

67. The Federalist No. 10 (James Madison).

68. *See* Karl R. Popper, The Open Society and Its Enemies (rev. ed. 1950) (providing a definition of "open society").

69. *See, e.g.,* City of Boerne v. Flores, 521 U.S. 507, 519–20 (1997)

70. McCulloch v. Maryland, 17 U.S. (4 Wheat.) 316, 407 (1819).

CHAPTER 2

1. Brown v. Board of Education, 347 U.S. 483, 489 (1954); Richard Kluger, Simple Justice 615 (1976) (quoting *Brown*, 345 U.S. at 972).

2. Kluger, Simple Justice, at 668–69.

3. Paul Finkelman, *The Constitution and the Intentions of the Framers: The Limits of Historical Analysis*, 50 U. Pitt. L. Rev. 349 (1989) (extended discussion of the limits of intentionalism and the use of history).

4. Michael Les Benedict, A Compromise of Principle: Congressional Republicans and Reconstruction 1863–1869, at 170 (1974).

5. Leon F. Litwack, North of Slavery: The Negro in the Free States, 1790–1860, at 279 (1961) (first quotation); Eugene Berwanger, The Frontier Against Slavery: Western Anti-Negro Prejudice and the Slavery Extension Controversy 4 (rev. ed. 2002) (second quotation); Jane H. Pease & William H. Pease, *Antislavery Ambivalence: Immediatism, Expedience, Race* 17 AM. Q. 682, 695 (1965), *reprinted in* 14 Articles on American Slavery: Antislavery 356, 369 (Paul Finkelman ed., 1989) (third quotation).

6. Raoul Berger, Government By Judiciary: The Transformation of the Fourteenth Amendment 10 (1977).

7. Hans Trefousee, Thaddeus Stevens: Nineteenth-Century Egalitarian 174 (1997).

8. Paul Finkelman, Millard Fillmore (2011).

9. U.S. v. Hanway, 26 F. Cas. 105, 110–13 (C.C.E.D. Pa. 1851); Trefousee, Thaddeus Stevens, at 14–15; Paul Finkelman, The Treason Trial of Castner Hanway, *in* American Political Trials 77, 82, 84–86, 89 (Michal Belknap ed., rev ed. 1994) (discussing the influence of Thaddeus Stevens in the Hanway trial).

10. Trefousee, Thaddeus Stevens, at 49–50.

11. *Id.* at 69 (quotation), 242.

12. Fugitive Slave Act of 1826, ch. L, 1826 Pa. Laws 150.

13. Prigg v. Pennsylvania, 41 U.S. (16 Pet.) 539, 625 (1842). *See* Paul Finkelman, *Story Telling on the Supreme Court:* Prigg v. Pennsylvania *and Justice Joseph Story's Judicial Nationalism,* 1994 Sup. Ct. Rev. 247, and Paul Finkelman, *Sorting Out* Prigg v. Pennsylvania, 24 Rutgers L.J. 605 (1993).

14. Act of March 3, 1847, ch. 159, 1847 Pa. Laws 206–8 (preventing kidnapping, preserving the public peace, and prohibiting the exercise of certain powers previously exercised by judges, and to repeal certain slave laws). *See generally* Paul Finkelman, An Imperfect Union: Slavery, Federalism, and Comity 137–39 (1981) (discussing the evolution of law in the North from allowing masters to visit free states while accompanied by slaves to immediately freeing all slaves voluntarily brought into free states); Paul Finkelman, Prigg v. Pennsylvania *and Northern State Courts: Anti-Slavery Use of a Pro-Slavery Decision,* 25 Civ. War Hist. 5 (1979) (discussing how Northern judges and legislators used Prigg as an excuse to avoid involvement in fugitive slave cases).

15. Act of March 1, 1780, ch. CXLVI, 1780 Pa. Laws 296 (providing for the gradual abolition of slavery); William Still, The Underground Railroad *in* Five Slave Narratives (William Loren Katz ed., 1968). Significantly, Pennsylvania, and most other Northern states, never tried to stop black immigration. Indeed, despite the reputation of the North as hostile to black immigration, only five states—Ohio, Indiana, Illinois, Iowa, and Oregon—ever tried to limit black immigration, and only Indiana, in the 1850s, actually implemented its laws to any effect. *See* Paul Finkelman, *Prelude to the Fourteenth Amendment: Black Legal Rights in the Antebellum North,* 17 Rutgers L.J. 415, 424–27, 429–44 (1986). *See, e.g.,* Commonwealth v.

Auld, 4 Pa. L.J. 515 (1850) (charging a master with the kidnapping of his runaway slave's children); A Review of the Trial, Conviction, and Sentence of George Alberti, for Kidnapping [1851], *reprinted in* 2 Fugitive Slaves and American Courts: The Pamphlet Literature 27 (Paul Finkelman ed., 1988); The Trial of Emanual Myers, of Maryland, for Kidnapping certain fugitive slaves, had at Carlisle, Pennsylvania, November, 1859 [1859], *reprinted in* 4 Fugitive Slaves and American Courts: The Pamphlet Literature 121 (Paul Finkelman ed., 1988).

16. Paul Finkelman, *The Strange Career of Race Discrimination in Antebellum Ohio*, 55 Case W. Res. L. Rev. 373–408 (2004).

17. Act of Jan. 5, 1804, 3 Ohio Laws 53 (1807) (providing for the regulation of "black and mulatto persons"); Act of Jan. 25, 1807, 5 Ohio Laws 53 (1807) (amending the act of Jan. 5, 1804 entitled "An Act Regulating black and mulatto persons"); Ohio Const. of 1802, art. IV § 1 (limiting the franchise to white males); Act of Feb. 9, 1831, 29 Ohio Laws 94 (1831) (relating to juries); Act of Feb. 10, 1829, 27 Ohio Laws 72 (1829) (providing "for the support and better regulation of common schools").

In 1800, Ohio had a black population of 337; it had grown by more than 550% to 1,899 by 1810, despite the fact that anti-immigration laws were on the books for 6 of those years. It more than doubled to 4,723 in the next decade, and doubled again in the next decade, reaching 9,568 by 1830; by 1840 the black population was 17,342, and in 1850, a year after the registration laws went off the books, the census found 25,279 blacks in the state, giving it the third largest free black population in the North. *See* United States Census, Negro Population, 1790–1915, at 57 (1915).

18. Berger, Government, at 10.

19. Dictionary of American Biography 49 (1964) (Brinkerhoff); Biographical Directory of the United States Congress 1774–1996 (1996) (Benjamin F. Wade); *id.* at 593 (James Ashley); Phyllis F. Field, William Dennison, *in* American National Biography 446–48 (1999).

20. Act of Feb. 26, 1839, ch. 37, 1838 Ohio Laws 38 (relating to fugitives from labor or service from other states).

21. Act of Jan. 19, 1843, ch. 41, 1842 Ohio Laws 13 (repealing an 1839 act relating to fugitives from labor and service from other states).

22. He was the District Attorney of Tuscarawas County from 1846–49. Biographical Directory of the United States Congress, at 663.

23. Resolution of Feb. 25, 1848, ch. 46 Ohio Laws 314 (declaring that the Ordinance of 1787, as relates to slavery, should be extended to the territory acquired from Mexico).

24. Act of Feb. 24, 1848, ch. 46, 1847 Ohio Laws 81 (providing for the establishment of Common Schools for the education of children of black and mulatto persons, and amending the March 7, 1838 act entitled, "An act for the support and better regulation of Common Schools, and to create permanently the office of Superintendent"); Finkelman, *Strange Career*, at 373–408. *See* for example, Chalmers v. Stewart, 11 Ohio 386 (1842), which involved a white parent complaining because blacks had been allowed to attend the public school.

25. *See* Howard N. Rabinowitz, *More Than the Woodward Thesis: Assessing the Strange Career of Jim Crow*, 75 J. of Am. Hist. 842, 845 (1988) (discussing this issue in the post-Civil War South). Rabinowitz "discovered" that what preceded segregation in the South "was normally exclusion" and that "ironically, segregation often therefore marked an improvement in the status of blacks."

26. Act of Feb. 10, 1849, ch. 47 Ohio Laws 17 (authorizing the establishment of separate schools for the education of colored children, and for other purposes).

27. *See* Kentucky v. Dennison, 65 U.S. (24 How.) 66, 68–69 (1861) (holding that the Federal Constitution does not impose an obligation on one state to "surrender its citizens or residents to any other state on the charge that they have committed an offence not known to the laws of the former...").

28. Republicans in New York and Connecticut, for example, attempted to create equal suffrage in their state. Finkelman, *Prelude to the Fourteenth Amendment*, at 430.

29. *Ex parte* Milligan, 71 U.S. (4 Wall.) 2, 16 (1866).

30. *See* David Dudley Cornish, The Sable Arm: Negro Troops in the Union Army, 1861–1865, at 29, 184 (1966) (discussing the policy and practice of integrating former slaves into the Union Army).

31. Reconstruction, 1865–1877, at 38 (Richard N. Current ed. 1965) (reprinting letter from Howell Cobb to General J. H. Wilson (June 14, 1865)).

32. U.S. Statutes at Large, XII, 589–92 (the Confiscation Acts). The Confiscation Act of July 17, 1862 "provided for the seizure of all the real and personal property of major rebel officeholders and all rebels who did not return to their allegiances within sixty days of a presidential warning proclamation." Benedict, A Compromise of Principle, at 247.

33. Paul Finkelman, *Lincoln, Emancipation and the Limits of Constitutional Change*, 2008 Sup. Ct. Rev. 349–87 (2009).

34. Reconstruction, 1865–1877, at 38.

35. Report of the Joint Committee on Reconstruction, 39th Cong., Resolution and Report of the Committee xiii (1st Sess. 1866).

36. *Id.* at xvii–xviii.

37. *Id.*

38. Act of Nov. 24, 1865, ch. 6, 1865 Ala. Laws 90 ("[p]rotect[ing] Freedmen in Their Rights of Person and Property in this State").

39. Act of Nov. 25, 1865, ch. 4, 1865 Miss. Laws 82 ("an Act for conferring Civil Rights on Freedmen, and for other purposes").

40. Act of Nov. 24, 1865, ch. 6, 1865 Ala. Laws 90 ("[p]rotect[ing] Freedmen in Their Rights of Person and Property in this State").

41. Rep. of the Joint Comm., Part IV: Florida, Louisiana, Texas, at 125.

42. Act of Nov. 24, 1865, ch. 6, 1865 Ala. Laws 90 ("an Act for amending the Vagrant Laws of the state").

43. Act of Nov. 25, 1865, ch. 4, 1865 Miss. Laws 82 ("an Act for conferring Civil Rights on Freedmen, and for other purposes").

44. Act of Nov. 22, 1865, ch. 5, 1865 Miss. Laws at 86 ("an Act for regulating the relation of Master and Apprentice, as it related to Freedmen, Free Negroes, and Mulattoes").

45. *Id.* at 90.

46. Act of Nov. 25, 1865, 1865 Miss. Laws 82 ("an Act for conferring Civil Rights on Freedmen, and for other purposes").

47. Rep. of the Joint Comm., at iv–vi; Rep. of the Joint Comm., Part IV, at 26; Rep. of the Joint Comm., Part III: Georgia, Alabama, Mississippi, Arkansas 85–86; Rep. of the Joint Comm., Part III, at 186.

48. James M. McPherson, The Struggle for Equality: Abolitionists and the Negro in the Civil War and Reconstruction 341 (1964).

49. Rep. of the Joint Comm., at xix; Rep. of the Joint Comm., Part I: Tennessee, at title page.

50. Rep. of the Joint Comm., Part I at, 107–08 (Hatch), 112, 120–21 (Fisk), 121 (Barnard).

51. Rep. of the Joint Comm., Part II: Virginia, North Carolina, South Carolina 4–5 (Turner), 7 (Underwood), 17 (Smith), 35 (sheriff).

52. Rep. of the Joint Comm., Part II, at 209 (Clapp).

53. Rep. of the Joint Comm., Part II, at 198; at 202–03 (Union Army captain), 206 (minister), 209–11 (Clapp).

54. *Id.* at 222–29, 234.

55. Rep. of the Joint Comm., Part IV, at 75–76.

56. Rep. of the Joint Comm., Part III, at 33, 42–43. Howard was the brother of the war hero, Major General Oliver Otis Howard, who at this time was the head of Freedman's Bureau.

57. In this sense it seems that the Court's decision in Lochner v. New York, 198 U.S. 45 (1905), was clearly wrong in determining that the idea of "freedom of contract" did not include the right to be exploited by powerful employers. That had been the situation in the South before the 14th Amendment. The Amendment was designed to prevent this.

58. McCulloch v. Maryland 17 U.S. (4 Wheat.) 316 (1819).

59. Rep. of the Joint Comm., Part II, at 4.

CHAPTER 3

1. Elizabeth A. Reilly, *Infinite Hope, Introduction to the Fourteenth Amendment: The 140th Anniversary of the Fourteenth Amendment,* 42 Akron L. Rev. 1003 (2009); Howard N. Meyer, The Amendment that Refused to Die, at xi (1973); James E. Bond, *The Original Understanding of the Fourteenth Amendment in Illinois, Ohio, and Pennsylvania,* 18 Akron L. Rev. 435 (1985).

2. A LEXIS search conducted on February 7, 2009 indicated that the Congressional Globe had been cited 212 times in U.S. Supreme Court cases, over 700 times in combined state and federal cases, and over 1,700 times in law journals. *See, e.g.,* Eric Foner, *Remarks at Conference on the Second Founding,* 18 J. Const. L. 1289, 1289 (2009).

3. There were two sessions of the 39th Congress, and the Congress was in recess from July 29, 1866–December 2, 1866. There was also a special session of the Senate from March 4–11, 1865. Biographical Directory of the United States Congress 1774–1789, at 179 (1989); Merrill D. Peterson, The Great Triumvirate: Webster, Clay and Calhoun (1987).

4. *See, e.g.,* Marsh v. Chambers, 463 U.S. 783, 790 (1983) ("An act 'passed by the first Congress assembled under the Constitution, many of whose members had taken part in framing that instrument, . . . is contemporaneous and weighty evidence of its true meaning.'" (quoting Wisconsin v. Pelican Ins. Co., 127 U.S. 265, 297 (1888) (omission in original)).

5. There were two sessions of the 38th Congress, which were held December 7, 1863–July 4, 1864 and December 5, 1864–March 3, 1865. The Senate met for a special session from March

4–14, 1863. Biographical Directory of the United States Congress, at 175; *Domestic Intelligence*, Harper's Weekly, Jan. 16, 1864, at 35.

6. Campaign of 1864, *in* National Party Platforms: 1840–1972, at 35 (Donald Bruce Johnson & Kirk H. Porter eds., 1973); The Ohio Platforms of the Republican and Democratic Parties From 1855 To 1881 Inclusive 23 (1881).

7. *See* David E. Kyvig, Ohio and the Shaping of the U.S. Constitution, *in* The History of Ohio Law 346 (Michael Les Benedict & John F. Winkler eds., 2004); E. B. Long & Barbara Long, The Civil War Day by Day: An Almanac: 1861–1865, at 630 (1971); *See* Constitutional Amendments 13, 14 (notes 1–940), U.S.C.S. 1–2 (Lawyers ed., LEXIS L. Pub. 1999).

8. William H. Barnes, History of the Thirty-Ninth Congress of the United States 577–624 (1969) (1868). Barnes provided biographical sketches of all members of the 39th Congress, indicating by typeface whether they were Republican or Democratic. The calculations are my own based upon Barnes' sketches. The numbers should be treated as only approximations—though hopefully close ones. For example, I have counted all the Representatives and Senators, but omitted the territorial delegates. Because of deaths, resignations, results from contested elections, and similar changes, the summary of all the Congressmen is both over-inclusive (it includes more than actually were serving at any one time) and under-inclusive (at any one point in time, it may not include others who served later.) When someone served in the 39th Congress in both the House and the Senate I counted them only once, in the house of Congress in which they first were elected. In spite of the fact that one may therefore need to recalculate the numbers for a given day or a given event, as an overall picture, these numbers should give a good idea of the distribution of power in the Congress.

There is, of course, also a question about parties. Most of the Congressmen are, as Barnes indicated, clearly affiliated with the Republican or Democratic Party. However, reference to other sources indicates that some were elected with party names like "Unionist," "Unconditional Unionist," etc. *See, e.g.,* Biographical Directory of the United States Congress: 1774–Present, http://bioguide.congress.gov/biosearch/biosearch.asp (last visited Mar. 23, 2009). The Biographical Directory indicates that there were seventeen Unconditional Unionists and eight Unionists in the 39th Congress. For purposes of this article, I have accepted Barnes' division of all members into Republican and Democrats as fairly accurate in that virtually all members of Congress were allied with one of the two major parties no matter what their individual party label.

9. Richard L. Aynes, *Enforcing the Bill of Rights Against the States: The History and the Future*, 18 J. Contemp. Legal Issues 77, 130–32 (2009) (detailing Johnson's motives, misstatements, and understanding of those misstatements).

10. According to U.S. Census data, only 9,371 degrees had been granted in 1870, the first year in which such information was recorded. National Center for Education Statistics, Digest of Education Statistics, available at http://nces.ed.gov/programs/digest/d07/tables/dt07_258.asp (last visited May 27, 2009). The total population at that time was 38,558,000. Natl Ctr. for Educ. Statistics, 120 Years of American Education: A Statistical Portrait 34 (Jan. 1993), http://nces.ed.gov/pubs93/93442.pdf. Merely as an illustration and without any claim of it as a representative sample, this is an account of the universities and law schools formally attended by members of Congress whose last names began with the letter "D;" 9 of the 17 members had received a college education:

William A. Darling (R-N.Y.): none.
Garrett Davis (D-Ky.): none.

Thomas T. Davis (R-N.Y.): Hamilton College (1831).
Henry Dawes (R-Mass.): Yale College (1839).
John L. Dawson (D-Penn.): Washington College (n.d.).
Joseph H. Defrees (R-Ind.): none.
Columbus Delano (R-Ohio): none.
Henry C. Deming (R-Conn.): Yale College (1836) and Harvard Law School (1838). He served
    as a Colonel in the 12th Connecticut Regiment during the war.
Charles Denison (R-Pa.): Dickinson College (1839).
Arthur A. Denny (R-Wash.): none.
James Dixon (R-Conn.): Williams College (1834).
Nathan F. Dixon (R-R.I.): Brown University (1833) and attended law schools at New Haven
    and Cambridge.
William E. Dodge (R-N.Y.): none.
Ignatius Donnelly (R-Minn.): none.
James R. Doolittle (R-Wis.): Geneva College (1834).
John F. Driggs (R-Mich.): none.
Ebenezer Dumont (R-Ind.): Indiana University (n.d.). He was a Colonel in the 7th
    Regiment of Indiana Volunteers.
Barnes, History of the Thirty-Ninth Congress, at 586–89.

11. My own quick count suggests that more than 160 were lawyers. The same appears to
have been true of the 38th Congress; for example, all nineteen member of the Ohio delegation had studied law. Margaret Leech & Harry J. Brown, The Garfield Orbit 157 (1978).

12. See Erving E. Beauregard, Reverend John Walker, Renaissance Man 69–71 (1990). John
Bingham attended Walker's Franklin College class in "General History," which studied the
Magna Carta, the English Petition of Right, the English Declaration Rights, writings of John
Locke, American history, the Declaration of Independence, the 5th Amendment Due Process
Clause, and other matters related to freedom and law. Other members of the 39th Congress
likely to have studied the same legal principles were Senator Edgar Cowan (class of 1839)
(R-Pa.), Senator Joseph S. Fowler (class of 1843) (R-Tenn.), and Representative William
Lawrence (class of 1838) (R-Ohio). Biographical Directory of the United States Congress, at
834, 1022, 1350.

13. Again, this example is provided without any claim about its representativeness. Benjamin
G. Harris (D-Md.) attended Yale College, Cambridge (Mass.) Law School, and apparently
studied law with a lawyer prior to being admitted to the bar in 1840. Biographical Directory
of the United States Congress, at 1137. Representative Philip Johnson (D-Pa.) apparently
studied law in an apprenticeship program and subsequently attended Union Law School in
Easton Pennsylvania before being admitted to the bar in 1848. Id. at 1270. Senator Charles
Sumner (R-Mass.) graduated from Harvard University (1830), from Harvard Law School
(1833), and was admitted to the bar in 1834, raising the possibility that he served in some
type of apprentice program in the intervening year. Id. at 1896. Charles Upson (R-Mich.)
studied at Yale Law School in 1844, moved to Michigan where he taught school, and served
as a deputy county clerk in a local court, and was admitted to the bar in 1847. Id. at 1966.
This raises the possibility that he either served in an apprenticeship program in Michigan
or his deputy clerkship served that purpose. Similarly, Elihu B. Washburn (R-Ill.) studied
law at both Kents' Hill Seminary (1836) and Harvard Law School (1839), but was not admitted to the bar until 1840. Id. at 2012. He worked in two different law offices before enrolling

in Cambridge Law School. Elihu Israel and Cadwallader Washburn: A Chapter in American Biography 164, 166 (Gaillard Hunt ed., reprt. 1969).

14. Using Barnes' biographical sketches, my own calculations indicate that 23.3% (14 of the 60 Senators) of the Senate and 41.8% (84 of the 201 House members) of the House had never been in Congress before the 39th Congress. Additionally, in the 38th Congress, it was said that 60% of the entering Congressmen were new to Congress. Leech & Brown, Garfield Orbit, at 157.

15. Biographical Directory of the United States Congress, at 179; Cong. Globe, 39th Cong., Special Session 1427 (1865); Cong. Globe, 39th Cong., 2d Session 2003 (1867).

16. *See* Benjamin B. Kendrick, The Journal of the Joint Committee of Fifteen on Reconstruction 155–69, 183–87 (1914); *see* Kyvig, Ohio and the Shaping of the U.S. Constitution, at 346; Michael Les Benedict, A Compromise of Principle: Congressional Republicans and Reconstruction 1863–1869, 31–32 (1974) (naming Bingham, Stevens, Colfax, Wilson, Justin S. Morrill, Elihu B. Washburn, George S. Boutwell (R-Mass.) and Roscoe Conkling (R-N.Y.)).

17. Benedict, A Compromise of Principle, at 32–33 (also listing John Sherman (R-Ohio), Lafayette Foster (R-Conn.), Lot M. Morrill (R-Maine), Ira Harris (R-N.Y.), and Benjamin F. Wade (R-Ohio)).

18. Richard L. Aynes, Ohio and the Drafting and Ratification of the Fourteenth Amendment, *in* 1 The History of Ohio Law 370 (Michael Les Benedict & John R. Winkler eds., 2004).

19. Drew Gilpin Faust, This Republic of Suffering: Death and the American Civil War, xi (2008); George W. Paschal, The Constitution of the United States Defined and Carefully Annotated 291–92 (1868); W.E.B. Dubois, Black Reconstruction in America 605 (Touchstone 1995) (1935); *Thirty-Ninth Congress*, Wash. News, Feb. 8, 1866, at 1, col. 4; Cong. Globe, 39th Cong., 1st Sess. 701 (Feb. 7, 1866).

20. On April 10, Secretary of War Edwin Stanton reported to President Johnson his estimate that the various rebel armies still had a total of 91,222 soldiers in the field. Michael W. Kauffman, American Brutus: John Wilkes Booth and the Lincoln Conspiracies 456 n.21 (2004).

21. William A. Tidwell, James O. Hall, & David Winfred Gaddy, Come Retribution: The Confederate Secret Service and the Assassination of Lincoln (1988); William A. Tidwell, Confederate Covert Action in the American Civil War: April '65 (1995); Kauffman, American Brutus; The Trial of the Conspirators to Assassinate President Lincoln: The Argument of Judge Advocate Bingham for the Government, *in* VIII American State Trials 495–645 (John D. Lawson ed., 1917) (John Bingham's speech as Judge Advocate at the Lincoln conspirators' trial).

22. Kauffman, American Brutus, Stewart Sifakis, Who Was Who in the Civil War 552 (1988), and Michael E. Banasik, Serving With Honor: The Diary of Captain Eathan Allen Pinnell Eighth Missouri Infantry (Confederate) 217 n.14, 227 (1999) (Mexico); Sifakis, Who Was Who, at 50 (England); A Brief History of the Confederate Colonies of Brazil: The Confederados, http://www.patsabin.com/lowcountry/confederados.htm (last visited Feb. 8, 2009), David I. Durham & Paul M. Pruitt, Jr., A Journey in Brazil: Henry Washington Hilliard and the Brazilian Anti-Slavery Society (2008) and Banasik, Serving With Honor, at 205 n.11 (Brazil).

23. VII Jefferson Davis: Constitutionalist: His Letters, Papers and Speeches 139 (Dunbar Rowland ed., 1923). *See also Case of Davis*, 7 F.Cas. 63 (C.C.D.VA. 1866–1871) (No. 3621A).

24. Long & Long, Civil War Day by Day, at 687.

25. *Id.* at 688–92.

26. *Id.* at 691; Sifakis, Who Was Who, at 460; Christopher D. Rucker, *The Pastor-Poet*, Civil War Times, Apr. 2005, at 12; Thomas Ayres, That's Not in My American History Book: A Compilation of Little-Known Events and Forgotten Heroes 125 (2000).

27. Long & Long, Civil War Day by Day, at 696.

28. *Id.* at 696–97; Constitutional Amendments, at 13–14.

29. Richard E. Beringer et al., Why the South Lost the Civil War 346 (1991).

30. Eric Foner, Reconstruction: America's Unfinished Revolution, 1863–1877, 261–63 (1988), at 262 (quotation).

31. Foner, Reconstruction, at 263.

32. Foner, Reconstruction, at 199, 342.

33. Long & Long, Civil War Day by Day, at 696–97.

34. Elihu Israel, at 237 (quotation); Hans L. Trefousse, Andrew Johnson: A Biography 310 (1989).

35. Trefousse, Andrew Johnson, at 36 (first quotation), 334 (second quotation).

36. 14 Stat. 1–809 (1865–1867).

37. 14 Stat. 27 (1866); Trefousse, Andrew Johnson, at 245–47.

38. 14 Stat. 173 (1866); Cong. Globe, 39th Cong., 1st sess. 3838, 3842 (1866).

39. Foner, Reconstruction, at 247, 249.

40. Richard L. Aynes, *Constricting the Law of Freedom: Justice Miller, The Fourteenth Amendment, and the* Slaughter-House Cases, 70 Chi-Kent L. Rev. 627, 660 n.228 (1994).

41. Ohio Platforms, at 24.

42. *Id.* at 27.

43. *The State and the Nation*, Cadiz Republican (Ohio), Aug. 15, 1866. The speech was given on August 8, 1866 (first quotation); The Cincinnati Commercial, Sept. 29, 1866, at 1 (second quotation).

44. Wager Swayne, The Ordinance of 1787 and the War of 1861: An Address Delivered Before the New York Commandery of the Military Order of the Loyal Legion 4 (1892). Swayne focused upon Section 1 of the Amendment and this allowed him refer to the key provisions of the 13th, 14th, and 15th Amendments as three paragraphs. *See id.* at 4–5.

45. The committee was approved by the Senate on December 9, 1861, and approved by the House the following day. Long & Long, Civil War Day by Day, at 147–48.

46. Kendrick, The Journal of the Joint Committee, at 37. The members of the Joint Committee were Senator William P. Fessenden (R-Me.), Chair; Senator Jacob M. Howard (R-Mich.); Senator James W. Grimes (R-Iowa); Senator George H. Williams (R-Or.); Congressman Justin S. Morrill (R-Vt.); Senator Ira Harris (R-N.Y.); Senator Reverdy Johnson (D-Md.); Congressman Thaddeus Steven (R-Pa.); Congressman John A. Bingham (R-Ohio); Congressman Roscoe Conkling (R-N.Y.); Congressman George S. Boutwell (R-Mass.); Congressman Elihu B. Washburn (R-Ill.); Congressman Henry T. Blow (R-Mo.); Congressman Henry Grider (D-Ky.);

and Congressman Andrew J. Rogers (D-N.J.). *Id.;* Benedict, A Compromise of Principle, at 32 (quote).

47. Kendrick, The Journal of the Joint Committee, at 264–65; Aynes, Ohio and the Drafting and Ratification of the Fourteenth Amendment, at 370–401 (work of the Joint Committee on Reconstruction), at 377 (estimate by Democratic candidate for Governor in Ohio, George W. Morgan); Meyer, The Amendment that Refused to Die, at 53 (indicating, without citation, that more than seventy amendments were introduced into the 39th Congress).

48. *The Union—In the Future,* Harper's Weekly, June 15, 1861, at 370 (quotations). The discussion of the officially sponsored mob action to expel Massachusetts Judge Samuel Hoar and his daughter from South Carolina because he wanted to contest South Carolina law against African American citizens of Massachusetts was a frequently discussed event in Congress. *See, e.g.,* Cong. Globe, 39th Cong., 1st Sess. 1263 (1866) (Representative John M. Broomall (R-Pa.)); Michael Kent Curtis, Free Speech, 'The People's Darling Privilege': Struggles for Freedom of Expression in American History 271–99 (2000) (on the free speech battles over Hinton Helper's *Impending Crisis* and over Rev. Daniel Worth).

49. Richard L. Aynes, *Unintended Consequences of the Fourteenth Amendment and What They Tell Us About Its Interpretation,* 39 Akron L. Rev. 289, 309, 320 (2006).

50. Cong. Globe, 39th Cong., 1st Sess. 2545 (1866) (House vote); *id.* at 3042 (Senate vote); Benedict, A Compromise of Principle, at 185–86 (discussing the caucus).

51. Cong. Globe, 39th Cong., 1st Sess. 3149 (1866) (House final vote); Benedict, A Compromise of Principle, at 186 (quotation).

52. Aynes, Ohio and the Drafting and Ratification of the Fourteenth Amendment, at 386 (omission in original) (citing *The Reconstruction Problem—Mr. Bingham's Speech,* N.Y. Times, Jan. 18, 1867, at 4).

53. Constitutional Amendments at 13 (Connecticut ratified on June 25, 1866, New Hampshire on July 6, 1866 and Tennessee on July 19, 1866).

54. Richard Nelson Current, Lincoln's Loyalists: Union Soldiers from the Confederacy 213–18, 342 (1992); Benedict, A Compromise of Principle, at 186.

55. *See The Fourteenth Amendment,* Marysville Tribune, Jan. 22, 1868 (reprinting an editorial from The Delaware Gazette) (arguing that because 22 of the 24 non-rebellious state legislatures had ratified the amendment, it was already in effect); Aynes, Ohio and the Drafting and Ratification of the Fourteenth Amendment, at 387.

56. Benedict, A Compromise of Principle, at 186, 211.

57. Trefousse, Andrew Johnson, at 271–75; Aynes, *Constricting the Law of Freedom.*

58. Trefousse, Andrew Johnson, at 253 (omission in original).

59. William Nelson, The Fourteenth Amendment: From Political Principle to Judicial Doctrine 60 (1988); Aynes, *Constricting the Law of Freedom,* at 396. Secretary of State William Seward declared that the Amendment was adopted on July 28, 1868. *Id.*

60. *The Truth Confessed,* Harper's Weekly, Jan. 16, 1864, at 34 (emphasis added).

61. Slaughter-House Cases, 83 U.S. 36, 129 (1872) (Swayne, J., dissenting).

62. Raoul Berger, Government By Judiciary: The Transformation of the Fourteenth Amendment 10 (1977).

63. Nelson, The Fourteenth Amendment, at 37; Kendrick, The Journal of the Joint Committee, at 185 (quotation).

64. Bingham was not talking about the 14th Amendment here, but rather about the 5th Amendment.

65. Cong. Globe, 37th Cong., 2d Sess. 1638 (1862).

66. Barnes, History of the Thirty-Ninth Congress, at 67; Cong. Globe, 39th Cong., 1st Sess. 216–22 (1866).

67. Barnes, History of the Thirty-Ninth Congress, at 68–70.

68. Cong. Globe, 37th Cong., 2nd Sess. 241 (1862).

69. Cong. Globe, 39th Cong., 1st sess. 156 (1866); *Eloquent Speech of Hon. John A. Bingham,* Cadiz Republican (Ohio), Aug. 15, 1866, 2, at col. 3.

CHAPTER 4

1. Cong. Globe, 39th Cong., 1st Sess. 1034 (1866). Bingham originally introduced a "joint resolution to amend the Constitution of the United States so as to empower Congress to pass all necessary and proper laws to secure to all persons in every State of the Union equal protection in their rights, life, liberty, and property . . . ." Cong. Globe, 39th Cong., 1st Sess. 14 (1865) on December 6, 1865. Joseph B. James, The Framing of the Fourteenth Amendment 48 (1956). It was referred to committee. The Joint Committee reported out this version in February 1866, a week after Johnson had vetoed the Freedmen's Bureau Bill. James, The Framing, at 84.

2. Cong. Globe, 39th Cong., 1st Sess. 1034.

3. *Id.* at 2765–66.

4. United States v. Guest, 383 U.S. 745, 784 (1966) (Brennan, J., concurring in part and dissenting in part) (quotation). *See* Robert Kaczorowski, *Revolutionary Constitutionalism in the Era of the Civil War and Reconstruction*, 61 N.Y.U. L. Rev. 863, 915, 918, 925 (1986) (the Amendment was designed to confer positive power, through a declaration of rights as positive law).

5. Michael Kent Curtis, No State Shall Abridge: The Fourteenth Amendment and the Bill of Rights (1986), exhaustively documents the content of Republican ideology, especially at pp. 26–56.

6. *E.g.*, Curtis, No State Shall Abridge, chapters 3, 5.

7. The Federalist No. 44 (James Madison).

8. Other methods included separating powers (The Federalist Nos. 48 (James Madison), 51 (Alexander Hamilton or James Madison)), using a bicameral form of legislature and relatively short terms of office (The Federalist No. 37 (James Madison)), especially in the popularly elected House of Representatives (The Federalist No. 53 (Alexander Hamilton or James Madison)), equal state representation in the Senate and state selection of Senators (The Federalist No. 62 (Alexander Hamilton or James Madison)), and Senate ability to check factions thus preventing unjust majoritarian rule (The Federalist No. 63 (Alexander Hamilton or James Madison)).

9. The Federalist No. 78 (Alexander Hamilton).

10. Kaczorowski, *Revolutionary Constitutionalism*, at 871–72.

11. Michael Kent Curtis, *Resurrecting the Privileges or Immunities Clause and Revising the Slaughter-House Cases Without Exhuming* Lochner: *Individual Rights and the Fourteenth Amendment*, 38 B.C. L. Rev. 1, 10 (1996) (emphasis added), (citing 2 The Bill of Rights, A Documentary History 1025, 1030–31 (Bernard Schwartz ed., 1971)).

12. Marbury v. Madison, 5 U.S. (1 Cranch) 137 (1803).

13. Barron v. Mayor and City Council of Baltimore, 32 U.S. 243 (1833), at 250 (quotation; emphasis added), at 248.

14. Dred Scott v. Sandford, 60 U.S. 393, 450 (1857), at 451–52 (quotation).

15. *Dred Scott* at 450.

16. Prigg v. Pennsylvania, 41 U.S. 539, 611–15 (1842); Act of the 12th of February 1793, ch. 51.

17. No Person held to Service of Labour in one State, under the Laws thereof, escaping into another, shall, in Consequence of any Law or Regulation therein, be discharged from such Service or Labour, but shall be delivered upon Claim of the Party to whom such Service or Labour may be due. U.S. Const. Art. IV, sec. 2, cl. 3. *Prigg* at 612 (first quotation) and 614 (second quotation).

18. *Prigg* at 611–12 (Union) and 614–17 (claim and delivery) (*see also* 541, argument of counsel).

19. *Prigg* at 620 (first quotation), 616, 615 (second quotation), 618–20 (the power to apportion representatives per the census flows from the express powers to apportion and to take the census; the power "to make laws to carry the stipulations of treaties into effect... result[s] from the duty of the national government to fulfil all the obligations of treaties;" the power to use habeas to enforce the guarantee against arrest for members of Congress; the power to legislate to secure habeas corpus or to suspend it as authorized is "by necessary implication, within the scope of the legislative power of congress" are offered as "cases where rights are intended to be absolutely secured, and duties are positively enjoined by the constitution.").

20. Commonwealth of Kentucky v. Dennison, 65 U.S. 66 (1860); *Barron* at 250, 247.

21. United States v. Cruikshank, 92 U.S. 542, 554–55 (1876) (emphasis added).

22. Curtis, No State Shall Abridge, at 48–54; James, The Framing, at 87. *But see* Kaczorowski, *Revolutionary Constitutionalism*, at 933–34.

23. Cong. Globe, 39th Cong., 1st Sess. 1034 (first, second and fourth quotations); *id.* at 1291 (third quotation); Curtis, No State Shall Abridge, at 62–63.

24. Cong. Globe, 39th Cong., 1st Sess. 2765–66.

25. William Rich, *Taking "Privileges or Immunities" Seriously: A Call to Expand the Constitutional Canon*, 87 Minn. L. Rev. 153, 171–72 (2002) (citing Cong. Globe, 39th Cong., 1st Sess. appx. at 135 (first quotation) and Cong. Globe, 39th Cong., 1st Sess. 1064 (second quotation)).

26. James, The Framing, at 97–98.

27. David Bogen, *Rebuilding the* Slaughter-House: *The Cases' Support for Civil Rights*, 42 Akron L. Rev. 1131, 1137 (2009) (citing Cong. Globe, 39th Cong., 1st Sess. 2459 (Rep. Stevens), at 2462 (Rep. Garfield); at 2465 (Rep. Thayer); at 2467 (Rep. Boyer); at 2498 (Rep. Broomall); at 2502, 2513 (Rep. Raymond)) (quotation).

28. Cong. Globe, 39th Cong., 1st Sess. 1294 (Wilson urging turning the proslavery arguments against themselves, making them into a force for good); *id.* at 1034 (Bingham).

29. Richard L. Aynes, *On Misreading John Bingham and the Fourteenth Amendment*, 103 Yale L.J. 57, 80 n.140 (1993) (citing *Ex parte Virginia*, 100 U.S. 339, 347 (1879)).

30. Garrett Epps, *The Antebellum Political Background of the Fourteenth Amendment*, 67 Law & Contemp. Probs. 175, 210 (Summer 2004) (first quotation); Cong. Globe, 39th Cong., 1st Sess. 1062 (Rep. Kelley) (second quotation).

31. Cong. Globe, 39th Cong., 1st Sess. 1294 (emphasis added).

32. Cong. Globe, 39th Cong., 1st Sess. Appx. 133 (Rogers); Michael McConnell, *Institutions and Interpretation: A Critique of* City of Boerne v. Flores, 111 Harv. L. Rev. 153, 176 (1997) (first quotation); Epps, *Antebellum Political Background*, at 210 (second quotation).

33. Cong. Globe, 39th Cong. 1st Sess. 1034 (Bingham); *id.* at 2766 (Howard); Kaczorowski, *Revolutionary Constitutionalism*, at 875, 877 (The 39th Congress was adopting the 14th Amendment at a time when "President Andrew Johnson, a Democratic Conservative, actually encouraged Southern resistance through his policy of appeasement. This continuing Southern hostility to the Union led Republicans and Southern Unionists to believe that the spirit that had led the South to secede had survived the Civil War."); McConnell, *Institutions and Interpretation*, at 176.

34. *Cruikshank*, 83 U.S. 36, 81 (1873) (dicta) (first quotation); *id.* at 554–55.

35. Civil Rights Cases, 109 U.S. 3 (1883); Harris v. United States, 106 U.S. 629, 640 (1883); Baldwin v. Franks, 120 U.S. 678 (1887); Hodges v. United States, 203 U.S. 1, 14 (1906); *see* Wilson Huhn, *The Legacy of* Slaughter-House, Bradwell, *and* Cruikshank *in Constitutional Interpretation*, 42 Akron L. Rev. 1051, 1077–78 (2009).

36. *E.g.*, Civil Rights Act of 1866, ch. 31, 14 Stat. 27 (1866) (originally entitled "An Act to protect All Persons in the United States in Their Civil Rights, and furnish the Means of their Vindication"); The Enforcement Act of 1870 (The Act of May 31, 1870), ch. 114, § 18, 16 Stat. 140 (1870) (originally entitled "An Act to enforce the rights of citizens of the United States"); Ku Klux Klan Act of 1871, ch. 22, §2, 17 Stat. 13 (1871) (originally entitled "An Act to enforce the Provisions of the 14th Amendment to the Constitution of the United States, and for other Purposes"); Civil Rights Act of 1875, ch. 114, §§3–5, 18 Stat. 336, 337 (1875) (originally entitled "An act to protect all citizens in their civil and legal rights"). Cong. Globe, 42nd Cong., 1st Sess. Appx. 84–85 (1871) (quotation).

37. Curtis, No State Shall Abridge, at 170, citing 4 Cong. Rec. 5585 (1876).

38. Congress had serious debates over using only the Section 5 power in the Civil Rights Act of 1964, fearing the limited scope of its Court-interpreted reach. The Commerce Power carried the day in Congress, and eventually in the Court. *See* Rebecca E. Zeitlow, *Belonging, Protection and Equality: The Neglected Citizenship Clause and The Limits of Federalism*, 62 U. Pitt. L. Rev. 281, 293–94 (2000) (citing A Bill to Eliminate Discrimination in Public Accommodations Affecting Interstate Commerce, 1963: Hearings on S. 1732 Before the Senate Comm. on Commerce, 88th Cong. 252 (1964)); *id.* at n.80 (testimony of Attorney General Robert Kennedy that "the law would be 'clearly constitutional' under the Commerce Clause, but not clearly under the 14th Amendment" (citing Hearings on S. 1732, 88th Cong. 28)); Heart of Atlanta Motel, Inc. v. United States, 379 U.S. 241 (1964) (upholding the public accommodations law as within Commerce Clause powers); Katzenbach v. Morgan, 384 U.S. 641, 650–51 (1966) ("[T]he McCulloch v. Maryland standard is the measure of what constitutes 'appropriate legislation' under § 5 of the 14th Amendment."); South Carolina v. Katzenbach, 383 U.S. 301, 326–27 (1966).

39. *E.g.,* City of Boerne v. Flores, 521 U.S. 507, 525 (1997) (separation of powers; Religious Freedom Restoration Act); Bd. of Trs. of the Univ. of Ala. v. Garrett, 531 U.S. 356, 374 (2001) (Title I of the Americans with Disabilities Act); United States v. Morrison, 529 U.S. 598, 625–27 (2000) (Violence Against Women Act); Kimel v. Fla. Bd. of Regents, 528 U.S. 62, 86, 91 (2000) (Age Discrimination in Employment Act); Coll. Sav. Bank v. Fla. Prepaid Postsecondary Educ. Expense Bd., 527 U.S. 666, 674 (1999) (Trademark Remedy Clarification Act); Fla. Prepaid Postsecondary Educ. Expense Bd. v. Coll. Sav. Bank, 527 U.S. 627, 647–48 (1999) (Patent and Plant Variety Protection Remedy Clarification Act); Nev. Dep't of Human Res. v. Hibbs, 538 U.S. 721, 735 (2003) (Family and Medical Leave Act); Tennessee v. Lane, 541 U.S. 509, 531 (2004) (Title II of the Americans With Disabilities Act). *E.g.,* Robert Kaczorowski, *The Supreme Court and Congress's Power To Enforce Constitutional Rights: An Overlooked Moral Anomaly,* 73 Fordham L. Rev. 153 (2004); Robert Kaczorowski, *Congress's Power To Enforce Fourteenth Amendment Rights: Lessons From Federal Remedies the Framers Enacted,* 42 Harv. J. on Legis. 187 (2005); Michael McConnell, *Institutions and Interpretation;* Rebecca Zietlow, *Congressional Enforcement of Civil Rights and John Bingham's Theory of Citizenship,* 36 Akron L. Rev. 717 (2003); Ruth Colker, *The Supreme Court's Historical Errors in* City of Boerne v. Flores, 43 B.C. L. Rev. 783 (2002); James W. Fox, Jr., *Re-readings and Misreadings:* Slaughter-House, *Privileges and Immunities, and Section Five Enforcement Powers,* 91 Ky. L.J. 67 (2002); Christopher Banks, *The Constitutional Politics of Interpreting Section 5 of the Fourteenth Amendment,* 36 Akron L. Rev. 425 (2003); Robert C. Post & Reva B. Siegel, *Legislative Constitutionalism and Section Five Power: Policentric Interpretation of the Family and Medical Leave Act,* 112 Yale L.J. 1943 (2003); Owen Fiss, *Between Supremacy and Exclusivity,* 57 Syracuse L.Rev. 187 (2007); Marci Hamilton, *What is Rehnquist Federalism?,* 155 U. Pa. L.Rev. 8 (2007); John Harrison, *State Sovereign Immunity and Congress's Enforcement Powers,* 2006 Sup. Ct. Rev. 353; John T. Valauri, *McCulloch and the Fourteenth Amendment,* 13 Temp. Pol. & Civ. Rts. L. Rev. 857 (2004).

40. *Boerne* at 522 (quotation) and 520 ("too much legislative power at the expense of the existing constitutional structure . . . [i]f Congress could define its own powers by altering the 14th Amendment's meaning . . ."); McConnell, *Institutions and Interpretation,* at 176–78; Aynes, *John Bingham,* at 71; Kaczorowski, *Revolutionary Constitutionalism,* at 866–67.

41. James, The Framing, at 101–04.

42. *Id.* at 113.

43. Kaczorowski, *Revolutionary Constitutionalism,* at 875; Curtis, No State Shall Abridge, at 14–15, 58–59, 134–36; James, The Framing, at 84, 97–98.

44. James, The Framing, at 84–85, 87 (citing Cong. Globe, 39th Cong., 1st Sess. 1034, 1064, 1088–90) and at 129–130 (citing Cong. Globe, 39th Cong., 1st Sess. 2542 (quotation)) ("a comparison of [Bingham's] remarks at this time with those made in February in explanation of his original amendment clearly demonstrates that his purpose had remained unchanged"). Although the modern Court has made much of the shift in language from the Bingham prototype using "secure" to the final wording of Section 5 using "enforce," *Boerne* at 520–22, nothing indicates this to have been a substantive change. Rather, Bingham appears to have used the words interchangeably in debating before Congress. When the language of "secure" was in the proposal first on the floor, Bingham responded to an opponent by asking, "who are opposed to *enforcing* the written guarantees of the Constitution." Cong. Globe, 39th Cong., 1st Sess. 813 (emphasis added). Discussing the Civil Rights Bill, Lawrence of Ohio used the words interchangeably, claiming that without congressional power to enforce them,

government would be powerless to secure or protect rights guaranteed in the Constitution. Curtis, No State Shall Abridge, at 77–78.

45. James, The Framing, at 47–48, 83–87.

46. James, The Framing, at 82–83 (Rogers voted against reporting the February version); Cong. Globe, 39th Cong., 1st Sess. Appx. 133 (Rogers); *id.* at 1034 (Bingham); James at 129 (citing *id.* 2538–39 (Rogers)).

47. James, The Framing, at 104–06 (citing Cong. Globe, 42nd Cong., 1st Sess. Appx. 84–85 (1871)).

48. Representative Hotchkiss argued, "This amendment proposes to leave it to the caprice of Congress; and your legislation upon the subject would depend upon the political majority of Congress...." Cong. Globe, 39th Cong., 1st Sess. at 1095; Kaczorowski, *Revolutionary Constitutionalism*, at 912–14: "Hotchkiss complained that by merely empowering Congress to enact laws for the protection of civil rights at some future date, the proposal actually left the citizen unprotected.... Hotchkiss wanted civil rights 'secured by a constitutional amendment that legislation could not override.' He sought an amendment that did more than merely authorize legislation; one that was self-executing, so that the protection of citizens' rights would not have to depend upon the uncertainty of future legislation. He added, 'Then if the gentleman wishes to go further, and provide by laws of Congress for the enforcement of these rights, I will go with him.'" (internal footnotes omitted).

49. *Boerne* at 517 (first quotation), 518 (second quotation), 535 (third quotation); Post & Siegel, *Legislative Constitutionalism.*

50. Curtis, No State Shall Abridge, at 83 (quotation) and 62.

51. Richard L. Aynes, *Ink Blot or Not: The Meaning of Privileges and/or Immunities*, 11 J. Const. L. 1295, 1305–07 (2009); Curtis, No State Shall Abridge, at 141 (quoting Lyman Trumbull, from Cincinnati Commercial, Sept. 3, 1866, at 2, col. 3) (first quotation) and at 140 (quoting General Martindale, from Albany Evening Journal, Sept. 21, 1866, at 1, col. 3) (second quotation).

52. Huhn, *Legacy*, at 1074–78.

CHAPTER 5

1. Slaughter-House Cases, 83 U.S. 36 (1873).

2. Akhil Reed Amar, *The Bill of Rights and the Fourteenth Amendment*, 101 Yale L.J. 1193, 1259 (1992).

3. Leo Pfeffer, This Honorable Court: A History of the United States Supreme Court 200 (1965).

4. For critics of Miller's position on the privileges or immunities clause *see* Michael Kent Curtis, *Resurrecting the Privileges or Immunities Clause and Revising the* Slaughter-House Cases *Without Exhuming* Lochner: *Individual Rights and the Fourteenth Amendment*, 38 B.C. L. Rev. 1 (1996); Michael Kent Curtis, No State Shall Abridge: The Fourteenth Amendment and the Bill of Rights (1986); Michael Conant, *Antimonopoly Tradition Under the Ninth and Fourteenth Amendments:* Slaughter-House Cases *Re-examined*, 31 Emory L.J. 785 (1982); Amar, *The Bill of Rights*; Richard L. Aynes, *On Misreading John Bingham and the Fourteenth Amendment*, 103 Yale L.J. 57 (1993); Bernard Schwartz, A History of the Supreme Court 159 (1993); William E. Nelson, The Fourteenth Amendment: From Political Principle to Judicial Doctrine 155–68

(1988); and Harold M. Hyman, "Slaughter-house Cases," *in* Encyclopedia of the American Constitution 1687–88 (Leonard W. Levy, Kenneth L. Karst, and Dennis J. Mahoney eds., 1986). For the view that the 14th Amendment did not incorporate the Bill of Rights *see* Charles Fairman, *Does the Fourteenth Amendment Incorporate the Bill of Rights? The Original Understanding*, 2 Stan. L. Rev. 5 (1949); Felix Frankfurter's concurring opinion in Adamson v. California, 332 U.S. 46, 59–68 (1947); Raoul Berger, Government by Judiciary: The Transformation of the Fourteenth Amendment (1977), chap. 8; and Berger, *Incorporation of the Bill of Rights in the Fourteenth Amendment: A Nine-Lived Cat*, 42 Ohio St. L.J. 435 (1981). For a third view, that Miller actually intended for the Bill of Rights to be incorporated into the 14th Amendment, *see* Robert C. Palmer, *The Parameters of Constitutional Reconstruction*: Slaughter-House, Cruikshank, *and the Fourteenth Amendment*, 1984 Ill. L. Rev. 739 (1984).

5. Richard L. Aynes, *Constricting the Law of Freedom: Justice Miller, The Fourteenth Amendment, and the* Slaughter-House Cases, 70 Chi.-Kent L. Rev. 627 (1994); Julius J. Marke, *The Banded Butchers and the Supreme Court: Herein of the* Slaughterhouse Cases, New York University Law Center Bulletin, XII (Spring 1964), 8 and 10; Pfeffer, This Honorable Court, at 199–200; and Russell W. Galloway, Justice For All? The Rich and Poor in Supreme Court History, 1790–1990, 67 (1991).

6. Xi Wang, The Trial of Democracy: Black Suffrage and Northern Republicans, 1860–1910, at 121–24 (1997); Robert G. McCloskey, The American Supreme Court 81 (2d ed., rev. and exp. by Sanford Levinson, 1994); Broadus Mitchell and Louise Pearson Mitchell, A Biography of the Constitution of the United States: Its Origin, Formation, Adoption, Interpretation 289–90 (1964); Aynes, *On Misreading John Bingham*, at 57–104; Michael W. McConnell, *The Forgotten Constitutional Moment*, 11 Const. Comm. 133 (1994); Loren Miller, The Petitioners: The Story of the Supreme Court of the United States and the Negro 105 (1966); Curtis, No State Shall Abridge, at 177–78; and Lou Falkner Williams, The Great South Carolina Ku Klux Klan Trials, 1871–1872, at 132–34 (1996).

7. Robert J. Kaczorowski, The Politics of Judicial Interpretation: The Federal Courts, Department of Justice and Civil Rights, 1866–1876, at 143, 159 (1985); and Loren P. Beth, *The* Slaughter-House Cases-*Revisited*, 23 La. L. Rev. 494, 501–04 (1963).

8. Michael Les Benedict, *Preserving Federalism: Reconstruction and the Waite Court*, Sup. Ct. Rev. 39–62 (1978); Carl Brent Swisher, Stephen J. Field: Craftsman of the Law 420 (1930); Richard C. Cortner, The Supreme Court and the Second Bill of Rights: The Fourteenth Amendment and the Nationalization of Civil Liberties 9–10 (1981); and Wendy E. Parmet, *From* Slaughter-House *to* Lochner: *The Rise and Fall of the Constitutionalization of Public Health*, 40 Am. J. of Legal Hist. 476 (1996).

9. New Orleans Daily Picayune, June 27, 1869. Louisiana Legislature, Act no. 118, March 8, 1869, appears in The Slaughter-House Cases, 83 U.S. 36, 38–43 (1873).

10. John Duffy, Pestilence in New Orleans, *in* The Past As Prelude: New Orleans, 1718–1968, at 107 (Hodding Carter ed., 1968); Paul Kens, Justice Stephen Field: Shaping Liberty from the Gold Rush to the Gilded Age, 118 (1997); Joe Gray Taylor, Louisiana Reconstructed, 1863–1877, at 6 (1974); Ronald M. Labbe, New Light on the Slaughterhouse Monopoly Act of 1869, *in* Louisiana's Legal Heritage 149–51 (Edward F. Haas ed., 1983); and Oliver Evans, New Orleans 51 (1959) (Audubon quotation).

11. New Orleans Bee, July 9, 1869; and The State of Louisiana, *ex rel.* S. Belden, Attorney General v. Wm. Fagan, et al., 22 La. Ann. 545, 552 (1870) (quotation).

12. Testimony of Dr. E. S. Lewis before the Louisiana House of Representatives Special Committee on the Removal of the Slaughter Houses in 1867, quoted in Kens, Justice Stephen Field, 118.

13. *State v. Fagan* at 553.

14. Labbe, New Light, at 150.

15. *State v. Fagan* at 551; Labbe, New Light, at 150; and William J. Novak, The People's Welfare: Law and Regulation in Nineteenth-Century America 230 (1996).

16. Herbert Hovenkamp, Enterprise and American Law, 1836–1937, at 119 (1991); Labbe, New Light, at 149–50; Evans, New Orleans, at 55–56; Duffy, Pestilence in New Orleans, at 107–11; Taylor, Louisiana Reconstructed, at 6; and Mitchell Franklin, *The Foundations and Meaning of the* Slaughterhouse Cases *[Part 2]*, 18 Tul. L. Rev. 222, 222–23 (1943).

17. John Duffy, A History of Public Health in New York City, 1866–1966, at 7–9, 24–25, 33, 39, 48 (1974).

18. Labbe, New Light, at 144–47; and New Orleans Bee, March 23, 1869.

19. Hovenkamp, Enterprise and American Law, at 123.

20. R. Delrieu, Les Abattoirs Publics de la Nouvelle-Orleans 17–18 (1869).

21. Mitchell Franklin, *Foundations and Meaning of the* Slaughterhouse Cases *[Part 1]*, 18 Tul. L. Rev. 34 (1943) and *[Part 2]*, at 225; and John W. Blassingame, Black New Orleans, 1860–1880, 60 (1973).

22. Franklin, *[Part 2]*, at 225; and Labbe, New Light, at 150–57. In 1862, for example, the neighboring town of Jefferson had ordered the slaughterhouses removed; but the war intervened, and the law was never carried out. New Orleans Bee, July 4, 1869.

23. Labbe, New Light, at 158; and Kens, Justice Stephen Field, at 119.

24. Labbe, New Light, at 158.

25. Pfeffer, This Honorable Court, at 198; Schwartz, History of the Supreme Court, at 159; Cortner, Supreme Court and the Second Bill of Rights, at 6; Kaczorowski, Politics of Judicial Interpretation, at 144; and Ella Lonn, Reconstruction in Louisiana, after 1868, 28 (1918).

26. New Orleans Daily Picayune, June 6, 1869, p. 8, c. 12; and New Orleans Bee, May 3, June 21, 1870; February 28, June 2, October 19, 1871; and March 21, 1872.

27. "The New Orleans press," legal historian Hebert Hovenkamp points out, "most of which represented the interests of the Old South, was responsible for the allegations of bribery and corruption, and historians have taken most of their facts at face value from these editorials." Hovenkamp, Enterprise and American Law, at 123. Besides newspaper allegations, historians have also relied on a piece of judicial dicta from the Louisiana Sixth District Court case in which Judge William H. Cooley said that he believed charges offered by a disgruntled Slaughterhouse Company employee. Durbridge v. Slaughterhouse Co., 27 La. Ann. 676 (1875). But Judge Cooley cannot be trusted. He had been a conservative Republican who left the party when he realized that the Radicals intended to push for civil rights for the freedmen, such as integrated schools and public accommodations. On the bench, Cooley regularly tried to thwart the acts of the legislature. "In fact so pronounced was the outspoken opposition of Judge Cooley to the legislation of the state," wrote the New Orleans Republican in June 1871, "that it became necessary for the lawmaking power to relieve him of jurisdiction in matters of injunction and mandamus, because his action threatened at one time to produce

great confusion if not positive conflict in matters of local law." New Orleans Republican, June 3, 1871. *See also* Charles Fairman, I Reconstruction and Reunion, 1864–1888, at 1321–24 (1971–1987); and Ted Tunnell, Crucible of Reconstruction: War, Radicalism, and Race in Louisiana, 1862–1877, at 122–24 (1984).

28. For examples of historians who have accepted the charges of bribery *see* Pfeffer, This Honorable Court, at 198; Schwartz, History of the Supreme Court, at 159; Cortner, Supreme Court and the Second Bill of Rights, at 6; Kaczorowski, Politics of Judicial Interpretation, at 144; and Franklin, *[Part 1]*, at 20–24.

29. The New Orleans Republican noted, for example, that in the past "the franchises of the state were granted in the most lavish fashion to gentlemen belonging to the superior race." New Orleans Republican, March 12, 1870. The prevalence of corruption in antebellum Louisiana is also widely acknowledged. Evans, New Orleans, at 59; Taylor, Louisiana Reconstructed, at 49, 82, 201, 251, 258; and Kens, Justice Stephen Field, at 119

30. Hovenkamp, Enterprise and American Law, at 119–20; Evans, New Orleans, at 62.

31. Labbe, New Light, at 151–52; Hovenkamp, Enterprise and American Law, at 120; Duffy, Pestilence in New Orleans, at 112; and Franklin, *[Part 2]*, at 221–23.

32. Tunnell, Crucible of Reconstruction, at 152 (quotation); and Lonn, Reconstruction in Louisiana, at 32.

33. Lonn, Reconstruction in Louisiana, at 32 (quotation); Taylor, Louisiana Reconstructed, at 189–96; and Michael Les Benedict, The Fruits of Victory: Alternatives in Restoring the Union, 1865–1877, at 44 (rev. ed., 1986).

34. Blassingame, Black New Orleans, at 49–50; Lonn, Reconstruction in Louisiana, at 17–18; and Taylor, Louisiana Reconstructed, at 178, 314–16, 318, 319, 343–45.

35. Lonn, Reconstruction in Louisiana, at 18; Labbe, New Light, at 154; New Orleans Republican January 19, 20, 22, and February 16, 1871; and New Orleans Bee, March 21, 1872. After the slaughterhouse company was launched, its officers tried to reach a compromise with the Gascon butchers who had sued to enjoin the company from asserting its rights under the 1869 act. The company placed some butchers on its board and gave stock to many individual butchers in return for dropping their lawsuits and relocating to the new slaughterhouse. A few butchers, however, refused this olive branch and the lawsuits continued. New Orleans Bee, June 21, 1870, and March 21, 24, 1872.

36. Eric Foner, Reconstruction: America's Unfinished Revolution 1863–1877, at 262–63 (1988) (Sheridan quotation); Samuel Miller to William Pitt Ballinger, August 29, 1869, Folder 6, Box 1, Samuel Freeman Miller Papers (Manuscript Division, Library of Congress, Washington, D.C.); Tunnell, Crucible of Reconstruction, at 104–07; and Taylor, Louisiana Reconstructed, at 106–10.

37. Tunnell, Crucible of Reconstruction, at 107 (quotation); and Taylor, Louisiana Reconstructed, at 146–47.

38. Taylor, Louisiana Reconstructed, at 151 (first quotation); Roger Fischer, The Post-Civil War Segregation Struggle, *in* The Past As Prelude: New Orleans, 1718–1968, at 293–94 (Hodding Carter ed., 1968); and New Orleans Bee, January 24, 1869 (second quotation).

39. Taylor, Louisiana Reconstructed, at 174; and New Orleans Commercial Bulletin, November 17, 1869 (quotation).

40. New Orleans Bee, January 1 and December 23, 1869, January 22, 1870, February 19, 1869, and July 14, 1869.

41. Blassingame, Black New Orleans, at 183; and Taylor, Louisiana Reconstructed, at 211.

42. New Orleans Daily Picayune, September 22, 1868; and New Orleans Bee, February 7, 1869.

43. New Orleans Bee, March 20, 1869, and April 28, 1870.

44. Tunnell, Crucible of Reconstruction, at 153 and 159.

45. New Orleans Bee, March 23, June 13 (first two quoted phrases) and June 22 (third quoted phrase), 1869, and February 28 and October 19 (last two quotations), 1871.

46. New Orleans Republican, March 22, 1870.

47. Franklin, *[Part 2]*, at 225; and New Orleans Bee, June 22, 13, and July 7, 1869 (the three quotations are from the three issues of the Bee in the order cited.)

48. Tony Freyer, John Archibald Campbell, *in* The Oxford Companion to the Supreme Court, 116–17 (Kermit Hall et al. eds., 1992).

49. Franklin, *[Part 2]*, at 229. For a more extensive analysis of Campbell's legal campaign against Louisiana's Reconstruction government *see* Michael A. Ross, *Obstructing Reconstruction: John Archibald Campbell and the Legal Campaign Against Louisiana's Republican Government*, 49 Civ. War Hist. 235 (2003). *See also* McCloskey, American Supreme Court, at 79; Harold M. Hyman and William M. Wiecek, Equal Justice Under Law: Constitutional Development, 1835–1875, at 475 (1982); and Freyer, *John Archibald Campbell*, at 116–17. Ross, *Obstructing Reconstruction*, at 235–53.

50. John A. Campbell to Nathan Clifford, June 25, 1871, Clifford Papers, Maine Historical Society (Portland, Maine); and McCloskey, American Supreme Court, at 79.

51. *Slaughter-House* at 45, 48, 60.

52. *Id.* at 51 and 53.

53. The legal team included former U.S. Senator Matthew H. Carpenter, a key supporter of the 14th Amendment, and Thomas J. Durant, a radical Louisiana Republican and one of the leaders of the Friends of Universal Suffrage. "In Boston he would be an Abolitionist of the Abolitionists," Whitelaw Reid said of Durant, "He speaks at negro meetings, demands negro suffrage, unites with negroes in educational movements, [and] champions negroes in the Courts." Tunnell, Crucible of Reconstruction, at 27; Taylor, Louisiana Reconstructed, at 75; Bernard Schwartz, History of the Supreme Court, at 159; and Michael Les Benedict, *Preserving Federalism*, at 59–60.

54. *Slaughter-House* at 78–79.

55. *Id.* at 64 and 71 (quotation).

56. In a recent article, Wendy E. Parmet, unlike most historians, presents a strong argument that a key motivation of the Court was to uphold the New Orleans law as a health measure. While she does not discuss Miller's interest in the sanitation movement, she does correctly conclude that the need to uphold health laws played a key role in Miller's opinion. Parmet's article, however, falls into the familiar trap of trying to provide a monocausal explanation of Miller's motivations in *Slaughter-House*. The need to uphold health measures was, indeed, crucial, but other influences such as the political context in Louisiana and the economic

agenda of Northern Republicans also played central roles. Parmet, *From* Slaughter-House *to* Lochner, at 476–505.

57. Hardin Weatherford, A Treatise On Cholera: With the Causes, Symptoms, Mode of Prevention and Cure, on a New and Successful Plane 11 (1833); Charles E. Rosenberg, The Cholera Years: The United States in 1832, 1849, and 1866, at 40 (1962); Samuel F[reeman]. Miller, An Inaugural Dissertation on Cholera Infantum Submitted to the Examination of the Trustees and Medical Professors of Transylvania University, for the Degree of Doctor of Medicine 9 (1838) (quotations) (copy in Transylvania University Archives, Lexington, Ky.); and Michael A. Ross, *Hill-Country Doctor: The Early Life and Career of Supreme Court Justice Samuel F. Miller in Kentucky, 1816–1849*, 71 Filson Club Hist. Q. 430, 445–51 (1997).

58. Miller, An Inaugural Dissertation, at 9 (quotation); and Ross, *Hill-Country Doctor*, at 434, 435, 446.

59. Keokuk (Iowa) Daily Gate City, April 20, 1863, November 5, 1858, November 29, 1859, December 9 (quoted phrase on pigs' cries) and 17 (quoted phrase on thousands of pigs), 1862.

60. *Id.* November 5, 1858; October 24, 1859 (final quoted phrase); August 4, 1860; June 12, 1862; June 21, 1862; December 9 ("porkopolis") and 17, 1862.

61. *Slaughter-House* at 63.

62. Richard D. Sears, The Day of Small Things: Abolitionism in the Midst of Slavery: Berea, Kentucky, 1854–1864, at 30–31 (1986); and H. Edward Richardson, Cassius Marcellus Clay: Firebrand of Freedom 19, 20, 32, 43 (1976).

63. Ross, *Hill-Country Doctor*, at 430–62; and Samuel Freeman Miller to William Pitt Ballinger, August 29, 1869, Miller Papers.

64. Beth, *The* Slaughter-House Cases-*Revisited*, at 487 and 490; and Robert J. Kaczorowski, The Nationalization of Civil Rights: Constitutional Theory and Practice in a Racist Society, 1866–1883, at 257 (1987).

65. *Slaughter-House* at 78.

66. Franklin, *[Part 1]*, at 53–73; and Tunnell, Crucible of Reconstruction, at 210. For a good general history of the last years of Reconstruction *see* Michael Les Benedict, The Fruits of Victory: Alternatives in Restoring the Union, 1865–1877, 53–63 (2d. ed., 1986). "As a result of the compromise [of 1877]," historian Joe Gray Taylor wrote, "the demise of the [Reconstruction] government in Louisiana was a foregone conclusion, but this was not so obvious in 1877 as it is today." Taylor, Louisiana Reconstructed, at 503.

67. *Slaughter-House* at 81.

68. *See* the remarks of Senators Morton and Howe in the Cong. Rec., 43d Cong., 1 Sess., 4147, 4148, 4149 (Senator Howe's remarks are on p. 4149); Cong. Rec., 43rd Congress, 1st Session, Appendix, 360–61 (first and fourth quotations from Senator Morton are on p. 361; second and third quotations on p. 360) (May 21–22, 1874).

69. Kaczorowski, Politics of Judicial Interpretation, at 199–229; Kaczorowski, Nationalization of Civil Rights, at 257–67; Xi Wang, Trial of Democracy, at 121–25; Aynes, *Constricting the Law of Freedom*, at 627–88; McCloskey, American Supreme Court, at 81; Mitchell & Mitchell, Biography of the Constitution of the United States, at 289–90; McConnell, *Forgotten Constitutional Moment*, at 115 and 133; Miller, The Petitioners, at 105; and Curtis, No State Shall Abridge, at 177–78.

70. *Slaughter-House* at 68.

71. *Id.*

72. *Id.* at 70.

73. Samuel Freeman Miller to William Pitt Ballinger, January 11, 1866, Folder 2, Box 1, Miller Papers.

74. *Slaughter-House* at 70.

75. Samuel Freeman Miller to William Pitt Ballinger, January 11, 1866, Miller Papers.

76. Samuel Freeman Miller to William Pitt Ballinger, August 29, 1869, Miller Papers.

CHAPTER 6

1. Slaughter-House Cases, 83 U.S. (16 Wall.) 36 (1872).

2. The Court did not apply the 2nd Amendment's right to bear arms to the states until its June 2010 decision in McDonald v. City of Chicago, 561 U.S. (2010).

3. For example, Southern legislatures reconstituted under President Andrew Johnson would still have countered the federal government, the North might still have tired of the effort to enforce the laws, segregation could still have developed, the state action doctrine might still have frustrated congressional action, and Campbell might have succeeded in blocking progressive legislation with an emphasis on property freedom that could even have invalidated civil rights laws aimed at private individuals.

4. *Slaughter-House* at 49–54, 79–81; *see* Michael A. Ross, Justice of Shattered Dreams: Samuel Freeman Miller and the Supreme Court During the Civil War Era 202 (2003); Jonathan Lurie, *Reflections on Justice Samuel F. Miller and the* Slaughter-House Cases*: Still a Meaty Subject*, 1 N.Y.U. J. L. & Liberty 355, 366–69 (2005); Michael A. Ross, *Obstructing Reconstruction: John Archibald Campbell and the Legal Campaign Against Louisiana's Republican Government, 1868–1873*, 49 Civ. War Hist. 235, 235–53 (2003).

5. United States v. Harris, 106 U.S. 629, 643–44 (1883); United States v. Cruikshank, 92 U.S. 542, 549 (1875); The Civil Rights Cases, 109 U.S. 3, 11 (1883); United States v. Guest, 383 U.S. 745, 757–60 (1966); United States v. Morrison, 529 U.S. 598, 621–23 (2000).

6. Section 1 is the focus of the 14th Amendment today, but contemporaries expected other Sections to have the most significant impact. They were designed to strip the old Confederacy of power and to reconstitute it with governments that were not corrupted by the evils of secession and slavery. Not yet ready to proclaim the right to vote regardless of race that would be advanced in the 15th Amendment, Section 2 protected against the effect of racial exclusion in the South by providing for a reduction in representatives in states that denied the vote. Section 3 of the 14th Amendment wiped out the old establishment and opened all political offices to new and untried individuals. It disqualified from holding state or federal office any person who previously took an oath to support the Constitution and then engaged in rebellion or aided it. Section 4 repudiated the debts of the Confederacy and prohibited payments for the loss or emancipation of slaves. Wealthy planters who had supplied the Confederacy were left with handfuls of worthless paper and lost the power that wealth had brought. *See, e.g.,* David E. Kyvig, Explicit and Authentic Acts: Amending the U.S. Constitution, 1776–1995, at 167–69 (1996).

7. For example, about thirty-seven percent of the House and twenty-five percent of the

Senate in the Louisiana legislature of 1869–71 were African American. Ronald M. Labbé & Jonathan Lurie, The Slaughterhouse Cases: Regulation, Reconstruction, and the Fourteenth Amendment 72 (2003). The Lieutenant-Governor, Oscar J. Dunn, was an African American. *See, e.g.*, Kwando M. Kinshasa, African American Chronology: Chronologies of the American Mosaic 55 (2006).

8. "[A] Northerner in the South after the American Civil War usu. seeking private gain under the reconstruction governments." Merriam-Webster's Collegiate Dictionary 189 (11th ed. 2003).

9. "[A] white Southerner acting in support of the reconstruction governments after the American Civil War often for private gain." Merriam-Webster at 1107.

10. 1869 La. Acts 37. This Act—derisively labeled as the "Social Equality Bill" by its opponents—"made it a criminal offense to deny African Americans entry to hotels, steamboats, railroad cars, barrooms, and other public places." "In the following month [after the 'Social Equality Bill'] the legislature passed a law to enforce the article in the 1868 constitution that required public schools in Louisiana to be open to all races. This further enraged whites, who labeled the enactment the 'School Integration Bill.'" Ross, Justice of Shattered Dreams, at 196–97.

11. 1869 La. Acts 170; Labbé & Lurie, The Slaughterhouse Cases, at 72–73, 103–6, 136–66.

12. Ross, *Obstructing Reconstruction*, at 241, 249–51. Transcript of Oral Argument at 3–30, Slaughter-House Cases, 83 U.S. (16 Wall.) 36 (1872), *in* 6 Landmark Briefs and Arguments of the Supreme Court of the United States: Constitutional Law 734, 736–63 (Philip B. Kurland & Gerhard Casper eds., 1975). Senator Matthew Carpenter represented the Slaughter-House incorporators. He also took a broad view of the substance of privileges and immunities, but argued that the Clause protected against racial discrimination and did not apply to the health concerns that led to the monopoly. David S. Bogen, *The Transformation of the Fourteenth Amendment: Reflections from the Admission of Maryland's First Black Lawyers*, 44 Md. L. Rev. 939, 1018–20 (1985).

13. *Slaughter-House* at 60–66.

14. *Slaughter-House* at 67–73.

15. *Slaughter-House* at 76 (quoting Corfield v. Coryell, 6 F. Cas. 546, 551–52 (C.C.E.D. Pa. 1823)), at 73–79 (second quotation).

16. *Slaughter-House* at 80–81.

17. Section 1 of the 14th Amendment overruled Dred Scott v. Sandford, 60 U.S. (19 How.) 393 (1856), by making all persons born in the United States citizens of the United States. Slaughter-House Cases, 83 U.S. at 73. *See* Cong. Globe, 39th Cong., 1st Sess. 2459 (1866) (statement of Rep. Stevens that provisions of Section 1 of the Amendment are all asserted in the organic law already, and Constitutional Amendment will prevent repeal of the Civil Rights Act); *id.* at 2511 (Rep. Eliot implicitly equated the Privileges or Immunities Clause with prohibiting state legislation discriminating against class); *id.* at 2539 (Rep. Farnsworth stated that Equal Protection was the only clause in Section 1 not already in the Constitution); *id.* at 2462 (statement of Rep. Garfield that the Amendment was to fix the Civil Rights bill in the Constitution); *id.* at 2465 (Rep. Thayer said "it is but incorporating in the Constitution of the United States the principle of the civil rights bill which has lately become a law…."); *id.* at 2467 (opposing the Amendment, Boyer said "the first section embodies the principles of

the civil rights bill. ..."); *id.* at 2498 (statement of Rep. Broomall that Congress voted for Section 1 "in another shape, in the civil rights bill. ..."); *id.* at 2502 and 2513 (statements of Rep. Raymond [Raymond had voted against the Civil Rights Bill as beyond congressional power and opposed other Sections of the proposed 14th Amendment, but supported Section 1, saying now the bill "comes before us in the form of an amendment to the Constitution, which proposes to give Congress the power to attain this precise result."]).

18. *Slaughter-House* at 49–54, 75–76; *see* Eugene Gressman, *The Unhappy History of Civil Rights Legislation*, 50 Mich. L. Rev. 1323, 1336–43 (1952).

19. *Slaughter-House* at 96–98 (Field, J., dissenting, joined by Chase, C.J., Bradley & Swayne, JJ.) (quotation); Ross, *Obstructing Reconstruction*, at 249 (citing The New Orleans Daily Picayune, May 16, 1869).

20. *Slaughter-House* at 97, 77–78, 82.

21. Bar membership: Bradwell v. State, 83 U.S. (16 Wall.) 130, 139 (1872); *In re* Taylor, 48 Md. 28, 32–34 (1877). Voting: James v. Bowman, 190 U.S. 127, 138 (1903); United States v. Harris, 106 U.S. 629, 638, 643 (1883); United States v. Cruikshank, 92 U.S. 542, 549 (1875). Violence: United States v. Morrison, 529 U.S. 598, 621–24 (2000); United States v. Lopez, 514 U.S. 549, 567–68 (1995) (holding that the Gun-Free School Zones Act exceeded Congress's Commerce Clause authority).

22. *Slaughter-House* at 77. Congressman John Bingham, the chief drafter of the 14th Amendment, understood that the Privileges and Immunities Clause secured the fundamental rights of citizens, including the individual rights in the Bill of Rights, against state abridgement. Cong. Globe, 42d Cong., 1st Sess. app. 84–85 (1871) (statement of Rep. Bingham); Michael Kent Curtis, No State Shall Abridge: The Fourteenth Amendment and the Bill of Rights (1986); Richard L. Aynes, Commentary, *Refined Incorporation and the Fourteenth Amendment*, 33 U. Rich. L. Rev. 289 (1999).

23. *See, e.g.,* Twining v. New Jersey, 211 U.S. 78, 93–97 (1908).

24. *See Slaughter-House* at 63; Bowman v. Chicago & N.W. Ry. Co., 125 U.S. 465, 489–91 (1888).

25. *Slaughter-House* at 63 (quoting Gibbons v. Ogden, 22 U.S. (9 Wheat.) 1, 203 (1824) and City of New York v. Miln, 36 U.S. (11 Pet.) 102 (1837); at 64 (citing United States v. DeWitt, 76 U.S. (9 Wall.) 41 (1870) and License Tax Cases, 72 U.S. (5 Wall.) 462 (1867)). The only one of these cases to hold federal legislation unconstitutional involved a federal tax statute that made it a misdemeanor to sell certain illuminating oil. The Supreme Court unanimously found the statute could not be supported as a revenue measure, and that it was beyond congressional power because it related exclusively to the internal trade of the states. The government's argument focused on the tax justification rather than the Commerce Clause. *DeWitt* at 44–45.

26. *Gibbons* at 26 (1824).

27. *See, e.g.,* Heart of Atlanta Motel, Inc. v. United States, 379 U.S. 241, 261 (1964) (upholding the public accommodations provisions with regard to hotels, motels, and similar establishments under Title II of the Civil Rights Act of 1964); Katzenbach v. McClung, 379 U.S. 294, 305 (1964) (upholding the public accommodations provisions with regard to restaurants under Title II of the Civil Rights Act of 1964).

28. Transcript of Oral Argument, at 7–8, *in* 6 Landmark Briefs and Arguments, at 734, 740–41, ("I conclude therefore... that wherever a law of a State, or a law of the United States,

makes a discrimination between classes of persons, which deprives the one class of their freedom or their property, or which makes a caste of them, to subserve the power, pride, avarice, vanity or vengeance of others, that this constitutes a case of involuntary servitude under the 13th Amendment to the Constitution."); *Slaughter-House* at 69.

29. *Slaughter-House* at 70; Ross, Justice of Shattered Dreams, at 115 (quotations); United States v. Cruikshank, 25 F. Cas. 707, 711–12 (C.C.D. La. 1874) (Bradley, Circuit Justice) (arguing the 13th Amendment power); Jones v. Alfred H. Mayer Co., 392 U.S. 409, 437–44 (1968); *see, e.g.*, Akhil Reed Amar, *Intratextualism*, 112 Harv. L. Rev. 747, 823 (1999).

30. *Slaughter-House* at 56 (abstract of oral argument) (emphasis omitted).

31. *Slaughter-House* at 80–81. If forced to confront the liberty issue at that time, Miller quite likely would have found against the butchers.

32. *Slaughter-House* at 118 (Bradley, J., dissenting) (stating "...above all, and including almost all the rest, the right of *not being deprived of life, liberty, or property, without due process of law.*"). *See, e.g.*, Duncan v. Louisiana, 391 U.S. 145, 154, 157–58 (1968) (holding that the right to jury trial in serious crimes applies to states). The delay may not have harmed civil rights significantly, because most of the important rights were recognized in state declarations and constitutional provisions, and the Supreme Court did not take an expansive view of those rights prior to incorporating them. For example, the Court incorporated the guarantee of freedom of speech in Gitlow v. New York, 268, U.S. 652, 666 (1925) but the abstract right of free speech did not restrain the government until the Court began to overturn convictions in 1937. DeJonge v. Oregon, 299 U.S. 353, 365 (1937); Herndon v. Lowry, 301 U.S. 242, 263–64 (1937).

33. *See, e.g.*, Griswold v. Connecticut, 381 U.S. 479 (1965); Roe v. Wade, 410 U.S. 113 (1973); Lawrence v. Texas, 539 U.S. 558 (2003).

34. *Slaughter-House* at 71–72 and 79–81.

35. *Slaughter-House* at 56 (abstract of oral argument); at 81 (quotation).

36. *See, e.g.*, Peter Westen, *The Empty Idea of Equality*, 95 Harv. L. Rev. 537, 548–56 (1982). Race is inherent, immutable, politically isolating, stigmatic, and has no inherent correlation to legitimate government purposes. Gender, alienage, and illegitimacy share many of these characteristics, and the Court carefully analyzes the situations where the characteristic does have a proper relationship to the government purpose.

37. *Slaughter-House* at 56 (abstract of oral argument).

38. Cong. Globe, 42d Cong., 2nd Sess. 496 (1872) (statement of Sen. Thurman) (quotation); *see* Bogen, *Transformation of the Fourteenth Amendment*, at 1020 n.272.

39. Strauder v. West Virginia, 100 U.S. 303 (1879); at 307–08 (quoting Slaughter-House Cases, 83 U.S. at 81); at 310; at 312 (Field, J. dissenting) (citing *Ex parte Virginia*, 100 U.S. 339, 349 (1879) (Field, J., dissenting)). *See also Ex parte Virginia*, 100 U.S. at 367. The broad vision of the Equal Protection Clause, traceable to the *Slaughter-House Cases* and *Strauder*, was mentioned by the Court when it struck down residential segregation ordinances in Buchanan v. Warley, 245 U.S. 60, 76–77, 82 (1917).

40. Nixon v. Herndon, 273 U.S. 536, 541 (1927) ("[I]t seems to us hard to imagine a more direct and obvious infringement of the Fourteenth. That Amendment, while it applies to all, was passed, as we know, with a special intent to protect the blacks from discrimination against them." (citing *Slaughter-House*, 83 U.S. 36; *Strauder*, 100 U.S. 303)).

41. *Slaughter-House* at 71.

42. *See, e.g.*, Baker v. Carr, 369 U.S. 186, 208–37 (1962).

43. Crandall v. State of Nevada, 73 U.S. (6 Wall.) 35, 44 (1867); United States v. Guest, 383 U.S. 745, 757–60 (1966); *Ex parte Yarbrough*, 110 U.S. 651, 660–67 (1884) (federal elections); *Crandall*, 73 U.S. (6 Wall.) at 44 (federal facilities); Hague v. C.I.O., 307 U.S. 496, 512–13 (1939) and United States v. Cruikshank, 92 U.S. 542, 552–53 (1875) (petition and assembly on federal matters).

44. Saenz v. Roe, 526 U.S. 489, 500–04 (1999) (quoting *Slaughter-House* at 80).

45. *Saenz* at 492–93, 500–03, 509–11.

46. *Slaughter-House* at 79 (quoting *Crandall*, 73 U.S. at 44 (1867)).

47. *Guest* at 747 (quoting 18 U.S.C. § 241 (1964)); at 757–59 (citing *Crandall* at 48–49); at 762–63 (Harlan, J., concurring in part and dissenting in part); *Slaughter-House* at 75, 77.

48. *Ex parte Yarbrough* at 663–64 (elections); *Crandall* at 44 (access); *Hague* at 512–13 (discussion).

49. *See* United States v. Crosby, 25 F. Cas. 701, 704–05 (C.C.D.S.C. 1871).

50. *Ex parte Siebold*, 100 U.S. 371, 383–84, 396 (1879).

51. *Ex parte Yarbrough* at 660–67, 666 (first quotation), at 662 (second quotation).

52. *Crandall* at 44.

53. *See In re Quarles*, 158 U.S. 532, 535–36 (1895) (recognizing the right to inform officials of violations of federal law); Logan v. United States, 144 U.S. 263, 285 (1892) (recognizing the right of prisoners in custody of federal marshal to be protected from "lawless violence"); United States v. Waddell, 112 U.S. 76, 80–81 (1884) (recognizing the right to access federal land grant). *See also* Risa E. Kaufman, *Access to the Courts as a Privilege or Immunity of National Citizenship*, 40 Conn. L. Rev. 1477, 1491 (2008) (arguing that *Crandall* reasoning leads to a right of access to the courts).

54. *Slaughter-House* at 79.

55. *Cruikshank* at 552–53.

56. *See, e.g.*, *Gitlow* at 666.

57. *See, e.g.*, Charles Lane, The Day Freedom Died: The Colfax Massacre, the Supreme Court, and the Betrayal of Reconstruction (2008).

58. *Cruikshank* at 555–57 (holding the indictment invalid because it did not allege a racial motivation for the interference with the vote); United States v. Reese, 92 U.S. 214, 216–22 (1875) (invalidating convictions by interpreting Sections 3 and 4 of the statute to apply to nonracial obstruction and holding that would not be warranted by the 15th Amendment and holding that the only federal privilege with respect to voting in state elections was to be free of racial discrimination). Justice Hunt dissented on the grounds that the Court incorrectly construed the statute, which he interpreted to apply only to racially motivated interference with suffrage. *Id.* at 242–45. (The Court subsequently questioned the propriety of the majority's statutory interpretation. *See* United States v. Raines, 362 U.S. 17, 24 (1960)).

The Court could have construed the statute and the indictments to apply only to racially based actions in these cases. Alternatively, they might have pursued the Guarantee Clause theory proffered *infra*. *See* Pamela Brandwein, Rethinking United States v. Cruikshank: Law and Politics in a Transitional Period (Nov. 14, 2008) (unpublished manuscript, presented at the 2008 Annual Meeting of the American Society for Legal History) (discussing Supreme Court's design to empower Congress to deal with racial violence).

59. *Slaughter-House* at 71 (quotation), 74–80; *Ex parte Yarbrough* at 666–67.

60. *Crosby* at 704 ("[T]he constitution has declared that the states shall make no distinction on the grounds stated in this first section. And, by this legislation, congress has endeavored, in a way which congress thought appropriate, to enforce it. . . . Congress may have found it difficult to devise a method by which to punish a state which, by law, made such distinction, and may have thought that legislation most likely to secure the end in view which punished the individual citizen who acted by virtue of a state law or upon his individual responsibility. If the act be within the scope of the amendment, and in the line of its purpose, congress is the sole judge of its appropriateness.").

61. *Cruikshank*, 25 F. Cas. At 712–714 ("Although negative in form, and therefore, at first view, apparently to be governed by the rule that congress has no duty to perform until the state has violated its provisions, nevertheless in substance, it confers a positive right which did not exist before. The language is peculiar. It is composed of two negatives. The right shall not be denied. That is, the right shall be enjoyed; the right, namely, to be exempt from the disability of race, color, or previous condition of servitude, as respects the right to vote.").

62. *Cruikshank*, 92 U.S at 555–56 ("[T]he 15th Amendment has invested the citizens of the United States with a new constitutional right, which is, exemption from discrimination in the exercise of the elective franchise on account of race, color, or previous condition of servitude. From this it appears that the right of suffrage is not a necessary attribute of national citizenship; but that exemption from discrimination in the exercise of that right on account of race, &c., is. The right to vote in the States comes from the States; but the right of exemption from the prohibited discrimination comes from the United States. The first has not been granted or secured by the Constitution of the United States; but the last has been);" United States v. Reese, 92 U.S. 214, 218 (1875) ("Previous to this amendment, there was no constitutional guaranty against this discrimination: now there is. It follows that the amendment has invested the citizens of the United States with a new constitutional right which is within the protecting power of Congress. That right is exemption from discrimination in the exercise of the elective franchise on account of race, color, or previous condition of servitude. This, under the express provisions of the second section of the amendment, Congress may enforce by 'appropriate legislation.'").

63. *Ex parte Yarbrough* at 663–65.

64. *Ex parte Yarbrough* at 661–65.

65. Reynolds v. Sims, 377 U.S. 533, 561–62 (1964).

66. James v. Bowman, 190 U.S. 127, 139 (1903).

67. *Guest* at 757–60; at 777–84 (Brennan, J., concurring in part and dissenting in part) (quotation; citations omitted); at 762 (Clark, J., concurring).

68. *See Ex parte Yarbrough* at 662–63.

69. *See* Brewer v. Hoxie Sch. Dist. No. 46, 238 F.2d 91, 100 (8th Cir. 1956)

70. Baker v. Carr, 369 U.S. 186, 209 (1962); Luther v. Borden, 48 U.S. (7 How.) 1, 42 (1849)

71. *See* Michael Les Benedict, Preserving the Constitution: Essays on Politics and the Con-

stitution in the Reconstruction Era 3, 11–12, 17 (2006); William M. Wiecek, The Guarantee Clause of the U.S. Constitution 166–243 (1972).

72. Texas v. White, 74 U.S. (7 Wall.) 700, 730 (1868).

73. Deborah Jones Merritt, *The Guarantee Clause and State Autonomy: Federalism for a Third Century*, 88 Colum. L. Rev. 1, 25 (1988).

74. *James v. Bowman* at 142; *Cruikshank*, 92 U.S. at 555–57; *Reese* at 217–18.

75. *Cruikshank*, 92 U.S. at 544 (citing Act of May 31, 1870, ch. 114, § 6, 16 Stat. 141) and 555–56. *See* Leslie Friedman Goldstein, *The Second Amendment, the* Slaughter-House Cases *(1873), and* United States v. Cruikshank *(1876)*, 1 Alb. Gov't. L. Rev. 365, 405–07 (2008), for a discussion of the *Cruikshank* Court's use of the Guarantee Clause.

76. *Guest* at 759 n.17.

77. *Cruikshank*, 92 U.S. at 552.

CHAPTER 7

1. Slaughter-House Cases, 83 U.S. 36 (1873); at 96 (Field, J., dissenting) (first quotation); at 129 (Swayne, J., dissenting) (second quotation); Robert H. Bork, The Tempting of America: The Political Seduction of the Law 166 (1990) (third quotation). *See, e.g.*, Richard L. Aynes, *Constricting the Law of Freedom: Justice Miller, the Fourteenth Amendment, and the* Slaughter-House Cases, 70 Chi.-Kent L. Rev. 627, 627 (1994) (noting that "'everyone' agrees the Court incorrectly interpreted the Privileges or Immunities Clause...")

2. *See, e.g.*, Michael Kent Curtis, *Historical Linguistics, Inkblots, and Life After Death: The Privileges or Immunities of Citizens of the United States*, 78 N.C. L. Rev. 1071, 1098–1124 (2000); D.O. McGovney, *Privileges or Immunities Clause, Fourteenth Amendment*, 4 Iowa L. Bull. 219, 233 (1918); Akhil Reed Amar, The Bill of Rights: Creation and Reconstruction 181–230 (1998); Michael Kent Curtis, No State Shall Abridge: The Fourteenth Amendment and the Bill of Rights (1986); Raoul Berger, *Incorporation of the Bill of Rights: A Reply to Michael Curtis' Response*, 44 Ohio St. L.J. 1 (1983).

3. Philip M. Hamer, *Great Britain, The United States, and the Negro Seamen Acts, 1822–1845*, 1 J. S. Hist. 3, 22–23 (1935); 5 State Documents on Federal Relations: The States and the United States 237–38 (Herman V. Ames ed., 1900).

4. *See* The Reconstruction Amendments' Debates 748 (Alfred Avins ed., 1967) (listing seventeen pages with references to the "Hoar incident in South Carolina" during debates surrounding promulgation of the Civil War Amendments). This account does not include a number of implied references to the same events. Cong. Globe, 39th Cong., 1st Sess. 1263 (1866) (discussing enactment of the Civil Rights Bill); *id.* at 158, 1034, 1090 (1866) (statements of Rep. Bingham).

5. *See* Hamer, *Negro Seamen Acts*, at 22–23. Supreme Court Justice William Johnson had previously issued a circuit court opinion stating that South Carolina's law violated both Commerce and Treaty Clause powers of Congress, but dismissed the case for lack of jurisdiction. *See* Elkison v. Deliesseline, 8 F. Cas. 493, 495–96, 498 (C.C.D.S.C. 1823) (No. 4,366). President Andrew Jackson and his Attorney General Roger Taney had refused to take action against South Carolina, with Taney expressing the view that "[t]he African race in the United States even when free... were not looked upon as citizens by the contracting parties who formed the Constitution" and were therefore not protected by the Privileges and Immunities Clause of Article IV. Don E. Fehrenbacher, Slavery, Law, and Politics: The Dred Scott Case

in Historical Perspective 38 (1981); Richard L. Aynes, *On Misreading John Bingham and the Fourteenth Amendment*, 103 Yale L.J. 57, 70–73 (1993).

6. Corfield v. Coryell, 6 F. Cas. 546, 551–52 (C.C.E.D. Pa. 1823) (No. 3,230).

7. *Compare* Johnson v. Tompkins, 13 F. Cas. 840, 850 (C.C.E.D. Pa. 1833) (No. 7416) (shifting from a comity to a substantive reading while upholding the use of force by slave owners to seize their "property" in non-slave states because of their entitlement to "all the privileges and immunities of citizens of any other states") *with* Dred Scott v. Sandford, 60 U.S. (19 How.) 393, 403 (1857) *and* Costin v. Washington, 6 F. Cas. 612, 614 (C.C.D.C. 1821) (No. 3266) (denying blacks the protections of citizenship and the clause).

8. *See, e.g.*, Cong. Globe, 39th Cong., 1st Sess. 1034 (1866) (statement of Rep. Bingham).

9. *Id.* app. at 256 (1866).

10. *Id.* at 2542–43 (1866).

11. *See* William J. Rich, *Privileges or Immunities: The Missing Link in Establishing Congressional Power to Abrogate State Eleventh Amendment Immunity*, 28 Hastings Const. L.Q. 235, 249–82 (2001) (providing a more detailed development of this background).

12. *Elkison* at 495–96; An Act to Revise, Consolidate, and Amend the Statutes Relating to Patents and Copyrights, ch. 230, 16 Stat. 198 (July 8, 1870); William J. Rich, *Taking "Privileges or Immunities" Seriously: A Call to Expand the Constitutional Canon*, 87 Minn. L. Rev. 153, 204, 216 (2002).

13. Crandall v. State of Nevada, 73 U.S. 35, 44 (1867) (striking down a capitation tax); the right was recently reinvigorated by the Supreme Court in Saenz v. Roe, 526 US 489, 498 (1999).

14. *Slaughter-House* at 96 (1873) (Field, J., dissenting).

15. *Slaughter-House* at 77, 79; *see* Rich, *Taking "Privileges or Immunities" Seriously*, at 167–73.

16. *See, e.g.*, Cong. Globe, 39th Cong., 1st Sess. App. 133 (1866) (Congressman Rogers challenging the broad extension of federal power represented by the Privileges or Immunities Clause); *id.* at 1034 (1866) (Congressman Bingham, assuring that "the proposed amendment does not impose upon any State of the Union, or any citizen of any State of the Union, any obligation which is not now enjoined upon them by the very letter of the Constitution"). *See, e.g.*, Charles Fairman, *Does the Fourteenth Amendment Incorporate the Bill of Rights?*, 2 Stan. L. Rev. 5, 36 (1949); Amar, The Bill of Rights, at 167–68.

17. *See* Raoul Berger, Government by Judiciary: The Transformation of the Fourteenth Amendment 30 (2d ed. 1997); David P. Currie, The Constitution in the Supreme Court 346–49 (1985).

18. Dred Scott v. Sandford, 60 U.S. 393 (1856).

19. Both sides of the *Slaughter-House* debate appear to agree on this point. *Slaughter-House* at 71 (majority) and at 95 (Field, J., dissenting)

20. Act of April 20, 1871 (Ku Klux Klan Act), ch. 22, §2, 17 Stat. 13 (1871) (first quotation); Cong. Globe, 42d Cong., 1st Sess. App. 81 (1871) (second quotation); 42 U.S.C. § 1983 (third quotation) (emphasis added).

21. *See, e.g.*, Charles L. Black, Jr., A New Birth of Freedom: Human Rights, Named and Unnamed 55 (1997) (characterizing Justice Miller's opinion in *Slaughter-House* as "probably

the worst holding, in its effect on human rights, ever uttered by the Supreme Court"). For a more favorable view of Justice Miller's perspective in *Slaughter-House, see* Michael A. Ross, Justice of Shattered Dreams: Samuel Freeman Miller and the Supreme Court during the Civil War Era 201–10 (2003) (describing Justice Miller's background as a physician, his support for public health measures, and his support for the biracial government in Louisiana that enacted the *Slaughter-House* regulations).

22. Ross, Justice of Shattered Dreams, at 200; Michael Franklin, *The Foundations and Meaning of the* Slaughter-House Cases, 18 Tul. L. Rev. 1, 52, 88 (1943); Aynes, *Constricting the Law of Freedom*, at 657; Rich, *Taking "Privileges or Immunities" Seriously*, at 179.

23. *Slaughter-House* at 79, 81.

24. *Slaughter-House* at 78–79 (quotation); *Crandall* at 44.

25. *Slaughter-House* at 78–79.

26. David S. Bogen, Slaughter-House *Five: Views of the Case*, 55 Hastings L.J. 333, 342, 376–77 (2003).

27. United States v. Cruikshank, 92 U.S. 542, 549 (1875) (citing *Slaughter-House* for a distinction between rights of state and national citizenship).

28. *Slaughter-House* at 79–80; Rich, *Privileges or Immunities: The Missing Link*, at 606–07.

29. *See* The Constitution of the United States of America: Analysis and Interpretation 1675 (Johnny H. Killian, George A. Costello & Kenneth R. Thomas eds., 2004).

30. *Slaughter-House* at 77–78.

31. *See, e.g.*, Gonzales v. Raich, 545 U.S. 1 (2005); Perez v. United States, 402 U.S. 146 (1971); Katzenbach v. McClung, 379 U.S. 294 (1964).

32. Thomas M. Cooley, The General Principles of Constitutional Law in the United States of America 245 (1880) (first quotation); McGovney, *Privileges or Immunities*, at 225 (second quotation); Todd Zubler, *The Right to Migrate and Welfare Reform: Time for* Shapiro v. Thompson *to Take a Hike*, 31 Val. U. L. Rev. 893, 917 (1997) (third quotation); Rich, *Privileges or Immunities: The Missing Link*, at 578–99; Rich, *Taking "Privileges or Immunities" Seriously*, at 284–92.

33. Saenz v. Roe, 526 U.S. 489, 502–03 (1999).

34. *See Cruikshank* at 549–50 (1875).

35. *See especially* Bd. of Trs. of the Univ. of Ala. v. Garrett, 531 U.S. 356, 364, 374 (2001); *see also* Fed. Mar. Comm'n v. S.C. State Ports Auth., 535 U.S. 743 (2002); Kimel v. Fla. Bd. of Regents, 528 U.S. 62 (2000); Alden v. Maine, 527 U.S. 706 (1999); Fla. Prepaid Postsecondary Educ. Expense Bd. v. College Sav. Bank, 527 U.S. 627 (1999); Seminole Tribe of Fla. v. Florida, 517 U.S. 44 (1996). *See generally* Rich, *Privileges or Immunities: The Missing Link*, at 575–77.

36. Pennsylvania v. Union Gas Co., 491 U.S. 1, 24 (1989) (Stevens, J., concurring) (noting that "numerous scholars have exhaustively and conclusively refuted the contention that the 11th Amendment embodies a general grant of sovereign immunity to the States"); Golden State Transit Corp. v. City of L.A., 493 U.S. 103, 112–13 (1989) (accepting the National Labor Relations Act as an example of "rights, privileges or immunities" protected by § 1983); Fla. Prepaid Postsecondary Educ. Expense Bd. v. College Savings Bank, 527 U.S. 627 (1999) (concluding that the Patent Clause could not be relied upon to abrogate the 11th Amendment);

Central Virginia Community College v. Katz, 546 U.S. 356 (2006) (concluding, by a 5–4 vote, that states are not immune from bankruptcy court orders).

37. *See* Rich, *Taking "Privileges or Immunities" Seriously*, at 210–19. For arguments in favor of positive rights, *see* Martha Nussbaum, Women and Human Development: The Capabilities Approach 111–61 (2000); Michael J. Sandel, Democracy's Discontent: America in Search of a Public Philosophy 124–28 (1996); Robin West, Progressive Constitutionalism: Reconstructing the Fourteenth Amendment 105 (1994). Ironically, the *Slaughter-House Cases* have been blamed for leading the courts down a path towards exclusive recognition of "negative" (rather than "positive") rights. *See* Michael J. Gerhardt, *The Ripple Effects of* Slaughter-House*: A Critique of a Negative Rights View of the Constitution*, 43 Vand. L. Rev. 409, 409–13 (1990).

38. This analysis would reverse conclusions reached by the United States Supreme Court in cases including *Kimel*, 528 U.S. 62 (2000) (Age Discrimination in Employment Act), *Garrett*, 531 U.S. 356 (2001) (Americans with Disabilities Act), *Alden*, 527 U.S. 706 (1999) (Fair Labor Standards Act) and *Fla. Prepaid*, 527 U.S. 627 (1999) (Patent rights) and restore the plurality conclusion of *Union Gas Co.*, 491 U.S. 1 (1989).

39. Cong. Globe, 39th Cong., 1st Sess. 2542 (1866) (statement of Rep. Bingham); *Slaughter-House* at 76–78.

CHAPTER 8

1. Slaughter-House Cases, 83 U.S. 36 (1873); Bradwell v. Illinois, 83 U.S. 130 (1873); Cruikshank v. United States, 92 U.S. 542 (1876).

2. *Slaughter-House* at 59–65; *see* Lochner v. New York, 198 U.S. 45, 61 (1905) (striking down a law prohibiting bakers from working more than sixty hours per week, stating: "[W]e think that such a law as this, although passed in the assumed exercise of the police power, ... is not, within any fair meaning of the term, a health law, but is an illegal interference with the rights of individuals....").

3. *Slaughter-House* at 73–76, 74 (first quotation), 76 (second and third quotations) (citing *Corfield*, 6 F. Cas. 546, 551–52 (C.C.E.D. Pa. 1823) (No. 3230).

4. *Slaughter-House* at 76.

5. *Slaughter-House* at 77–78. See Richard L. Aynes, *Constricting the Law of Freedom: Justice Miller, the Fourteenth Amendment, and the* Slaughter-House Cases, 70 Chi.-Kent L. Rev. 627, 627–29 (1994) (collecting views of scholars on the *Slaughter-House* Court's interpretation of the Privileges and Immunities Clause).

6. *See* 2 The Works of John C. Calhoun 242–43 (Richard Krenner Crallé ed.) (1888) (Calhoun stated: "Notwithstanding all the pomp and display of eloquence on the occasion, every citizen is a citizen of some State or territory, and, as such, under an express provision of the constitution, is entitled to all privileges and immunities of citizens in the several States; and it is in this, and in no other sense, that we are citizens of the United States); *Slaughter-House* at 95 (Field, J., dissenting); Charles L. Black, Jr., A New Birth of Freedom 32 (1997).

7. George C. Wallace, Governor, 1963 Inaugural Address (Jan. 14, 1963), available at http://www.archives.state.al.us/govs_list/inauguralspeech.html. Governor Wallace said: Today I have stood, where once Jefferson Davis stood, and took an oath to my people. It is very appropriate then that from this Cradle of the Confederacy, this very Heart of the Great Anglo-Saxon Southland, that today we sound the drum for freedom as have our generations

of forebears before us done, time and time again through history. Let us rise to the call of freedom-loving blood that is in us and send our answer to the tyranny that clanks its chains upon the South. In the name of the greatest people that have ever trod this earth, I draw the line in the dust and toss the gauntlet before the feet of tyranny . . . and I say . . . segregation today . . . segregation tomorrow . . . segregation forever.
Statement by Alabama Clergymen on Racial Problems in Alabama (Apr. 12, 1963), available at http://www.stanford.edu/group/King/frequentdocs/clergy.pdf ("We are now confronted by a series of demonstrations by some of our Negro citizens, directed and led in part by outsiders.").

8. Martin Luther King, Jr., Letter from a Birmingham Jail (Apr. 16, 1963), available at http://www.mlkonline.net/jail.html.

9. Interview by Katie Couric with Joe Biden and Sarah Palin, U.S. Vice-Presidential Nominees, (Oct. 1, 2008), available at http://www.cbsnews.com/stories/2008/10/01/eveningnews/main4493062.shtml.

10. Palko v. Connecticut, 302 U.S. 319, 324–25 (1937) (Cardozo, J.) ("In these and other situations immunities that are valid as against the federal government by force of the specific pledges of particular amendments have been found to be implicit in the concept of ordered liberty, and thus, through the 14th Amendment, become valid as against the states.").

11. Cruzan v. Director, Mo. Dep't of Health, 497 U.S. 261, 293 (1990) (Scalia, J., concurring).

12. *See* Allgeyer v. Louisiana, 165 U.S. 578, 591 (1897); Bernard Schwartz, A History of the Supreme Court 179–82 (1993) (describing "Due Process and Liberty of Contract").

13. *See* Adamson v. California, 332 U.S. 46, 71–72 (1948) (Black, J., dissenting) (contending that one of the chief purposes of the 14th Amendment was to make the Bill of Rights applicable against the States, and assembling historical evidence in support of that proposition); Michael Kent Curtis, No State Shall Abridge: The Fourteenth Amendment and the Bill of Rights (1986).

14. Meyer v. Nebraska, 262 U.S. 390 (1923) (parental rights); Stromberg v. California, 283 U.S. 359 (1931) (freedom of speech); Near v. Minnesota, 283 U.S. 697 (1931) (freedom of the press); Cantwell v. Connecticut, 310 U.S. 296 (1940) (freedom of religion); Lawrence v. Texas, 539 U.S. 558, 574 (2003) (intimate personal choices). In a number of decisions from different eras, the Supreme Court has echoed the language of the Declaration. *See* Marbury v. Madison, 5 U.S. 137, 176 (1803); *Meyer* at 399; Loving v. Virginia, 388 U.S. 1, 12 (1967); Planned Parenthood of Southeastern Pennsylvania v. Casey, 505 U.S. 833, 846 (1992) (O'Connor, Souter & Kennedy, JJ.).

15. *Bradwell* at 131–33; *see* Richard L. Aynes, Bradwell v. Illinois: *Chief Justice's Dissent and the "Sphere of Women's Work,"* 59 La. L. Rev. 521, 525 (1999).

16. *Bradwell* at 139.

17. *Slaughter-House* at 71 (first quotation), 81 (second quotation).

18. *Bradwell* at 141–42 (Bradley, J., concurring in the judgment).

19. Bowers v. Hardwick, 478 U.S. 186 at 196–97 (1986) (Burger, C.J., concurring).

20. United States v. Virginia (VMI), 518 U.S. 515 (1996); at 566–68, 601–03 (Scalia, J., dissenting); 566 (first and second quotation); 602–3 (third quotations including VMI Code); 603 (last quotation).

21. *VMI* at 567 (first quotation), 568 (second quotation).

22. Plessy v. Ferguson, 163 U.S. 537, 550 (1896) (upholding Louisiana statute requiring segregation of the races on trains).

23. Goesaert v. Cleary, 335 U.S. 464 (1948); Reed v. Reed, 404 U.S. 71 (1971); Romer v. Evans, 517 U.S. 620 (1996); Lawrence v. Texas, 539 U.S. 558 (2003).

24. *Lawrence* at 572 (first quotation), at 577–78 (second quotation) (quoting Bowers v. Hardwick, 478 U.S. 186, 216 (1986) (Stevens, J., dissenting)). *See VMI* at 567 (Scalia, J., dissenting) (acknowledging that the majority of the Court does not agree with his tradition approach).

25. *Lawrence* at 572, 574, 577–78.

26. Barbier v. Connelly, 113 U.S. 27, 32 (1885).

27. Railway Express Agency v. New York, 336 U.S. 106, 115 (1949) (Jackson, J., concurring).

28. *Cruikshank* at 548–49; Charles Lane, The Day Freedom Died: The Colfax Massacre, The Supreme Court and the Betrayal of Reconstruction (2008).

29. Lane, The Day Freedom Died, at 65–66, 70; Charles Lane, *To Keep and Bear Arms*, Wash. Post, Mar. 22, 2008, at A13, available at http://www.washingtonpost.com/wp-dyn/content/article/2008/03/21/AR2008032102540.html.

30. *Cruikshank* at 548, 551–57.

31. *Cruikshank* at 549.

32. *Cruikshank* at 551.

33. *Cruikshank* at 548, 551, 552 (quotation).

34. *Cruikshank* at 553–54 (emphasis added).

35. *See* B.F. Butler, To Protect Loyal and Peaceable Citizens of the United States, H.R. Rep. No. 41–37, at 1–4 (1871) (describing dozens of assaults and murders of blacks and their white allies across the South).

36. *See* Civil Rights Act of 1866, ch. 31, 14 Stat. 27 (codified at 42 U.S.C. §§ 1981–1982 (2000)) (originally entitled "An Act to protect All Persons in the United States in Their Civil Rights, and furnish the Means of their Vindication"); Ku Klux Klan Act of 1871, ch. 22, § 2, 17 Stat. 13 (codified at 42 U.S.C. § 1985, 18 U.S.C. § 241 (2000)) (originally entitled "An Act to enforce the Provisions of the 14th Amendment to the Constitution of the United States, and for other Purposes"); Civil Rights Act of 1875, ch. 114, §§ 3–5, 18 Stat. 335 (codified at 42 U.S.C. § 1984 (2000)) (originally entitled "An act to protect all citizens in their civil and legal rights").

37. *See, e.g.*, Abraham Lincoln, President, Second Inaugural Address (Mar. 5, 1865). Lincoln stated:
One-eighth of the whole population were colored slaves, not distributed generally over the Union, but localized in the Southern part of it. These slaves constituted a peculiar and powerful interest. All knew that this interest was somehow the cause of the war. To strengthen, perpetuate, and extend this interest was the object for which the insurgents would rend the Union even by war, while the Government claimed no right to do more than to restrict the territorial enlargement of it. Neither party expected for the war the magnitude or the duration which it has already attained. . . .

38. Cong. Globe, 39th Cong., 1st Sess. 1757 (1866) (statement of Sen. Lyman Trumball, floor manager of the 14th Amendment) ("How is it that every person born in these United States owes allegiance to the Government? . . . [T]he meaning of American citizenship. . . . [is that] [t]his government, . . . has certainly some power to protect its own citizens in their own country. Allegiance and protection are reciprocal rights."); *id.* at 1263 (1866) (remarks of Rep. John H. Broomal) "The rights and duties of allegiance and protection are corresponding rights and duties. Upon whatever square foot of the earth's surface I owe allegiance to my country, there it owes me protection, and wherever my Government owes me no protection I owe it no allegiance and can commit no treason.;" Cong. Globe, 42nd Cong., 1st Sess. 85 (1871) (John Bingham quoted Daniel Webster as having said, "[t]he maintenance of the Constitution does not depend on the plighted faith of the States as States to support it. . . . It relies on individual duty and obligation. . . . On the other hand, the Government owes high and solemn duties to every citizen of the country. It is bound to protect him in his most important rights and interests."). *See also* Daniel A. Farber & Suzanna Sherry, A History of the American Constitution 430–33 (2d ed. 2005) (describing the Republican Party's linkage of allegiance and protection); Rebecca E. Zietlow, *Congressional Enforcement of Civil Rights and John Bingham's Theory of Citizenship*, 36 Akron L. Rev. 717, 740 (2003); Alan R. Madry, *State Action and the Due Process of Self-Help; Flagg Bros. Redux*, 62 U. Pitt. L. Rev. 1, 40 (2000); Wilson Huhn, *The State Action Doctrine and the Principle of Democratic Choice*, 34 Hofstra L. Rev. 1379, 1403–04 (2006).

39. *See, e.g.,* Steven J. Heyman, *The First Duty of Government: Protection, Liberty, and the Fourteenth Amendment*, 41 Duke L.J. 507, 553–54 (1991) (noting that John Bingham, the leading drafter of the 14th Amendment, and other Republicans, considered the adoption of the Amendment as ensuring the constitutionality of the Civil Rights Act of 1866); *see also* Aynes, *Constricting the Law of Freedom*, at 631; Richard L. Aynes, *The Continuing Importance of John A. Bingham and the Fourteenth Amendment*, 36 Akron L. Rev. 589, 610 (2003); Frank J. Scaturro, The Supreme Court's Retreat from Reconstruction: A Distortion of Constitutional Jurisprudence 78–79 (2000).

40. *See* Civil Rights Cases, 109 U.S. 3, 26–27 (1883) (Harlan, J., dissenting) (stating, "the court has departed from the familiar rule requiring, in the interpretation of constitutional provisions, that full effect be given to the intent with which they were adopted."). *See generally* Huhn, *The State Action Doctrine*, at 1430–43 (assembling authorities supporting the proposition that the framers of the 14th Amendment intended to clothe Congress with the authority to prohibit individuals from interfering with the fundamental rights of American citizens).

41. *Cruikshank* at 554–59.

42. *See* Douglas Linder, Lynchings: By State and Race, 1882–1968, http://www.law.umkc. edu/faculty/projects/ftrials/shipp/lynchingsstate.html (last visited Jan. 31, 2009) (citing statistics provided by the Archives at Tuskegee Institute showing large numbers of lynchings in the period following *Cruikshank*); C. Vann Woodward, The Strange Career of Jim Crow 43 (1966) ("[I]t was, after all, in the 'eighties and early 'nineties [of the nineteenth century] that lynching attained the most staggering proportions ever reached in the history of that crime."); *see also* Gunnar Myrdal, An American Dilemma 560–61 (1944) (describing lynching in America, almost all of which occurred in the Southern and border states); Douglas Linder, The Trial of Joseph Schipp, et al.: An Account, http://www.law.umkc.edu/faculty/projects/ftrials/shipp/trialaccount.html (last visited Jan. 31, 2009) (describing the 1906 lynching of Ed Johnson in Tennessee and the subsequent trial of Sheriff Joseph Schipp and other members of the mob in the United States Supreme Court for criminal contempt).

43. *See Plessy*, 163 U.S. 537 (1896) (separate railroad cars for blacks and whites); Williams v. Mississippi, 170 U.S. 213 (1898) (poll tax, literacy test, disqualification for certain crimes, and residency requirements designed to disqualify African Americans from voting); Gong Lum v. Rice, 275 U.S. 78 (1927) (separation of the races in the public schools); Blyew v. United States, 80 U.S. 581 (1872) (Strong, J.) (no federal jurisdiction to hear murder case where Kentucky law prohibited blacks from testifying as witnesses to crimes committed by whites); United States v. Reese, 92 U.S. 214 (1876) (Waite, C.J.) (Section 3 of the first Enforcement Act construed broadly to render it unconstitutional under the 15th Amendment); Harris v. United States, 106 U.S. 629, 640 (1883) (Wood, J.) (provision of Ku Klux Klan Act unconstitutional); The Civil Rights Cases, 109 U.S. 3 (1883) (Civil Rights Act of 1875 unconstitutional); Baldwin v. Franks, 120 U.S. 678 (1887) (Ku Klux Klan Act unconstitutional insofar as it applies to private action); Hodges v. United States, 203 U.S. 1, 14 (1906) (Brewer, J.) (Civil Rights Act of 1866, no constitutional power to reach private action); United States v. Morrison, 529 U.S. 598 (2000) (Violence Against Women Act unconstitutional as applied to private acts of gender violence); Cumming v. Bd. of Educ. of Richmond County, 175 U.S. 528 (1899) (no injunction against local authorities who had closed the separate secondary school for African Americans while continuing to operate a school for white students); Pace v. Alabama, 106 U.S. 583 (1883) (state law that punished interracial marriage constitutional). *See generally* Woodward, Strange Career of Jim Crow, at 71, 145.

44. Hugo Black joined the Court on August 19, 1937, and Stanley Reed was added on January 31, 1938. Felix Frankfurter, Robert Jackson, and William Douglas were also appointed by Roosevelt. All five were still members of the Court in May 1954 *See* Oyez Project, Hugo L. Black Biography, http://www.oyez.org/justices /hugo_l_black (last visited Jan. 31, 2009); Oyez Project, Stanley Reed Biography, http://www.oyez.org/justices/stanley_reed (last visited Jan. 31, 2009); *see also* Oyez Project, http://www.oyez.org/courts/warren/war1 (last visited Jan. 31, 2009) (listing justices from the first term of the Warren Court). *See* Missouri *ex rel.* Gaines v. Canada, 305 U.S. 337 (1938) (ordering the School of Law of the State University of Missouri to admit an African American student); Brown v. Bd. of Educ., 347 U.S. 483, 495 (1954) ("We conclude that in the field of public education the doctrine of 'separate but equal' has no place."); Heart of Atlanta Motel, Inc. v. United States, 379 U.S. 241 (1964) (upholding Congress's power under the Commerce Clause to enact the Civil Rights Act of 1964); Katzenbach v. McClung, 379 U.S. 294 (1964).

45. *E.g.*, Bd. of Trs. of the Univ. of Ala. v. Garrett, 531 U.S. 356, 374 (2001) (Title I of the Americans with Disabilities Act); Kimel v. Fla. Bd. of Regents, 528 U.S. 62, 86, 91 (2000) (Age Discrimination in Employment Act); Coll. Sav. Bank v. Fla. Prepaid Postsecondary Educ. Expense Bd., 527 U.S. 666, 674 (1999) (Trademark Remedy Clarification Act); Fla. Prepaid Postsecondary Educ. Expense Bd. v. Coll. Sav. Bank, 527 U.S. 627, 647–48 (1999) (Patent and Plant Variety Protection Remedy Clarification Act).

46. United States v. Kras, 409 U.S. 434, 460 (1973) (Marshall, J., dissenting).

CHAPTER 9

1. Slaughter-House Cases, 83 U.S. 36, 57 (1873).

2. Richard L. Aynes, Unintended Consequences of the Fourteenth Amendment, *in* Unintended Consequences of Constitutional Amendment 110–40 (David E. Kyvig ed., 2000).

3. *See* Jonathan Truman Dorris, Pardon and Amnesty Under Lincoln and Johnson—The Restoration of the Confederates to Their Rights and Privileges 1861–1898, at 370 (1953).

4. *See* Harold Melvin Hyman, Era of Oath: Northern Loyalty Tests During the Civil War and Reconstruction (1954).

5. *See* Charles Fairman, 6 The Oliver Wendell Holmes Devise: History of the Supreme Court of the United States: Reconstruction and Reunion 1864–88, at 607–12 (1971).

6. John Niven, Salmon P. Chase: A Biography 383–396 (1995); Frederick J. Blue, Salmon P. Chase: A Life in Politics 250–53 (1987); J.W. Schuckers, The Life and Public Services of Salmon Portland Chase 266, 519–20 (1878). Chase believed that his planned visit could provide further evidence to support a presidential proclamation that would secure equal and universal suffrage. Blue, Salmon P. Chase, at 250.

7. Jefferson Davis: Constitutionalist: His Letters, Papers and Speeches 139 (Dunbar Rowland ed., 1923); Case of Davis, Chase 1, 7 F. Cas. 63 (C.C.D. Va. 1867). Both the Federal Case and the Rowland accounts are prints from reports of the case prepared by Bradley T. Johnson, Esq. A partial report appears in 3 Am. Law. Rev. 368. Rowland cites the case as "From Decisions of Chief Justice Chase in the Circuit Court of the United States for the Fourth Judicial Circuit, 1867–1871. By Bradley T. Johnson of the Virginia bar, 1876;" Hans L. Trefousse, Andrew Johnson: A Biography 211 (1989); 5 The Salmon P. Chase Papers, Correspondence 1865–1873, at 43 (John Niven et al. eds., 1998) (letter from W.T. Sherman to Chase, dated May 6, 1985).

8. Jefferson Davis: Constitutionalist, at 139; Roy F. Nichols, *United States vs. Jefferson Davis*, 31 Am. Historical Rev. 266, 268 (1926); Schuckers, Life, at 524; The Salmon P. Chase Papers at 49 (quotation).

9. Michael Les Benedict, *Salmon P. Chase as Jurist and Politician: Comment on G. Edward White, Reconstructing Chase's Jurisprudence*, 21 N. Ky. L. Rev. 133, 135 (1993); Charles Wilson, *The Original Chase Organization Meeting and the Next Presidential Election*, 23 Miss. Valley Hist. Rev. 61, 62 (1936); Niven, Salmon P. Chase.

10. Robert McElroy, Jefferson Davis: The Unreal and the Real 510–11 (Smithmark Publishers 1995) (1937); William J. Cooper, Jefferson Davis, American (2000).

11. Niven, Salmon P. Chase, at 396; Henry Luther Stoddard, Horace Greeley: Printer, Editor, Crusader 229 (1946); James M. McPherson, Battle Cry of Freedom: The Civil War Era 849 (1988); Dorris, Pardon and Amnesty, at xx and 281–94.

12. Niven, Salmon P. Chase, at 395, 409; Les Benedict, *Salmon P. Chase*, at 140.

13. "[Charles] Sumner assures me Chase has gone into [the South] to promote negro suffrage. I have no doubt that Chase has that and other schemes for Presidential preferment in hand in this voyage." Gideon Welles, The Diary of Gideon Welles 304 (1911) (citing entry by Welles of May 10, 1865).

14. For a complete discussion of Chase's presidential ambitions, *see* Blue, Salmon P. Chase, at 283–307.

15. Nichols, *U.S. vs. Jefferson Davis*, at 266.

16. In her memoirs, Varina Davis, the wife of Jefferson Davis reports a correspondence in which Davis wrote:
During the interval between the announcement . . . of the secession of Mississippi and the receipt of the official notification which enabled me to withdraw from the Senate, rumors were in circulation of a purpose, on the part of the United States Government, to arrest

members of Congress preparing to leave Washington on account of the secession of the States which they represented.
Varina Davis, 2 Jefferson Davis: Ex-President of the Confederate States of America: A Memoir 2–3 (1890). Varina's footnote states "Mr. Davis remained a week in Washington, hoping that he might be the person arrested." *Id.* at 3. Had this course of conduct occurred, the issue of secession could have ultimately made its way to the United States Supreme Court.

17. George Fort Milton, The Age of Hate: Andrew Johnson and the Radicals 152 (1930).

18. Schuckers, Life, at 533; Dorris, Pardon and Amnesty, at 95; J.G. Randall, The Civil War and Reconstruction 707 (1937) (first omission in original); Eric L. McKitrick, Andrew Johnson and Reconstruction 3 (1960).

19. Wm. Davis, Jefferson Davis, at 131; Cooper, Jefferson Davis, at 119; McElroy, Jefferson Davis, at 69–70.

20. Garret Epps, Democracy Reborn: The Fourteenth Amendment and the Fight for Equal Rights in Post-Civil War America 27 (2006).

21. The compact theory of the Union is a theory relating to the development of the Constitution, claiming that the formation of the nation was through a compact by all the states individually, and that the national government is consequently a creation of the states. *See* Alpheus Thomas Mason, *The Nature of Our Federal Union Reconsidered*, 65 Pol. Sci. Q. 502 (1950). A leading exponent of this theory was John C. Calhoun, a person that Jefferson Davis closely identified with politically and philosophically. *See id.* Proponents of the theory relied heavily on the Kentucky and Virginia Resolutions written secretly by Thomas Jefferson and James Madison in 1798. *See id.* For a complete discussion of the South's position relative to the compact theory, *see* Albert Taylor Bledsoe, Is Davis a Traitor; or Was Secession a Constitutional Right Prior to the War of 1861? (1907). For Jefferson Davis's view of the compact theory, *see* Jefferson Davis, 1 The Rise and Fall of the Confederate Government 171–78 (1990). For a more recent interpretation of the same argument, *see* James Ronald Kennedy and Walter Donald Kennedy, Was Jefferson Davis Right? (1998).

22. Dred Scott v. Sandford, 60 U.S. 393 (1857).

23. Don E. Fehrenbacher, The Dred Scott Case: Its Significance in American Law and Politics 417–48 (1978) (providing a chapter-long discussion of the attacks on Taney and the Supreme Court as a result of the decision); David F. Hughes, *Salmon P. Chase: Chief Justice*, 18 Vand. L. Rev. 569, 581–82 (1965); William Blair, Why Didn't the North Hang Some Rebels? The Postwar Debate Over Punishment for Treason 5 (2004); Donald E. Collins, The Death and Resurrection of Jefferson Davis 19 (2005) ("Although [Davis] heartily desired a trial that he hoped to use as a platform to vindicate the rightness of the path he had chosen in 1861—states' rights, the right of secession, and the Confederacy—it never came.") Davis essentially went to his grave arguing that his position on States' Rights was correct. He devotes most of his two volume memoirs to this argument.

24. Albert Bushnell Hart, Salmon Portland Chase 352 (1899).

25. McElroy, Jefferson Davis, at 526. There is a great deal of information written about Davis's imprisonment. Originally he was held with a 24 hour guard and lights were kept on at all times. Charles M. Blackford, *The Trials and Trial of Jefferson Davis*, 29 S. Hist. Soc. Papers 45, 52 (1901). For a while he was held in leg irons. *Id.* But gradually, his confinement was eased. *See* McElroy, Jefferson Davis, at ch. XXVII–XXVIII.

26. McElroy, Jefferson Davis, at 539.

27. Nichols, *U.S. vs. Jefferson Davis*, at 270.

28. Report of the Twelfth Annual Meeting of the Virginia State Bar Association 241 (Eugene C. Massie ed., 1900). O'Conor volunteered his services at the request of a number of lawyers of similar views because practically all Southern lawyers were at that time barred from practicing in the federal courts because of the Ironclad Oath requirement. This requirement was ultimately thrown out by the U.S. Supreme Court in Cummings vs. Missouri, 71 U.S. 277 (1867) and *Ex parte Garland*, 71 U.S. 333 (1867).

29. Hudson Strode, Jefferson Davis—Tragic Hero—The Last Twenty-Five Years 1864–1889, at 242 (1955).

30. Cooper, Jefferson Davis, at 539–40; McElroy, Jefferson Davis, at 539–40.

31. Niven, Salmon P. Chase, at 394–96; *Ex parte Milligan*, 71 U.S. 2, 123 (1866).

32. Trefousse, Andrew Johnson, at 211.

33. Nichols, *U.S. vs. Jefferson Davis*, at 266–67; Cooper, Jefferson Davis, at 541, 559.

34. Act for the Punishment of Certain Crimes Against the United States, ch. 9, §14, 1 Stat. 112 (1790).

35. *See* Dorris, Pardon and Amnesty, at 4.

36. *Id.*

37. An Act to Suppress Insurrection, to Punish Treason and Rebellion, to Seize and Confiscate the Property of Rebels, and for Other Purposes, 12 Stat. 589 (1862).

38. *See* Dorris, Pardon and Amnesty, at 4–5.

39. *Case of Davis* at 78.

40. David K. Watson, *The Trial of Jefferson Davis: An Interesting Constitutional Question*, 24 Yale L.J. 669, 670 (1914).

41. Schuckers, Life, at 534.

42. Charles Warren, 3 The Supreme Court in United States History 207 (1922) (citing *Philadelphia Inquirer*, May 12, 1866). The decision to try Davis in Richmond raised the question of whether or not "a jury [could] be procured in Virginia or any state of the late Confederacy which would find Davis guilty[.]" Nichols, *U.S. vs. Jefferson Davis*, at 267.

43. Cooper, Jefferson Davis, at 554, 559, 563.

44. For background information on Underwood, *see* Fairman, OWH Devise: Reconstruction, at 601–07. *See also* Crandall A. Shifflett, John C. Underwood—A Carpetbagger Reconsidered, 1860–1873 (1971) (unpublished dissertation, Univ. of Va.); Nichols, *U.S. vs. Jefferson Davis*, at 268.

45. Johnson wrote Chase on August 11, 1865: "I would be pleased to have a conference with you in reference to the time, place and manner of trial of Jefferson Davis, at your earliest convenience." Robert B. Warden, An Account of the Private Life and Public Service of Salmon Portland Chase 645 (1874).

46. Niven, Salmon P. Chase, at 395; The Salmon P. Chase Papers, at 64 (letter from Chase to Charles Sumner dated August 20, 1865); Hart, Salmon Portland Chase, at 353; Fairman, OWH Devise: Reconstruction, at 177.

47. Jefferson Davis: Constitutionalist, at 141–42; *see also Case of Davis* at 78.

48. Nichols, *U.S. vs. Jefferson Davis*, at 269 n.12; *Case of Davis* at 63–65, 81–88; Jefferson Davis: Constitutionalist, at 142; Horace Henry Hagan, *United States vs. Jefferson Davis*, 25 Sewanee Rev. Q. 220, 222 (1917) (referring to the 1862 Act as the Treason Act of 1862).

49. Jefferson Davis: Constitutionalist, at 142–44.

50. The Salmon P. Chase Papers at 70 (letter from Chase to Johnson, dated October 12, 1865).

51. Reply to the Attorney General to the Resolution of the State Relative to the Prosecution of Jefferson Davis for Treason, XI Op. Att'y Gen. 411 (1869).

52. Schuckers, Life, at 536–37.

53. Jefferson Davis: Constitutionalist, at 142, 150–51; Watson, *Trial of Jefferson Davis*, at 671.

54. Kennedy & Kennedy, Was Jefferson Davis Right?, at 104; Strode, Jefferson Davis, at 279, 307–8. Strode is decidedly pro Davis and pro Southern. He makes the only reference to the composition of this grand jury that I can locate, which is the reason I used the adjective "allegedly." Strode cites a letter from Mrs. Robert E. Lee, dated May 6, 1866 to a friend in which she states, "Have you read Underwood's charge to the grand jury, 5 of whom are negroes?"

55. On this occasion Davis was represented by Messrs. James T. Brady, William B. Reed, James Lyons, and Robert Ould. Blackford, *Trial of Jefferson Davis*, at 61–62; Jefferson Davis: Constitutionalist, at 152.

56. McElroy, Jefferson Davis, at 564–65; *Case of Davis* at 70.

57. *Case of Davis* at 71–72; Hart, Salmon Portland Chase, at 352.

58. The Salmon P. Chase Papers, at 183 (letter from Chase to Thomas W. Conway, printed in N.Y. Tribune, Sept. 19, 1870).

59. Schuckers, Life, at 542 (Letter from Chase to Schuckers, dated September 24, 1866).

60. Hart, Salmon Portland Chase, at 299 (showing Chase wrangling with the President Lincoln over military matters); *id.* at 353 (saying that Chase "had no heart in the prosecution" of Jefferson Davis); Jefferson Davis: Constitutionalist, at 141–42 (stating Underwood's former position that "the technical treason of its beginning should be ignored," and indicating that this changed after an interview with the President.); *see* Patricia Hickin, *John C. Underwood and the Antislavery Movement in Virginia 1847–1860*, 73 Va. Mag. Hist. & Biography 156 (1965).

61. Hickin, *Underwood*, at 156–59, 165; Nichols, *U.S. vs. Jefferson Davis*, at 268 n. 7; Fairman, OWH Devise: Reconstruction, at 601.

62. Hickin, *Underwood*, at 159; Patricia Hickin, John Curtis Underwood and the Antislavery Crusade 1809–1860 (1961) (unpublished dissertation, Univ. of Va.) 63–64, 136.

63. Richard Lowe, Republicans and Reconstruction in Virginia 1856–70, at 9, 34 (1991); Hickin, *Underwood*, at 165–66; Hans Louis Trefousse, Historical Dictionary of Reconstruction 235 (1991).

64. Shifflett, *Underwood*, at 15–16. *See also* Journal of the Executive Proceedings of the Senate of the United States of America, Volume XI 481 (Government Printing Office 1887) (Letter dated July 26, 1861).

65. *See* Hickin, *Underwood*; Lowe, Republicans and Reconstruction, at 12–14.

66. Fairman, OWH Devise: Reconstruction, at 601; Blue, Salmon P. Chase, at 264; Niven, Salmon P. Chase, at 434.

67. *See* Hickin, *Underwood.*

68. Fairman, OWH Devise: Reconstruction, at 602 (citing Richmond Dispatch, May 7, 1867).

69. McVeigh v. United States, 78 U.S. 259, 266–67 (1871); Fairman, OWH Devise: Reconstruction, at 823–28.

70. Chase was an early proponent of the use of the writ of habeas corpus in antislavery litigation. For a few examples, *see* Niven, Salmon P. Chase, at 51, 62.

71. Fairman, OWH Devise: Reconstruction, at 602–05.

72. The Salmon P. Chase Papers, at 285–86 (letter from Chase to Underwood dated November 19, 1868), at 292 (letter from Chase to Underwood dated January 14, 1869). On May 3, 1869 when Chase sat as the Circuit Judge in Richmond, he reversed the prior decisions made by Underwood. Fairman, OWH Devise: Reconstruction, at 603–606.

73. The question of the effect of Section 3 of the 14th Amendment on office holders who had taken an oath to support the Constitution and then engaged in the rebellion is discussed in U.S. v. Powell, 27 F. Cas. 605, 606 (C.C. N.C. 1871). *See also* Griffin's Case, 11 F. Cas. 7 (C.C. Va. 1869); State v. Watkins, 1869 La. LEXIS 367, at 1–2 (La. 1869).

74. Jefferson Davis: Constitutionalist, at 138; Hart, Salmon Portland Chase; Schuckers, Life.

75. Blue, Salmon P. Chase, at 264; Nichols, *U.S. vs. Jefferson Davis,* at 271.

76. Nichols, *U.S. vs. Jefferson Davis,* at 269–75.

77. *Id.* at 273–74.

78. Chester L. Barrows, William M. Evarts: Lawyer, Diplomat, Statesman 172 (1941).

79. Cooper, Jefferson Davis, at 545; Gaines M. Foster, Ghosts of the Confederacy 15 (1988).

80. Nichols, *U.S. vs. Jefferson Davis,* at 273–74. For an account of the actual transfer and the proceedings relative to the bond hearing, *see* McElroy, Jefferson Davis, at 581–88.

81. Blue, Salmon P. Chase, at 265–66; Fairman, OWH Devise: Reconstruction, at 608–09.

82. Nichols, *U.S. vs. Jefferson Davis,* at 279–80. For an in depth discussion of the inner workings of the trial, *see* Gene Smith, High Crimes and Misdemeanors: The Impeachment and Trial of Andrew Johnson 236–63 (1977); *see* Steven G. Calabresi and Christopher S. Yoo, *The Unitary Executive During the Second Half-Century,* 26 Harv. J.L. & Pub. Pol'y 667, 757 (2003).

83. Richard Henry Dana, *The Reasons for Not Prosecuting Jefferson Davis,* 64 Proc. Mass. Hist. Soc'y 201–9 (1930–1932); Nichols, *U.S. vs. Jefferson Davis,* at 276–78.

84. *Case of Davis* at 88; Samuel Shapiro, Richard Henry Dana, Jr. 1815–1882, at 137 (1961).

85. Nichols, *U.S. vs. Jefferson Davis,* at 279–80; Niven, Salmon P. Chase, at 429–32; The Salmon P. Chase Papers, at 227.

86. Niven, Salmon P. Chase, at 432; Blue, Salmon P. Chase, at 283–85, 297.

87. McElroy, Jefferson Davis, at 589–611.

88. Niven, Salmon P. Chase, at 409 (citing letter from Chase to Schuckers of May 15, 1866).

89. Watson, *Trial of Jefferson Davis,* at 674; *Case of Davis* at 89.

90. *Case of Davis* at 88–89.

91. Hart, Salmon Portland Chase, at 353.

92. *Case of Davis* at 89–90, 94.

93. *Case of Davis* at 91; Cooper, Jefferson Davis, at 565–66; Nichols, *U.S. vs. Jefferson Davis,* at 280; McElroy, Jefferson Davis, at 604.

94. Blue, Salmon P. Chase, at 266, 297, 300; Dorris, Pardon and Amnesty, at 379–80.

95. *Case of Davis* at 10; Nichols, *U.S. vs. Jefferson Davis,* at 283. "Following the disagreement of the circuit court on this motion and its certification of division to the Supreme Court, Evarts proposed to enter a *nolle prosequi* in the circuit court if the defendant's counsel would agree to drop the motion to quash. This was agreed to." Brainerd Dyer, The Public Career of William M. Evarts 108 (1933).

96. Proclamation No. 15, 15 Stat. 711 (Dec. 25, 1868) (published online at John T. Woolley & Gerhard Peters, The American Presidency Project, available at http://www.presidency.ucsb.edu/ws/print.php?pid=72360 (last visited Mar. 26, 2009)); Dorris, Pardon and Amnesty, at 357–58; Fairman, OWH Devise: Reconstruction, at 788; Trefousse, Andrew Johnson, at 346.

97. Nichols, *U.S. vs. Jefferson Davis,* at 284; Hagan, *U.S. vs. Jefferson Davis,* at 224.

98. J. Davis, Rise and Fall of the Confederate Government.

99. *See id.* at vi (foreword by James M. McPherson).

100. S.J. Res 16, 95th Cong. (1978) (enacted).

CHAPTER 10

1. Bradwell v. Illinois, 83 U.S. 130 (1873); Chi. Legal News, June 14, 1873, at 454 (discussing the Supreme Court's decision to uphold the Illinois Supreme Court's decision to deny Myra Bradwell's law license application) (quotation); *A Woman Admitted to the Bar in Missouri,* Chi. Legal News, Apr. 3, 1870, at 212; Karen Berger Morello, The Invisible Bar: The Woman Lawyer in America 1638 to the Present, at 37–38 (1986) (Iowa, Missouri, Michigan, Maine, and Utah).

2. *Bradwell* at 141 (Bradley, J., concurring).

3. *See* Rogers M. Smith, *"One United People": Second-Class Female Citizenship and the American Quest for Community,* 1 Yale J.L. & Human. 229, 260–61 (1989); Joan Hoff, Law, Gender, and Injustice: A Legal History of U.S. Women (1991); Nancy T. Gilliam, *A Professional Pioneer: Myra Bradwell's Fight to Practice Law,* 5 L. & Hist. Rev. 105 (1987); Frances Olsen, *From False Paternalism to False Equality: Judicial Assaults on Feminist Community, Illinois 1869–1895,* 84 Mich. L. Rev. 1518, 1527–29 (1986); Deborah L. Rhode, Justice and Gender: Sex Discrimination and the Law 21–22 (1989); William Wiecek, The Lost World of Classical Legal Thought: Law and Ideology in America, 1886–1937, at 150 (1998); 2 Charles Warren, The Supreme Court in United States History Volume 1836–1918, at 550 (1935); 4 Charles Fairman, The Oliver Wendell Holmes Devise: History of the Supreme Court of the United States: Reconstruction and Reunion 1864–88, at 1364–68 (1971); Richard L. Aynes, Bradwell v. Illinois: *Chief Justice Chase's Dissent and the "Sphere of Women's Work,"* 59 La. L. Rev. 521, 537–38 (1999); *e.g.,* John E. Nowak & Ronald D. Rotunda, Constitutional Law 827 (6th ed. 2000); Douglas W. Kmiec et al., The American Constitutional Order: History, Cases, and Philosophy 1179 (2d ed. 2004); Kathleen M. Sullivan & Gerald Gunther, Constitutional Law 648 (4th ed. 2001).

4. *Bradwell* at 141 (1873) (Bradley, J., concurring). *See, e.g.,* Geoffrey R. Stone et al., Constitutional Law 622 (5th ed. 2005); Kmiec et al., American Constitutional Order, at 1399; Sullivan & Gunther, Constitutional Law, at 648; Walter F. Murphy et al., American Constitutional Interpretation 744 (1986) (citing the decision in *Bradwell* as part of the Court's "judicial indifference to the rights of persons who were not white males"); Nowak & Rotunda, Constitutional Law, at 827–28 ("The views quoted here [by Justice Bradley] were representative of the attitudes women met when they attempted to challenge sex-based classifications."). *See also* Ellen Carol DuBois, Taking the Law into Our Own Hands: *Bradwell, Minor,* and Suffrage Militance in the 1870s, *in* Visible Women: New Essays on American Activism 30 (Nancy A. Hewitt & Suzanne Lebsock eds., 1993); Jane M. Friedman, America's First Woman Lawyer: The Biography of Myra Bradwell 21 (1993). For discussions of the concept of separate spheres, *see* Barbara Welter, *The Cult of True Womanhood: 1820–1860,* 18 Am. Q. 151 (1966); Nancy F. Cott, The Bonds of Womanhood: "Woman's Sphere" in New England, 1730–1835 (1977); Carroll Smith-Rosenberg, *The Female World of Love and Ritual: Relations between Women in Nineteenth-Century America,* 1 Signs 1 (1975)

5. *The XIV Amendment and Our Case,* 5 Chi. Legal News, Apr. 19, 1873, at 354.

6. Paul Brest et al., Processes of Constitutional Decisionmaking: Cases and Materials 1179–80 (5th ed. 2006); Louis Fisher, American Constitutional Law 945–54 (3d ed. 1999); DuBois, Taking the Law, at 20 n.4; Gilliam, *A Professional Pioneer,* at 115 n.3. For a discussion of Virginia Minor and her case, Minor v. Happersett, *see* DuBois, at 22.

7. Friedman, America's First Woman Lawyer, at 11 n.4; *Death of Mrs. Myra Bradwell,* 28 Am. L. Rev. 278 (1894); *Myra Bradwell* 26 Chi. Legal News, Feb. 17, 1894, at 200–02; *see* Ellen Carol DuBois, Feminism and Suffrage: The Emergence of an Independent Women's Movement in America 1848–1869, at 162–202 (1978) (describing the first split in the women's rights movement, which occurred in 1869, over whether to support the 15th Amendment that granted suffrage to African American men, but not to women); DuBois, Taking the Law, at 21 n.5 (quotation).

8. Eleanor Flexner & Ellen Fitzpatrick, Century of Struggle: The Woman's Rights Movement in the United States 145–46 (enl. ed. 1996).

9. *See* Gilliam, *A Professional Pioneer,* at 115 n.3.

10. Wiecek, Lost World, at 3 n.3, 175, 177–80 (quotation); *see* Robert W. Gordon, Legal Thought and Legal Practice in the Age of American Enterprise 1870–1920, *in* Professions and Professional Ideologies in America 70 (Gerald L. Geison ed., 1983) (arguing that elite lawyers during this time fought against an instrumental approach to law and advocated instead a scientific, formalist approach); Morton J. Horwitz, The Transformation of American Law 1870–1960: The Crisis of Legal Orthodoxy 3, 109–42 (1992); Kermit L. Hall, The Magic Mirror: Law in American History 223 (1989).

11. Sociological jurisprudence is philosophy that the law be viewed "within a broad social context rather than as an isolated phenomenon" and that "legislation and court adjudications [should] take into account the findings of other branches of learning, particularly the social sciences." Justice William O. Douglas, Jurisprudence, Microsoft® Encarta® Online Encyclopedia (2008), available at http://encarta.msn.com/encyclopedia_761558172/Jurisprudence. html. The term was coined by Roscoe Pound in the first decade of the twentieth century. Wiecek, Lost World, at 191–93 n.3.

12. Bradwell was ultimately admitted to both the Illinois and the Supreme Court bars.

Friedman, America's First Woman Lawyer, at 30 n.4. But women did and continue to face discrimination within the legal profession and society. Smith, *"One United People,"* n.3. The obstacles were and are even greater for women of color. Janet E. Gans Epner, American Bar Association Comm. on Women in the Profession, Visible Invisibility: Women of Color in Law Firms (2006). But there have been incremental advances. By 1950 every state in the Union admitted women lawyers. Morello, Invisible Bar, at 37–38. In 1971 the Supreme Court began using the Equal Protection Clause to strike down sex discrimination. Reed v. Reed, 404 U.S. 71, 76–77 (1971). In 1981 the first woman Justice was appointed to the United States Supreme Court. Morello, Invisible Bar, at 218.

13. Friedman, America's First Woman Lawyer, at 35–36 n.4, 41; *Myra Bradwell*, at 200 n.7; *All Dabble in the Law*, Chi. Daily Trib., May 12, 1889, at 26 (quotation) (Bradwell dating the beginning of her formal legal studies at 1857 "about five years after our marriage I determined to read [law] in good earnest.")

14. Dorothy Thomas, Myra Colby Bradwell, *in* 1 Notable American Women 1607–1950: A Biographical Dictionary 223–24 (Edward T. James ed., 1971); *Myra Bradwell*, at 201 n.7; Stephen M. Buechler, The Transformation of the Woman Suffrage Movement: The Case of Illinois, 1850–1920, at 58–59 (1986).

15. *Myra Bradwell*, at 200 n.7; Caroline K. Goddard, Bradwell, Myra Colby, *in* Women Building Chicago 1790–1990: A Biographical Dictionary 112–13 (Rima Lunin Schultz & Adele Hast eds., 2001); Friedman, America's First Woman Lawyer, at 77–79 n.4; 6 Industrial Chicago: The Bench and Bar 642 (1896); *The Laws of 1869*, 1 Chi. Legal News, Mar. 13, 1869, at 188; *The Myra Bradwell Case*, Chi. Daily Trib., Apr. 20, 1873, at 8 (describing the Chi. Legal News as "the best law-newspaper in the country").

16. The doctrine of coverture tied women's legal status to her marital or kin relationships. A married woman was thought to become one with her husband, a union that effectively rendered her civilly dead. *See* Norma Basch, In the Eyes of the Law: Women, Marriage, and Property in Nineteenth-Century New York 17–19, 20–24 (1982); Linda E. Speth, The Married Women's Property Acts, 1839–1865: Reform, Reactions, or Revolution?, *in* Women and the Law: A Social Historical Perspective Volume II: Property, Family and the Legal Profession 69–70 (D. Kelly Weisberg ed., 1982); Carole Shammas, *Re-Assessing the Married Women's Property Acts*, 6 J. Women's Hist. 9, 10 (1994); Sandra F. VanBurkleo, "Belonging to the World": Women's Rights and American Constitutional Culture 108–10 (2001). For example, in one of her first issues Bradwell reported that Mary E. Magoon was practicing law in the lower courts in North English, Iowa (where a law license was not required). *Female Lawyer*, Chi. Legal News, Feb. 27, 1869, at 172.

17. Industrial Chicago, at 642 n.15; Friedman, America's First Woman Lawyer, at 78 n.4.

18. Bear v. Hays, 36 Ill. 280, 281 (1865). *See Husband and Wife—Property of Latter Under Law of 1861*, Chi. Legal News, Oct. 17, 1868, at 22 (specifying the inequalities that persisted in the Illinois property laws). *Law Relating to Women*, Chi. Legal News, Oct. 31, 1868, at 37; Chi. Legal News, Jan. 9, 1869, at 117 (informing readers that New Hampshire passed a married earning act and asserting: "We hope, before the adjournment of the present legislature, they will have that right in Illinois."); *Talk with the Legislature*, Chi. Legal News, Feb. 27, 1869, at 172; *Married Women's Separate Property Under Act of 1861*, Chi. Legal News, Nov. 13, 1869, at 53. The law was approved March 24, 1869. It established that married women's wages were their sole and separate property, but specified that the act did not give a wife "any right to compensation from any labor performed for her minor children or husband." An Act in

Relation to the Earnings of Married Women, Laws of the State of Illinois Enacted by the General Assembly 255 (1869). *See generally* Amy Dru Stanley, From Bondage to Contract: Wage Labor, Marriage, and the Market in the Age of Slave Emancipation 176–77, 197–203 (1998).

19.   Buechler, Transformation, at 68–75 n.14. Kate Doggett, Rev. E.J. Goodspeed, and Rebecca Mott were also elected to attend the ERA convention. *Chicago Woman Suffrage Convention,* Chi. Legal News, Feb. 20, 1869, at 164. *See* DuBois, Feminism and Suffrage, at 162–202, 165 n.7 (describing the first split in the women's rights movement, which occurred in 1869, over whether to support the 15th Amendment that granted black suffrage to African American men, but not to women).

20.   DuBois, Feminism and Suffrage, at 198–99 n.7; *Woman's Suffrage. Election of Delegates to the National Convention at Cleveland,* Chi. Trib., Nov. 14, 1869, at 1 (quotation).

21.   2 The Selected Papers of Elizabeth Cady Stanton and Susan B. Anthony: Against an Aristocracy of Sex: 1866 to 1873, at 284 (Ann D. Gordon ed., 2000); *Conventions,* N.Y. Times, Nov. 25, 1869, at 1; Buechler, Transformation, at 86 n.14; *Woman's Suffrage,* Chi. Trib., Jan. 5, 1870, at 4 (quotations).
Some members of the committee who were also members of the Cook County Woman Suffrage Association (CCWSA) did act on the idea of a Northwestern Suffrage Association. Five months after the meeting the CCWSA published an initial call for a meeting in Chicago for anyone interested in the possibility of forming a Northwestern association. *Female Suffrage,* Chi. Trib., May 19, 1870, at 1. A Northwestern Association was established on May 25, 1870, but it appears that it was sympathetic to Susan B. Anthony and the NWSA and not neutral. *See Woman Suffrage,* N.Y. Times, Dec. 1, 1870, at 5; *Woman's Suffrage Convention of the Northwestern Franchise Association,* Chi. Trib., May 26, 1870, at 3.

22.   *The Woman Suffrage Associations—Illinois Advocates Urge Union,* N.Y. Times, Nov. 21, 1870, at 2; *Woman Suffrage,* Chi. Trib., Nov. 27, 1870, at 3; *Woman's Suffrage,* Chi. Trib., Jan. 5, 1870, at 4 (quotation); *Female Suffrage: Meeting of the Executive Committee of the Illinois Association,* Chi. Trib., Apr. 19, 1871, at 3; Buechler, Transformation, at 104 n.14.

23.   *Female Suffrage: Meeting of the Executive Committee of the Illinois Association,* Chi. Trib., Apr. 19, 1871, at 3. The term "free divorce" was used interchangeably with "easy divorce" and often in connection with the concept of "free love." Free-Love and Free-Divorce, Every Saturday: A Journal of Choice Reading, July 22, 1871, at 75; *War in the Woman Suffrage Camp. Mrs. Henry H. Stanton. Free Divorce and Free Love,* Chi. Trib., Nov. 13, 1870, at 2; *Taking the Back-Track,* Chi. Trib., Apr. 14, 1872, at 5; *Judge Farwell on Divorce,* Chi. Trib., Sept. 22, 1872, at 4; *Woman and Easy Divorce,* The Independent, Dec. 28, 1871, at 4. It was also called "freedom of divorce." Editorial Article, Chi. Trib., Jan. 27, 1871, at 2; *see also* Stanley, From Bondage to Contract, at 178 n.18. Free love embraced the concept of women's sexuality and advocated that women had the right to decline sexual intercourse. Barbara Goldsmith, Other Powers: The Age of Suffrage, Spiritualism, and the Scandalous Victoria Woodhull, 208 (1998). Opponents to free love described it as "free lust." Editorial Article 2, Chi. Trib., Nov. 14, 1870, at 2. Free divorce referred to state laws that broadened the grounds under which either or both the husband and wife could sue for divorce. (*See* for example *Free Trade in Divorce,* N.Y. Times, Apr. 17, 1872, at 4, that describes a proposed bill in New York that would have allowed divorce on the grounds that one of the parties was "unhappy or uncomfortable.") Those who opposed divorce except on the grounds of adultery or extreme cruelty criticized these laws, arguing that they destroyed the institution of marriage that they insisted was the

"foundations of the social order." *Divorces in Illinois*, Chi. Trib., Feb. 23, 1873, at 6; *The World of Amusement*, Chic. Trib., Jan. 29, 1871, at 2 (arguing that "divorce[] made easy...makes a farce of marriage...kills the home...dissevers the family...[and] is an outrage upon the child"). *See also* Nancy F. Cott, Public Vows: A History of Marriage and the Nation 106–111 (2000). Proponents of liberal divorce laws, which included Elizabeth Cady Stanton, argued that denying divorce to women denied their liberty and caused harm to the family. *"Woman's Right" to Divorce*, N.Y. Times, May 18, 1870 at 2; Norma Basch, Framing American Divorce: From the Revolutionary Generation to the Victorians 68–69 (1999).

24. *Female Suffrage: Meeting of the Executive Committee of the Illinois Association*, Chi. Trib., Apr. 19, 1871, at 3; A.J. Grover, The Bible Argument Against Woman Stated and Answered from a Bible Standpoint (1870). Charles Waite similarly challenged Christianity and the Bible. Charles B. Waite, History of the Christian Religion to the Year Two Hundred, at iii–iv, 1–15 (3d ed. 1881). Elizabeth Cady Stanton shared the position that Christianity and the Bible had a deleterious effect on the position of women. In 1895, after almost a decade of work, she published the Woman's Bible. Ellen Carol DuBois, Woman Suffrage and Women's Rights 160, 163–65, 170 (1998).

25. *Woman Suffrage: First Annual Convention of the Cook County Woman Suffrage Association: Resolutions Offered that Woman is Already Entitled to the Franchise*, Chi. Trib., Mar. 11, 1871, at 3; *Woman Suffrage: Reception to Mrs. Stanton and Miss Anthony: The Former Addresses a Few Words to Her Friend*, Chi. Trib., June 9, 1871, at 4; *see also* 3 The Selected Papers of Elizabeth Cady Stanton and Susan B. Anthony 152, 153 n.5 (Ann D. Gordon ed., 2003) (reprinting a letter from Anthony to Elizabeth Boynton Harbert urging Harbert to become President of the IWSA to replace Jones, who had moved to Europe and could no longer lead the NWSA; with Jones gone, Anthony feared the AWSA sympathizers within the IWSA might take control of the state association).

26. Buechler, Transformation, at 104 n.14.

27. *Female Suffrage: Meeting of the Executive Committee of the Illinois Association*, Chi. Trib., Apr. 19, 1871, at 3. Jane Graham Jones succeeded Waite as President of the IWSA. Buechler, Transformation, at 104 n.14. Jones was also committed to Anthony. *See* 3 Selected Papers of Stanton and Anthony, at 152 n.25.

28. Bradwell also used the Chi. Legal News presses to serve as the Woman's Journal's western agent, publishing the paper every Saturday. *The Woman's Journal*, Chi. Legal News, Jan. 15, 1870, at 124. Lucy Stone, Mary Livermore, and Julia Ward Howe, all leaders of the AWSA, were the editors of the Journal.

29. Before the split, Bradwell met with Elizabeth Cady Stanton in Springfield, Illinois in late February 1869 and described her as one of the "great apostles" of the woman suffrage movement. *Suffrage and Springfield*, Chi. Legal News, Feb. 27, 1869, at 172. She met with Susan B. Anthony in Chicago in March 1870. She described the encounter as "a very pleasant visit" and published her full support for Anthony's proposed 16th Amendment to the Constitution. *Susan B. Anthony*, Chi. Legal News, Mar. 12, 1870, at 188. After Bradwell left the IWSA she attended at least two national meetings of the NWSA. *See Washington*, Chi. Daily Trib., Dec. 1872, at 2; *The Women*, Chi. Daily Trib., May 7, 1879, at 3. Bradwell and Anthony also exchanged a handful of letters from 1873 to 1888 that reflected their continued, albeit strained, relationship. Friedman, America's First Woman Lawyer, at 184–89 n.4.

30. *Mrs. Bradwell's Poem*, Chi. Trib., July 2, 1871, at 2.

31. Morello, Invisible Bar, at 11 n.1; Louis A. Haselmayer, *Belle A. Mansfield*, 55 Women Lawyers J. 46–47 (1969); Dorothy Thomas, Arabella Mansfield, *in* 2 Notable American Women 1607–1950: A Biographical Dictionary 492, 493 (Edward T. James ed., 1971). Mansfield used her legal expertise to advance the women's rights movement in Iowa. In August of 1870 she drafted a "Constitution for the Henry County Woman Suffrage Association." She continued to teach as well as give various lectures on legal issues such as "The Principles of Government" and "The Origin of Law" and furthered her legal education at Iowa Wesleyan University receiving her Bachelor of Laws degree in June 1872. At the first national meeting of women lawyers at the Isabella Clubhouse in Chicago during the World's Fair of 1893, Mansfield gave an address on her admission to the bar and was given an honorary membership to the National League of Women Lawyers founded during the Fair. Haselmayer, at 49 (quoting a letter from John Mansfield published in the Iowa Classic, Dec. 1872, at 17).

32. *A Married Woman Admitted to the Bar in Iowa*, Chi. Legal News, Oct. 16, 1869, at 20.

33. *A Woman Cannot Practice Law or Hold Any Office in Illinois*, Chi. Legal News, Feb. 5, 1870, at 145; *All Dabble in the Law*, n.13.

34. Friedman, America's First Woman Lawyer, at 37 n.4, 40; *All Dabble in the Law*, n.13 (quotations); *see* Aynes, Bradwell v. Illinois, at 536 n.3.

35. *All Dabble in the Law*, n.13 ("The world, too, has begun to learn the lesson that it is not necessary for a woman to break up all family ties and sacrifice womanly attributes and graces in order to succeed in other trades than the honored one of housewife.") (quoting Myra Bradwell).

36. *See In re* Bradwell, 55 Ill. 535 (1869).

37. *See A Woman Cannot Practice Law*, at 145 n.33.

38. Adam Winkler describes these arguments as "living constitutionalism." Adam Winkler, *A Revolution Too Soon: Woman Suffragists and the "Living Constitution,"* 76 N.Y.U. L. Rev. 1456, 1463 (2001) (explaining that Living Constitutionalism requires that the Constitution must be interpreted "in light of society's changing needs and conditions rather than solely the Framers' intent"); Benjamin N. Cardozo, The Nature of Judicial Process 82–83 (1921).

39. *A Woman Cannot Practice Law*, at 145–46 n.33. The letter from the Supreme Court Reporter was dated October 6, 1869. Bradwell filed her second brief on November 18, 1869.

40. *Id.* at 145–46; Olsen, *From False Paternalism*, at 1524 n.3. Bradwell also argued that for her in particular, coverture was not a barrier to her ability to engage in business transactions since the Illinois legislature had granted her a special charter to operate the Chi. Legal News. *See also* Winkler, *A Revolution Too Soon*, at 1481 n.38, 1482 n.141.

41. *A Woman Cannot Practice Law*, at 146 n.33. However, at this time Iowan Mansfield, a married woman, was the only woman admitted to any state bar in the United States.

42. Morton J. Horwitz, Transformation of Constitutional Law, *in* 6 Encyclopedia of the American Constitution 2712 (Leonard W. Levy & Kenneth L. Karst eds., 2d ed. 2000); Paul W. Kahn, Legitimacy and History: Self-Government in American Constitutional Theory 32–64 (1992); Winkler, *A Revolution Too Soon*, at 1463 n.38; Wiecek, Lost World, at 19 n.3, 44; *see also* Morton J. Horwitz, The Transformation of American Law, 1780–1860, at 178–80 (1977); William E. Nelson, *The Impact of the Antislavery Movement Upon Styles of Judicial Reasoning in Nineteenth Century America*, 87 Harv. L. Rev. 513, 521–24 (1974).

43. *A Woman Cannot Practice Law*, at 146 n.33.

44. *Id.*

45. *See* Horwitz, Transformation of American Law, at 3 n.10, 109–10, 142; Hall, Magic Mirror, at 223 n.10. *See* Oliver Wendell Holmes, *The Path of Law*, 10 Harv. L. Rev. 457 (1897); Wiecek, Lost World, at 191–93 n.3,; Roscoe Pound, *Mechanical Jurisprudence*, 8 Colum. L. Rev. 605, 609 (1908) (quotation); *see generally* Roscoe Pound, *The Need of a Sociological Jurisprudence*, 19 Green Bag 607 (1907); Cardozo, Nature of Judicial Process, at 82–83 n.38 (quotation).

46. Winkler, *A Revolution Too Soon*, at 1457–58 n.38, 1479. Although there are no known correspondences between Bradwell and Stanton specifically discussing this argument of judicial interpretation, there is evidence that the two women interacted during this period and there is a letter Anthony wrote to Bradwell in 1873 after her prosecution for voting in which she asks Bradwell "What are we going to do or say next?" and writes "How I would love to talk of our Constitutional position and work for the future." Friedman, America's First Woman Lawyer, at 184 n.4 (letter from Anthony to Bradwell dated July 30, 1873). This letter was written after Bradwell withdrew from the IWSA. It offers the possibility that Bradwell and Anthony had previously talked about their constitutional arguments. This possibility is supported by the similarities in the arguments of Bradwell, Stanton, and Minor three years earlier, before the splintering of the IWSA. Further, Anthony published an article on October 7, 1869 announcing that Bradwell was about to apply for her law license. *What Women are Doing*, The Revolution, Oct. 7, 1869, at 218. Bradwell had just submitted the application in October and just received the letter from the Court Reporter denying her application. Bradwell had not yet published this information in the Chi. Legal News. Bradwell submitted her second brief to the Illinois Supreme Court on November 16, 1869, but she did not publish copy of it until February 5, 1870. *See A Woman Cannot Practice Law*, at 146 n.33. Stanton made her argument to the Senate Committee on the District of Columbia in January 1870. Winkler, at 1479.

47. Winkler, *A Revolution Too Soon*, at 1480–81 n.38, 1483; 2 History of Woman Suffrage 407–520 (Elizabeth Cady Stanton, Susan B. Anthony & Matilda Joselyn Gage eds., 1881); *see* Kelly v. Owen, 74 U.S. 496 (1868).

48. DuBois, Taking the Law, at 21–22 n.4; Winkler, *A Revolution Too Soon*, at 1476–77 n.38; 2 History of Woman Suffrage, at 407–11 n.47; 2 Selected Papers of Stanton and Anthony, at 273–75 n.21. Although Minor's argument did not include the new method of constitutional interpretation that included consideration of changed social circumstance, it did call for a broad interpretation of the Constitution and it included a plea for justice. *Dear Revolution (Letter by Francis Minor)*, The Revolution (Oct. 21, 1869); 2 Selected Papers of Stanton and Anthony, at 275 ("That justice and equity can only be attained by having the same laws for men and women alike." (Francis Minor to the *Revolution*, Resolution 5, Oct. 14, 1869)). Suffragists quickly seized on the New Departure argument and put it into practice by demanding the vote. DuBois, at 117–18 n.7.

49. DuBois, Taking the Law, at 30 n.4; Gilliam, *A Professional Pioneer*, at 114 n.3; *A Woman Cannot Practice Law*, at 146 n.33.

50. *A Woman Cannot Practice Law*, at 146 n.33.

51. *Id.*

52. 2 Selected Papers of Stanton and Anthony, at 296 n.21; Winkler, *A Revolution Too Soon*, at 1480, 1483 n.38.

53. Goldsmith, Other Powers, at 248–55 n.23; Winkler, *A Revolution Too Soon*,at 1484, 1489, 1485 n.38 (quoting Victoria C. Woodhull's testimony before the Judiciary Committees of the Senate and House of Representatives of the Congress of the United States).

54. United States v. Anthony, 24 F. Cas. 829 (N.D.N.Y. 1873); 2 History of Woman Suffrage, at 653, 657–58, 667–68, 691 n.47; Winkler, *A Revolution Too Soon*, at 1506, 1511–12, 1514 n.38; Flexner & Fitzpatrick, Century of Struggle, at 159–60 n.8; Rogers M. Smith, Civic Ideals: Conflicting Visions of Citizenship in U.S. History 341 (1997). Bradwell published the decision in Anthony's case and then wrote two editorial notes criticizing the decision, Chi. Legal News, June 21, 1873, at 466 and Chi. Legal News, July 19, 1873, at 498.

55. *See, e.g., Mrs. Lockwood's Case*, 11 Chi. Legal News, Nov. 16, 1878, at 70.

56. *In re Goodell* 39 Wis. 232 (1875); *see* Catherine B. Cleary, *Lavinia Goodell: First Woman Lawyer in Wisconsin*, 74 Wisc. Mag. of Hist. 243 (1991); Virginia G. Drachman, Sisters in Law: Women Lawyers in Modern American History 22–23 (1998); *Can a Woman Practice Law in Wisconsin?*, Chi. Legal News, Jan. 1, 1876, at 116 (quotations). For contemporary discussions of the case *see Should Women Practice Law in Wisconsin*, 8 Chi. Legal News, March 25, 1876, at 215 (where Bradwell dissects Ryan's opinion); *Women as Lawyers—Mrs. Goodell's Case*, Cent. L.J. 186 (Mar. 24, 1876) (arguing that women should have the chance to practice law); Editorial Notes, Indep., Mar. 23, 1876, at 16 (describing Ryan's decision as "stupid, illiberal, and mean").

57. *See Shall Women Be Admitted to Practice Law in the Federal Courts?*, Chi. Legal News, Mar. 23, 1878, at 215; *Shall Women Be Admitted to the Bar?*, Chi. Legal News, Mar. 30, 1878, at 224–25; *The Admission of Women to the Bar*, Chi. Legal News, Feb.15, 1879; *Women as Lawyers*, Chi. Legal News, May 11, 1878, at 271–72; *Women's Right to Practice in the U.S. Courts*, Chi. Legal News, Feb. 10, 1877, at 169. Morello, Invisible Bar, at 31, 33 n.1; Drachman, Sisters in Law, at 27 n.56; Fairman, OWH Devise, at 1366 n.3. *See also* Jill Norgren, *Before It Was Merely Difficult: Belva Lockwood's Life in Law and Politics*, 23 J. Sup. Ct. Hist. 16, 29 (1999); Lee Ann Potter, *A Bill to Relieve Certain Legal Disabilities of Women*, 66 Soc. Educ. 117, 119 (2002); Frances A. Cook, Belva Ann Lockwood: For Peace, Justice, and President, May 13, 1997, available at http://stanford.edu/group/WLHP/papers/lockwood (quotation).

58. Belva Lockwood, In Support of House Bill 1077, Entitled "A Bill to Relieve Certain Disabilities of Women," *in* James Kirby, 1 The Legal News 185 (1878) (quotation). *See Shall Women Be Admitted to the Bar?* at 225 n.57; Morello, Invisible Bar, at 34 n.1; *Mrs. Lockwood's Victory*, Chi. Legal News, Mar. 2, 1878, at 191; *Women's Right to Practice*, at 169 n.57.

59. 20 Stat. 292 (1879); *Women as Lawyers*, at 272 n.57; *Admission of Women to the Bar*, at 181 n.57. Throughout Sargent's political and legal career, he was a champion of women's rights. A close friend of Susan B. Anthony's, in 1878 he introduced the "Anthony Amendment" to Congress, the woman suffrage amendment that was ultimately enacted as the 19th Amendment in 1920. Flexner & Fitzpatrick, Century of Struggle, at 165 n.8.

60. Virginia G. Drachman, Women Lawyers and the Origins of Professional Identity in America 243 (1993).

61. *In re Bradwell*, 55 Ill. 535 (1869). *A Woman Cannot Practice Law*, at 147 n.33; *see also* Olsen, *From False Paternalism*, at 1518–41 n.3.

62. *A Woman Cannot Practice Law*, at 147 n.33; *see also* Buechler, Transformation, at 64 n.14.

63. Gilliam, *A Professional Pioneer*, at 117, 119 n.3. Bradwell did, nonetheless, praise Carpen-

ter's argument on her behalf. *Senator Carpenter's Argument—Liberty of Pursuit*, Chi. Legal News, Jan. 20, 1872, at 108.

64. *Supreme Court of the United States*, Chi. Legal News, Jan. 20, 1872, at 108–09; E. Bruce Thompson, Matthew Hale Carpenter: Webster of the West 101 (1954); Smith, Civic Ideals, at 260 n.3; Hoff, Law, Gender, and Injustice, at 168–69 n.3; Gilliam, *A Professional Pioneer*, n.3. *See also* DuBois, Taking the Law, at 19–40 n.4.

65. *Senator Carpenter's Argument*, n.63.

66. *The Political Aspect of the Question*, Chi. Trib., Feb. 8, 1872, at 5.

67. Friedman, America's First Woman Lawyer, at 185 n.4 (emphasis deleted) (letter from Anthony to Bradwell dated June 30, 1873).

68. *More Supreme Court Decisions*, Boston Daily Advertiser, Apr. 16, 1873, at 1; Gilliam, *A Professional Pioneer*, at 126 n.3; Warren, Supreme Court, at 550 n.3.

69. *The XIV Amendment and Our Case*, Chi. Legal News, May 10, 1873, at 390.

70. Nineteen state courts refused to admit grant women a license to practice law without an act from their legislatures. Drachman, Sisters in Law, at app. 1 n.56 (listing the date of admission of the first woman lawyer in each state and the District of Columbia and whether the admission was approved by the state court or if an act of the state legislature was required to overcome the court's refusal to admit women to its bar).

71. Ellen Martin, *Admission of Women to the Bar*, 1 Chi. L. Times 76, 76–77 (1887) (quoting the Examining Committee Report); *see* Thomas, Notable American Women, at 492–93 n.31.

72. *A Woman Lawyer at Last*, Newark Advocate (Newark, OH), July 9, 1869, at 1, col. H; *The Athens of Iowa Ahead*, Morning Republican (Little Rock, AR), July 14, 1869, at col. A.

73. *A Married Woman*, at 20 n.32 (quoting from the *Mount Pleasant Journal*); Daily National Intelligencer & Washington Express (D.C.), Oct. 26, 1869, at col. H.

74. *Personal and General*, Frank Leslie's Illustrated Newspaper (NY), Nov. 27, 1869, at 171, col. C; *All Sorts and Sizes*, Bangor Daily Whig & Courier, Nov. 13, 1869, at col. F; *see also* The News and Observer (Raleigh, NC), Aug. 16, 1892, at col. A (discussing Mansfield being admitted to the bar); *Notes*, The Daily Inter Ocean (Chi.), Aug. 27, 1892, at 11, col. B; *Current Comment*, St. Paul Daily News, Aug. 30, 1892, at 4, col. C; *America's Female Lawyers*, The Atchison Daily Globe (Atchison, KS), Sept. 20, 1892, col. E.

75. *See* Ga. Weekly Telegraph & Ga. Journal & Messenger, Nov. 15, 1870, at col. D (reprinting an article from the Rockford Register).

76. *See Personal*, The Milwaukee Sentinel, Nov. 10, 1871, at col. C.

77. The Daily Patriot (Concord, NH), Nov. 23, 1871, at col. B.

78. The law they drafted in the fall of 1871, was "[a]n act to secure to all persons freedom in the selection of occupation, profession or employment." S. 275, 27th Sess., at 1024–1026 (Ill. 1872).

79. *Miss Alta M. Hulett's Lecture*, Rockford Register, Dec. 2, 1871, at 1 (reporting that the night of Hulett's debut the Hall was "filled to its utmost capacity . . . [with] not a foot of standing room unoccupied" and that "over four hundred persons went away unable to get inside"); *Miss Alta M. Hulett's Lecture*, Rockford Journal, Dec. 2, 1871, at 1–2 (reporting that Hulett "spoke for an hour and a half and during the whole time she held [the audience's]

strict attention and drew from them repeated rounds of applause."). *See also Miss Hulett's Lecture*, Rockford Gazette, Nov. 30, 1871.

80. *A Feminine Dred Scott Case*, The Independent, Mar. 10, 1870, at 4.

81. Gilliam, *A Professional Pioneer*, at 123 n.3.

82. *The Myra Bradwell Case*, Chi. Trib., Apr. 20, 1873, at 8; *Woman's Right to Practice Law*, Chi. Daily Trib., May 11, 1873, at 8 (first quotation); *A Feminine Dred Scott Case*, at 4 n.80 (second quotation); *see also Women Practice in the Courts—A Test Case*, N.Y. Times, Mar. 16, 1873, at 1 (reprinting an article from the Chi. J. which was published before the Supreme Court rendered its decision, offering support for Bradwell's argument that women are citizens and can practice law). Note that there were some who did not support separate spheres but were critical of Bradwell and the woman's movement for bringing this case when it was apparent that they would lose. Warren, Supreme Court, at 550 n.1 n.3 (quoting The Nation, Apr. 24, 1873).

83. *Admitted to Practice*, Milwaukee Daily Sentinel, June 19, 1874, at 5, col. C (quotations); *see also* The Galveston Daily News, July 23, 1874, at col. D (noting that Goodell "is said to be a lady of good education, fine appearance, and modest bearing"); *About Women*, Lowell Daily Citizen and News (MA), June 29, 1874, at col. C; *General Intelligence*, Boston Investigator, July 8, 1874, at 6, col. D; *Personalities*, Cleveland Daily Herald, July 3, 1874, at 4, col. F (noting Goodell was admitted "after passing a very creditable examination").

84. *See In re Goodell*, 39 Wis. 232, 244–45 (1875); *see also Supreme Court of Wisconsin*, Chi. Legal News, Mar. 11, 1876, at 196, 199.

85. *See Miss Goodell's Application Denied*, Chi. Legal News, Mar. 4, 1876, at 191 (reprinting the Wisconsin State Journal article) (first and third quotation); *see also Female Lawyers*, Milwaukee Daily Sentinel, Feb. 24, 1876, at 7, col. A (reprinting Ryan's opinion with an extended headline which reads "Female Lawyers. Opinion of Chief Justice Ryan in the Case of Miss Lavinia Goodell. The Reasons for Refusing Her Application to the Bar. Law That Is About a Thousand Years Old") (second quotation); *see also Mr. Mosness on Judge Ryan's Opinion*, Chi. Legal News, May 13, 1876, at 271 (letter by Mosness to Bradwell arguing that the Chief Justice of the Wisconsin court's "prejudice against women in the practice of law" influenced him to "disregard the plain provision of the statute"). In 1877, with the support of every lawyer in her county, Goodell secured a law that prohibited sex as grounds for denying a law license. *See* Cleary, *Lavinia Goodell*, at 265 n.56.

86. Milwaukee Daily Sentinel, Apr. 25, 1879, at 4, col. B (discussing Lavinia Goodell's application to the bar).

87. Inter Ocean (Chi.), Jan. 31, 1877, at 4, col. F (summarizing article from N.Y. World).

88. *Woman Lawyers*, Bismarck Daily Trib., June 20, 1891, at 2, col. D.

89. Helene Silverberg, Gender and American Social Science: The Formative Years 13–14 (1998); Felice Batlan, *Law and the Fabric of the Everyday: The Settlement Houses, Sociological Jurisprudence, and the Gendering of Urban Legal Culture*, 15 S. Cal. Interdisc. L.J. 235 (2006); Ira Harkavy & John L. Puckett, *Lessons from Hull House for the Contemporary Urban University*, 68 Soc. Service Rev.299 (Sep., 1994); Andrew R. Timming, *Florence Kelley: A Recognition of Her Contributions to Sociology*, 4 J. Classical Soc. 289 (Nov. 2004).

90. Smith, Civic Ideals, at 270 n.3.

91. 208 U.S. 412 (1908); Susan D. Carle, *Gender in the Construction of the Lawyer's Persona,* 22 Harv. Women's L.J. 239, 245 (1999); Ronald K.L. Collins & Jennifer Friesen, *Looking Back on Muller v. Oregon,* 69 A.B.A. J. 294 (1983).

92. Judith A. Baer, The Chains of Protection: The Judicial Response to Women's Labor Legislation 66 (1978).

93. Mary Becker, *The Sixties Shift to Formal Equality and the Courts: An Argument for Pragmatism and Politics,* 40 Wm. & Mary L. Rev. 209, 212, 214–16, 222–29 (1998).

94. Morello, Invisible Bar, at 34–35 n.1 (federal court practice); Elizabeth Pleck, *Feminist Responses to "Crimes Against Women, 1868–1896,* 8 Signs 451 (1983) (criminal laws); Susan M. Hartmann, The Other Feminists: Activists in the Liberal Establishment 58–61 (1998) and Linda Kerber, No Constitutional Right to Be Ladies: Women and the Obligations of Citizenship 169–70 (1998) (Dorothy Kenyon and jury service); Catherine Waugh McCulloch, "Trial by Jury," *The Woman Citizen* at 488 (Oct. 2, 1920) and Gretchen Ritter, *Jury Service and Women's Citizenship Before and After the Nineteenth Amendment,* 20 Law Hist. Rev. 479 (2002) (Catherine Waugh McCulloch's work and arguments).

95. I Dissent 127 (Mark Tushnet ed., 2008).

96. Quong Wing v. Kirkendall, 223 U.S. 59, 63 (1912); see also Fay v. New York, 332 U.S. 261 (1947); Hoyt v. Florida, 368 U.S. 57 (1961).

97. *Quong Wing* at 64–65 (Lamar, J., dissenting).

98. Goesaert v. Cleary, 335 U.S. 464, 468 (1948) (Rutledge, J., dissenting).

99. *See* Leslie W. Gladstone, Women's Issues in Congress: Selected Legislation 1832–1998, *in* Women and Women's Issues in Congress 11 (Janet V. Lewis ed., 2000) (listing and describing federal laws that granted women rights though the nineteenth and twentieth centuries).

100. Equal Pay Act of 1963, Pub. L. No. 88-38, 77 Stat. 56 (codified as amended at 29 U.S.C. 206 90d (2000)). *See also* Cynthia Harrison, On Account of Sex: The Politics of Women's Issues, 1945–1968, at 899 (1988).

101. *See, e.g.,* Reed v. Reed, 404 U.S. 71 (1971) (finding a statute that required a preference for a male administrator for a decedent's estate was an equal protection violation); Frontiero v. Richardson, 411 U.S. 677 (1973) (finding denial of housing and medical benefits to the families of female military officers was an equal protection violation); Craig v. Boren, 429 U.S. 190 (1976) (introducing intermediate scrutiny as a midpoint between strict scrutiny and a rational basis standard); United States v. Virginia, 518 U.S. 515 (1996) (applying a stronger "skeptical scrutiny" standard). *See also* Ruth Bader Ginsburg, *Constitutional Adjudication in the United States as a Means of Advancing the Equal Stature of Men and Women Under the Law,* 26 Hofstra L. Rev. 263, 267–68 (1997).

102. *See* Catherine A. MacKinnon, Sexual Harassment of Working Women (1979); Lynn Hecht Schafran, *Is the Law Male?,* Trial, Aug. 1995, at 18; Lynn Hecht Schafran, *Is the Law Male?: Let Me Count the Ways,* 69 Chi.-Kent L. Rev. 397 (1993); Serena Mayeri, *Constitutional Choices: Legal Feminism and the Historical Dynamics of Change,* 92 Cal. L. Rev. 761, 827–34 (2004); Reva B. Siegel, *Text in Contest: Gender and the Constitution from a Social Movement Perspective,* 150 U. Pa. L. Rev. 297 (2001); Martha Albertson Fineman, The Illusion of Equality: The Rhetoric and Reality of Divorce Reform (1991); Leslie Bender, *Is Tort Law Male?: Foreseeability Analysis and Property Managers' Liability for Third Party Rapes of Residents,* 69

Chi.-Kent L. Rev. 313 (1993); Sylvia A. Law and Patricia Hennessey, *Is the Law Male?: The Case of Family Law*, 69 Chi.-Kent L. Rev. 354 (1993); Dorothy E. Roberts, *Rape, Violence, and Women's Autonomy*, 69 Chi.-Kent L. Rev. 359 (1993); Sarah E. Burns, *Is the Law Male?: The Role of Experts*, 69 Chi.-Kent L. Rev. 389 (1993).

CHAPTER 11

1. U.S. Const. amend. XIV, § 1. The first sentence is commonly known as the Citizenship Clause and the first part of the second sentence as the Privileges or Immunities Clause. For background on the framing and initial treatment of these clauses, *see* Richard L. Aynes, *Unintended Consequences of the Fourteenth Amendment and What They Tell Us About Its Interpretation*, 39 Akron L. Rev. 289, 290–300 (2006).

2. U.S. Const. amend. XIV, § 2. This section was a compromise designed by congressional Republicans to prevent Southern whites from denying suffrage to blacks under state laws while also gaining more seats in Congress by claiming African Americans in the numeric calculations for apportionment, which would have resulted in greater Southern white dominance in the House of Representatives than was true before the Civil War, when enslaved blacks counted as three-fifths of a person for apportionment purposes. Such a goal could have been achieved by simply basing representation on the number of qualified voters in each state. That, however, would have forced Northern states to choose between enfranchising women and unnaturalized immigrants or having a smaller proportionate representation, especially as white men migrated west. The particularly convoluted, race-based language of the Amendment protected Northern interests while preventing an immediate Southern democratic resurgence. *See* Eric Foner, Reconstruction: America's Unfinished Revolution, 1863–1877 at 252 (1988). It also caused an almost irreparable rift between advocates of women's suffrage and the Republican party by specifying protection only for male suffrage. *Id.* at 255.

3. U.S. Const. amend XIV, § 3. This section also enabled Congress to remove this disability by two-thirds vote. *Id.* Congress did so in 1872. *See* Act of May 22, 1872, ch. 193, 17 Stat. 142 (removing political disabilities imposed by the 14th Amendment). This section was generally considered a mild punishment for confederates, replacing as it did a disenfranchisement of confederates through 1870. Foner, Reconstruction, at 253–54.

4. Saenz v. Roe, 526 U.S. 489 (1999). The Citizenship Clause played a significant role in the Court's analysis. *Id.* at 506–07. But the specific right of citizens to move into another state and be treated equal to those already residing there is a narrow right. Lawrence H. Tribe, *Saenz Sans Prophecy: Does the Privileges or Immunities Revival Portend the Future—or Reveal the Structure of the Present?*, 113 Harv. L. Rev. 110, 197–98 (1999).

5. Akhil Amar, America's Constitution: A Biography 381–82 (2005); Rebecca E. Zietlow, Enforcing Equality: Congress, the Constitution, and the Protection of Individual Rights 6 (2006). *See* Kenneth L. Karst, Belonging to America: Equal Citizenship and the Constitution (1989).

6. *E.g.*, Karst, Belonging to America at 134–46 n.5, 189–216; Zietlow, Enforcing Equality, at 150–51 n.5.

7. *See generally* Larry D. Kramer, The People Themselves: Popular Constitutionalism and Judicial Review (2004); Mark Tushnet, Taking the Constitution Away from the Courts (1999). Professor Zietlow's book is in this vein as well, although she focuses mainly on congressional speakers. *See* Zietlow, Enforcing Equality, at 9, 145–59 n.5. For examples of historical legal

scholarship that looks beyond governmental actors, *see* William Forbath, Law and the Shaping of the American Labor Movement (1991); William Forbath, *The New Deal Constitution in Exile*, 51 Duke L.J. 165 (2001); James Gray Pope, *The Thirteenth Amendment versus the Commerce Clause: Labor and the Shaping of American Constitutional Law, 1921–1957*, 102 Colum. L. Rev. 1 (2002).

8. On the diverse aspects of civil society evident in Tocqueville and Hegel, *see* John Ehrenberg, Civil Society: The Critical History of an Idea 121–32 (discussing Hegel), 160–69 (1999) (discussing Tocqueville); Jean L. Cohen & Andrew Arato, Civil Society and Political Theory 91–116 (1992) (discussing Hegel); Jeffrey C. Alexander, The Civil Sphere 99–101 (2006) (discussing Tocqueville). Hegel's analysis of civil society arises mainly in G. W. F. Hegel, Elements of the Philosophy of Right §§ 182–256 (Allen W. Wood ed., H. B. Nisbet trans., 1991). Tocqueville discusses aspects of civil society throughout both volumes of Democracy in America. *See* Alexis de Tocqueville, Democracy in America 205–23, 590–616 (Arthur Goldhammer trans., 2004).

9. Nancy L. Rosenblum & Robert C. Post, Introduction to Civil Society and Government 1, 3 (Nancy L. Rosenblum & Robert C. Post eds., 2002). Their definition is structured as a contrast to government, which is "a domain of common purpose and identity."

10. Linda C. McClain & James E. Fleming, *Some Questions for Civil Society-Revivalists*, 75 Chi-Kent L Rev 301, 309 (2000) (citing, inter alia, Council on Civil Society, A Call to Civil Society: Why Democracy needs Moral Truths (1998); Seedbeds of Virtue: Sources of Competence, Character, and Citizenship in American Society (Mary Ann Glendon & David Blankenhorn eds. 1995)). *See also* Rosenblum & Post, Civil Society, n.9.

11. Linda C. McClain & James E. Fleming, *Foreword: Legal and Constitutional Implications of the Calls to Revive Civil Society*, 75 Chi.-Kent L. Rev. 289, 292 (2000) (discussing the variety of views of civil society).

12. Matthew Mancini, Alexis de Tocqueville and American Intellectuals: From His Times to Ours ix–x (2006).

13. Jean L. Cohen, American Civil Society Talk, *in* Civil Society, Democracy, and Civic Renewal 55–56 (Robert K. Fullinwider ed., 1999) (arguing that the concept of civil society often presumes a focus on the voluntary associations of private life and omits any consideration of the public sphere or the integrated relations of government and civic life).

14. Jürgen Habermas, The Public Sphere: An Encyclopedia Article, *reprinted in* Critical Theory and Society: A Reader 136 (Stephen Eric Bronner & Douglas MacKay Kellner eds., 1989) (1964). *See also* Jürgen Habermas, The Structural Transformation of the Public Sphere: An Inquiry into a Category of Bourgeois Society (Thomas Burger & Frederick Lawrence trans., Massachusetts Institute of Technology 1989) (1962).

15. Nancy Fraser, Rethinking the Public Sphere: A Contribution to the Critique of Actually Existing Democracy, *in* Habermas and the Public Sphere 109 (Craig Calhoun ed., 1992). But this "shared vision of the good . . . blocked as potential topics of deliberation the arrangements that sustained actual exclusions from the public sphere." Robert Asen & Daniel C. Brouwer, Introduction, *in* Counterpublics and the State 1, 5–10 (Robert Asen & Daniel C. Brouwer eds., 2001). *See also* Mary P. Ryan, Gender and Public Access: Women's Politics in Nineteenth-Century America, *in* Habermas and the Public Sphere, at 259; Carol C. Gould, Diversity and Democracy: Representing Differences, *in* Democracy and Difference: Contesting the Boundaries of the Political 171, 172–76 (Seyla Benhabib ed., 1996); Geoff Eley, Nations, Publics, and Political Cultures: Placing Habermas in the Nineteenth Century, *in* Habermas

and the Public Sphere, at 289; Catherine R. Squires, *Rethinking the Black Public Sphere: An Alternative Vocabulary for Multiple Public Spheres*, 12 Comm. Theory 446, 466 (2002).

16. Alexander, Civil Sphere, at 276, 279 n.8.

17. Peggy Cooper Davis, Neglected Stories: The Constitution And Family Values 221 (1997).

18. Act of April 9, 1866, ch. 31, § 1, 14 Stat. 27 (protecting the civil rights of United States citizens). The Act provided: [A]ll persons born in the United States and not subject to any foreign power, excluding Indians not taxed, are hereby declared to be citizens of the United States; and such citizens, of every race and color, without regard to any previous condition of slavery or involuntary servitude, except as a punishment for crime whereof the party shall have been duly convicted, shall have the same right, in every State and Territory in the United States, to make and enforce contracts, to sue, be parties, and give evidence, to inherit, purchase, lease, sell, hold, and convey real and personal property, and to full and equal benefit of all laws and proceedings for the security of person and property, as is enjoyed by white citizens, and shall be subject to like punishment, pains, and penalties, and to none other, any law, statute, ordinance, regulation, or custom, to the contrary notwithstanding. *See generally* Foner, Reconstruction; Eric Foner, Free Soil, Free Labor, Free Men: The Ideology of the Republican Party Before the Civil War (1995); James D. Schmidt, Free to Work: Labor Law, Emancipation, and Reconstruction, 1815–1880 (1998); Amy Dru Stanley, From Bondage to Contract: Wage Labor, Marriage, and the Market in the Age of Slave Emancipation (1998); James W. Fox, Jr., *Democratic Citizenship and Congressional Reconstruction: Defining and Implementing the Privileges and Immunities of Citizenship*, 13 Temp. Pol. & Civ. Rts. L. Rev. 453, 460–66 (2004).

19. Morton J. Horwitz, The Transformation of American Law, 1780–1860, at 211 (1977).

20. *See* Foner, Reconstruction, at 54.

21. *Id.* at 54 and 364–79.

22. Foner, Reconstruction, at 370–73; Theda Skocpol, *The Tocqueville Problem: Civic Engagement in American Democracy*, 21 Soc. Sci. Hist. 455, 460 (1997) (drawing connections between Jacksonianism, expanded suffrage, and Tocquevillian associationalism); Leon F. Litwack, North of Slavery: The Negro in the Free States, 1790–1860 (1961) (explicating the segregationist and white supremacist nature of Northern antebellum society).

23. *See* Foner, Reconstruction, at 289.

24. Philip S. Foner and George E. Walker performed a tremendous service in compiling the materials from the state and national black conventions of the nineteenth century. *See* 1 Proceedings of the Black State Conventions, 1840–1865 (Philip S. Foner & George E. Walker eds., 1979); 1 Proceedings of the Black National and State Conventions, 1865–1890 (Philip S. Foner & George E. Walker eds., 1986).

25. Eric Foner, *Rights and the Constitution in Black Life during the Civil War and Reconstruction*, 74 J. Am. Hist. 863, 867–69 (1987); Tocqueville, Democracy, at 215–23 n.8 (political associations), 604–609 (civil and political associations).

26. *See* Elizabeth Regosin, Freedom's Promise: Ex-Slave Families and Citizenship in the Age of Emancipation (2002).

27. *See generally* 1 Proceedings, 1840–1865; 1 Proceedings 1865–1890; Foner, Reconstruction, at 112.

28. *See, e.g.*, 1 Proceedings, 1865–1890, at 80–81; 2 Proceedings of the Black State Conventions, 1840–1865 302 (Philip S. Foner & George E. Walker eds., 1979); Foner, Reconstruction,

at 180, 251–61, 289 *See also* Foner, *Rights and the Constitution,* at 872–73 n.25; Xi Wang, *Black Suffrage and the Redefinition of American Freedom,* 17 Cardozo L. Rev. 2153, 2179–95 (1995–1996). John Mercer Langston, Freedom and Citizenship 110 (1969) (1883) (quotation). For Langston, and for other men advocating black rights during this period, "manhood" was often used synonymously with citizenship. *E.g.,* Address of the Colored State Convention to the People of the State of South Carolina, *in* 2 Proceedings, 1840–1865, at 299.

29. Foner, *Rights and the Constitution,* at 867–69 n.25. A similar point could be made about Northern free blacks who had developed a nascent, enclave-like civil society that included black churches (especially the A.M.E. Church) and a black press in the North as part of the black abolitionist movement. These civil society organizations and activities helped fuel both the abolitionist movement and the subsequent movement for black citizenship and suffrage. On antebellum Northern black society generally, *see* Patrick Rael, Black Identity & Black Protest in the Antebellum North (2002); James Oliver Horton & Lois E. Horton, In Hope of Liberty: Culture, Community, and Protest Among Northern Free Blacks, 1700–1860 (1997); Litwack, North of Slavery, n.22; Jane H. Pease & William H. Pease, They Who Would Be Free: Blacks' Search for Freedom, 1830–1861 (1974).

30. The South Carolina Convention of 1865 is discussed in 2 Proceedings, 1840–1865, at 286–304; *see id.* at 298 (first quotation), 298–99 (second quotation); Foner, *Rights and the Constitution,* at 870 n.25 (autonomy quotation).

31. 1 Proceedings, 1865–1890, at 147–48 (discussing the Proceedings of Pennsylvania Convention, 1865).

32. Foner, Reconstruction, at 365–70.

33. *Id.* at 372.

34. 2 Proceedings, 1840–1865, at 302; *see also* Langston, Freedom and Citizenship, at 110 n.28. On the Sherman land grant and the forty-acres-and-a-mule idea, *see generally* Claude F. Oubre, Forty Acres and a Mule: The Freedmen's Bureau and Black Land Ownership (1978).

35. 2 Proceedings, 1840–1865, at 291, 302. Tocqueville discusses a range of components of civil society, including press (book I, chapter 11), political associations (book I, chapter 12), public associations (book II, chapter 5), and, to some extent, religion (book II, chapters 9 & 12). *See* Tocqueville, Democracy, n.8.

36. In November 1865, the National Equal Rights League held its first meeting in Cleveland. *See* 1 Proceedings, 1865–1890, at 40. The Pennsylvania Convention was itself the Annual Meeting of the Pennsylvania State Equal Rights League. *Id.* at 132. In Georgia, the convention that met in January, 1866 referred in its opening to the Georgia Equal Rights Association. *Id.* at 232.

37. Foner, Reconstruction, at 64, 117; Jonathan M. Bryant, How Curious a Land: Conflict and Change in Greene County, Georgia, 1850–1885, 104–118 (1996) (discussing activities of Equal Rights Associations in Georgia). On the Union Leagues, *see generally* Michael W. Fitzgerald, The Union League Movement in the Deep South: Politics and Agricultural Change During Reconstruction (1989).

38. *See, e.g.,* Fitzgerald, Union League, at 117 n.37 (noting "interconnection between political insurgency and labor concerns in League-sponsored mass activity"). *See generally* 1 Proceedings, 1840–1865; 1 Proceedings, 1865–1890.

39. Fitzgerald, Union League, at 127–28 n.37; *see* Foner, *Rights and the Constitution,* at 874 n.25.

40. Foner, *Rights and the Constitution,* at 874 n.25.

41. *Id.*

42. Foner, Reconstruction, at 282.

43. Foner, Free Soil, at 878–80; Foner, Reconstruction, at 346–92; *see, e.g.,* Joseph William Singer, *No Right to Exclude: Public Accommodations and Private Property,* 90 Nw. U. L. Rev. 1283, 1342 (1996); Foner, Reconstruction, at 281–82. Massachusetts passed the first major state desegregation law. *Id.* at 28 and 370–71.

44. Foner, Reconstruction, at 368, 373.

45. Slaughter-House Cases, 45 83 U.S. 36 (1872).

46. Civil Rights Cases, 109 U.S. 3 (1883).

47. Foner, Reconstruction, at 454–59. For a history of the prosecution of the Klan in this period, *see* William S. McFeely, Amos T. Akerman: The Lawyer and Racial Justice, *in* Region, Race, and Reconstruction: Essays in Honor of C. Vann Woodward 395 (J. Morgan Kousser & James M. McPherson eds., 1982).

48. 2 Proceedings, 1840–1865, at 284–304.

49. *See, e.g.,* David A. Crocker, Civil Society and Transitional Justice, *in* Civil Society, Democracy, and Civic Renewal, *supra,* at 375 n.21; Civil Society and Political Change in Asia: Expanding and Contracting Democratic Space (Muthiah Alagappa ed., 2004).

50. James W. Fox, Jr., *Intimations of Citizenship: Repressions and Expressions of Equal Citizenship in the Era of Jim Crow,* 50 How. L.J. 113 (2006).

51. *Id.* at 135–37; 152–61.

52. *Id.* at 161–188; *see, e.g.,* Leon F. Litwack, Trouble In Mind: Black Southerners In The Age of Jim Crow, 150–67 (1998); *cf.* Fredrick C. Harris, Will the Circle be Unbroken? The Erosion and Transformation of African-American Civic Life, *in* Civil Society, Democracy, and Civic Renewal, at 317 n.13.

53. This, essentially, is the regime represented by the Supreme Court's fin-de-siècle jurisprudence simultaneously upholding the activist state actions of white supremacy (*e.g.,* Plessy v. Ferguson, 163 U.S. 537 (1896), *overruled by* Brown v. Bd. of Educ. of Topeka, Shawnee County, Kan. 347 U.S. 483 (1954)),and uprooting state protections of labor in order to protect industrial capitalism (*e.g.,* Lochner v. People of the State of N.Y., 198 U.S. 45 (1905), *overruled in part by* Day-Brite Lighting Inc. v. State of Mo., 342 U.S. 421 (1952), *and* Ferguson v. Skrupa, 372 U.S. 726 (1963)); Alexander, Civil Sphere, at 269–73 n.8.

54. Alexander, Civil Sphere, at 265–385 n.8 (discussing race and civil repair); *see, e.g.,* Alfred L. Brophy, Reconstructing the Dreamland: The Tulsa Riot of 1921, Race, Reparations, and Reconciliation 79 (2002) (discussing the importance of law, constitutionalism, and equal citizenship in the Oklahoma black community of the 1910s); Houston A. Baker, Jr., Critical Memory and the Black Public Sphere, *in* The Black Public Sphere: A Public Culture Book 23 (The Black Public Sphere Collective ed., 1995) ("[T]he Constitution of the United States and the American national flag were valued sites of patriotism and pride for the black public sphere.").

55. Foner, Reconstruction, at 364–79.

56. *E.g.,* Jean Bethke Elshtain, *Will the Real Civil Society Please Stand Up?,* 75 Chi-Kent L. Rev. 583, 583–84 (identifying individual moral leaders, but ignoring social movements in civil

society). Robert Putnam is much more attentive to the historical development of voluntary associations, including within black communities. *See, e.g.*, Robert D. Putnam, *Bowling Alone* 390–91 (2000). However, because Putnam tends to view voluntary associationalism as something unique or separate from social movements and group political consciousness, his analysis misses the importance of the connections between civil society organizations and the public sphere. *See also* Gerald Gamm & Robert D. Putnam, *The Growth of Voluntary Associations in America, 1840–1940*, 29 J. Interdisciplinary Hist. 511 (1999).

57. 2 Proceedings, 1840–1865, at 286–304.

58. Bryant, How Curious a Land, at 104 n.37.

59. Although a topic for another day, this myth of separation of the private civil sphere from the public governmental sphere was one of the greatest legal-constitutional roadblocks to equal citizenship erected by the Supreme Court in the *Civil Rights Cases* and related opinions.

Index